FRENCH CUISINE FOR ALL

Books by Louisette Bertholle

FRENCH CUISINE FOR ALL
SECRETS OF THE GREAT FRENCH RESTAURANTS
MASTERING THE ART OF FRENCH COOKING (*with Julia Child and Simone Beck*)

LOUISETTE BERTHOLLE

French Cuisine for All

Translated by Mary Manheim
With the Help of the Author

Drawings by Earl Thollander

DOUBLEDAY & COMPANY, INC.
GARDEN CITY, NEW YORK   1980

French edition published by Éditions Albin Michel under the title
    Une Grande Cuisine pour tous
Copyright © 1976 by Opera Mundi, Paris

Library of Congress Cataloging in Publication Data

Bertholle, Louisette.
    French Cuisine For All.

    Translation of Une grande cuisine pour tous.
    Includes index.
    1. Cookery, French.   I. Title.
TX719.B419713 641.5'944

ISBN: 0-385-13087-2
Library of Congress Catalog Card Number 78-1235
English Translation and Illustrations Copyright © 1980 by Doubleday & Company, Inc.

to Henri

Contents

Whenever the name of a recipe is followed by an asterisk (*) in the text, the recipe is included elsewhere in the book. Consult the Index for page numbers.

Acknowledgments

In preparing the present book the author was helped by a number of people who contributed friendship and encouragement, confidence, inspiration, and knowledge.

I would especially like to thank Julia Child and Simone Beck, my companions in the adventure of cookery.

Another person I wish to thank is Camille Cadier, our assistant at the École des Trois Gourmandes, who over the years helped us with her skill, tact, and understanding.

I owe a debt of gratitude to all my friends in the Cercle des Gourmettes—to our late president, Madame Poussard, to our new president, Madame Jean Marcel Régnier, and to the entire membership as well—for their constant efforts to maintain the high standards of French cuisine.

I would like especially to express my admiration and gratitude to our chef, Madame Aimée Cassiot, who represents the finest in French cookery—a true *cordon bleu* if there ever was one!

Appreciation and thanks go to Steven Spurrier, whose knowledge of regional wines has been a help to me.

For his inexhaustible kindness and patience, I thank my butcher, Christian Prosper, a true artist and craftsman.

Introduction

For more than three years I enjoyed a most unusual opportunity to observe the recent trends in French cuisine, during my work on *Secrets of the Great French Restaurants*. More than 350 restaurants with stars in the *Michelin Guide* provided me with 1686 recipes, which I was able to study, evaluate, and when necessary try out. My contact with this fascinating mosaic of French gastronomy made me aware of the changes that have taken place in the last twenty years.

It was then that I conceived the idea of this book. Its purpose is to acquaint the home cook with the advantages of a new way of cooking, which may best be described as simple, refined, and natural.

I have tried to make my book as nearly complete as possible, including a chapter on cooking techniques and terms. I believe that this section is essential, for it provides access to the subtle variations that give the new French cuisine its distinction. I am convinced that many a painful blunder will be avoided, not only by neophytes, but by enlightened amateurs as well, if they consult it before going to work on any of the recipes.

A chapter on various condiments and herbs, seasonings and spices used in French cooking will also provide useful and interesting information.

In this book the reader will not always find the familiar recipes that appear in most other French cookbooks: *gratin dauphinois* and *gratin savoyard,* for example, are replaced by other, less known gratins. Among the entrees, I have given preference over the capricious classical soufflé to mousselines and unmolded soufflés, which can wait for a little while before being served. Even so, I have included a few recipes for these soufflés and have provided helpful pointers and safeguards against failure.

I have provided some notes on oils and vinegars that are the principal ingredients in salad dressings, as well as recipes for homemade aromatic oils and vinegars that can lend a personal and distinctive note to the seasoning of salads and of vegetables served as hors-d'oeuvre.

I am sure you will find many useful hints in the chapter Selection, Arrangement, and Decoration of Serving Dishes, which is accompanied by such decorative recipes as the one for an edible baking dish cover!

One chapter is devoted to eggs. In it, I hope, the reader will find reasons for giving egg dishes, sometimes regarded as dull, the place they deserve.

Vegetable purées are very much in fashion. They are delicious accompaniments and they lend elegance to the simplest of dishes. The recipes truly belong to the new, simple, more natural type of French cooking.

The classical sauces for fish, meat, poultry, game, and vegetables have not been neglected, as they are indispensable to fine cuisine. But in addition, I have included some of my "little sauces," which are simple, easy to make, and delicious, and they can be used for many dishes. I also recommend *jus lié*, a recent development of a sauce (much lighter than the old-style *jus lié*); it has my full approval and is to be found in the chapter on poultry.

This book reflects not only the changes that have occurred in the living art of cuisine, but also my own preferences; it is the product of my own choices and reflections. Above all, I regard it as an attempt to let my readers in on my love affair with cookery. I shall not try to convert them to my own tastes, but if, in reading and making use of my recipes, some are imbued with my passion for the culinary art, my aim of providing people who like to cook with a key to the French *art de vivre*—namely, the art of fine but simple cookery—will have been attained.

FRENCH CUISINE FOR ALL

PART I

The Basics of French Cuisine

To brown (*dorer*) To cook meats, poultry, some vegetables, etc., in hot fat until they turn golden brown. Also: to set cooked food under a broiler or place in the oven until the top is lightly glazed and golden. (Note: the French language contains many words describing the various shades of browning desired—*blondir, pincer, rissoler,* and others—whereas in English we merely say "brown" or "lightly brown.")

Étuver (Note: There is no precise English translation for this word.) To stir-cook vegetables, such as zucchini, endive, lettuce, onions, carrots, in butter or other fat. After 4 to 5 minutes, a very small amount of water, bouillon, or cream should be added if necessary, to prevent any coloration. The pan is then covered and the vegetables cooked, steamed, over low heat until done.

To sweat (*suer*) To cook a vegetable briefly, as a preliminary step, in butter or other fat until the juices are released and appear as beads on the surface of the vegetable. The cooking is then continued as in *étuver* (given above). Also: to place a chicken in a preheated 350° F. oven for about 15 minutes until it has turned a pale ivory color and beads of natural juice appear on the skin. This step is called for in certain recipes.

OVEN COOKING

To roast (*rôtir*) To cook in an oven by exposure to dry heat, a method of cooking used especially for meat, poultry, game, and large fish. Roasting is not a simplified method of cooking; on the contrary, it requires extreme care and attention, even subtlety.

Roasting Red Meats, such as Beef and Lamb

These meats should be seared in a burning hot oven to seal in the juices. The heat is then lowered and the roast is cooked until the center is tender and the juices run pink when the meat is pricked. Overcooked beef or lamb loses its juice and nutritive value and tends to be tasteless and sometimes stringy.

Preparing Roast Beef, Roast Leg of Lamb*

The meat should be roasted in a heavy roasting pan not much larger than the meat itself. If the pan is too large, the juices spread out thinly and burn. If possible, the roasting pan should be equipped with a rack. The pan should be brushed with a thin layer of peanut oil, then dotted with 3 or 4 pats of butter. It is not a good idea to grease a roasting pan exclusively with butter, for it burns too easily. If you do use butter, always mix it with a little peanut oil. In former times, roasting pans were greased with clarified butter, which does not burn, but nowadays cooks use butter pats and oil, which are quicker.

  Large cuts of beef should be barded, that is, tied with strips of fat before they are roasted. Suet and bacon are recommended for beef and veal; bacon for pheasant and chicken; fatback or salt pork for venison and wild game birds. That part of the roast not covered with barding fat should be lightly rubbed with peanut oil, then with softened butter. Do not rub meat to be roasted with melted butter, which would simply run to the bottom of the pan, dry out, and burn.

The roast should be placed in a preheated oven about 3½–4 inches from the bottom.

The roast should be salted twice during the cooking process, once just *before* it is turned and again *after* it has been turned. After turning the roast, add about 4 tablespoons of boiling water to the roasting pan. Pour the water along the sides of the pan so that it does not touch the roast. The water will moisten the essential juices running out of the roast and prevent them from burning. These juices are a natural product of meat that is roasted; they are often used to enrich sauces.

Baste the meat with the pan juices three or four times during the roasting.

When the meat is removed from the oven, it should be placed on a board and allowed to settle for 5 to 8 minutes before being carved. This makes the carving easier.

Roasting White Meats, such as Pork and Veal

These meats should be barded before roasting, as with red meats. The roasting pan should be greased with peanut oil and margarine. The roast should be seasoned with salt and pepper, then placed in the pan and put in a moderate oven (350° F.). Turn the meat regularly until it is nicely colored on all sides. Then add ½–1 cup of boiling water, pouring it around the edges of the pan so as not to touch the meat. Toward the end of the cooking, place a piece of aluminum foil over the roast to prevent it from drying out. The meat is done when the juices run perfectly clear. Place the meat on a board and let it settle for a few minutes before carving.

Spit-roasting in the Oven

This is one of the best ways to cook large pieces of meat such as rib roast and leg of lamb. It is especially good for poultry. A spit-roasted chicken, for instance, keeps its full flavor. Under its crisp skin the meat will be tender and juicy. Do not forget to spoon up all the juices released when the chicken is carved, and add them to the gravy.

DEGREASING BOUILLONS, JUICES, AND SAUCES

The cooked fat resulting from simmering, sautéing, and browning is indigestible and harmful to the human organism. If eaten day after day, it can cause any number of ailments.

Even though I do not believe that special diets are effective, I do think that the elimination of cooked fat by degreasing is necessary to make our food more digestible and to reduce its caloric content. On occasion I have removed a half cup of cooked fat from a braising sauce—sheer poison for the system had it not been gotten rid of. All bouillons, ragouts, juices, and sauces require degreasing.

Degreasing Bouillon

For meat and poultry bouillons, skim off all the fat-impregnated impurities for the first 20 to 30 minutes of cooking. Once the bouillon is cooked, strain it through a colander lined with a double thickness of dampened cheesecloth on which you have placed an ice cube. The fat will collect and coagulate around the ice. Then quickly blot up any remaining fat by drawing narrow strips of paper toweling over the surface of the bouillon.

Degreasing a Juice

Remove the roast (meat, poultry, game) from the roasting pan and let the juice stand for several minutes until the fat has risen to the surface. Tilt the pan and remove the fat with a spoon.

Deglazing

Deglazing a pan, scrape up the coagulated pan juices by pouring in hot liquid such as wine or water and stirring the bottom of the pan with a small whisk or a fork. The juice is now ready to be poured in a heated sauce bowl (after you have adjusted the seasoning).

Degreasing a Sauce or Food Cooked in a Sauce

For the first part of the degreasing process I recommend a method that I have never seen anyone else use or have even seen explained in writing. Conceivably, it is my own invention.

When the sauce has finished cooking, move the saucepan or casserole in such a way that only half of it remains simmering on the heat. The fat will make its way to the side that is not simmering, and there it will rise to the surface where it can be removed with a spoon. After this partial degreasing, remove the saucepan or casserole completely from the heat. When the remaining fat rises to the surface, spoon it off. If the sauce is very rich, you may still see small particles of fat on the surface. Remove these by drawing narrow strips of paper toweling quickly over the surface of the sauce, using each strip only once.

MORE KITCHEN PROCEDURES

Poêler   There is no exact English equivalent for this procedure, but it is simple and easy to understand. It is used mainly for poultry and for older partridge or pheasant. The verb *poêler* is sometimes translated as "to casserole," but this is not entirely correct.

A chicken or game bird is first browned in a mixture of hot peanut oil and butter in a casserole, either in the oven or on top of the stove. When it has begun to color, remove it from the casserole and tie some barding fat around it to keep it from drying out. Replace the bird in the casserole along with 3 or 4 pats of butter, pour 4 tablespoons of red port wine, Madeira, dry sherry or dry vermouth around the edges of the casserole, add a *Bouquet garni** and cover the bird with a piece of aluminum foil. Cover the casserole. Heat on top of the stove until the liquid reaches the boiling point, then set it in a moderate oven until the bird is tender and the juice runs clear. During the cooking, turn the bird first on one side, then on the other. If necessary, add a little boiling hot bouillon to the pan juices (about 4 tablespoons). The bird will then cook in its own fragrant steam. When it is done, remove the casserole from the oven and discard the *bouquet garni.* Place the bird on a board for a few minutes before carving. Deglaze it (term defined above), then degrease the pan juices, strain them into a warmed sauce bowl, and keep them hot while you carve the bird.

To braise (*braiser*)   To cook meat, fish, or a vegetable (especially cabbage) in a heavy braising pan or heavy-bottomed enameled casserole that has been lined with braising ingredients such as bacon rinds, sliced carrots, and cut-up onions. After the braising ingredients are stir-cooked in a little fat, the meat, fish, or vegetable is laid on top of them, wine and hot bouillon are added, and the mixture is brought to a boil on top of the stove. A *bouquet garni* (and possibly other seasoning) is added, the pan or casserole is covered and placed in a slow oven until the food is tender and succulent.

To gratiné (*gratiner*)   To cover already cooked food with cream, bread crumbs, grated cheese, butter, and cook it in a hot oven or under the broiler until the top is golden brown.

To glaze (*glacer*)   To put already cooked food in a very hot over or under the broiler for 30–60 seconds in order to give the surface a lustrous, golden-brown finish. Also: to brush pastry, cakes, etc., with lightly beaten egg yolk diluted with a drop or two of water, and place in the oven until the top glistens.

To refresh (*rafraîchir*)   To cool blanched vegetables by rinsing them under the cold water tap or plunging them into cold water for a few seconds. This stops the cooking and helps to set the color.

To skim (*dépouiller*)   To remove the impurities that foam to the surface of simmering or boiling liquids or sauces. This is done with a spoon or a skimmer.

Condiments, Herbs, Seasonings and Spices

ALLSPICE (also known as Jamaica pepper)
This is the dried and ground berry of the allspice, or pimento, tree (*Pimenta officinalis*) of the East Indies. It has a wonderful aroma and a deliciously pungent flavor resembling combined cloves, nutmeg, and cinnamon. Except for certain exotic dishes, it is not widely used in France.

AROMATIC PEPPER
An evenly proportioned mixture of black pepper, white pepper, and allspice. These are pounded or ground together and are used in some fish soups, onion soups, and in summer vegetables such as zucchini and eggplant, in terrines and pâtés, and as a flavoring for duck, brown sauces, and other foods.

BASIL
An aromatic herb, *Ocimum basilicum.* Basil grows beautifully in pots but, being an annual, must be planted anew each spring. It will last all through the summer and until the first frosts. The taste of the oval-shaped basil leaf is unique. It is hard to describe, but one can detect in it the flavors of anise, clove, mint, and perhaps a touch of allspice. With its delicate white flowers, it is one of the prettiest of aromatic plants. If mincing is required in a recipe, always cut basil leaves with scissors. It is delicious in all kinds of spring salads, especially tomato salad and cucumber salad. Pounded with garlic and olive oil, it gives *Pistou** its inimitable flavor.

BASTARD SAFFRON (see Safflower)

BAY LEAF
The shiny, deep green leaf of the laurel, or bay, tree (*Laurus nobilis*), known in antiquity as "Daphne's tree" or "Apollo's laurel." In the story told by Ovid, Daphne is pursued by Apollo, who has fallen in love with her. Frightened and unwilling, she runs away. Just as she feels his breath on her neck, she cries out to her father, a river god, to help her, and he obliges in a strange way by changing her into a laurel tree. According to legend, Apollo took the laurel tree as a symbol of victory and glory, and that is why heroes were crowned with wreaths of laurel leaves.

All this is ancient history. Today we revere the bay leaf for its pungent taste and aroma. It is one of the basic ingredients of *Bouquet garni,** and is used in court bouillons, marinades, ragouts, or in any dish requiring a good strong flavor. Bay leaf is at its best when freshly dried. Green bay leaves have a hard, bitter, almost acrid taste. One bay leaf (rarely two leaves) is ample for flavoring a court bouillon or a fish soup. When recipes call for a half or smaller piece of a leaf, this amount must not be exceeded.

BLACK PEPPER (see Pepper)

BOUQUETS GARNIS

A *bouquet garni* is an assortment of fresh or dried herbs, or a combination of both, tied together or slipped into a small cheesecloth bag and added to soups, sauces, bouillons, and other foods for extra flavoring. The *bouquet* should be added when the liquid has begun to boil or simmer strongly, and it should always be removed before the dish is served.

Bouquet garni classique

> 1 sprig parsley with its stem and sometimes its root
> 1 sprig thyme, dried or fresh
> ½–1 bay leaf

Bouquet garni with fresh herbs
Bouquet garni aux herbes fraîches

> 1 small sprig parsley
> 2 small sprigs chervil
> 1 small sprig tarragon
> ½ bay leaf
> 1 sprig thyme

Bouquet garni provençal

> 1 sprig thyme
> 1 branch rosemary
> a piece of fennel or a small fennel shoot
> 1 bay leaf

NOTE: *These are the three most common types of* bouquets garnis. *Where other ingredients are included, they are mentioned in the recipe.*

CAPERS

Capers are the tart flower buds of a prickly shrub (*Capparis spinosa*) grown in Mediterranean regions. The best are the small round ones produced in the Var and Bouches-du-Rhône country of France. They are preserved in small jars and are used in certain white sauces that need a little more flavor, and especially in sauces served with fish.

CAYENNE PEPPER

Also called red pepper, this is a very hot, pungent, brick-red powder made by drying and grinding the fruits and seeds of various hot pepper plants. Only an infinitesimal amount should be used—as much as will stay on the point of a knife, and no more. It is used to heighten the flavor of various fish soups. For example, it is added to *Crab Sauce à l'Américaine** and it will sharpen the taste of cottage cheese.

CHERVIL

Chervil resembles parsley in the triangular groupings of its leaves, but it is a lighter green and has a more fragile texture. It is similar to tarragon in its anise-like taste, and for this reason the two herbs complement each other when used together.

Sprinkled on soups, finely minced chervil adds a refreshing taste. It is also delicious with spring salads and boiled or sautéed new potatoes. In season it can be added to a *bouquet garni* (see *Bouquet garni* with Fresh Herbs*). In short, you can use it as you use parsley, but, unlike parsley, it is at its best only in the spring. Cream of Chervil Soup* is one of the most delicious of spring soups.

CHIVES

A plant, *Allium schoenoprasum,* having dark green multiple stems that look like rushes. The delicate, slightly garlicky taste of these stems adds a delicious flavor to green salads, potato and tomato salads. And what is more appetizing than an omelet made with freshly cut chives? Always use scissors when cutting chives. This method avoids crushing the stems and keeps the juices in. Snip off the tops and root ends of the stems before using them. Chives are used only in raw foods or as a last-minute addition to cooked foods, because cooking them for any length of time makes them bitter.

CINNAMON

Cinnamon is the highly aromatic bark of several trees of the genus *Cinnamomum,* a member of the laurel family growing mainly in tropical Asia. The rich brown bark rolls up naturally when it is stripped from the trees. It has a delicious, penetrating fragrance and a sweet-pungent taste. In France it is used only in pastries, particularly with apples, and in *pain perdu* (a kind of French toast).

CLOVES

A spice consisting of the dried flower buds of a widely cultivated tropical tree (*Eugenia caryophyllata*). It has a penetrating pungent taste and should be used with discretion. An onion studded with a clove or two gives a marvelous fragrance to various bouillons—in fact, what would a beef *Pot-au-feu** do without this addition? It can also be used in marinades for game and for studding ham.

CORIANDER

This is a spice made from the dried pale pink aromatic seeds of the coriander plant (*Coriandrum sativum*). Its taste is highly individual, peppery and slightly sweet. It is used in Italian and Greek cooking for fish and vegetables (see Vegetables *à la Grecque**) and in certain French Mediterranean dishes, as well as in some types of sausages and pâtés.

CURRY POWDER

A hot, pungent powder made by blending a variety of spices. Its extraordinary symphony of fiery flavors is perceived by the taste buds only after the food with which it has been used is swallowed. The best curry powder is imported from India. The most common spices used in curry powder are black pepper, dried ginger, mustard seed, cumin, poppy seed, dried garlic, turmeric, and cinnamon. It is used in various Indian-style rice dishes and can be added to sauces for lamb, chicken, veal, crab, and other foods.

DILL

An herb, *Anethum graveolens,* with a very fresh, tart taste. Both the seeds and feathery stalks are used. It is sometimes added to the aromatic broth for Vegetables à la grecque,* to some marinades, and to some *bouquets garnis.**

EAST INDIAN SAFFRON   (see Turmeric)

FENNEL

A genus of aromatic plants of the Umbelliferae family. Its bulbs (or hearts) and shoots are eaten raw or cooked. Fennel grows wild along seaside roads in the Mediterranean region, and it occurs throughout Provence as well as on the sandy cliffs and bluffs of Brittany. To my taste, the fennel with the strongest anise flavor is to be found in Corsica.

Fennel has many uses in French cooking. Its seeds are used in flavoring capers or gherkins. Fish are often broiled on a bed of fennel shoots. To use fennel in a court bouillon or sauce, split the shoot in two lengthwise in order to release the anise flavor that is concentrated in its center. When the hearts, or bulbs, of cultivated fennel are cooked, they are a delicious vegetable with an anise flavor (see Fennel Hearts Braised in Butter*). The hearts can also be sautéed and served with various kinds of broiled fish. The little fennel shoots that sprout from the top of the heart can be chopped fine and used to season green salads and potato salad. Minced even finer, they can serve as a substitute for dill (which is difficult to grow) and sprinkled on boiled or steamed potatoes. Another delicious dish is Gratin of Potatoes with Fennel Shoots.*

FOUR SPICES

Known in French as *quatre épices,* this is an aromatic mixture of ground white pepper, ground ginger, grated nutmeg, and ground cloves. It is similar in flavor to allspice. This spice will be hard to find in the United States, but you can mix your own at home.

    4 tablespoons ground white pepper
    3 teaspoons ground ginger
    3½ teaspoons grated nutmeg
    1 teaspoon ground cloves

Mix together and store in a small bottle. Keep it tightly corked.

GARLIC

Garlic is one of the most ancient of bulb plants, the ancestor of the onion and the shallot. It is thought to have originated in the Central Asian steppe region and may have been brought to the West by the Mongols. It belongs to the genus *Allium* and the family Liliaceae. Its bulb, which is enclosed in a white or pinkish covering, is composed of smaller, separately wrapped bulbs known as cloves. This skin is very bitter when cooked and should be removed before using the clove (there are one or two exceptions to this, notably in roasting a leg of lamb, when the garlic cloves, unpeeled, are crushed and placed in the roasting pan). The strong smell of garlic is due to its oil. Though it belongs to the same family as the lily, their scents are not in the least related. The acrid, persistent smell of garlic is one of its disadvantages, since it lingers after the dish flavored with garlic has been eaten. This can be a social hazard!

In France, garlic is associated with the sun and with the fragrant dishes of Provence. It should be used with discretion. Sometimes a small piece of the clove is enough. Care must be taken in cooking garlic, because it burns easily. It should be cooked very gently in oil or butter over a low flame along with whatever foods it is flavoring. A better idea is to make a garlic paste and add it to the dish after it has cooked.

Garlic Paste

This method of preparing garlic lessens its strong flavor. Cut two peeled garlic cloves in halves or quarters. Using a garlic press, squeeze them into a mortar or heavy bowl. Add a tablespoon of olive oil or peanut oil and pound with a pestle. When the garlic is completely crushed, stir it with a wooden spatula until a paste has formed. If you prefer, use a tablespoon of butter instead of oil.

Garlic is added to all marinades, especially marinades for game, the number of garlic cloves depending on the quantity of marinade. When meat, especially game, is slowly cooked (in ragouts, for example), the amount of garlic can be increased. Speaking of her native Burgundy, the great writer Colette tells us of a recipe for wild hare in which thirty garlic cloves (and the same number of shallots) were used. The hare was stewed gently for seven or eight hours, by which time the garlic had melted into the juice and its flavor had blended with all the others. Garlic is a zestful addition to summer vegetables, eggplant, zucchini, to crip winter salads, and might almost be called indispensable in the making of fish soups and Salt Cod with Garlic and Cream* (*Brandade de morue*). It is delicious in *Ratatouille.**

GHERKINS
These are a species of cucumber (*Cucumis anguria*) that in their natural state have a rather insipid taste. Preserved in wine vinegar to which a few peppercorns, small onions, and a sprig or two of tarragon have been added, they turn into an appetizing condiment very popular in France. Gherkins add a note of piquancy to many sauces, and a few of them are always served with beef *Pot-au-feu.** They are also used to garnish cold cuts, especially cold roast pork and ham.

GINGER
A plant of the genus *Zingiber,* native to Asia, now widely cultivated for its pungent, aromatic rootstalk. It is not a common kitchen spice in France except for those cooks who specialize in Oriental cooking or in dishes such as Lacquered Roast Pork.*

Unpeeled fresh ginger ("black ginger") can be used in marinades and sauces in which it is sautéed quickly to release its flavor. Scraped and peeled ginger ("white ginger") is very often candied or preserved and used in chutneys, pickles, or in desserts and candies. The dried rootstalk is ground and used as a condiment.

GREEN PEPPER (see Pepper)

HERBE À TORTUE
A mixture of finely ground herbs consisting of oregano, basil, savory, fennel seed, and rosemary. It is used to flavor certain bouillons and in preparing calf's head, tongue, and tripe.

JAMAICA PEPPER (see Allspice)

JUNIPER BERRIES
These are the berry-like, blue fruit of the evergreen juniper tree, which bears only once in two years. The bittersweet taste lends itself deliciously to Braised Cabbage,* to Sauerkraut,* and to the sauces of game birds.

LEEK
A plant, *Allium porrum,* that is closely related to the onion and has a long white slender bulb and thick, dark green leaves. It has been cultivated since antiquity. It is said to have a beneficial effect on the voice and is often recommended for singers and public speakers. The leek is also believed to have diuretic and disintoxicating properties. It is sometimes called "the poor man's asparagus," though one wonders why, since it is both expensive and seasonal and can only be eaten fresh.

It is one of the main ingredients in vegetable soups and poultry bouillons. In Northern France a tart is made from the white part of leeks. They are delicious served with Baked Whiting.*

MACE
Mace is the dried red or pale yellow husk of the nutmeg seed. It tastes like a mixture of nutmeg and cinnamon and is used in pickling and in marinades.

MARJORAM
The dried and crushed leaves of *Majorana hortensis,* it has a rich, almost nutty taste. It is used in marinades, in ragouts (particularly ragouts of lamb), and sometimes as a seasoning for stuffed tomatoes.

MIGNONNETTE
This is a homemade spice consisting of crushed black peppercorns, crushed white peppercorns, and a small amount of crushed coriander seeds. It has a strong, hearty taste and is especially good with broiled steak.

MINT
Any of several varieties of the genus *Mentha.* It has a biting, invigorating taste. It is used very little in French cooking. In this book I have included a recipe of Anglo-Saxon origin for a sauce (used with Leg of Lamb*) made with fresh mint leaves. They can also be chopped and sprinkled over cucumber salad. Lightly dried, mint can be used to give a pleasant aroma to Mint Vinegar.*

MIXED HERBS (see *Herbe à tortue*)

NUTMEG
This is the aromatic oval-shaped seed of the tree *Myristica fragrans,* widely cultivated in the East and West Indies and elsewhere in the tropics. Grayish-brown in color (sometimes coated with a white preservative powder), it has a perfectly delicious taste. It should always be freshly grated. Nutmeg is used in white sauces, cheese dishes, and various vegetables *au gratin.*

ONION

A biennial plant of the Liliaceae family, cultivated the world over for its sharp-tasting bulb. It is one of the oldest of plants, and it was so revered in Egypt that a cult was dedicated to it. The onion is covered with several layers of skin. The countryfolk in some parts of France believe that, when onions have more than the usual number of layers, the winter will be long and hard. The raw flesh has a sharp, pungent odor and a taste that is lessened by cooking.

There are several varieties of onions; the most common is the coppery-skinned yellow onion. There is also the strongly flavored red-skinned, slightly flat Italian onion, and the mild, almost sweet, light-colored Spanish onion. Green (or spring) onions are sold in bunches, along with their green stems. They have a fresh, piquant taste and are used as a garnish in springtime menus or as an hors d'oeuvre. They are delicious dipped in salt and eaten with bread and butter. The green stems can be used in making soup when leeks are not obtainable.

OREGANO

A wild species of marjoram with a stronger, spicier flavor. Dried and crushed, it is used particularly in Italian dishes. Try to imagine a pizza without oregano!

PARSLEY

Parsley is the herb *Petroselinum crispum,* thought to have originated in Sardinia. In French cooking it is the most widely used of all herbs. There are two main varieties: the one having small, flat leaves, and the other having crinkly, curly leaves. Since the latter is more decorative, it is preferable as a garnish.

Parsley has a pronounced taste, and there is practically no sauce that does not benefit by its use. It figures in every *bouquet garni,** that inevitable accompaniment of ragouts, and soups. It has diuretic and digestive properties and is rich in vitamins and protein. When garnishing a platter or plate with parsley, you will obtain a better effect by using one or two small bunches rather than by strewing sprigs all over the platter. Finely chopped parsley sprinkled over uninteresting-looking foods adds color and zest, and when used on tomatoes or carrots it provides a gay color contrast. Fried parsley is a superb garnish, but it is not easy to make. I have a childhood memory of fried parsley that was both green and crisp, and I have never been able to duplicate it exactly.

Fried Parsley

>   1 cup parsley sprigs
>   1⅛ cup of peanut oil

The main thing to know about frying parsley is that the sprigs must be absolutely dry. To clean them, place them under cold running water, shake, and wipe each one dry. Unless you can succeed in getting the parsley perfectly dry, it is very risky to wash it.

Gather the parsley sprigs into small bunches, leaving each with stems about ½ inch long. Heat the oil in a small, heavy-bottomed saucepan. When the oil begins to sizzle, take hold of the bunches by the stems and lower them into the oil. Stir them, turn them over, remove them with a slotted spoon before they begin to darken, and place them on a double thickness of paper towels, where they will immediately

---

stiffen. Salt them while they are still hot and place them very gently (otherwise they will fall to pieces) on the dish they are to garnish.

PEPPER

Pepper is the most widely used of all the spices. French cuisine would be inconceivable without it. Though they look different, black pepper and white pepper are basically the same. Black pepper is grayish-black and slightly wrinkled in appearance because the berry is dried in the husk. White pepper is the same berry stripped of its husk before drying, hence it is more expensive. It is white and glossy and has a distinct but delicate taste, less sharp than black pepper.

Black pepper is used in most French cooking. White pepper is reserved for use in light-colored sauces and on white meats, eggs, and fish so as not to mar the appearance of the dishes with little black flecks.

Green peppercorns come from berries picked before they are fully ripe, hence the green color. They have a characteristic fresh, tangy flavor. They can be bought preserved in cans or jars but will not keep long unless the container is wrapped in aluminum foil and refrigerated. The best way to buy them is dried and vacuum-packed. They are used to season sautéed steaks, roast duck or goose, leg of lamb, in short, as a seasoning for rich, dark succulent meats and not for such meats as roast veal or chicken. To prepare and use green peppercorns: Peel the peppercorns or crush them lightly so as to release the flavor. Do not insert them into the meat or fowl; simply add them to the roasting pan when the meat is halfcooked, continuing to baste frequently. Two tablespoons of crushed green peppers are ample for a roast duck. It is not a good idea to use green peppercorns too often. They should be saved for special occasions.

Selecting the right kind of pepper and figuring out the exact amount to use require experience. Pepper is at its best when freshly ground. For this reason I specify the use of freshly ground pepper throughout this book. In some preparations—for example, marinades and fish bouillons (which are to be strained)—I recommend pounding the pepper with a wooden mallet to intensify the taste.

QUATRE ÉPICES   (see Four Spices)

RED PEPPER   (see Cayenne Pepper)

ROSEMARY

A decorative evergreen shrub, *Rosmarinus officinalis,* that has blue flowers and needle-shaped grayish-green leaves used in flavoring. Its heady fragrance scents the countryside in Provence, especially on the shores of the Mediterranean, where the leaves are covered with a fine white powder (perhaps caused by the evaporation of sea salt). Bees love the small delicate flowers and use them to produce a deliciously flavored honey. Rosemary is used in many Provençal dishes.

SAFFLOWER

Also known as bastard saffron, this is an herb resembling a thistle. The heart of its large orange-colored flower contains two substances, one yellow and one red, which when blended combine to make a light red dye. The edible safflower oil is made from the seeds of the plant.

SAFFRON

A spice made from the dried orange stigmas of the saffron crocus (*Crocus sativus*). It has existed since ancient times in the Far East, Near East, and parts of Africa; it was introduced into Europe by the Arabs. In France it was first used in the Mediterranean region for flavoring the wonderful fish stew *bouillabaisse.* The saffron stigmas gathered toward the end of the summer are at first a bright yellow, but as they dry they turn a deeper, almost orange color. This spice releases its penetrating flavor and color as soon as it is added to a hot liquid.

Saffron is used in many dishes; for example, Indian-style curried chicken, certain shellfish, and in Mussel Pilaf with Saffron and Curry.* True saffron is the most expensive spice used in French cuisine. Elizabeth David, the English cooking expert and writer, tells us in *Spices, Aromatics and Condiments* that it takes 170,000 flowers to make one pound of saffron.

SAGE

A plant (*Salvia officinalis*) that was considered sacred in antiquity. The Egyptians are thought to have used it in embalming because of its antiseptic properties. It bears small mauve flowers, but only the leaves of branches that have not borne flowers are dried and used as an herb. It is very popular in Italy, especially with veal and fish Flounder Fillets with Sage.*

SALT

Salt, or sodium chloride ($NaCl$), is the most ancient and indispensable of seasonings. It is a natural product. Formerly, most of the world's supply consisted of sea salt produced by the evaporation of sea water. Today, most of our salt is mined; in its crude form it is known as rock salt.

In French cooking both coarse rock salt and coarse sea salt are used. Coarse salt is put in soups and in water used to blanch vegetables. Coarse sea salt is recommended for salting the water in which fish are to be poached—this makes a remarkable difference in the taste of the fish. Fine table salt is made from both sea salt and rock salt. Fine sea salt, with its hint of iodine flavor, is delicious sprinkled on fish fillets after cooking.

In France coarse salt is served on the side with beef *Pot-au-feu.** There is nothing more delicious than to crunch coarse salt along with your bread and meat!

SAVORY

There are two varieties of this aromatic herb: *Satureja hortensis,* known as summer savory, and *S. montana,* or winter savory. Both have a delicate flavor resembling thyme with a slight whiff of mint.

Savory is added to the *Bouquets garnis** used in cooking lentils and dried beans of all sorts, because it combats the flatulence often caused by these foods. It is also used in various ragouts as well as in marinades for game and venison.

SCALLIONS

Scallions are a variety of spring onion having a slim bulb and dark green leaves. They are especially good (finely cut with scissors) in green salads.

SHALLOTS

The shallot is a plant (*Allium ascalonicum*) cultivated for its edible coppery-red bulb, not unlike the garlic bulb in shape. In taste it is halfway between garlic and onion. It is said that shallots were cultivated in Charlemagne's imperial gardens and were considered a great novelty. The craze for cooking with shallots reached its peak around 1960 (about the time when the brown sauces were going out). You would have thought the shallot had been invented to suppress all other tastes in cooking, to turn, as it were, French cuisine into a "shallot cuisine." In the early 1960s no one would have dared to sauté anything without adding the proper amount of finely minced shallots. I know. I did it myself, and I taught my pupils to do so.

The taste of shallot is both delicate and zestful and can transform the most banal of dishes. But beware: it has a very domineering personality, and if too much is used it can completely overwhelm the taste of any food it is used with. So be as sparing with it as you are with garlic. One or two finely minced shallots are usually enough in any dish. Putting them through a garlic press is a better idea than mincing them. Parisian cooks use a great many shallots in all sorts of dishes and sauces. Sometime ago, when the Paris food market was still in central Paris, one of the late-night restaurants served a traditional onion soup that was more full-bodied and flavorsome than any other I had ever tasted. One night I learned the chef's secret: just before serving the soup he squeezed a little raw shallot through the garlic press directly on top of the soup. Not a trace of shallot was to be seen—but what a delight the soup was to smell and to taste!

Shallots are also used in the reduction of the vinegar that forms the base of Béarnaise Sauce* and similar sauces. It is a necessity in most court bouillons, in the sauces used to accompany freshwater fish, and in marinades for game. If you cannot find shallots, substitute the minced white part of green onions (one onion for each shallot). Add finely minced garlic to the onion and bind it with a drop or two of peanut oil. This will not have the true fragrance of shallot, but it will come very close to it.

TARRAGON

Tarragon (*Artemisia dracunculus*) is thought to have been brought to the West by the Crusaders. A sixteenth-century French botanist called it *herbe dragon* (dragonwort), and in the seventeenth-century, Jean La Quintinie, a French agronomist, sang its praises.

For us, tarragon is associated with the springtime. It has a very subtle flavor, suggesting anise with slightly acid overtones. Tarragon seasons green salads wonderfully and is also (especially when fresh) ideal for *Bouquets garnis.** To my taste, it reaches its peak of perfection in Béarnaise Sauce,* and I sometimes slip a sprig or a few leaves of tarragon in with the garlic used in roasting a leg of lamb, thus making the taste of garlic less obvious. It harmonizes well with the flavor of poultry and other white meats and makes the best of all aromatic vinegars (see Tarragon Vinegar*).

THYME

Cultivated thyme in a small aromatic plant (*Thymus vulgaris*) with grayish-green leaves. It is sometimes used as a scented border in gardens. It secretes an essential oil that has diuretic and antiseptic properties. Wild thyme[1] (*Thymus serpyllum*) has a strong, heady fragrance and grows in many regions (especially in Provence and the Mediterranean countryside). The thyme that grows on seaside cliffs is so spicy and pungent it almost goes to your head, and it somewhat resembles curry powder.

Thyme is used in *bouquets garnis,** in sauces, ragouts, marinades, and homemade aromatic oils (see Oils).

Fresh thyme has a sharper, more pungent taste than dried thyme. It is at its best when it just begins to dry. To dry your own thyme: Cut the thyme branches on a sunny day in early summer. Place it on paper towels and put it in a darkened room. It will dry quickly and keep all its aroma. When the leaves dry and detach themselves from the branch, place them in a wide-necked jar and close it firmly. Plastic bags are useless for keeping dried herbs. Most of the common herbs, bay leaf and tarragon, for example, can be dried in this way. They will keep for ten to twelve months.

TURMERIC

Also known as East Indian saffron, this is an East Indian herb (*Curcuma longa*). Its rootstalk is dried and ground into powder. It has a tangy, sharp, peppery taste and is used especially in making curry powder. In French cooking turmeric is used in the preparation of arrowroot.

VANILLA

The vanilla plant is a genus of climbing orchids native to tropical America and is now cultivated widely in other tropical places such as Guadeloupe, Java, and the island of Réunion. It is cultivated for its highly scented pods, which are responsible for the sweet, aromatic taste of many foods. The finest pods are long (8 to 11 inches) and flexible, with a slightly frosted appearance. Vanilla is used in the manufacture of chocolate and other confections, in custards, cakes, icings, creams, and any number of other delicious sweet things.

---

[1] Wild thyme is more common in France than in the United States, though it can be found in certain regions.

Oils

PEANUT OIL

The oils chiefly used in French cuisine are peanut oil and olive oil. Some people prefer olive oil for its rich, characteristic flavor, but peanut oil is more widely used precisely because it is tasteless and odorless. Another advantage of peanut oil is that it can be kept for a long time. It should be stored at slightly below room temperature (around 56° F.). One of its greatest virtues is that it does not burn as easily as butter. For this reason it is wise to add a small amount of peanut oil to the butter used in sautéing. It is recommended particularly for making dressings for tender green salads or for salads composed of green vegetables of taste so delicate it might be overpowered if a stronger oil were used. For deep-fat frying, peanut oil is by far the most satisfactory.

It is important to know how to select peanut oil. If the label on the bottle states that the oil is PURE or NATURAL, and specifies that the oil is made entirely from peanuts, you can buy it with confidence. Pure peanut oil can be heated to 310° F. without burning. Some peanut oils are labeled simply SUPERIOR, and it is wise to be suspicious of these, because more often than not they have been mixed with another type of oil. The mixture may be entirely satisfactory, but you cannot be absolutely sure.

OLIVE OIL

Olive oil is the most ancient of all oils used in cooking and seasoning. The olive tree (*Olea europaea*) originated in Asia and was known throughout antiquity. It is thought to have been brought to the Mediterranean regions by Phocaean Greeks, who came from Asia Minor and founded the city of Marseilles.

Once opened, a bottle or can of olive oil (unlike peanut oil) does not keep for a very long time. So unless you are a devotee, you are wiser to buy it in small amounts. The finest olive oil has its vintages like wine. The best vintage olive oil comes from Salon-de-Provence, Grasse, and Nice. There are three categories of olive oil:

Virgin Olive Oil

Virgin olive oil is obtained in a first pressing by the cold-press method. "Extra fine" virgin olive oil contains 1 per cent of acidity, and "fine" virgin olive oil 1½ per cent. Virgin olive oil is particularly digestible because of the oleic acid it contains. It can be used in sautéing as well as deep-fat frying (but be warned: it does give off a strong odor).

Pure Refined Olive Oil

This contains 1.5 per cent to 1.8 per cent of acidity. It is obtained by hot-pressing the virgin oil extracted in the first pressing along with the oil cake from which the pits have been removed. It has a stronger, fruitier taste than virgin oil and is slightly green in color.

Ordinary Olive Oil

This contains 3 per cent of acidity and is obtained by mixing virgin olive oil with refined olive oil.

NOTE: *It is inadvisable to reuse any oil, especially olive oil, after deep-fat frying. It contains harmful impurities that cannot be completely removed even by being strained.*

WALNUT OIL

The walnuts from trees in Auvergne, and in the Bourbonnais and Limousin regions, furnish most of the walnut oil in France. The oil is extracted by the cold-press method from green walnuts only. Because it contains 5 per cent of linoleic acid, it burns easily and does not keep for any length of time. But, freshly pressed, it makes a delicious dressing for crisp fall or winter salads such as endive, beet, or celery root. If walnut oil begins to have a strong taste and smell, add a little peanut oil.

AROMATIC OILS

It is easy to make one's own aromatic oils (all of which have olive oil as their base). These fragrant oils are used particularly in French Mediterranean and Provençal cooking. The advantage of preparing them at home is that you can make them in small quantities (pints or half pints) and thus need not worry about deterioration in flavor or change in color. If you like mixing your salads at the table, these oils can be served in covered earthenware pots.

Garlic Oil *Huile d'ail*

> 6–8 cloves garlic (depending on their size and your taste for garlic)
> 2 cups olive oil

Remove the cloves of garlic from the bulb. Do not peel them. Simply place them in an empty bottle, add the oil, and cork well. Always use a new cork. Put the bottle in a cool place for about 15 days before using, turning the bottle once a day without shaking it. This method is used for all the following aromatic oil recipes.

Garlic oil is delicious on pieces of French bread, with or without butter. It makes a delicious dressing for tomatoes, celery root, green peppers, and for crisp winter salads where it replaces *the Chapon* (Garlic Crusts). It can also be used in Mushroom Caps Sautéed in Butter,* Potato Salad,* and Salade niçoise.**

Oil with Herbs from Provence   *Huile aux herbes de Provence*

- 2 cups olive oil
- 4 or 5 bay leaves
- 2 or 3 sprigs thyme
- 1 or 2 fennel shoots split lengthwise

The method is the same as in Garlic Oil* (Huile d'oil—recipe above). This oil can be used in baking or broiling fish. Sprinkle the fish with the oil, using a sprig of the macerated thyme. The same method can be used in barbecuing fish and meats, for if only the dried herbs are used they tend to turn black and produce a bitter flavor.

Oil with Savory   *Huile de sarriette*

An aromatic oil with an extremely delicate taste. These ingredients will fill a small earthenware pot. Remember to cover it carefully.

- 1⅛ cups olive oil
- 5–6 branches dried savory

The method is the same as in Garlic Oil.* This oil is used on all sorts of dry cheeses (which have been first sprinkled with a little freshly ground pepper). It is superb with goat or ewe cheeses, if you can find them in specialty shops. Serve it with farmer's cheese and green onions as a cocktail snack.

Limes Preserved in Olive Oil   *Citrons verts confits dans l'huile d'olive*

I heartily recommend this delicious Moroccan aromatic oil. It consists of limes studded with cloves and preserved in olive oil. Keep a jar in your refrigerator and use it to impart a new taste to roast duck, or, for that matter, roast chick or pork.

Use a jar with a good screw-on top that will hold at least 3 cups.

- 5–6 limes (depending on their size), well washed and dried, each lime studded with 5 or 6 cloves
- 2 cups olive oil

Place the limes in the jar, add the oil (which should completely cover the limes), screw on the cover, and refrigerate.

The limes will be ready to use in two or three months. They will be slightly faded, their color having gone into the oil, but wonderfully preserved. The oil may be used as a dressing for various salads, and, for example, Vegetables à la Grecque.* The best way to use the preserved limes is with Roast Duck.*

Vinegars

VINEGARS

Vinegar (or sour wine, from French *vin aigre*) is a liquid condiment produced by the acetic fermentation of wine or other alcohol-containing liquid. It seems to have existed since early times. The Chinese made it from rice spirits some three thousand years ago. Mohammed forbade the faithful to drink wine but recommended vinegar. The Bible bears witness to its use in the ancient Middle East. In the West vinegar is as old as the wine it was made of. Roman soldiers in combat refreshed themselves with posca, a mixture of water and vinegar sometimes flavored with mint leaves. In the Middle Ages vinegar, often seasoned with spices, made its appearance in French cuisine; bread dipped in vinegar is mentioned as a garnish for soups. Vinegar became so important a product in France that Charles VI, in 1394, issued an edict recognizing the Corporations des Vinaigriers (vinegar makers) and granted its members the right to hawk the vinegar made from their vintage.

Alcohol Vinegar   *Vinaigre d'alcool*

A very strong vinegar rarely used in French cooking (and then mainly in preserving). In salad dressings it causes the leaves to wilt immediately, and it is considered harmful to delicate stomachs.

Cider Vinegar   *Vinaigre de cidre*

This is a mild vinegar with an apple taste. Though it has its devotees in France, it is not as popular as wine vinegar.

Malt Vinegar   *Vinaigre de malt*

A bitter-tasting vinegar made from the wastes of barley left over from brewing. It is much appreciated in England and in the United States but is little known in France.

Wine Vinegar   *Vinaigre de vin*

The first wine vinegar goes back to the Roman occupation of the Loire Valley. The good red and white wines of the region incurred natural oxidation in the course of their long, slow journey down the river, and they arrived in due course, not as wine, but as vinegar. This seems to have been the origin of "the Orléans method," first described by Jean Chaptal in 1807. Since then, thanks largely to the discoveries of Louis Pasteur, the method has been perfected and the acidification process speeded up.

The most commonly used vinegar is red wine vinegar. It should be sharp in taste with just a little of the bouquet of the wine it is made from. The best is Orléans vinegar, famous throughout the world. Other excellent (but, alas, expensive) vinegars include champagne vinegar and sherry vinegar. The latter, with its strong taste of muscat grapes, is used in sauces accompanying fish or poultry and in various marinades. A few drops of it can be used to deglaze* the pan in which a duck or chicken has been roasted.

To vary the taste of salads and the dressings used on them, you can make a variety of aromatic vinegars at home.

AROMATIC VINEGARS

Shallot Vinegar for Winter *Vinaigre d'échalote pour l'hiver*

    5 or 6 shallots
    1 teaspoon white peppercorns
    1 quart wine vinegar

With a sharp knife remove the pink layer of shallot skin. Do not break the thin white skin underneath. Add the shallots and the peppercorns to the vinegar and cork the bottle tightly. Let this mixture macerate for 12 to 15 days, for the first 5 or 6 days turning the bottle once a day. Filter the vinegar into another bottle or jar and close tightly. For a stronger taste add 1–3 cloves of garlic.

Shallot vinegar is an excellent accompaniment to oysters or shellfish. It can also be used in making dressings for crisp winter salads. A small quantity can be added to marinades for game and wild fowl.

Tarragon Vinegar *Vinaigre à l'estragon*

Pick the tarragon branches on a sunny day in the early summer. Put them in a dry place for about 5 days, or until they have just begun to dry.

    1 quart of wine vinegar
    2 sprigs half-dried tarragon (or 1 long sprig broken in two)

Pour the vinegar into a clear glass bottle or jar, add the tarragon, and close tightly. Macerate for from 15 days to 3 weeks, then remove the tarragon.

Elderberry Flower Vinegar *Vinaigre de sureau*

Pick clusters of the blossoms before the fruit has formed. Dry them for 10 days if the weather is dry and for 2 weeks if it is humid.

>   1 quart wine vinegar
>   4–6 clusters dried elderberry flowers

Pour the vinegar in a clear glass bottle, add the dried blossoms, and close tightly. Macerate for 2 weeks. Then filter the vinegar, without shaking the bottle, into another clear bottle.

This vinegar can be used in Green Bean Salad.* It can also replace lemon juice in cooking duck or partridge. It can be used with discretion in marinades and some sauces for game.

Mint Vinegar *Vinaigre de menthe*

A fragrant, refreshing vinegar that can be used in dressings for cucumber salad and fennel hearts. You can even make a drink out of it by adding water and sugar.

>   1 quart wine vinegar
>   2 sprigs half-dried mint
>   2 teaspoons sugar

Follow the method in the preceding recipe.

Cherries in Vinegar *Cerises au vinaigre*

A delicious condiment used for accompanying beef *Pot-au-feu,** stewed chicken, cold roast pork, cold roast duck. Large sweet cherries (Bing or Queen Anne) are the best for this vinegar. If you want a very strong condiment, use alcohol vinegar, otherwise use Tarragon Vinegar.* Make this vinegar in small jars (3 or 4 at a time, so they can be placed on the table.

FOR ABOUT 1 CUP WINE VINEGAR USE:

>   ¼ pound sweet red cherries (not too ripe)
>   1 cup tarragon vinegar or alcohol vinegar
>   1 sprig half-dried tarragon
>   15 black peppercorns
>   a few coriander seeds

Wipe each cherry carefully with a clean cloth. Leave about ½ inch of stem on each cherry. Place the cherries in the jar, add the vinegar, tarragon, peppercorns, and coriander seeds. Seal tightly and put in a cool, dark place. The cherries will be ready to use in about 6 weeks or when they have lost their color, but the longer you keep them the better they will be. After a year the vinegar becomes mild and delicious.

Butters

THREE METHODS OF PREPARING BUTTER USED IN COOKING

NOTE: *For each recipe in this book that calls for butter, sweet butter is to be used.*

Clarified, or Drawn, Butter *Beurre clarifié*

Place 5 tablespoons of butter in a saucepan. Heat until it boils up and foams (without coloring). Remove from heat, tilt the saucepan, and with a spoon remove the impurities that have risen to the surface. It is these impurities that burn when butter is cooked at high temperatures. The resulting butter will be very clear and can be heated to much higher temperatures than unclarified butter can.

Clarified butter is used in cooking crêpes and in sautéing delicate meats such as brains, sweetbreads, and breasts of chicken. In the old days it was used for coating roasts before baking.

Creamed Butter *Beurre en pommade*

Put 5 tablespoons of butter in a bowl (the butter should be at room temperature) and with a fork crush it against the sides of the bowl until it has the consistency of face cream. Before using it, beat it into a soft mass with a small whisk.

Kneaded Butter *Beurre manié*

This consists of an equal amount of butter and flour worked together with a fork. It is used as a binding for a sauce or for pan juices.

to thicken a sauce

>   2 tablespoons butter
>   2 tablespoons flour

Work together with a fork until a smooth paste has formed. Beat small portions one after the other into the sauce. *Beurre manie* can be used to bind all fine sauces, particularly when the original thickening is inadequate.

to thicken pan juices

The method is the same but the quantities are different: 1 tablespoon butter and 1 tablespoon flour. If a very small amount of sauce or pan juice is to be thickened, use 2 teaspoons flour and 2 teaspoons butter.

SAVORY BUTTERS *Beurres travaillés*

Butters flavored with aromatic herbs or seasoned with garlic or shallot can replace sauces for broiled meats or fish or for fish cooked *au naturel.* They can also be served with blanched or stewed vegetables. Savory butters flavored with shellfish and smoked fish are delicious used as spreads for canapés or crackers. All flavored butters can be made in advance and kept covered in the refrigerator.

The procedure for making these tasty flavored butters is almost always the same: Cut all herbs with scissors and mince all other ingredients—shellfish, fish, fowl liver, or wild game liver—and put these through a food mill[1] along with the amount of butter indicated in the recipe. Work the ingredients together with a spatula until a smooth mixture is formed.

Herb Butter *Beurre d'herbes*

7½ tablespoons creamed butter
1 tablespoon scissored chervil
1 tablespoon scissored parsley
1 tablespoon scissored chives
1 tablespoon green onion (or other onion) put through a garlic press
salt to taste
freshly ground pepper to taste

Herb butter is used on broiled steak or veal. It is delicious with potatoes that are boiled in their jackets and then peeled, with sautéed potatoes, and with green beans.

Tarragon Butter *Beurre d'estragon*

The taste of tarragon is so delicate and subtle it would be a shame to add any other herbs.

2–3 drops Tarragon Vinegar*
salt
freshly ground pepper
3 tablespoons fresh tarragon leaves finely cut with scissors
7½ tablespoons butter, cut in pieces

---

[1] In some cases a blender may be substituted.

Add the vinegar, salt, and pepper to the minced tarragon leaves and put through the finest disk of a food mill, along with the pieces of butter. Work into a smooth paste with a wodden spatula and refrigerate.

Use tarragon butter as a topping for fillets of sole au naturel, for sautéed veal chops, calf's liver. Another idea: top broiled tomato halves with a little of this delicious butter.

Green Butter with Tarragon   *Beurre vert à l'estragon*

Green butter . . . what could be more spring-like? It is made of tarragon butter to which a little *vert d'épinards* (given below) has been added. Prepare the butter as in the preceding recipe.

making the vert d'épinards

Add a good handful of well-washed fresh spinach to a saucepan of boiling water. Salt the water and cook the spinach for about 2 minutes. Drain thoroughly. Place the spinach in a square of clean cheesecloth. Pick up the four corners of the cloth and twist and squeeze the juice out over a bowl. Extract all the juice you can. Work 2 tablespoons of the spinach juice into the tarragon butter with a wooden spatula. Adjust for seasoning. Cover and refrigerate.

Provençal Butter   *Beurre provençale*

> 5 tablespoons butter
> 2 shallots, squeezed through a garlic press, or the same amount of raw onion squeezed through a garlic press
> 1–2 cloves garlic, squeezed through a garlic press and pounded with 1 tablespoon olive oil
> 2 tablespoons finely minced fresh or dried herbs: chervil, parsley, tarragon, or basil
> salt
> freshly ground pepper

Work the butter into a smooth mass with a fork, then mix in all the other ingredients and work the mixture until it is smooth.

Shallot Butter   *Beurre d'échalote*

> 2 tablespoons shallot very finely minced or put through a garlic press
> ½ cup creamed butter

Work the shallots into the butter, cover, and place in the refrigerator.

This is enough butter to top 6 slices of calf's liver (broiled or sautéed). It is excellent with broiled ham steak.

Red Wine Butter Flavored with Shallot   *Beurre marchand de vin*

A special butter for broiled or sautéed steaks.

   1½ cups full-bodied dry red wine
   2 heaping tablespoons minced shallot
   1 pinch salt
   1 good pinch (taken with 3 fingers) Mignonnette*
   ½ cup creamed butter

Place the wine and shallot in a heavy-bottomed enameled saucepan and reduce almost completely—that is, until there is just the merest glaze on the bottom of the pan. Transfer this glaze to a bowl. When the glaze is cool, add the salt and mignonnette. Work in the butter with a wooden spatula. Cover and refrigerate. Spread hot steaks with the butter just before serving.

Lemon Butter   *Beurre citronné*

   juice of ½–1 lemon, depending on your taste for lemon
   ½ cup cold butter, cut in small pieces
   salt
   freshly ground pepper

Put the lemon juice in a small enameled saucepan and add 2 pieces of butter. Place over low heat and whisk in the rest of the butter, 2 pieces at a time. Do not let the butter boil or become transparent. When all the butter has been beaten in, remove pan from heat and continue to beat for another minute. Add salt and pepper to taste and pour in a sauce bowl.

Snail Butter   *Beurre d'escargot*

   ½ cup butter, cut in small pieces
   1 heaping tablespoon shallot squeezed through a garlic press
   2 cloves garlic squeezed through a garlic press
   1 heaping tablespoon finely scissored parsley
   salt
   freshly ground pepper

Put the first 4 ingredients through a food mill,[1] blend with a wooden spatula, add salt and pepper to taste. Cover and refrigerate.

This butter is used to garnish snails in their shells (as well as large mussels cooked in the same fashion as snails). It can also be used to butter baked or broiled fish. It is delicious on mushrooms and various summer vegetables.

[1] A blender may be used instead of a food mill in this recipe.

Mustard Butter   *Beurre de moutarde*

> ½ cup creamed butter
> 2 tablespoons strong Dijon mustard
> 3 or 4 drops lemon juice (or 3 drops champagne vinegar or sherry vinegar)

Work ingredients into a smooth paste, cover, and refrigerate.

A delicious butter topping for broiled fish, especially sardines and herrings. It goes wonderfully with pork sausages and sautéed pork chops.

Anchovy Butter   *Beurre d'anchois*

> 6·small boneless, skinless anchovy fillets
> ½ cup butter, cut in small pieces

Chop the anchovies and put them through a food mill along with the pieces of butter. Blend with a wooden spatula and add:

> 1 tablespoon heavy cream
> freshly ground pepper (1 or 2 turns of the mill)
> a few drops lemon juice or a small amount freshly grated nutmeg

NOTE: *Do not add salt*

Mix into the anchovy purée, cover, and refrigerate.

Anchovy butter is delicious on broiled red mullet.

Shrimp Butter   *Beurre de crevettes*

> ¼ pound cooked, peeled, and deveined shrimp
> ½ cup butter, cut in small pieces

Chop the shrimp and put them through a food mill along with the pieces of butter. Blend with a spatula. Cover and refrigerate.

Shrimp butter can be used for buttering broiled or poached fish or as a spread for canapés.

Smoked Salmon Butter   *Beurre de saumon fumé*

> 2 slices smoked salmon, cut in pieces with a stainless steel knife
> ½ cup butter, cut in small pieces

Put the smoked salmon along with the pieces of butter through a food mill. Blend into a smooth mass with a wooden spatula. Cover and refrigerate.

Chicken Liver Butter *Beurre de foies de volaille*[1]

8 tablespoons butter
4–5 chicken livers
4 tablespoons cognac
salt
freshly ground pepper

Heat 3 tablespoons of the butter in a small skillet, add the chicken livers, and sauté them, stirring constantly. Flake them with cognac, stir, and remove from heat. (The livers should cook for a few minutes only. They should not be browned, as this will toughen them.) Salt and pepper the livers and put them through a food mill, along with their cooking juices and the remaining butter, cut in small pieces. Blend the purée with a wooden spatula. Spread the butter on the canapés and reheat just before serving.

The canapés can be used as a garnish for breasts of chicken and turkey.

NOTE: *For other butters (including dessert butters) see the Index.*

[1] Three duck livers or one turkey liver may be substituted for the chicken livers.

Sauces

COLD SAUCES *Sauces froides*

Cold sauces are varied in color and flavor; they can be mild or pungent or spicy. Practically all of them are based on mayonnaise. These sauces are used to enhance cold foods that would be too plain or too dry without them. Leftover chicken or fish, hard-boiled eggs, or simply boiled potatoes served hot seem to cry out for a cold sauce. Some of these sauces can be used to turn mussels, shrimp, crab meat, or lobster into salad, with or without other ingredients.

Mayonnaise *Sauce mayonnaise*

Mayonnaise consists of egg yolk, mustard, salt, and pepper into which oil is beaten progressively. A small amount of vinegar or lemon juice (or both) is added at the end.

Things to Know About Making Mayonnaise

Cold is the enemy of mayonnaise. All ingredients should be at room temperature—they should never come directly from the refrigerator. If the oil or the eggs are cold, dip the bowl to be used in making the mayonnaise into warm water. Be sure to dry it carefully.

The thickness of the mayonnaise depends on the amount of egg yolk used. For a good firm mayonnaise, use *less* rather than *more* egg yolk.

The taste and consistency of mayonnaise depend on the kind of oil used. Olive oil tends to make the sauce oilier than peanut oil, and is used especially in the South of France, particularly in Garlic Mayonnaise* (*Sauce Aïoli*). If you wish, you can use half olive oil and half peanut oil.

making the mayonnaise

MAKES ABOUT 1¾ CUPS

  1 large egg yolk (or 2 small yolks)
  1 tablespoon mustard (either mild or strong Dijon)
  salt
  freshly ground pepper
  1½ cups peanut oil
  1 tablespoon wine vinegar or 2 tablespoons lemon juice

Put the egg yolk (or yolks) in a bowl and add the mustard, salt, and pepper. Stir these together with two or three strokes of a wooden spatula and allow to rest for 40 or 50 seconds. Beating with a whisk or electric beater, add the oil drop by drop, increasing the amount of oil to a thin stream, then a thicker stream as the sauce gains body. When the mayonnaise has reached the proper consistency, beat in the vinegar or lemon juice (or a combination of the two), and finally bind in one or two thin streams of oil. Taste and adjust for seasoning. Fresh walnut oil may also be used in making mayonnaise. It is especially good with celery salad, potato salad, winter salads of Belgian endive, celery root, and beets.

About Keeping Mayonnaise a Day or Two

Lightly powder the top of the mayonnaise with flour (using a sugar shaker) and store it in the refrigerator. The oil in the mayonnaise, which has a tendency to rise, will be absorbed by the flour and a light crust will form. Remove this crust just before serving the mayonnaise and you will find your mayonnaise exactly as if freshly made.

About Serving Mayonnaise on a Warm Day

If you plan to serve mayonnaise on a summer day, especially out of doors or on the terrace, try this method for keeping it intact:

Put a heaping tablespoon of cream cheese in a bowl and beat the mayonnaise in little by little. When the mayonnaise has been completely absorbed, taste for seasoning (you may wish to add more mustard or pepper). Then put it in a cool place until time to serve it. If it has to stand for any length of time, put it in the refrigerator.

NOTE: *Warning about mayonnaise in picnic dishes*

Foods prepared with mayonnaise should not *be taken to picnics, not even in a portable cooler. Illness-causing bacteria grow rapidly when the temperature rises above 40°F. If you are planning a picnic, try the recipe for Mayonnaise Without Eggs (recipe follows).*

Mayonnaise Without Eggs   *Mayonnaise sans oeufs*

If you are planning a picnic, try this recipe.

MAKES ABOUT 1½ CUPS

2 tablespoons evaporated milk
1–1¼ cups peanut oil
1 teaspoon mustard
juice of ½ lemon
salt
freshly ground pepper

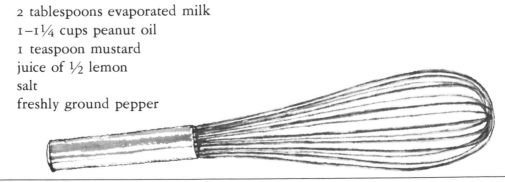

Put the evaporated milk in a bowl and beat in the oil, first drop by drop, then in a thin stream. When the sauce has reached the proper consistency, add the mustard, lemon juice, salt, and pepper. If the color seems drab, tint the sauce green or pink with a drop or so of vegetable coloring.

Garlic Mayonnaise *Sauce aioli*

MAKES ABOUT 1¾ CUPS

3–6 cloves garlic, depending on how garlicky you want your mayonnaise
2 egg yolks
1½ cups olive oil
salt
freshly ground white pepper
lemon juice to taste

Put the garlic in a mortar or heavy bowl along with a few drops of olive oil and pound to a smooth paste. Add the egg yolks, working them into the paste with a wooden spatula. Add the olive oil very slowly as for Mayonnaise.* Season with salt and pepper and a small amount of lemon juice. Keep the *aioli* in a cool place until ready to use.

Pimento Mayonnaise *Bayonnaise*

This delicious sauce is from Bayonne, in southwestern France. It consists of mayonnaise mixed with pimentos, seasoned with onion, and heightened with Cayenne pepper. It is excellent with poached fish (such as fresh tuna, fresh or salt codfish), served hot or cold, or with jumbo shrimp or with lobster, or as a dressing for crab meat salad served in avocado halves.

MAKES ABOUT 2 CUPS

1 cup freshly made Mayonnaise,* with olive oil and lemon juice
3 large canned pimentos
2 tablespoons heavy cream
2 tablespoons cognac
salt
freshly ground pepper
2 tablespoons ketchup
1 teaspoon onion squeezed through a garlic press
a dash of mild paprika
a (smaller) dash of Cayenne pepper

preparing the pimentos

Drain the pimentos thoroughly and blot them dry with a paper towel. Mince them. Place a strainer lined with cheesecloth over a large bowl. Grind the minced pimentos through a food mill (using the finest disk) onto the cheesecloth. Pick up the corners of the cheesecloth and twist the cloth tightly so as to extract the juice. Place the cheesecloth back on the strainer to catch the last drops of juice, so that the purée of pimento will be as free of liquid as possible. This can be done several hours ahead of time.

making the mayonnaise

Add the cream, cognac, ketchup, pressed onion, salt, and pepper to the mayonnaise. Taste for seasoning. Put the well-drained purée of pimento in a bowl and, using a wire whisk, beat in the mayonnaise, starting with a small quantity and increasing the amount as you beat. Add the paprika and the Cayenne pepper. Adjust seasoning if necessary. Place in the refrigerator until time to serve.

Anchovy Mayonnaise   *Sauce Collioure*

An anchovy mayonnaise I came across in the Pyrénées-Orientales. It is garnished with small shrimp. This is delicious with *Crudités niçoises** or Hard-Boiled Eggs.*

MAKES ABOUT 2 CUPS

6 canned anchovy fillets, well drained
1½ cups Mayonnaise* made with olive oil and lemon juice
lemon juice to taste
a taste garlic (optional)
4 tablespoons peeled, cooked, deveined small shrimp

NOTE: *Do not add salt*

Cut the anchovies into very small pieces and, with a food mill set over a bowl and using the finest disk, mash them into a purée. Using a wire whisk, beat the mayonnaise into the bowl of anchovy purée. Add lemon juice to taste and the garlic squeezed through a garlic press. Stir in the shrimp. Place the sauce in a serving bowl.

This sauce may be used to accompany raw vegetables such as cucumbers, tomatoes, artichoke hearts, fennel hearts, celery hearts, cauliflower, and radishes.

Horseradish Sauce   *Sauce raifort*

A mustard-flavored sauce with the sharp tang of freshly grated horseradish. Serve it with boiled meats, especially *Pot-au-feu,** and with smoked fish.

MAKES ABOUT 1½ CUPS

---

2 slices fresh white bread with crusts removed
4 tablespoons cold milk
1 cup heavy cream
3 tablespoons freshly grated horseradish
1 teaspoon white wine vinegar
1 tablespoon strong Dijon mustard
a pinch of sugar
a pinch of salt
freshly ground pepper

Soak the bread in the cold milk, squeeze it out, and put it through a food mill, using the finest disk. Beat in all the other ingredients until the sauce is well blended and smooth. Refrigerate for 20–30 minutes before serving. (Prepared horseradish may be substituted for fresh, but all the vinegar must be rinsed out and the horseradish carefully blotted dry.)

Cold Sauce with Curry Powder *Sauce froide au curry*

Another sauce useful for serving with hors-d'oeuvre. It can also be used as a dressing for various salads: rice salad, hard-boiled egg, mussel, or chicken salad. To the chicken salad add a tender stalk or two of crisp celery, diced.

MAKES ABOUT 1½ CUPS

3 tablespoons cream cheese
freshly ground pepper
1 cup Mayonnaise* made with lemon juice
2 tablespoons heavy cream
1 tablespoon onion squeezed through a garlic press
½ apple, peeled and grated
1–2 teaspoons curry powder

Put the cream cheese in a bowl and mash it with a fork until it is smooth. Pepper it lightly. Using a wire whisk, beat the mayonnaise in small amounts into the cream cheese. Mix in the heavy cream, onion, grated apple, and curry powder. Beat lightly for a few seconds. Place in the refrigerator so that it will become firm.

Béatrice Sauce *Sauce Béatrice*

A highly original cold sauce, and one of my favorite "little sauces." It has a mayonnaise base but contains more mustard, lemon juice, and pepper than usual. The beaten egg whites make it light and fluffy but thick enough for saucing.

MAKES ABOUT 2 CUPS

2 egg yolks

2 tablespoons mild mustard (tarragon mustard if possible)

salt

freshly ground black pepper

1¼ cups peanut oil

2 egg whites

3 tablespoons lemon juice

a little freshly ground white pepper

a pinch of curry powder (taken with 3 fingers)

Make Mayonnaise* of the egg yolks, mustard, salt, black pepper, and oil. In a second bowl beat the egg whites, to which a pinch more salt has been added, until stiff peaks form. Gradually add to the mayonnaise along with the lemon juice, white pepper, and curry powder. Adjust seasoning. Remember, the taste of lemon predominates in this sauce. Transfer to a bowl and keep in a cool place until ready to serve.

This recipe makes enough sauce to cover 6 cold poached eggs. It is also excellent served with slightly warm asparagus, cold poached fish fillets and warm artichoke hearts.

Soft-Boiled Egg Sauce   *Sauce de Sorges*

The base of soft-boiled eggs gives this sauce a particular smoothness. In the Périgord region the eggs are sometimes cooked under hot ashes, which give them the rustic savor of a wood fire. The proportion of egg yolks varies from one recipe to another.

MAKES ABOUT 2 CUPS

4 soft-boiled eggs (3–3½ minutes, depending on their size)

a pinch of salt

freshly ground pepper (2 turns of the pepper mill)

1–2 shallots, peeled and squeezed through a garlic press

¾ cup of peanut oil or olive oil

1 cup beef bouillon for recooking the soft-boiled egg whites

1 tablespoon minced parsley

1 tablespoon wine vinegar

Crack open the soft-boiled eggs (the yolks should be very soft). Scoop out the yolks, reserve the white, put the yolks into a warmed bowl, and add the salt, pepper, and shallots. Stir for a minute with a wooden spatula, then beat in the oil (as for Mayonnaise*) until the sauce is thick. Bring the bouillon to a simmer and cook the soft-boiled egg whites in it. Strain and chop them finely and add to the egg yolk sauce along with the parsley and vinegar. Beat well, place in a saucedish, and serve.

Orange Mayonnaise with Cream   *Sauce maltaise à l'orange*

This is an orange-flavored mayonnaise lightened with cream. It is particularly delicious with warm or cold asparagus or with cold roast pork or veal.

MAKES ABOUT 1¾ CUPS

    1 cup Mayonnaise* made with lemon juice
    grated rind of 1 orange
    juice of half this orange
    3 tablespoons heavy cream[1]

To the mayonnaise, which should be very firm, add the grated orange rind and the orange juice. Beat in the cream. Taste for seasoning, adding salt and pepper if necessary.

PINK SAUCES   *Sauces roses*

Sauce Françoise

A sweet and pungent sauce with a mayonnaise base, delicious with deep-fried fish. It is perfect as a cocktail dip for shrimp, mussels, and little balls of fried fish stuck on toothpicks.

MAKES ABOUT 2 CUPS

    1 egg yolk
    2 teaspoons strong Dijon mustard
    salt
    freshly ground pepper
    1 cup olive oil
    1 tablespoon cognac
    2 tablespoons Worcestershire sauce
    2 tablespoons ketchup
    ½ teaspoon Tabasco sauce
    a dash of liquid hot red pepper seasoning

Make a Mayonnaise* with the egg yolk, mustard, salt, pepper, and oil. When it is the proper consistency, add the rest of the ingredients one after the other, beating well after each addition. Transfer to a sauce bowl and keep in a cool place.

---

[1] You may substitute the stiffly beaten white of 1 egg for the cream. Remember to add a pinch of salt before beating the white.

Sauce Perrine

To be sure that the seasoning of this sauce is right, taste it while making it.

MAKES ABOUT 1¾ CUPS

> 1 small (3-ounce) package cream cheese
> ¾ cup heavy cream
> salt
> freshly ground pepper
> 2 tablespoons ketchup
> 1 or 2 dashes Worcestershire sauce
> a pinch of curry powder
> salt and pepper if necessary, after tasting
> a splash of milk if necessary, for thinning the sauce

Work the cream cheese and cream together in a bowl, add the salt and pepper. Place the bowl in the middle of a shallow dish filled with ice cubes, add the rest of the ingredients, beating after each addition. Adjust seasoning. The sauce will thicken in the refrigerator. Remove it after 1 hour.

NOTE: *If you wish a stronger sauce—to serve with cocktail sausages, for example—add 2 teaspoons to 1 tablespoon of Dijon mustard.*

GREEN SAUCES *Sauces vertes*

Tartar Sauce *Sauce tartare*

Serve tartar sauce with deep-fried or sautéed fish of all kinds.

MAKES ABOUT 2 CUPS

> 2 raw egg yolks
> 2 teaspoons Dijon mustard
> salt
> freshly ground pepper
> 6 hard-boiled egg yolks, mashed
> 1½ cups peanut oil
> 2 tablespoons wine vinegar
> 1–2 tablespoons lemon juice
> 3 tablespoons chives finely cut with scissors

Mix the raw egg yolks with the mustard, salt, and pepper. Add the mashed hard-boiled egg yolks, mixing well. Then beat in the oil as for Mayonnaise.* Stir in the vinegar, lemon juice, and chives. Keep in the refrigerator until time to serve.

Green Mayonnaise   *Mayonnaise verte*

2 cups firm Mayonnaise* seasoned with mild mustard and a combination of
    wine vinegar, lemon, salt, and freshly ground pepper
½ cup spinach leaves, washed and picked over
2 tablespoons fresh chervil
2 tablespoons tarragon leaves
1 tablespoon heavy cream (optional)

Blanch the spinach for 3–5 minutes. Drain and blot dry. Plunge the chervil and tarragon into boiling water for 1–2 minutes, drain and blot dry. Mix the spinach and herbs together and put them through a food mill, using the finest disk. Fold the resulting purée into the mayonnaise. Stir in cream.

Watercress Sauce   *Sauce cressonière*

This mayonnaise sauce owes its fresh green color to watercress, spinach juice (*Vert d'épinards**), and fresh herbs. It is delicious served with Trout in Aspic.

a small bunch of watercress, washed and carefully dried
2 tablespoons finely minced fresh tarragon leaves
2 tablespoons finely minced chervil leaves
3 hard cooked egg yolks, mashed
1½ cups firm Mayonnaise* seasoned with lemon and tarragon vinegar
4 tablespoons *vert d'épinards*

Pick the leaves off the watercress stems and put them with the herbs through a food mill twice, using the finest disk. With a wooden spatula work this purée into the mashed egg yolks, then beat very gradually into the mayonnaise along with the *vert d'épinards.* Taste for seasoning, adding more lemon or pepper if necessary.

WHITE SAUCES   *Sauces blanches*

White sauces consist of butter, flour, milk, and seasonings. Do not add more flour than is indicated in the recipes. The sauces should be light and delicate in consistancy rather than thick and heavy. They are used particularly to sauce braised vegetables, fish fillets, and certain egg dishes, which are often placed in the oven to brown.

    The base of white sauce is the *roux,* which serves as the thickening agent. A *roux* is a combination of butter and flour cooked over low heat and stirred constantly with a wooden spatula. The color of a *roux* (and therefore of the sauce) depends on how long you cook the butter and flour. The sauces made from a white *roux* are always white.

The Liquid Used in White Sauces

This is nearly always milk, though once in a while milk is replaced by the clear water in which a vegetable has been cooked, thus imparting the flavor of the vegetable to the sauce. The *roux* should always be removed from the heat while the liquid is beaten in, after which the saucepan is put back on the heat until it boils, for about one minute. The sauce should be smooth, not lumpy!

Béchamel Sauce *Sauce béchamel*

This is the base of all white sauces. Always use a heavy-bottomed enameled saucepan, a wooden spatula, and a wire whisk.

MAKES ABOUT 1¼ CUPS

the roux

> 1½ tablespoons butter
> 1½ tablespoons flour

the liquid

> 1⅛ cups hot milk
> salt
> freshly ground pepper
> freshly grated nutmeg

For a thicker *béchamel* sauce—to be used, for example, as the base of a soufflé—the proportions are: 2 tablespoons butter, 2½ tablespoons flour, 1 cup hot milk.

making the sauce

Melt the butter in the saucepan and add the flour. With the spatula stir the butter and flour together until it boils and becomes frothy but not darkened. Remove from the heat and let it stand for a few seconds, then pour in the hot milk all at once, beating vigorously with the whisk. Place the saucepan on a low flame, let it bubble up two or three times, remove from heat, and add the seasonings. If you wish to enrich the sauce, beat in 2–3 tablespoons of butter off the heat.

Mornay Sauce *Sauce Mornay*

MAKES ABOUT 1½ CUPS

Make a Béchamel Sauce* as in the preceding recipe. Remove from heat and add 2 tablespoons of grated Swiss cheese, or ⅔ tablespoon of grated Swiss cheese with ⅓ tablespoon of grated Parmesan cheese. To enrich this sauce, add 2 tablespoons of heavy cream or 1 tablespoon of butter.

Béchamel Sauce with Cream   *Sauce crème*

Prepare a Béchamel Sauce,* making sure that you add no more flour than is indicated. It should be just thick enough to coat a spoon lightly. Before serving, add 4 tablespoons of heavy, cream, place over heat, bring to a boil, remove from heat, and add seasonings, not forgetting the freshly grated nutmeg!

VARIATION: **Béchamel Sauce with Curry**   *Sauce crème au curry*

> 1 recipe of Béchamel Sauce with Cream (above)
> 1 tablespoon curry powder mixed with 2 tablespoons heated heavy cream
> a very small dash of Cayenne pepper
> 2 tablespoons grated Swiss cheese

Place these ingredients in a small, heavy-bottomed saucepan and beat together. Heat over a low flame, stirring gently, until hot. Do not boil.

BLOND SAUCES   *Sauces blondes*

Blond sauces used to go by the unattractive name of "fat white sauces." This was to distinguish them from the white (or *béchamel*) sauces, which use milk or the clear liquid in which vegetables have been cooked. "Fat" sauces use bouillon made from chicken or veal (and sometimes fish) as a liquid, and this gives them a slightly darker color. These sauces eventually became known as blond sauces, which is much more aesthetic!

Blond sauces are based on a *velouté,* which consists of a blond *roux* moistened with bouillon.

Velouté Sauce

the blond roux

> 2 tablespoons butter
> 2 tablespoons flour

the liquid

> 1½ cups bouillon made from chicken or white meat, such as veal (see *Fond blanc lié** below), or from fish, heated and carefully degreased*
> ½ cup of the same bouillon, cold, added by spoonfuls while the sauce is cooking
> freshly ground pepper
> salt only after tasting (the bouillon may be salty enough)

SAUCES   41 *making the velouté*

In a heavy-bottomed enameled saucepan make a *roux* of butter and flour as described in the Béchamel Sauce.* Remove the *roux* from the heat and with a wire whisk beat in the heated chicken bouillon. Place on low heat and simmer for 10–15 minutes. While it is simmering, add the cold bouillon by spoonfuls. This will bring the impurities to the surface, where they can be skimmed off. Add freshly ground pepper and salt if necessary.

Velouté of White Meat   *Fond blanc lié*

The *fond blanc lié* is made in the same manner as the *velouté* sauce above, but with the addition of 3 pounds of veal bones, 1 or 2 chicken giblets (optional), and enough water to cover the bones. Add 15 minutes to the cooking time.

Fish Velouté   *Velouté de poisson*

An excellent sauce for serving with fillets of fish.

MAKES ABOUT 2½ CUPS

the blond roux

> 2 tablespoons butter
> 2½ tablespoons flour

the liquid

> 3 cups Fish Stock*
> 3–4 raw mushrooms, chopped

Proceed as in the basic recipe for Velouté Sauce,* simmering for about 25 minutes. Fish *velouté* is usually finished with a *Liaison suprême.**

NOTE: *Two tablespoons of capers may be added to the sauce at the end of cooking. Another suggestion is to stir in ½ cup dry white wine or ½ cup dry sherry or vermouth.*

Sauce financière

This is a rich Velouté Sauce* garnished with mushrooms, olives, tongue, formerly served only with *vol-au-vent,* now used to accompany many dishes, particularly Roast Chicken with *Sauce Financière,** a dish as practical as it is delicious. (Leftover chicken, boned and cut in small pieces and added to 2½ cups of *sauce financière,* can serve 4–5 people. Surround the platter with *Fleurons** or triangular Croutons.*)

MAKES ABOUT 3½ CUPS

⅓ pound mushroom caps

1–2 tablespoons butter

⅔ cup pitted green olives, blanched for a few minutes to rid them of
    excess salt

salt

freshly ground pepper

a few drops of lemon juice

2 thick slices smoked beef tongue

3 cups Velouté Sauce* made from chicken bouillon[1]

Wash the mushrooms and pat them dry. If they are large, cut them in quarters;
otherwise leave them whole. Sauté in the 1–2 tablespoons of butter. Add the
olives, salt, pepper, and lemon juice, set aside. Cut the tongue in thin strips.
(NOTE: *smoked ham, also cut in thin strips, may be substituted for the tongue.*)
Incorporate these ingredients into the warmed chicken velouté sauce, place
over low heat for 8–10 minutes, stirring occasionally with a wooden spatula.

to make a richer version of the sauce

2 lamb's brains, poached in salted water for about 15 minutes, or 1 calf's brain
    poached in salted water for about 20 minutes

salt

freshly ground pepper

2 tablespoons butter for sautéing the brains

4 tablespoons Madeira

3 tablespoons heavy cream

Slice the poached brains, add salt and pepper. Lightly sauté them in the butter
and add to the velouté sauce. Place over low heat for about 8 minutes, stirring
occasionally with a wooden spatula. Just before serving, stir in the Madeira and
cream. Adjust for seasoning and transfer to a heated sauce bowl.

NOTE: *You may substitute a poached and sautéed sweetbread for the brains.*

Aurora Sauce *Sauce aurore*

A fine, delicate sauce made rosy with tomato paste.

MAKES ABOUT 2½ CUPS

2½ cups chicken Velouté Sauce* made from chicken bouillon

2–3 tablespoons tomato paste

*Bouquet garni classique** with parsley stems

---

[1] This makes enough sauce for a poached or fried chicken; 2 cups of the same sauce makes enough for a
3-pound veal roast.

Beat the tomato paste into the velouté sauce, add the *bouquet garni,* and place over low heat. Simmer for about 15 minutes, stirring and skimming off any impurities that rise to the surface. Remove from heat, discard the *bouquet garni,* and add:

> 3 tablespoons butter
> 3–4 tablespoons heavy cream
> a pinch of salt
> a smaller pinch of sugar
> freshly ground pepper
> a small amount of freshly grated nutmeg

Place over low heat just long enough to bind the ingredients, stirring with a wooden spatula. Do not let the sauce boil. Beat before serving.

This sauce is an excellent accompaniment for Ham Mousseline,* Loaf of Chicken Liver, Bresse Style,* for spooning over Poached Eggs on Croutons,* or for saucing fish fillets.

BROWN SAUCES *Sauces brunes*

Brown sauces are used in all sorts of ragouts such as *Navarins* (Lamb Stew*), in many game dishes, in *Coq au vin* (Chicken in Wine*), and in recipes using dark-fleshed fowl. The base of most brown sauces is the brown *roux,* which is really no more difficult to make than a white *roux,** though it does require a little more time, patience, and care.

Brown Roux *Roux brun*

There are two kinds of sauces using a brown *roux:* simple brown *roux* sauce and brown *roux* sauce with *mirepoix.**

Simple Brown Roux Sauce

MAKES ABOUT 3 CUPS

> 2 tablespoons lard, or 1 tablespoon butter and 1 tablespoon peanut oil
> 2½ tablespoons flour
> 3 cups hot Beef Bouillon*

In a heavy saucepan melt the lard or the butter and oil over low heat. Stir in the flour. Continue to work in the flour gently and patiently, without increasing the heat, until the mixture changes to the color of a hazelnut. Remove from heat and slowly beat in the hot bouillon.

Brown Sauce with Mirepoix   *Sauce roux brun à la mirepoix*

This sauce is more highly seasoned and is lighter in color than the preceding one. *Mirepoix* is used as a base for many sauces. To the bacon or ham and the vegetables called for in this recipe, sometimes a piece of bay leaf and a sprig of dried thyme are added. The proportions vary, depending on the amount and type of sauce that is being made.

MAKES ABOUT 3 1/2 CUPS

2 tablespoons lard, or 1 tablespoon butter and 1 tablespoon peanut oil
1/8 pound lean bacon or boiled ham, diced
1 carrot, chopped fine
1 onion, chopped fine
1 stalk celery, diced
1–2 shallots, chopped (optional)
2 pinches of sugar
2 1/2–3 tablespoons flour
2–3 cups dry white wine or full-bodied red wine
2–3 cups hot Beef Bouillon,* degreased*
freshly ground pepper
1 clove garlic, crushed
1 tablespoon tomato paste
1 *Bouquet garni classique**
salt

In a heavy saucepan heat the lard or the butter and oil. Add the bacon or ham, vegetables, and just one pinch of sugar. Stir-cook for about 10 minutes, or until the ingredients are barely soft and have just begun to brown. Sprinkle in the flour and let it brown, stirring with a wooden spatula and scraping the bottom of the pan. Beat in the wine gradually, bring to a boil, and, still beating, add the hot bouillon, pepper, garlic, tomato paste, the other pinch of sugar, and the *bouquet garni.* Reduce heat and simmer, uncovered, for 35–40 minutes, stirring occasionally. Strain into a saucepan through a strainer, pressing against the vegetables with the back of a spoon to extract their flavors and juices. Scrape into the sauce the purée that has collected on the outside of the strainer.

Delicate Brown Sauce   *Roux brun fin*

In certain dishes, such as *Civet de lièvre** and *Coq au vin,** a brown sauce can be made by sprinkling the pieces of meat or poultry with flour and browning them in hot fat, stirring and turning the pieces until they are golden brown. This can be done either on top of the stove or under the broiler (not too close to the heat). When the meat is brown, add the liquid indicated in the recipe. Thickening and enriching are completed by adding one recipe of *Beurre manié** at the end of the cooking.

Sauce ragoût See Simple Brown Roux Sauce.

Game Sauce *Sauce civet*

MAKES ABOUT 3 CUPS

2 tablespoons lard, or 1 tablespoon butter and 1 tablespoon peanut oil
2½ tablespoons flour
2 cups dry white wine or full-bodied red wine
2 cups hot Beef Bouillon,* degreased*

Heat the lard or the butter and oil in a heavy saucepan. Stir in the flour. Continue to stir until the mixture turns the color of a hazelnut. Beat in the wine, bring to a boil and boil for 1 minute. Reduce heat, add hot bouillon and simmer for about 15 minutes, stirring occasionally.

Demi-Glace

This is a concentrated meat stock used to give body and to enrich other sauces and bouillons. Making this used to be a complicated affair, but the modern method below will cause you very little trouble.

FOR 1 CUP OF DEMI-GLACE

9 cups brown meat stock, thoroughly degreased*

Place the stock in a heavy-bottomed enameled saucepan, bring slowly to a boil, lower heat, and simmer, uncovered, until it has reduced to 2 cups. Strain the stock through a fine sieve into another heavy-bottomed saucepan. Place over low heat and continue to simmer, watching carefully and stirring, for as it reduces and thickens it will have a tendency to stick to the bottom of the pan and burn. When the stock is thick and syrupy enough to coat a spoon, remove it and let it cool to lukewarm, stirring two or three times. You should have about 1 cup of demi-glace. Pour into a jar, cover, and place in the refrigerator, where it will keep for 10 days to 2 weeks.

WHIPPED SAUCES OF EGG AND BUTTER

These are sauces of distinction. Though they are rich and fine and delicate, their only drawback is their fragility. Great care must be taken in making them.

The sauces are made with egg yolk and butter and seasoned with either vinegar or lemon juice. No thickening of any sort is used. They are particularly sensitive to heat; if they are overheated the egg yolks are apt to curdle. Because of this, they should always be made in a double boiler or a pan set over hot water. To be extra sure that they do not overheat, it is wise to place an asbestos mat or flame controller over the burner.

These sauces enhance the simplest of dishes; for example, a plain poached fish or a slice of broiled meat. They are used on asparagus, artichoke hearts, sweetbreads—in fact, there is no end to the number of dishes they can improve.

Serving These Whipped Sauces

Because of their delicate nature it is unwise to serve them piping hot. Just a little warmer than lukewarm is the proper temperature.

What to Do if They Must Stand for a While

Gently beat the sauce a few seconds after removing it from the heat. This will cool it and prevent it from continuing to cook. The sauce should remain over hot water that must not exceed 120° F.—barely lukewarm. Beat the sauce lightly two or three times. But the sauce should not be allowed to stand for any length of time—just long enough for you to arrange a platter or slice meat.

Hollandaise Sauce   *Sauce hollandaise*

Of all the egg-and-butter sauces, hollandaise sauce is the most distinctive. It is flavored with lemon juice to which water has been added.

MAKES ABOUT 1¼ CUPS[1]

3 egg yolks
1 tablespoon lemon juice mixed with 1 tablespoon cold water
¾–1 cup butter, divided into pieces
freshly ground pepper
salt

A heavy-bottomed enameled pan is required for making the sauce. Put the egg yolks, lemon juice, and water in the saucepan. Stir them together with a wooden spatula. Add a piece of butter (amounting to about 3 tablespoons) and some pepper (2 turns of the pepper mill). Do not salt at this time. Place the saucepan in a pan of warm water and set it on low heat. Beat the mixture with a wire whisk, adding the pieces of butter gradually until all of it has been absorbed and the sauce begins to thicken. If the sauce seems to be thickening too rapidly or there is the least sign of curdling, remove the pan from the water and beat in ½ tablespoon of cold water or a tiny pinch of crushed ice (this operation can be done once only). The completed sauce should be smooth and just thick enough to coat a spoon. Add salt and, if necessary, a little more pepper and lemon.

---

[1] Four egg yolks and 1⅛ cups of butter will make about 1¾ cups of sauce.

Hollandaise Sauce with Thickening *Sauce hollandaise liée*

This method is used in restaurant cooking or at home when the sauce must be made ahead of time and reheated. The thickening should be as undetectable as possible. There are two methods of thickening hollandaise sauce:

1. Add 1 tablespoon of fairly thick Velouté Sauce* to the egg yolks before beating in the butter.
2. In the saucepan dissolve 1 teaspoon of arrowroot in 3–4 tablespoons of milk that has been boiled and cooled. Beat in the egg yolks, a tablespoon of butter, and the lemon juice. Place the saucepan in a pan of warm water and proceed with the recipe.

    With either of these methods your hollandaise may be reheated more or less safely, though it is still a delicate matter. Remember to beat the sauce constantly while reheating.

Mousseline Sauce *Sauce mousseline*

Mousseline sauce is hollandaise sauce to which whipped cream has been added just before serving. Light and frothy, it is delicious served with asparagus, artichoke hearts, and avocados. It can be used as an accompaniment to various poached fish. When used with fish, *mousseline* sauce may be garnished with a few capers.

MAKES ABOUT 3 CUPS (ENOUGH FOR 5–6 PEOPLE)

2½ cups Hollandaise Sauce*
½ cup heavy cream

After preparing the hollandaise sauce, add 1 teaspoon of finely shaved ice to the cream and beat until it forms soft peaks. Gradually incorporate the cream into the sauce. Taste for seasoning, and add a little more lemon juice if you wish.

Béarnaise Sauce *Sauce béarnaise*

An incomparably fragrant sauce, similar to hollandaise in its lightness. Béarnaise sauce consists of a reduction of good wine vinegar with added shallots and herbs, the essential herb being fresh tarragon. (If fresh tarragon is unobtainable, a tablespoon of dried tarragon leaves will do.) The proportion of butter to eggs is 6 tablespoons of butter per egg yolk.

MAKES ABOUT 1¼ CUPS[1]

[1] Use 4 egg yolks and 1 cup of butter for about 1¾ cups of sauce.

wine and herb base

  ½ cup red wine vinegar

  3 shallots, chopped fine

  1 tablespoon finely cut fresh tarragon leaves, or 1 heaping teaspoon
     crushed dried tarragon leaves

optional herbs

  a sprig of chervil

  a small piece of bay leaf

  a sprig of fresh or dried thyme

  white or black pepper, crushed

remaining ingredients

  3 egg yolks

  ¾–1 cup butter, cut in pieces

  salt to taste

Put the vinegar, shallots, and herbs in a heavy-bottomed enameled saucepan and reduce until you have 1½–2 tablespoons of liquid. Strain it, pressing against the herbs with the back of a spoon in order to extract all the flavor. Pour the liquid back into the saucepan, add the egg yolks, and stir together with a wooden spatula. Add a piece of butter and place the saucepan in a pan of warm water over low heat, using an asbestos mat as a safeguard. Using a wire whisk, beat in the rest of the butter gradually until it is completely absorbed. At this moment add salt—just a little at first—then taste.

NOTE: *If you are use fresh tarragon, add a few extra leaves, cut fine with scissors, just before pouring the sauce into the serving bowl.*

Choron Sauce   *Sauce choron*

A Béarnaise Sauce* with tomato paste added. Make the *béarnaise* and add 1–2 tablespoons of tomato paste. This sauce makes an excellent accompaniment to poached eggs, broiled fish, and broiled steaks (especially steak fillets).

Valois Sauce   *Sauce valois*

A *béarnaise* sauce enriched by meat glaze, commonly known as "demi-glace." This sauce is especially good with broiled meats.

MAKES ABOUT 1⅓ CUPS

  1 recipe Béarnaise Sauce*

  2 teaspoons Demi-Glace*

Make the *béarnaise* sauce and just after the final beating, while the sauce is still standing over hot water or is in a double boiler, stir in the demi-glace very gently until it has melted. Pour the sauce into a warmed sauce bowl.

White Butter Sauce   *Beurre blanc*

Beurre blanc originated in the Loire-Atlantique department. Indeed, it may have been "invented" in Nantes. It is a creamy, butter-colored sauce much appreciated for its lightness and delicacy. Like other Whipped Sauces of Egg and Butter,* it is served just a little warmer than lukewarm.

MAKES ABOUT 2 CUPS

4 tablespoons dry white wine or 4 tablespoons lemon juice
4 tablespoons wine vinegar
1 tablespoon finely minced shallot or 1 tablespoon minced green onion
a good pinch of coarse salt
freshly grated white pepper
1⅓–1¾ cups butter, divided into 15 pieces
a few drops of lemon juice

Place the wine or lemon juice, vinegar, shallot or onion, and seasonings in a heavy-bottomed enameled saucepan and reduce over medium heat to about 1 tablespoon. Remove pan from heat and beat in 2 pieces of butter. Place pan over very low heat. Rapidly and steadily whip the *beurre blanc* with a wire whisk, regularly adding fresh pieces of butter as soon as the previous ones have melted. Continue beating until all the butter has been used up.

The sauce will look opaque and foamy. To eliminate the foam, place the sauce in a bowl and beat lightly with the whisk. The result will be a creamy sauce, lighter looking than other whipped sauces. Add a few drops of lemon juice. Taste for seasoning.

If, during the cooking, the sauce takes on the transparent appearance of melted butter, your sauce is ruined beyond repair. But if you catch it in time you can retrieve it by placing the saucepan on a marble slab and whisking in several drops of lemon juice. This causes the particles of solid matter to remain in suspension rather than sink to the bottom of the pan as when butter is melted.

Beurre blanc *is used to sauce all sorts of poached or broiled fish. It is delicious with asparagus, artichoke hearts, broccoli, and hearts of fennel.*

Cream of Mushroom Sauce   *Sauce à la crème de champignons*

¾ pound firm mushrooms, stem ends discarded
4 tablespoons butter
3 shallots, minced fine
4–5 tablespoons heated milk
3¼ cups heavy cream
salt
freshly ground pepper
a pinch of curry powder

Wash and dry the mushrooms and slice thin. Place them, along with the butter and shallots, in a no-stick skillet, stir-fry for 5 minutes. Drain the resulting juice into a bowl and replace it with the milk. Cover the pan and simmer over low heat, stirring now and then, until the mushrooms are soft. Drain this liquid into the bowl. Put the mushrooms in a blender and run at high speed for 1 minute. Add to the bowl containing the other liquid. Put the heavy cream in a heavy-bottomed enameled saucepan and set over low heat. Bring gently to a boil, stirring constantly with a wooden spatula until slightly reduced and thick. Remove from heat, stir in the seasonings and the mushroom mixture. Adjust for seasoning. Place over very low heat for 1–2 minutes, stirring constantly.

Pastry Dough

CRUST PASTRY DOUGHS

Short Crust Lining Dough *Pâte à foncer*

For pâtés and meat pies.

    1¾ cups all-purpose flour
    2 teaspoons salt
    6 tablespoons butter
    4 tablespoons lard
    1 small egg
    about 3 tablespoons cold water

Short Crust Pastry Dough with Butter *Pâte brisée fine au beurre*

For savory tarts and for quiches.

    1³/₄ cups all-purpose flour
    1 teaspoon salt
    ³/₅ cup butter
    1 small egg
    about 3 tablespoons cold water

Short Crust Pastry Dough with Margarine *Pâte brisée à la margarine*

For all sorts of savory tarts and tartlets indispensable for cocktail snacks and buffets. I use this recipe regularly, and always with success. It reheats beautifully.

    1¾ cups all-purpose flour
    ¾ cup margarine
    1 heaping teaspoon salt
    1 egg
    about 4 tablespoons cold water

Sugar Crust Pastry Dough *Pâte sablée sucrée*

For fruit tarts and tartlets and any number of desserts.

> 1¾ cups all-purpose flour
> ½ teaspoon salt
> 1 scant tablespoon sugar
> ½ cup plus 3–4 tablespoons butter
> 1 egg diluted with 1–3 tablespoons cold water

making the pastry dough

The same procedure is used for all the preceding types of pastry dough.

Sift the flour into a bowl, make a well in the center, and mix in the salt (and sugar if you are making *pâte sablée*). Make another well and add the fat, cut in small pieces. Using your fingers or a wide-pronged fork and working lightly and rapidly, mix the fat into the flour until the dough has the texture of coarse sand when rubbed between the fingers. Add part of the liquid (some of the water and the egg) and work in until the dough begins to become compact. Still working, add the rest of the water and egg, then form the dough into a ball. If cracks form or the dough separates, add a little more cold water. Wrap the dough in parchment paper and let it rest in the refrigerator for at least 1 hour. This last step is absolutely indispensable if you want a firm, easy-to-roll dough.

PUFF PASTRY *Pâte feuilletée*

It takes at least three hours to make classical six-turn puff pastry. This includes resting the dough. The result of this long effort is perfectly delicious, providing the pastry is eaten as soon as it emerges from the oven. It is very hard to reheat classical puff pastry, because it has a tendency to fall to pieces and scatter crumbs everywhere.

I don't want to subject you to the many operations in making classical puff pastry. Confidentially, though I like to remember preparing it, I now prefer to make a simpler puff pastry—also called half-pastry or rough-puff pastry—which is not nearly as complicated, takes far less time, and can be reheated without falling apart. This simple puff pastry can be used in exactly the same way as the classical kind—for example, *Pithiviers,* * *Vol-au-vent,* patty shells, and Napoleons.*

Simple Puff Pastry *Pâte demi-feuilletée à quatre tours*

This recipe makes about 1 pound of puff pastry.

> ⅞ cup butter, or half this amount butter and half magarine
> 1¾ cups all-purpose flour
> 1⅓ teaspoons salt (for savory puff paste) or 1 teaspoons salt (for sweet puff pastry)
> 3–4 tablespoons cold water (a little more if necessary)

Divide the butter into 2 equal portions and place both in refrigerator. Sift the flour into a large bowl and mix in the salt. Make a well in the center and add half the butter, cut in small pieces. Knead lightly with a fork or the fingertips of one hand, adding some of the water as you knead. Work rapidly without trying to get a perfectly smooth mixture. Form the dough into a ball, dust lightly with flour, cover with wax paper, and place in refrigerator until it is good and firm.

Lightly flour a marble or plastic work surface and place the dough on it. With a rolling pin flatten the dough into a rectangle about ½ inch thick. Flatten the remaining half of the butter into a rectangular shape that will cover about ⅓ of the dough. Enclose the butter by folding the sides then the ends over the butter, making a kind of package. Seal the edges by pressing them with a rolling pin. Cover the dough and place in the refrigerator for 30–40 minutes, until it is well rested and firm.

Remove the dough from the refrigerator, place it on the work surface, and roll it out into a rectangle. Fold it into three (folding both ends) and seal as before. You will now have a three-layered "brick." Roll, fold, and seal one more time. The dough has now been "turned" twice, and, to remind yourself, you might want to make two little indentations in the dough with the tips of your second and third fingers. Cover the dough and return it to the refrigerator for 15–20 minutes. Repeat this process a second time (you will now have turned the dough four times), then put the dough back in the refrigerator. It will be ready for use after a rest of 20–30 minutes.

Simple puff pastry will keep for a week in the refrigerator if it is well enclosed in aluminum foil. And it will keep a month in the freezer. Thaw it at room temperature or let it stand in the refrigerator overnight.

Choux Pastry   *Pâte à choux*

Choux pastry can be used in a multitude of ways, not only in delicate, fine desserts, but in entrees and hors-d'oeuvre as well. Nothing sets off a wine like the Crown of Choux with Cheese* served in the Beaujolais country or farther north in Burgundy. The little puffs, the *choux,* freshly made and served cold, can be used as cases for Duxelles of Mushrooms* with Mayonnaise,* or crab salad accompanied by a rose-colored sauce—*Sauce Françoise** or Pimento Mayonnaise,* for example. How elegant and yet how simple to make!

Among the desserts, small tender puffs filled with *Crème patissière** or *Pralin** are an everyday affair, but those glorious pyramid-shaped pieces known as *Profiteroles** are a dessert to mark an occasion!

You will need a heavy-bottomed enameled saucepan for this.

MAKES ABOUT 24 PUFFS

1 cup water

⅓ cup butter

1 teaspoon salt (for savory puffs) or 1 scant teaspoon salt and a small pinch of sugar (for sweet puffs)

1 cup all-purpose flour

4 whole eggs plus 1 egg white

1 egg yolk beaten with 3 drops water, for glazing

Preheat oven to 400° F.

Put the water, butter, salt (and sugar if necessary) into the saucepan and bring to a boil. As soon as the butter is melted, remove the pan from heat and add the flour all at once. Stir vigorously with a wooden spatula until the paste forms a solid mass. Put the saucepan back on very low heat, stir until a light but colorless film of paste forms on the bottom of the pan. Remove the pan from heat and add the eggs one by one, beating each egg until it has been completely absorbed into the mixture before adding the next one. Then add the unbeaten egg white, half at a time, and beat until completely mixed. This will add to the lightness and dryness of the pastry. Leave in the saucepan until it has cooled to room temperature.

cooking the pastry

Using a pastry bag or spoon (I prefer using a spoon), place small portions of dough on a lightly buttered baking sheet. Allow plenty of space between them, since they double in size when baked. Dip a pastry brush into the egg yolk and paint the top of each *choux* (puff); do not let the egg run over the sides, as this will prevent them from rising properly. Bake for about 20 minutes. The *choux* should be nicely puffed, light, and crisp. Remove them with a spatula and place on a rack to cool.

Cheese Puffs   *Choux secs au fromage*

NOTE: *The ingredients for the glaze are the same as in the preceding recipe: 1 beaten egg yolk diluted with 3 drops of water.*

MAKES ABOUT 20–25 PUFFS

1 recipe of Choux Pastry*

1¼ cups grated Swiss cheese

¼ teaspoon freshly grated nutmeg

freshly grated pepper (1–2 turns of the pepper mill)

⅛ cup grated Swiss cheese, set aside

Preheat oven to 350° F.

As you make the *choux* dough, after you have added the eggs stir in the 1¼ cups of grated cheese, nutmeg, and pepper. Spoon small portions of the dough on a lightly buttered baking sheet, placing them well apart. Brush the top of each puff with the egg yolk and sprinkle with a little of the ⅛ cup of grated cheese. Bake for about 20 minutes. Serve warm.

These make a delicious entrée served with Mornay Sauce* or Crème de fromage.*

Crown of Choux with Cheese *Gougère au fromage*

This light, appetizing crown of puffs can be served just as it emerges from the oven, or accompanied by a cheese sauce, or cut in two horizontally and filled with Mornay Sauce.*

FOR 6 PEOPLE

1⅓ cups water
³⁄₅ cups butter
a tiny pinch of salt
1¾ cups all-purpose flour
4 large eggs plus 1½–2 egg whites
¾ cup finely minced Swiss cheese (set 1½ tablespoons aside)
1 egg yolk, diluted with 3 drops water
Preheat oven to 350° F.

Prepare a *choux* dough made of the first 4 ingredients above, following the directions in the recipe for Choux Pastry.* Add the eggs per instructions, then stir in the ¾ cup of minced cheese. Lightly butter a baking sheet and drop the dough by spoonfuls onto it to form a circle. Brush the top of each with the egg and water mixture. Place on top a little of the set-aside minced cheese. Bake for about 35 minutes. The *gougére* will double in bulk with baking. Serve it warm, still in its crown shape. The puffs should be cut apart at the table.

ideas for embellishing warm puffs when served as hors-d'oeuvre or entrees

Garnish them with a thick Mornay sauce, adding a little more pepper and some freshly grated nutmeg. If you wish to enrich the sauce, add a beaten egg yolk to the base. Another excellent garnish is Duxelles of Mushrooms* (about 1½ cups). A shell fish garnish can be made by using Mornay sauce as a base, enriching it with a beaten egg yolk and adding ¼ pound of fresh or canned crab meat or ¼ pound of peeled, cooked, and deveined shrimp, finely cut. Cold puffs served as an entree or hors-d'oeuvre can be stuffed with *Tapénade** or with Mayonnaise* to which have been added 1 tablespoon of cognac and ¼ pound of fresh or canned crab meat.

Arrangement and Decoration

Careful presentation is an important element in French cuisine. Without it the finest cooking cannot be regarded as truly successful.

CHOICE OF SERVING DISHES

Certain serving dishes are better suited to certain foods than others: the materials they are made of, their color and form can all contribute to attractive presentation and ease in serving. In choosing them one must think of the practical as well as the aesthetic side. One point to remember is that hot dishes must be served hot, and that is why I recommend the use of metal serving dishes whenever possible. These can be heated in a hot oven before the food is put in them and can be kept hot while the dish is being arranged and served. At the table an electric hot tray is sometimes advisable. The best of cooking leaves one dissatisfied when it is served lukewarm.

Virtually all known metals make good serving dishes: silver, silver-plated alloys, stainless steel (which is expensive but even more heat-resistant than silver and much easier to take care of), and of course copper.

A meat roast should be sliced and placed on an oval metal platter surrounded by its garniture.

Deep round metal serving dishes (always preheated) are used for dishes served with a sauce, such as ragouts and fricassees.

Vegetables, especially mixed vegetables, look dull when served in a pastel-colored or, even worse, on a flowered porcelain dish. It is best to serve vegetables in a deep round or oval metal dish.

The same sort of dish can be used for purées. Stuffed tomatoes *à la provençale* and shirred eggs are most attractive when served in a shallow copper baking dish.

Porcelain platters can be used for serving hors-d'oeuvre, cold entrees, cold stuffed eggs and tomatoes, cold meats and fish. I am not a devotee of matched dinner services. I find it more personal and elegant to use unmatched plates and dishes, bought here and there. Sometimes their very form and color suggest what to use them for.

While you cook a dish, it is advisable to be thinking of the most practical and attractive way to serve it.

FINISHING TOUCHES AND DECORATIONS

These are indispensable in serving a dish. Compare a hard-boiled egg, served by itself on a plate, and half a hard-boiled egg placed on a lettuce leaf. Now put a little pinch of mixed herbs on top of the egg. These two extra touches give the dish a professional, finished look.

If you are serving a platter of hot roast meat slices, do not arrange a collar of lettuce leaves around the meat. It is much more attractive to place a small bunch of stemmed, unseasoned watercress at one end of the platter. If the meat is to be the main course, you might surround it with halves of broiled tomatoes topped with finely cut mixed herbs. The tomatoes and watercress form an interesting color contrast. Braised fennel hearts, clusters of cooked cauliflower, glazed carrots, onions, or turnips can also be used as garnishes for roast meat.

A platter of chicken cut in pieces may be decorated with artichoke hearts garnished with *duxelles* of mushrooms, green peas (French or English style), or stuffed mushrooms.

A platter on which a cold fish is served may be garnished with slices or quarters of peeled tomatoes, half slices of fluted lemon, and a small bunch of parsley may be placed in the gill. Do not overload the platter with decorations. The effect will be much more pleasing if the garnishes are widely spaced, as in the border of a flower garden.

THE USE OF LEMON AND HERBS

Fluting a Lemon

Wash and dry the lemon. With a fluting knife cut off regularly spaced lengthwise strips of peel. Cut the lemon in slices, then cut the slices in half. Place them around a platter, the indented edges facing the outer edge of the dish.

Mixed Herbs

Herbs must not be strewn indiscriminately on food. A much better effect is obtained by putting the barest pinch of finely cut mixed herbs on a boiled potato than by scattering them all over the potato. The same principle applies to the use of parsley. Place small amounts of finely cut parsley on selected elements, not on the whole dish.

about 35 minutes.

Croutons *Croûtons*

Croutons are an ideal garnish for sauced foods. They are made from slices of white bread from which the crusts have been removed (because they have a tendency to burn). They are cut in various shapes but are all made according to the same principle.

making croutons

Burned croutons are met with only too frequently. This happens when they have been cooked over too high heat for too long. Croutons must be cooked quickly but over very moderate heat. To achieve crisp, golden croutons, begin by drying the bread over moderate heat on top of the stove, using a toasting grill. If you dry the bread in the oven, the croutons will be too dry and brittle. The best fat to use in cooking them is margarine, which is odorless and burns less easily than butter. If butter is used, it should be in combination with oil.

FOR 12 CROUTONS

2 tablespoons butter and 2 tablespoons peanut oil, or 3–4 tablespoons margarine

12 slices firm white bread, crusts removed

Heat the fat in a skillet but do not let it darken. When it is hot, add the dried bread slices. Let them absorb the butter for a moment, then shake the skillet a little. Turn them and if necessary add a little more fat. The second side takes only an instant to cook. When the croutons are golden brown, remove them from the skillet, place on paper towels, and salt immediately. If they are made in advance, they may be reheated before serving. Simply place them in a 350° F. oven, heat off, for a minute or so.

Croutons can be rectangular, triangular, round, or they can be diced. The diced croutons are used for soups and as garnish for omelets or scrambled eggs.

Canapés

Usually larger than croutons, canapés are used as a base for such foods as poached or scrambled eggs and sautéed mushrooms. Spread with Chicken Liver Butter* they make an elegant base on which chicken breasts or wild fowl can be placed.

In making canapés, cut the bread slices ¼ inch thick and remove the crusts. Square canapés usually measure about 2½ inches square, and rectangular canapés about 3½ by 2½ inches. Tiny cocktail canapés measure about 1½ inches square. *Preheat oven to 350° F.*

browning the canapés

Dry the bread slices on top of the stove, using a toasting grill, then butter each piece. Place them in the oven until they are golden brown. Salt while still hot. Canapés can be made in advance and reheated before serving. Use the same method as for reheating croutons.

Puff Pastry Crescents *Fleurons*

These are small croissants made of simple puff pastry. They are elegant garnishes and are used in fine French cooking. They are almost always served with fish fillets in sauce, sweetbreads, and chicken fricassee.

FOR 6 PEOPLE

½ pound Simple Puff Pastry* (enough for 12 fleurons)
1 egg yolk diluted with 3 drops water
Preheat oven 375° F.

Roll the dough ¼ inch thick. Cut out rounds with a fluted 3-inch cutter. With one stroke of the cutter through the middle of the round, form a crescent. Form another crescent with the cutter by turning the remaining piece of dough around and cutting through it. Reserve the scraps for re-forming into a ball and rolling out again. Using a pastry brush, paint the tops of the crescents with the egg and water mixture.

baking the fleurons

Place the crescents on a slightly dampened baking sheet and bake for 10–12 minutes, or until they are puffed and golden. Put them on a rack to cool. To reheat before serving, place them in a hot oven (heat off). For serving, make a border of *fleurons* around the platter but not touching any sauce. They will keep for 4 or 5 days in the refrigerator in a covered container.

Savory Tartlets *Croustades*

These are made of simple puff pastry and are baked in small molds about 3 inches in diameter, large enough and deep enough to hold, for example, a poached egg and its sauce, as in Poached Eggs in Croustades with Sauce Choron.*

FOR 6 PEOPLE

about ½ pound Simple Puff Pastry*
Preheat oven to 365° F.

For this recipe you will need 6 lightly buttered tartlet molds as described above.

Roll the dough about ⅛ inch thick (no more). Cut 6 rounds, using a cutter or thin-rimmed glass. Line the tartlet molds with the dough, pressing it firmly against the bottom and sides. Prick the dough on the bottom of each mold with a fork. Cut a round of parchment paper and place it over the dough at the bottom, and on top of this place a few small pebbles to keep the dough from puffing. Bake for about 12 minutes. Remove the *croustades* from the molds and cool on a rack. They are easier to reheat if you keep them in the refrigerator, well-covered, until the next day.

Oval Tartlets and Round Tartlets   *Barquettes et Croûtes*

These oval or round pastries give a distinctive touch to the simplest foods. Filled with Duxelles of Mushrooms* or purée of spinach, they are an excellent accompaniment to ham. Filled with *Ratatouille,** they go deliciously with hot or cold roast of veal.

FOR 6 PEOPLE

1 recipe for Short Crust Pastry Dough with Butter*
Preheat oven to 350° F.

For this recipe you will need 12 small oval or round (or 6 of each) molds, lightly buttered.

Roll the dough about ⅛ inch thick (no more). Here is a little suggestion for cutting tartlet molds rapidly: Place the molds side by side in three rows. Lay the rolled-out dough on the molds and go over it once with the rolling pin. The dough will be cut by the pressure of the rolling pin against the sharp edges of the mold, and you will have the proper amount for lining each mold. Line the molds, pressing the dough firmly against the bottom and sides with the thumbs. Prick the dough on the bottom of the molds with a fork, cover the dough on the bottom with a piece of parchment paper cut to fit, and place several small pebbles on top. Bake for 10–12 minutes. Remove the tartlets from the molds, place on a rack to cool, and store, well covered, in the refrigerator until the next day.

A Baking Dish Cover Made of Pastry   *Couvercle en pâte*

A very elegant way of covering a baking dish of chicken *financière,** chicken Marengo,* *coq au vin,** or any number of sumptuous casserole dishes. But how in the world do you go about making an edible pastry cover to replace the regular cover of a baking dish? It is not as complicated as you may think. First of all, you need:

the cover of a baking dish
a sheet of aluminum foil
¾ pound Simple Puff Pastry* or Short Crust Pastry with Butter* (½
    pound pastry for the cover; the rest for decorations)
1 egg yolk diluted with 3 drops water
Preheat oven to 375° F.

Around the cover of a baking dish, closely fit a sheet of aluminum foil (glossy side up). It should follow the form of the cover exactly. Press the edges of the foil underneath the cover.

Roll the dough in an oval shape ¼ inch thick. Place the baking dish cover on the dough and cut around it. Then, still following the outline of the cover, cut a strip about ½ inch wide and set it aside. Place the dough on the cover, on top of the aluminum foil. Mold it well. Then form an edging with the cut-out strip, brushed with cold water to facilitate sticking. Score this strip with a knife.

Roll out the remaining dough ¼ inch thick. Make small rounds with a cutter and form these into leaf shapes, cutting "veins" with the point of a knife. Wet a pastry brush with cold water and brush the leaves. Arrange them in a circle in the middle of the dough cover. Brush the beaten egg and water mixture over the entire dough cover. Go over the veins of the leaves with the point of a knife. Score each side of the cover.

Bake for 15–20 minutes, checking after 15 minutes to see how it is progressing. After baking, remove the pastry cover, including the aluminum foil, from the real cover. Let it cool for a few minutes, then remove the foil. Place on a rack to finish cooling. Reheat by placing in a 400° F. oven, heat off.

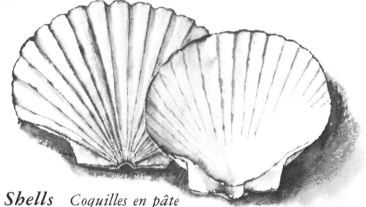

Pastry Scallop Shells   *Coquilles en pâte*

It goes without saying that you will garnish these pastry shells with scallops in a rich sauce, but you can also fill them with sauced leftover fish or, for a more elegant occasion, with pieces of lobster covered with Crab Sauce *à l'Américaine.** For a grand dinner, place a thin slice of truffle on top of the garnished shell.

To make the shells you will need 12 scallop shells. If real scallop shells are unobtainable, substitute metal or Pyrex ones. You will also need 6 pieces of buttered parchment paper cut to fit the shell.

FOR 6 PEOPLE

1 recipe for Short Crust Pastry with Butter*
Preheat oven to 375° F.

Roll the dough about ⅛ inch thick. Cut it into 6 pieces and fill the molds, pressing hard with the thumbs and making sure that the dough covers every part of the mold, even the extremities. Prick the dough with a fork. Lay the cut-out paper over the dough in each mold, then place a second mold over the paper, pressing down firmly. Bake for 10 minutes, then remove the second scallop mold and the paper and allow to bake for 5 more minutes to ensure that the insides of the shells are cooked. Let the shells cool slightly before unmolding them. To unmold, loosen the edges delicately with the point of a knife. Place them on a rack to finish cooling. The pastry shells may be stored, well covered, in the refrigerator until the next day.

Beverages

WINE TODAY

Unlike other good things that were cheaper and better in times gone by, wine is having its golden age today. There has been enormous progress in the techniques of viticulture and wine making. Today the grapes are in perfect condition when they go into the vats, and the fermentation process is subject to close supervision, so that risks are reduced to a minimum. Rapid transportation has also helped to improve the quality of our wine.

The choice of wines is now more varied than ever, and there are wines admirably suited to all the dishes that go to make up present-day cuisine. In the past the repertory was limited to the classical wines of the best known regions: Bordeaux, Burgundy, Champagne. Sometimes three or even four of these choice wines were served at the same meal, something that seems unthinkable today. On the one hand, a succession of rich dishes makes it impossible to appreciate good wine, and on the other hand the palate, after the first two wines, is no longer sensitive enough to savor a third. Today our meals are lighter, very often based on a single choice dish. The wine is selected to go with this main dish, and a second wine, if any, is not brought on until the cheese or dessert course.

The enjoyment of good wine was formerly an aristocratic privilege. Today more and more acceptable wines are being sold at moderate prices. Yet strange to say, this democratic trend has not brought standardization.

Though the great old vintage wines will always be a source of rare pleasure, we have in recent years developed a taste for regional wines. In former days many of these *vins de pays,* because of their low alcoholic content, did not travel well and were seldom seen outside their home country. Modern transportation has made it possible to ship them without difficulty. They are produced in increasing quantities, and a wide selection of them is available. We like them for their natural quality, often preferring them to the famous vintages because the new, lighter cuisine calls for light, dry wines.

Our choice of wine will depend not only on the dish to be accompanied, but also on our humor, on the season and the weather. Wine should be served cooler in summer than in winter. In hot weather we should avoid full-bodied red wines and favor light red wines, rosés, and dry white wines.

There is a recent tendency to drink red wine with fish, and why indeed should a fish course not be accompanied by a light, dry, well-chilled red wine (unless there is cream in the fish sauce). The wines of the Loire and Champagne regions are excellent with fish. With fish soups and bouillabaisse a light red wine or a rosé is preferable to white wine. Habit or tradition often makes us neglect some splendid discoveries. Unusual combinations of wines and foods often provide unsuspected savors that delight the palate.

A FEW POINTERS

Temperature

We often read that certain wines should be served *chambré,* that is, at room temperature. Today this recommendation has lost its meaning; it dates from the days before central heating, when wines were brought up from cellars where the temperature was scarcely above freezing point and "warmed" in dining rooms where, except in midsummer, the prevailing temperature was seldom above sixty degrees Fahrenheit.

Red Wines

It is advisable to serve red wines of the great vintages at a temperature of about sixty-five degrees. The newer and lighter the wines are, the cooler they should be served; a temperature of around fifty degrees is advisable for new Beaujolais and Burgundy and for fruity regional wines.

White Wines

Dry white wines and rosés should be served at a temperature not exceeding forty-eight degrees, a degree or two warmer if they are rich in bouquet. Sweet white wines, the great white Bordeaux—Graves, Château-Cheval Blanc, Léognan, Château Laville, Haut-Brion, to name a few—should be served at a temperature not exceeding forty-eight degrees.

Serve Sauternes—Château d'Yquem and Bommes—at a temperature of forty-five degrees. At this temperature Sauternes harmonize splendidly with *foie gras*.

Champagne

Champagne should be iced and served at a temperature of forty-five degrees, or somewhat cooler when extra dry. I have a predilection for champagne decanted into a carafe. This method of serving, adopted by certain restaurants, seems to bring out its crisp flavor.

Extreme temperatures are fatal to wines. When the wine is served too cold, the bouquet is lost; too much warmth brings out a taste of alcohol and sometimes of acidity.

Uncorking

Though in the long run air is the enemy of wine, brief contact with the air is needed to release the bouquet and flavor after the long confinement in the bottle. All wines gain by being uncorked some minutes before drinking. In the case of wines from one to five years old, fifteen minutes will suffice. New wine should be opened somewhat longer in advance, and fine vintage wines should be uncorked as much as thirty minutes before serving, but no more, for once in glasses they will be further exposed to the air and the danger of oxidation. As a general rule wine should not be uncorked too much in advance, for once oxidation has set in the wine is ruined.

When Wine Should Be Decanted

Wine is decanted (that is, transferred to a carafe) when a deposit has formed at the bottom of the bottle as a result of age. We decant to prevent this deposit from being poured into the glasses with the wine. This in general is the best way to serve the fine old Bordeaux wines, which tend more than others to form a deposit. It is also advisable to decant wine that has been brought up from the cellar just before serving.

The wine basket, much used in restaurants because it lends a picturesque touch to the activity of the wine waiter, is useful for bringing wine up from your own cellar. When one is used, the wine should be decanted or else the bottle should be removed and placed in an upright position.

Wineglasses

What is a good wineglass? All good wineglasses have stems. There are two possible shapes: the "balloon" and the "tulip." Either should be made of fine glass (though crystal is not absolutely necessary). The wine drinker should be able to hold the glass by the stem, raise it toward the light, and savor its aroma before actually tasting it.

Since wineglasses should not be filled more than two thirds, the minimum capacity should be about five ounces.

What are we to think of the heavy wineglasses that have recently made their appearance? They do not help us to taste wine. Thick glass makes for too much space between the upper and lower lip. Semi-crystal glasses are fine enough to do honor to any wine. Since crystal glasses are very expensive, I suggest that, instead of buying sets, you acquire your glasses as you run across them in antique and bric-a-brac shops. Such a collection of unmatched glasses will add charm to your table setting.

The Cellar

Few people today possess those good old cellars floored with beaten earth, where the temperature varied from forty to fifty degrees, according to the season. But many of us take pleasure in collecting wines, and with a little thought it is still possible to install a satisfactory wine cellar. Here are the precautions to be taken: the space devoted to your wines must be sufficiently high and wide to accommodate the rack needed to store your bottles lying down. This is necessary to keep the wine in permanent contact with the cork and avoid exposure to the air. The space for storing wine must be dark, shielded from electric light as well as daylight, and far from any source of heat, such as hot water pipes. An unused closet can serve as a wine cellar if you are able to keep it cool. A wine cellar must be equipped with a thermometer. If the temperature exceeds fifty degrees, the wine will age too quickly and will not keep.

WHAT WINES TO SERVE WITH WHAT FOODS

Soups

Wine is not served with soup, except for bouillabaisse and soups garnished with fish. With these serve a light red wine or a rosé.

Shellfish

Serve a dry white wine, though in the Gironde region oysters are often accompanied by a Léognan or Sauternes. Today it has become fashionable to eat oysters, mussels, clams, and other shellfish with a well-chilled light, red wine. Personally I prefer a Gewurztraminer or Muscadet.

Fish

Fish is generally accompanied by white wine: dry in the case of baked fish or fillets in butter; somewhat richer white wines in the case of fish served with rich sauces. If there is red wine in a fish sauce, a red wine may be chosen.

Poultry—White Meat

With chicken and turkey serve fine red wines rich in bouquet but not too full-bodied. Among the Bordeaux, a Médoc; among the Burgundies, a Mâcon or a Beaune. Among the regional wines, a Beaujolais Villages, Sancerre or a Chinon.

Poultry—Dark Meat

Serve good full-bodied red wines: a red Burgundy or a Côtes-du-Rhone or, among the Bordeaux, a Saint-Émilion.

White Meat

With white meats serve white or red wine or rosé, according to the season and the circumstances. The simpler the dish, the lighter the wine should be. Roasted meats, more than anything else, bring out the full flavor of fine wine.

Pink Meat

The savor of lamb and mutton is enhanced by a light regional wine: a Loire or Saône wine, a Beaujolais Villages or Côtes-du-Rhone rather than a traditional Bordeaux.

Red Meat

Do not drink white wine with red meat. A rosé may be acceptable in a pinch, but only if made from dark grapes. All good red wines are suitable, a full-bodied Bordeaux or Burgundy is an excellent choice. If you select a regional wine, it should be at least five years old.

Charcuteries[1]

With roast or braised pork, serve regional red wines or good rosé. With roast or braised ham, serve good red wines or a fine white wine such as Meursault.

Game

Red wine is served with all game. Game birds call for lighter, more subtle wine than venison and other ground game. With partridge and pheasant serve fine red wine rich in bouquet—among the Burgundies, Beaune, Volnay, Chambertin. Among the Bordeaux, a fine château wine. With venison and other ground game, serve a full-bodied vintage wine, a Burgundy if possible: Gevrey-Chambertin, Côtes-de-Nuits, or Vosne. Among the Côtes-du-Rhone, Châteauneuf-du-Pape. Among the regional wines, a Cahors more than five years old.

Salad

Do not serve wine with salad, and if you have some left in your glass refrain from drinking it. Both salad and wine would suffer.

Cheese

Cheese can be served with the wine that has been drunk in the course of the meal or with a somewhat more full-bodied wine. Do not serve a subtle wine with a strong cheese. It is a good idea to choose a wine originating in the same region as the cheese: they always go well together.

Dessert

Such great white Bordeaux as Sauternes, Barsac, and Monbazillac are excellent dessert wines. Other possibilities are a regional wine such as Jurançon or a well-chilled demi-sec champagne. Other good dessert wines are white port wine, sherry (not too dry), amontillado, Frontignan, Muscatel, or Banyuls, all well chilled. These wines, underestimated as table wines, contribute a welcome change at the end of a good meal.

---

[1] Pork products.

SOME REFRESHING AND BRACING DRINKS

Sangría

FOR A 2-QUART PITCHER

  1 bottle good, full-bodied red wine
  1 orange, washed and dried
  1 lemon, washed and dried
  2 peaches, peeled and pitted
  2–3 tablespoons sugar
  2 cups club soda
  ice cubes

Pour the wine into the pitcher and add the fruit, cut in slices or quarters. Stir in the sugar. Just before serving, add the carbonated water and ice cubes, stirring gently.

NOTE: *a bottle of Provençal rosé may be substituted for red wine. This makes a lighter, fruitier drink.*

Sangría fantaisie

Stronger than the preceding drink, this version of sangría makes an excellent apértif or summer cocktail.

FOR A 2-QUART PITCHER

  1 bottle good, full-bodied red wine
  1 orange, washed and dried
  1 lemon, washed and dried
  1 ounce cognac[1]
  1 ounce Cointreau
  2 tablespoons sugar
  2 cups club soda
  ice cubes

[1] If you prefer the drink stronger, use 2 ounces each of cognac and Cointreau.

Pour the wine into the pitcher and add the fruit, cut in slices or quarters, the cognac, Cointreau, and sugar. Stir. Just before serving, add the carbonated water and ice cubes, stirring gently.

Cup au vin blanc

Another refreshing drink, made with Alsatian-type dry white wine. Use a 2-quart pitcher.

MAKES 6–7 CUPS

1 bottle dry white wine
1 orange, washed and dried
1 lemon, washed and dried
2 peaches, peeled and pitted
5–6 large whole strawberries
1 small piece cucumber skin
2 tablespoons sugar
2 cups carbonated water
ice cubes

Pour the wine into the pitcher and add the oranges, lemons, and peaches, cut in slices or quarters, and the strawberries, left whole. Add the cucumber skin and stir in the sugar. Just before serving, add the carbonated water and ice cubes, stirring gently.

Cup au champagne

A delicious summer drink for a garden party or buffet. Use a 2-quart pitcher.

MAKES ABOUT 7 CUPS

rind of 1 orange
rind of 1 lemon
5 or 6 large whole strawberries (optional)
3 lumps sugar impregnated with Angostura bitters
1 bottle dry or extra-dry champagne
1–2 ounces cognac
1–2 ounces Cointreau or Grand Marnier
2 cups carbonated water
ice cubes

Put the fruit rinds, strawberries, and sugar lumps into the pitcher. Pour in the champagne and liqueurs, stir, and put in the refrigerator for 2–3 hours. Just before serving, add the carbonated water and ice cubes, stirring gently.

Punch au thé

A good strong punch to give you strength when out hunting or picnicking in early spring, or braving the wild winds at sea. For this you will need a 2-quart thermos bottle.

First make a pot of tea using 4 tea bags or 4 teaspoons of black tea and about a quart of boiling water. Add ¼–½ cup of sugar. While the tea is steeping, flame 1 cup of rum, seed and remove the membranes from a slice of lemon. Strain the tea into the thermos bottle. Add the rum and lemon slice. Close the bottle tightly. Shake it before pouring drinks.

PART II

Le Repas

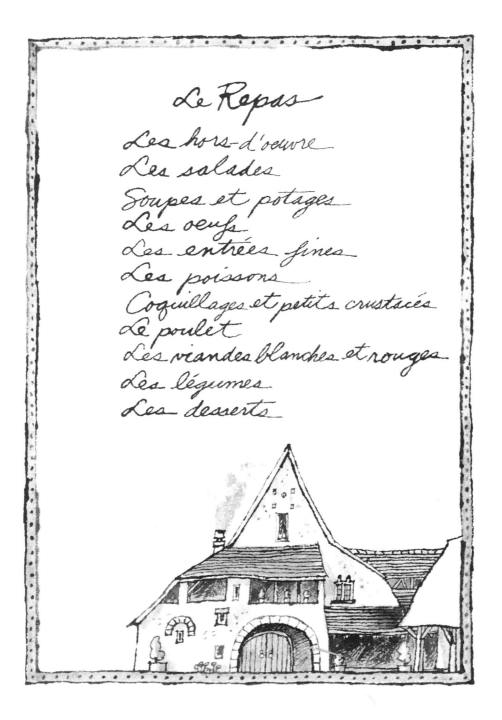

Le Repas
Les hors-d'oeuvre
Les salades
Soupes et potages
Les oeufs
Les entrées fines
Les poissons
Coquillages et petits crustacés
Le poulet
Les viandes blanches et rouges
Les légumes
Les desserts

Les hors-d'oeuvre

Either of these two sherbets is ideal for starting a meal on a hot summer day.

Tomato Sherbet   *Sorbet à la tomate*

This is a delicate, spicy sherbet that is quickly and easily made. Served in champagne cups, it is coated with a sweet and pungent tomato sauce. A pinch of fresh basil may be added.

FOR 6 PEOPLE

First place 6 champagne glasses in the refrigerator to chill and cloud. Place a metal serving bowl in the refrigerator about 15 minutes before using it.

ingredients for the sherbet

>   4½ cups canned tomato juice
>   a good squeeze of lemon juice
>   a dash of celery salt
>   freshly ground pepper
>   1 egg white

making the sherbet

Pour the tomato juice into the chilled bowl, add the seasonings, and taste. Add the egg white and beat the mixture with a wire whisk. Place the bowl in the freezer for 1 hour, or until the mixture is thickened. Beat it with an electric beater, then put it back in the freezer until completely firm.

making the spiced tomato sauce

>   10–12 tablespoons ketchup
>   1 small can spiced tomato sauce
>   a dash of liquid hot red pepper seasoning
>   a good squeeze of lemon juice
>   1 tablespoon finely cut fresh basil leaves (using scissors)

Place the ketchup in a bowl, add the spiced tomato sauce and the hot red pepper seasoning, tasting as you add. Mix in the lemon juice. Taste again. If you feel that it needs some salt, add a little. The sauce should be bright red, hot, and spicy, providing a sweet and pungent taste contrast to the bland tomato sherbet.

serving the sherbet

Place 2 scoops (or 2 rounded tablespoons) of sherbert in each chilled glass. Spoon the sauce over each scoop of sherbet so that each one looks like a small tomato. Decorate the top of each "tomato" with a pinch of the basil leaves (if the fresh herb is not available, use a dot of minced parsley).

Cantaloupe Sherbet   *Sorbet au melon*

Before beginning this recipe, put 6 champagne glasses in the refrigerator to chill and cloud. Put a metal serving dish in the refrigerator about 15 minutes before using it.

FOR 6 PEOPLE

3 ripe large cantaloupes
sugar to taste
juice of ½ lemon
freshly ground pepper (1 turn of the mill)
2 egg whites for binding the melon purée
a few drops red port wine
mint leaves or 6 half slices of fluted lemon for garnish

Scoop out the flesh of the cantaloupes and purée in a blender at low speed. Place the purée in a bowl and add sugar. Stir in the lemon juice, pepper, and egg whites. Beat the mixture thoroughly with a wire whisk or electric beater, place in the chilled serving bowl, and put in the freezer for 1 hour. Remove the bowl, beat the sherbet again, and replace in the freezer until ready to serve.

Place 2 scoops or 2 rounded tablespoons of sherbet in each chilled champagne glass. Sprinkle each scoop with 1 or 2 drops of port wine—no more, because alcohol will cause the sherbet to melt. Decorate the sherbet with mint leaves or place a slit lemon slice on the rim of each glass.

Celery Stuffed with Roquefort Cheese Paste
Côtes de céleri garnies de pâte de roquefort

Prepared in advance and kept in the refrigerator until ready to serve, this delicious hors-d'oeuvre can also be used as a cocktail snack.

8 crisp celery stalks

Cut the root end and leafy top from the celery and wash well in cold water. With the aid of a knife pull the strings from the outer side of each stalk, then cut the stalks into 2½ -inch lengths (about 2 bites each).

Roquefort cheese paste

⅓ cup crumbled Roquefort cheese
3½–4 tablespoons butter cut in small pieces
1 tablespoon cognac
2 tablespoons red port wine or medium-dry sherry
freshly ground pepper
salt if necessary
a dash of paprika or Cayenne pepper

In a bowl mash the cheese and butter with a fork. Mix in the remaining ingredients, blend with a wooden spatula until smooth, and taste to see if salt is needed. Place in the refrigerator for 2 or 3 minutes, then spread on the celery pieces so as to form domes, smoothing the surface with a knife. Sprinkle a tiny bit of paprika or Cayenne pepper on top.

Celery Root with Mustard Sauce *Céleri-rave rémoulade*

Raw celery root cut in julienne* strips is an excellent winter hors-d'oeuvre. It is usually dressed with mustard sauce, which is not at all difficult to make. It can also be dressed with mayonnaise that is highly seasoned with mustard and lightened with cream. The preparation of the celery root remains the same whichever dressing you choose.

FOR 4–6 PEOPLE

1 small celery root, or half of a large one

Peel the celery root deeply, cut it in quarters, and rub each quarter with a half lemon. This prevents oxidation, which causes the skin to darken. Using a strong, sharp knife, cut the quarters into julienne strips about the thickness of matchsticks.

Mustard Sauce *Sauce rémoulade*

3 tablespoons Dijon mustard
salt
1 cup peanut oil
freshly ground pepper
1 tablespoon red wine vinegar
a squeeze of lemon juice
a pinch of curry powder (optional)

Place the mustard and salt in a bowl and mix. Add about 2 tablespoons of oil in thin streams, beating vigorously with a wire whisk. Beat in the rest of the oil, a little at a time, until the sauce has thickened (it should not be as thick as mayonnaise). Add the pepper, then the vinegar, drop by drop, beating all the time. Mix in the lemon juice and curry powder. If a thicker sauce is desired, make Mayonnaise,* using the same amount of mustard as in *sauce rémoulade*. Beat in 1 tablespoon of heavy cream at the end. Dress the celery root with either of these sauces and place in a shallow serving bowl.

Mixed Celery Root Salad   *Salade de céleri-rave composée*

An excellent winter hors-d'oeuvre or salad, this goes beautifully with cold veal, cold pork, and pâtés. It can be enhanced with optional ingredients, noted at the end of the recipe.

FOR 6 PEOPLE

¾–1 cup Mayonnaise,* made with strong Dijon mustard and lemon juice
1 scant tablespoon heavy cream
1 small celery root, peeled and cut as in preceding recipe
1 good eating apple, peeled and cut in fine slices
1 medium-size beet, cooked, peeled, and diced
12 walnut halves
1 small celery stalk, minced, for garnish
2–3 celery leaves, minced, for garnish

optional ingredients

3 Belgian endives, cut in slices or quarters
3 artichoke hearts, cooked and diced
6 large raw mushroom caps, coated with lemon juice and sliced

Stir the cream into the mayonnaise. Mix in all the other ingredients, using just enough mayonnaise to coat them. Transfer to a shallow salad bowl and top with minced celery and leaves.

Mixed Vegetable Salad with Mayonnaise
Macédoine de légumes en mayonnaise

This classic hors-d'oeuvre, sometimes called Russian salad, is made of cooked vegetables, and usually some raw ones, dressed with mayonnaise. A *macédoine* consists of diced carrots, turnips, green beans cut in small bits, green peas, and *flageolets* (a French variety of green kidney bean).

Preparing the vegetables is a long process, since each should be cooked separately. I recommend using canned *macédoine,* which can be turned into an hors-d'oeuvre that is just as delicious and attractive as any you have slaved over yourself. It is possible to find cans of imported *macédoine* of vegetables in the United States.

Macédoine can be used as an accompaniment for cold meats, chicken in aspic, for example, and is more successful for a buffet than is a green salad, which wilts rapidly.

FOR 6–10 PEOPLE

3 medium-size boiling potatoes
2–3 tablespoons French Dressing with Mustard*
2 large cans *macédoine* of vegetables
2 celery hearts, diced
12 radishes, sliced
1½ cups well-seasoned Mayonnaise*

garnish for the salad

1 hard-boiled egg yolk, crumbled
2 tablespoons mixed minced parsley, chervil, and tarragon
12 radishes, grated
a few raw onion rings

Cook the potatoes in their jackets. Peel and dice them. While they are still warm, mix in the French dressing. Set aside. Drain the cans of *macédoine* and rinse the contents with warm water. Spread them out on a kitchen towel, pat dry. Place them in a shallow salad bowl. Add the potatoes, diced celery hearts, and sliced radishes. The radishes add crispness and color to the salad. Mix in the mayonnaise, being careful not to crush the vegetables.

Even the surface of the salad with a knife and sprinkle the garnish on top.

optional additions to the salad

6–8 raw mushrooms, sliced; or 6–8 pitted black olives, cut in two; or ½ cup cooked beets, diced; or 1 apple, peeled, rubbed with lemon, and diced

This salad makes a delicious first course for a summer day if you add

2 or 3 hard-boiled eggs, chopped; leftover cold fish, chopped and boned; or leftover cold chicken, boned and cut in small pieces; or a 6-ounce can of crab meat, shredded

Hard-Boiled Egg Salad   *Salade d'oeufs durs*

A substantial hors d'oeuvre perfect for serving with meals out of doors. The recipe calls for anchovy mayonnaise, but if you prefer use mayonnaise seasoned with curry powder or substitute French dressing with herbs for the mayonnaise.

FOR 6 PEOPLE

9–10 hard-boiled eggs (plus 1 hard-boiled egg for decoration)
1½ cups Anchovy Mayonnaise*
6 anchovy fillets (rolled with capers if possible)
1 handful black olives
6 red radishes, sliced thin

Peel the eggs, slice evenly, and place in a shallow oval dish. Lightly mix in the anchovy mayonnaise (or whatever dressing you have chosen). Decorate the top of the salad (leveled with a spatula) with the reserved hard-boiled egg, cut in 6 slices, the rolled anchovy fillets, the black olives, and the radishes.

Cucumbers with Mint   *Concombres à la menthe*

This is a cool-tasting summer hors-d'oeuvre.

FOR 4–6 PEOPLE

2 slender cucumbers (slender ones have fewer seeds)
1 recipe Simple French Dressing*
10 mint leaves
6 fluted half-slices lemon

Peel and slice the cucumbers. Draw out the excess liquid by placing them between paper towels and pressing lightly with the flat of the hand. Place the cucumbers in a shallow serving dish and stir in the French dressing. Cut the central vein from the mint leaves and cut them finely with scissors. Stir the cucumber slices again and sprinkle them with the mint. Decorate the rim of the dish with the fluted half-slices of lemon.

Cucumbers with Cream and Lemon Dressing   *Concombres à la crème*

FOR 4–6 PEOPLE

2 slender cucumbers
1 recipe of Cream and Lemon Dressing*

Prepare the cucumbers as in the preceding recipe. Stir in the cream and lemon dressing.

An elegant way of serving this hors-d'oeuvre is to place lettuce leaves in the form of a flower on a small platter and arrange the dressed cucumbers on top. Sprinkle with minced fresh chervil and tarragon, or garnish with a few black olives or 5–6 thin strips of peeled tomato.

STUFFED CUCUMBER BOATS *Barquettes de concombres*

These make elegant summer hors-d'oeuvre. They must be served very cold so the cucumbers are firm and crisp. The filling, given in the recipe following, is added just before serving.

Cucumbers Stuffed with Tuna and Anchovies
Concombres garnis de thon et d'anchois

FOR 6 PEOPLE

2 large, firm cucumbers
½ cup canned tuna, shredded
6 fillets of anchovies, minced
2–3 tablespoons butter or 2–3 tablespoons Mayonnaise*
a few drops lemon juice or vinegar
freshly ground pepper
several small black olives
2 teaspoons minced fresh chervil and tarragon[1]

NOTE: *Do not add salt to the filling until you have tasted it.*

Peel the cucumbers and slice in two lengthwise. Scoop out the pulp containing seeds, thus creating boat shapes. Sprinkle the hollows with salt, put them upside down on paper towels to absorb excess moisture, then place them in the refrigerator.

making the filling

Work the tuna and anchovy fillets together with a fork. Stir in the butter or mayonnaise, the lemon juice or vinegar, and some pepper. Taste for salt. Just before serving, pile the filling into the cucumber boats in the form of domes. Decorate the tops with small black olives and herbs or parsley. Place the filled cucumbers on an oval platter that has been garnished with lettuce leaves or slices of peeled tomato. Place a sharp knife for slicing on the side of the platter.

[1] If fresh chervil and tarragon are unavailable, use finely minced parsley.

Cucumbers Filled with Crab Meat   *Concombres garnis de chair de crabe*

  2 large, firm cucumbers
  ½ cup well-drained, flaked crab meat
  3–4 tablespoons well-seasoned Mayonnaise*
  1 tablespoon ketchup
  a few drops Worcestershire sauce
  a few drops lemon juice
  salt
  freshly ground pepper
  10 seeded black olives, minced fine, or 1 canned pimento, drained, dried,
     and minced

Prepare the cucumbers as in the preceding recipe. Mix the remaining ingredients together and adjust seasoning. Just before serving, heap the filling in the cucumbers. Top with olive or pimiento garnish.

This filling and the preceding one can also be used for whole peeled tomatoes.

Raw Mushroom Salad with Cream   *Salade de champignons à la crème*

FOR 6 PEOPLE

  1 pound small, firm mushrooms
  juice of ½ lemon
  freshly ground pepper
  a pinch of ground coriander
  a small pinch of curry powder
  salt to taste
  3 tablespoons heavy cream

Rinse the mushrooms several times. Drain and pat dry with a towel. Cut them into thin slices, place in a bowl, and stir in the lemon juice. Add pepper, spices, and salt to taste. Add the cream, stirring it in very carefully so as not to bruise the mushrooms. Place in the refrigerator for a few minutes. Accompany with fresh French bread and butter.

This hors-d'oeuvre can also be used as a canapé spread. Drain off any excess liquid before spreading it on canapés.

Raw Mushrooms with Mayonnaise *Champignons crus en mayonnaise*

        1 pound mushrooms
        ¾ cup Mayonnaise*
        1 tablespoon lemon juice
        1 tablespoon heavy cream
        a pinch of curry powder
        1 tablespoon mixed minced parsley, chervil, and tarragon (optional)
        salt

Prepare the mushrooms as in the preceding recipe. Stir in the lemon juice, cream, curry powder, and herbs into the mayonnaise. Add salt if needed.

Vegetables à la Grecque *Légumes à la grecque*

These are an excellent cold hors-d'oeuvre. They are made of vegetables cooked in a previously reduced aromatic broth, then they are allowed to marinate in the broth until cool. Mushrooms, small white onions, artichoke hearts, celery hearts, fennel hearts, or young leeks can all be prepared *à la grecque*.

basic recipe for the aromatic broth

        4½ cups cold water
        ½ cup olive oil
        juice of ½–1 whole lemon
        1 carrot, sliced lengthwise
        1 onion, stuck with a clove
        1 stalk celery, sliced lengthwise
        2 slices fennel heart with shoots if possible
        a few coriander seeds
        a few dillseeds
        a few peppercorns
        salt
        1 *Bouquet garni,** including thyme, rosemary, sage, 2 bay leaves, and
            oregano or marjoram
        a pinch of saffron
        a pinch of curry powder

Simmer these ingredients in an enameled saucepan for 20–25 minutes. Strain into a heavy-bottomed enameled saucepan.

Mushrooms à la Grecque   *Champignons à la grecque*

1½ pounds small mushrooms
1 recipe cold aromatic broth (given above)

Stem the mushrooms and wash them thoroughly. Add a little lemon juice to the last washing water. Drain on paper towels and pat dry, then cut them in quarters. Place them in the cold aromatic broth, heat, and bring to a boil. Turn down heat and simmer for 10 minutes. Remove the saucepan from heat and let the mushrooms cool in the broth.

serving the mushrooms **à la grecque**

Remove the mushrooms from the broth with a slotted spoon and place in a shallow porcelain or earthenware serving dish. Taste the broth. It might be necessary to add a little more lemon, pepper, or olive oil (if you add more olive oil, beat it in carefully). Pour the broth over the mushrooms. A garnish of mixed herbs might be added.

Small White Onions à la Grecque with Tomato Sauce
Petits oignons à la grecque à la sauce tomate

36–40 small white onions
aromatic broth (given above)
1 scant cup Tomato Fondue,* or 3 tablespoons tomato paste
1 tablespoon olive oil
a pinch of sugar
a pinch of ground coriander
a pinch of curry powder

Peel the onions, making a cross in the root end with a knife to allow the flavor of the broth to penetrate. Simmer them in the broth until tender (test for tenderness with the point of a knife). Cool them in the broth, remove with a slotted spoon, and place in a porcelain or earthenware serving dish. Pour the tomato fondue or tomato paste in a heavy-bottomed enameled saucepan. Using a whisk, beat the broth in very slowly. Simmer until somewhat reduced. Add the olive oil, sugar, coriander, and curry powder, simmer for a few minutes until the sauce is fairly thick. Pour over the onions, let them cool before serving.

Small White Onions with Seedless Raisins
Petits oignons aux raisins de Smyrne

This dish bears a resemblance to Small White Glazed Onions* and onions *à la grecque* (see Vegetables à la Grecque). It is a delicious accompaniment to cold ham, chicken, and duck.

FOR 6 PEOPLE

> a handful of seedless raisins
> 1 cup hot tea
> 1 cup beef bouillon
> ¾ cup dry white wine
> a few coriander seeds
> freshly ground pepper
> 1 *Bouquet garni,** including a sprig each of thyme and rosemary, 1 bay leaf, and a small piece of fennel
> salt (only after tasting the broth)
> 24–30 small white onions, peeled, making a cross in the root end with a knife
> 3 tablespoons butter cut in pieces
> 4 tablespoons boiling water
> a good pinch of sugar

Place the raisins in a small enameled saucepan. Cover with the hot tea, bring to a boil, and cook for 1 minute. Remove from heat and let the raisins macerate until they are soft and plump. Strain and set aside.

Put the beef bouillon, white wine, coriander seeds, and pepper in a heavy-bottomed enameled saucepan. Bring to a boil, add the *bouquet garni*, turn down heat, and simmer for 10–15 minutes. Taste for salt. Strain and set aside.

Place the onions in a small, heavy frying pan or saucepan. They should be somewhat crowded together. Add the pieces of butter. Place on moderate heat and cook, turning the onions frequently so they become coated with butter. (This will prevent them from falling apart.) Add the boiling water and sugar. Cover the pan and cook briskly for 5 minutes. Lower heat, add the raisins and broth, cook very slowly for 15–20 minutes, until the onions are very tender and the liquid is reduced. Place in a shallow porcelain dish. Serve cool, not ice cold.

Tomato Salad *Salade de tomate*

It seems absurd to tell anyone how to make tomato salad. Doesn't everyone know? And yet, when I think of some of the "tomato salads" I have been served, I believe that a few words of advice may be in order.

It is absolutely necessary to peel the tomatoes. This can be done in two ways.

peeling tomatoes

If your tomatoes are garden-fresh and sun-ripened, it seems a shame to plunge them (even if only for a few seconds) into boiling hot water. Instead, wash them under the cold water tap and dry them carefully with a towel. Then, starting from the top of the tomato, scratch out four lines in the skin with the point of a knife, as though dividing the tomato into quarters, being careful not to cut into the flesh. Insert the knife along these scratched-out lines and peel the tomato. Next, remove the stem by cutting out a cone at the core end. If the tomatoes you are using are hard and not very red (these are signs that they have been picked and shipped before fully ripened), it will be impossible to peel them in this manner. Instead, plunge them one by one into a saucepan of boiling hot water (off heat) for 20–30 seconds, then peel them.

cutting tomatoes

There is nothing so unattractive and insipid-tasting as tomato slices full of watery hollows. The best method for cutting tomatoes is to cut them in two vertically, then to cut each half into sections. Remove the seeds and drain off excess moisture by placing the sections on paper towels. Arranged on a plate and, with dressing, tomatoes cut in this manner look and taste appetizing.

dressing for tomatoes

For tomatoes the best is French Dressing with Mustard.* If possible, use tarragon mustard and Tarragon Vinegar.* Either olive oil or peanut oil may be used.

garnishing tomatoes

Any garnish of mixed herbs is recommended, particularly chives, chervil, and tarragon. To give a tomato salad more substance, add 1 or 2 hard-boiled eggs, sliced, a few black olives, or a few rings of raw onion.

COLD STUFFED SMALL TOMATOES
Petites tomates farcies froides

These are among the most charming of all hors-d'oeuvre, especially if they are nicely served. They can be prepared somewhat in advance.

Tomatoes Stuffed with Pimentos   *Tomates aux poivrons*

FOR 6 PEOPLE

    12 firm-fleshed small tomatoes
    3 canned pimentos
    3 hard-boiled eggs, minced
    ½ celery heart, minced
    a good pinch of curry powder
    salt
    freshly ground pepper
    4 tablespoons Mayonnaise,* with extra mustard, for binding the filling

Peel the tomatoes and cut a thin slice off the core end. Scoop out the flesh with a teaspoon and place the tomatoes upside down on paper towels to drain off excess liquid. This procedure is used in all recipes for stuffed raw tomatoes.

Drain the pimentos on a double layer of paper towels and blot them dry. Mince them. Place them in a bowl, add the hard-boiled eggs, celery heart, curry powder, salt, and pepper. Gently stir in the mayonnaise.

Wipe out the inside of each tomato with a piece of paper towel before you add the filling. The tomatoes may be served on a plate garnished with lettuce leaves. They may be kept in the refrigerator for one hour.

The pimento filling may also be used to fill hard-cooked eggs, cut in two lengthwise. Mash the yolks and add them to the pimento mixture. Fill the whites.

Small Tomatoes with Tapénade   *Petites tomates à la tapénade*

Tapénade is a Provençal delicacy. The ingredients vary slightly, depending on the region, but anchovies, black olives, and capers are always included.

FOR 6–8 PEOPLE

    12 anchovy fillets, put through the finest disk of a food mill
    1½ cups pitted black olives, minced
    2 tablespoons minced capers
    3–4 hard-boiled egg yolks, mashed
    a few drops lemon juice

---

3 cloves garlic, pounded into a paste with 2 tablespoons olive oil
freshly ground pepper
12 small tomatoes, prepared for stuffing as in the preceding recipe
sprigs of parsley

NOTE: *Do not add salt.*

With a wooden spatula work the anchovies, olives, capers and egg yolks together. Mix in the lemon juice and garlic paste, add the pepper. Adjust for seasoning. Refrigerate the *tapénade* for at least 20 minutes before stuffing the tomatoes (which have been wiped out with a piece of paper towel). Arrange the tomatoes on a platter and decorate each with a sprig of parsley.

Small Tomatoes with Cream Cheese and Chives
Petites tomates gervaises

Tomatoes with a highly spiced cream cheese filling . . . very nice for a summer luncheon or dinner on the terrace.

FOR 4 PEOPLE

2 8-ounce packages cream cheese
1 tablespoon strong Dijon mustard
2–3 tablespoons heavy cream
2 tablespoons onion squeezed through a garlic press, or 2 spring onions, minced
3 tablespoons finely scissored chives
1 tablespoon ketchup
freshly ground pepper
a dash of Tabasco sauce
salt
8 firm-fleshed small tomatoes prepared for stuffing (see Cold Stuffed Small Tomatoes)

Place the cream cheese and mustard in a bowl and work into a paste with a fork. Work in the cream. Stir in the onion, chieves, ketchup, pepper, Tabasco sauce, and salt to taste. Adjust for seasoning. Fill the tomatoes. Place them on a plate garnished with unseasoned watercress. Refrigerate for a few minutes before serving.

Lentil Salad   *Salade de lentilles*

A bowl of lentils seasoned with French dressing is excellently suited to a buffet, especially a country buffet.

FOR 6–8 PEOPLE

2 pounds cooked lentils

dressing for lentil salad

    1 tablespoon Dijon mustard

    7 tablespoons peanut oil

    2 tablespoons wine vinegar

    salt

    freshly ground pepper

garnish for lentil salad

    10–12 half slices fluted lemon

    2 tablespoons minced parsley

    2 onions, cut into rings

Place the lentils in a shallow bowl. Prepare the dressing as in the recipe for French Dressing with Mustard.* Mix into the lentils. Arrange the lemon slices around the edge of the bowl and sprinkle them with parsley. Decorate the top of the salad with onion rings.

Potato Salad   *Salade de pommes de terre*

This is one of the most delicious of all salads, and it can be served as an hors-d'oeuvre or as an accompaniment to another dish.

    Never cook potatoes for salad in advance. The potatoes should be cooked in their jackets, peeled, sliced, and dressed while warm. Choose medium-size boiling potatoes, the kind that do not fall apart when cooking. Do not refrigerate the salad after making it. It should be served slightly warm.

FOR 6 PEOPLE

    2¼ pounds boiling potatoes

    1 tablespoon coarse salt for water

    ½ cup Simple French Dressing* with a little extra mustard

    1 shallot, squeezed through a garlic press

    3–4 tablespoons Mayonnaise*

    2 tablespoons mixed minced parsley and chervil, or 2 tablespoons finely
        scissored chives

Place potatoes in a roomy kettle and cover them with cold water. Add the salt and bring to a boil over moderate heat. Cook for 16–18 minutes after they have started boiling. To test for doneness, prick a potato with a larding needle. If the needle enters easily, the potato is done. Or remove a potato from the water and press it between thumb and index finger; if done, the potato will give slightly to the touch. With a slotted spoon remove the potatoes from the water one by one. Peel and cut in slices or pieces. Place in a salad bowl and pour the French dressing over them. Mix lightly, using two wooden spoons.

Stir the shallot into the mayonnaise, add to the salad, a tablespoon at a time, mixing after each addition. Stop adding mayonnaise when the potatoes are lightly coated. Sprinkle with herbs and serve warm.

The following two recipes are based on potato salad.

Potato Salad with Périgord Sauce
Salade de pommes de terre à la sauce du Périgord

A sumptuous salad for a special occasion. Your guests will know immediately that the sauce contains some truffle. This salad goes wonderfully with cold turkey or cold baked ham.

FOR 6 PEOPLE

Périgord sauce   ABOUT 1½ CUPS

> 3 hard-boiled egg yolks, mashed
> salt
> freshly ground pepper (optional)
> 3 tablespoons heavy cream
> 4 tablespoons peanut oil
> juice of ½ lemon
> 1–2 tablespoons cognac
> 1 medium-size canned truffle, peeled, minced, and arranged in 2 small
>   piles

Place the mashed egg yolks in a bowl, add salt and pepper. Work in the cream little by little with a wooden spatula. Add the oil as for Mayonnaise.* When the sauce has reached the proper consistency, stir in the lemon juice, cognac, and one of the piles of minced truffle.

> 1 recipe Potato Salad (see preceding recipe)

Prepare the potato salad but without French dressing. Place the slices or pieces of warm potatoes in a salad bowl and lightly mix in the Périgord sauce. Taste for salt. Sprinkle the top with the rest of the minced truffle.

Salade Niçoise with Basil   *Salade niçoise au basilic*

An appetizing summer hors-d'oeuvre, colorful, succulent, and filling. Composed of tomatoes, potatoes, green beans, green peppers, and fennel hearts, it is garnished with hard-boiled eggs, anchovies, black olives, fresh basil, and a few rings of raw onion.

FOR 6 PEOPLE

1½ pounds tomatoes, peeled, seeded, and quartered

⅔ pound green beans, blanched for 10 minutes only

3 green peppers, cut in half vertically, cored, seeded, and sliced fine

2 fennel hearts, sliced thin

2 recipes of French Dressing with Mustard* (made with tarragon vinegar if possible)

⅔ pound potatoes, cooked in their jackets, peeled, sliced, and seasoned with Simple French Dressing* while still warm

3 hard-boiled eggs, cut in half

6 anchovy fillets rolled around capers

a few rings of raw onion

a few small black olives

2 tablespoons scissored fresh basil

assembling and serving the salad

Dress the tomatoes, green beans, green peppers, and fennel hearts separately with the French dressing with mustard. Arrange, along with the dressed potatoes, in a large shallow dish in small piles, making a pattern of colors: green, white, red. Place the hard-boiled egg halves, garnished with the rolled anchovy fillets, around the edge of the dish. Decorate the top of the salad with rings of onion, black olives, and basil. Place in the refrigerator, covered, until serving time.

Accompany the salad with cold rosé wine and French bread and butter. This is an ideal summer meal, especially if served out of doors.

Mediterranean Style Raw Vegetables   *Crudités niçoise*

A platter of raw vegetables served unseasoned. The dressing is passed, and each person seasons the choice of salad to his or her own taste. It goes without saying that the vegetables used, as well as the dressing, can be varied.

FOR 6 PEOPLE

2 celery hearts, washed and trimmed

6 unpeeled small tomatoes

6 spring onions with about 1½ inches of stem

3 fennel hearts, cut in half

3 hearts romaine lettuce (or other variety)

3 or 4 small artichoke hearts (optional)

cauliflower flowerets

2 medium-size green peppers, halved, seeded, and sliced

½ bunch red radishes

Place the celery hearts in a small glass filled with water in the center of a shallow wooden salad bowl or round earthenware platter. Arrange the vegetables around the glass of celery, making contrasting color combinations. At least two dressings should be served with the vegetables.

Sauce Béatrice* A pleasant light sauce seasoned with mustard and lemon juice
Sauce Françoise* or *Sauce Perrine* Both of these sauces are colored pink with tomato. The first is more highly seasoned than the second. Both are ideal with *crudités*.
Sauce Collioure Anchovy Mayonnaise* enhanced with curry powder. It is garnished with tiny gray shrimps and pleasantly refreshed with grated raw apple.
Sauce Bellini, also called *bagna cauda,* which means "hot bath" in Piedmontese, is a hot sauce in which the *crudités* are dipped as they are eaten. This procedure brings out the characteristic flavor and aroma of each vegetable. Pierre Bellini, a Franco-Italian restaurant owner in Paris, is the originator. When he saw me trying to fathom the secret of his sauce, he kindly gave me the recipe.

Sauce Bellini

MAKES ABOUT 2¾ CUPS

6–8 cloves garlic
2½ cups olive oil
12 whole anchovy fillets
2 heaping tablespoons heavy cream

For this recipe you will need a deep flameproof casserole and a small alcohol burner.

Peel the garlic and cut in thin slices. Heat the olive oil until it sizzles, add the garlic, turn down heat, and cook for a minute or two without letting the garlic brown. Add the anchovies and simmer for another minute or two, stirring with a wooden spatula. Remove the saucepan from heat and beat in the cream. Pour the sauce into the casserole and place over the alcohol burner. This is the "hot bath" into which the raw vegetables are dipped.

Chicken Liver Mousse with Port Wine
Mousse de foies de volaille au Porto

A creamy mixture of chicken livers flavored with herbs, port wine, and cognac, for garnishing canapés or small pastry tarts. It can also be molded into a roll, refrigerated, then cut in slices and served along with other hors-d'oeuvre.

ENOUGH FOR 12–15 SMALL CANAPÉS

12–15 fresh chicken livers
freshly ground pepper
¼ pound fresh pork fat, diced
½ cup red port wine
2 tablespoons cognac
2 tablespoons butter
a small piece from a sprig of thyme, fresh or dried
a small piece of bay leaf
salt
8 tablespoons fresh white bread crumbs
1 tablespoon heavy cream

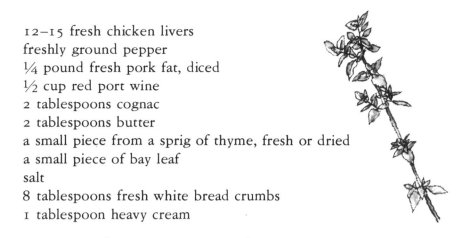

Prepare the chicken livers as in Chicken Livers in Aspic.* Season them with pepper. Marinate the livers and pork fat in the wine and cognac for 20 minutes or so. Remove with a slotted spoon and pat dry. Set the marinating liquid aside.

Butter a skillet. Add the pork fat and place the skillet over moderate heat until the fat has more or less melted. Add the livers and herbs and sauté quickly, no more than 2–3 minutes, so the interiors of the livers remain rosy-pink. Remove the livers, season with salt and set aside.

Pour into the skillet the wine and cognac in which the livers have marinated. Reduce slightly over moderate heat and add the bread crumbs. Cook for a minute or so, then remove from heat and discard the herbs and any visible pieces of pork fat. Put the liver and bread crumb mixture through a food mill, using the finest disk. Place the resulting mousse in an earthenware bowl, and with a wooden spatula work in the cream little by little. Taste and adjust seasoning, cover the bowl with aluminum foil, and refrigerate.

Potato and Smoked Herring Salad
Salade de pommes de terre et de harengs fumés

A substantial winter hors-d'oeuvre.

FOR 6 PEOPLE

1 recipe Potato Salad*
4–5 Fillets of Smoked Herring Marinated in Oil,* cut in pieces
1 tablespoon minced parsley
1 large beet, cooked, peeled, and diced
4 or 5 onion rings

Place the potato salad and the herring pieces in a salad bowl and mix lightly together. A small amount of the marinade from the herrings may be added. Top the salad with the parsley, beets, and onion rings.

Beef Salad, Paris Style   *Salade de boeuf à la parisienne*

A classical hors-d'oeuvre composed of highly seasoned boiled beef and potato salad.

FOR 6 PEOPLE

½–⅔ pound boiled beef (leftover *Pot-au-feu** meat is fine)
6 tablespoons beef bouillon (a bouillon cube will do for this)
1 recipe French Dressing with Mustard*
1 recipe of Potato Salad*
2 tablespoons minced parsley
5 or 6 onion rings

Dice the meat and heat it in the bouillon. Remove from heat and let it stand for 2–3 minutes, then strain. Season the meat with the mustard dressing. Mix this salad lightly with the potato salad so as not to crush the potatoes. Garnish with the parsley and onion rings.

NOTE: *If the salad seems dry, add a few tablespoons of mayonnaise.*

Tuna Mousse   *Mousse de thon*

FOR 6 PEOPLE

6 canned anchovies, chopped (reserve oil in can)
3 cloves garlic, squeezed through a garlic press, pounded into a paste with 2 tablespoons olive oil
2 tablespoons heavy cream
¾ cup crumbled canned tuna (reserve oil in can)
a few drops lemon juice
a pinch of curry powder
a pinch of ground coriander

NOTE: *Add salt only after tasting.*

Place the chopped anchovies and the garlic paste in a small, heavy-bottomed enameled saucepan. Set over low heat, stir in the cream, tuna, lemon juice, and spices. Simmer gently for a few minutes, stirring constantly with a wooden spatula. Mix in a little of the reserved tuna oil and anchovy oil, remove from heat. Set aside to cool.

Chill a serving bowl by placing it in another, larger, bowl filled with ice cubes.

Grind the cooled tuna mixture through a food mill[1] (using the finest disk) into the ice-cold bowl. Beat in 2–3 more tablespoons heavy cream or 2 tablespoons Creamed Butter.*

[1] A blender may be used instead of a food mill.

Canned Sardine Pâté *Pâté de sardines en boîte*

Serve this appetizing hors-d'oeuvre on a platter along with others, or use it as a spread for canapés or sandwiches. The pâté can be made well in advance. It will keep for 24 hours in the refrigerator.

FOR 6 PEOPLE

3 cans skinless sardines (6 sardines in oil in each can)
1 clove, crushed and pulverized
freshly ground pepper
a pinch of ground coriander
a few drops lemon juice
2 tablespoons olive oil
2 tablespoons butter

ingredients for the garnish

several very thin strips of pimento or peeled tomato
2 or 3 sprigs parsley
3 slices fluted lemon, cut in half

Drain the sardines, cut off the tails, but do not remove the backbones. Place them in a bowl and mash with a fork. Add the spices, lemon juice, and olive oil, put through a blender. Work in the butter with a fork, taste for seasoning. Place in the refrigerator.

serving the pâté

Place the sardine pâté on a small hors-d'oeuvre dish and with a spatula level the surface. Using the point of a knife, make diamond-shaped patterns, and mark these with the strips of pimento or tomato. Place the sprigs of parsley around the pâté and border the dish with the lemon slices.

Fillets of Smoked Herring Marinated in Oil
Filets de harengs fumés, marinés à l'huile

An excellent winter hors-d'oeuvre. It can also be used as a spread for canapés or buttered rye bread, then decorated with triangles cut from the flesh of a lemon.

FOR 6 PEOPLE

6 fillets smoked herring
3 or 4 slices onion
3 or 4 rounds raw carrot
2 sprigs thyme
1 small bay leaf
a few peppercorns
enough peanut oil to cover the herrings

NOTE: *Do not add salt.*

Place the herrings in a shallow porcelain or glass dish. Distribute the slices of onion and carrot on top of and around the fillets, add the thyme, bay leaf, and peppercorns. Cover with peanut oil. Fit a piece of aluminum foil over the dish. Allow to marinate for 2 or 3 days before serving. Serve with pumpernickel and butter or with buttered toast.

If you would like a more substantial hors-d'oeuvre, serve the herrings with Belgian Endive Salad,* Field Salad,* or warm Potato Salad.*

Mackerel with White Wine   *Maquereaux au vin blanc*

A marinated hors-d'oeuvre that will keep for a week in the refrigerator.

FOR 6 PEOPLE

6 small mackerel, cleaned, heads removed
salt
freshly ground pepper
1 small carrot, sliced thin
1 medium-size onion, sliced thin
1 lemon, sliced
½ small chili pepper
12 coriander seeds
2 cloves
1 cup dry white wine
3 tablespoons wine vinegar
1 *Bouquet garni classique**

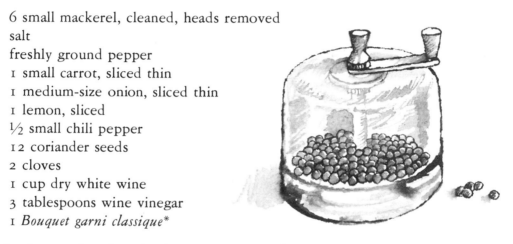

Wash the mackerel and place them in a flat, rectangular flameproof pan. Sprinkle with salt and pepper. Arrange the carrot, onion, and lemon slices on and around the fish. Add the spices, white wine, and vinegar. The mackerel should be just covered with liquid. Cover the pan with a piece of aluminum foil and marinate for 20 minutes. Remove the foil, place pan on medium heat, and bring to a boil. Add the *bouquet garni.* Let the liquid bubble for a few minutes, then turn off heat. Cool the mackerel in the marinade. Remove the *bouquet garni* before serving.

Salads

There are many varieties of salad greens, and their dressing depends a good deal on the kind chosen. Salad making is both a science and an art. We often relegate the task to someone who knows nothing about cooking, thinking, "It can't go wrong." How far from the truth! There is an adage that in order to make a salad one must be three persons: a prodigal with oil, a miser with vinegar, and a wise man with salt. How many of us today really know how to dress a salad?

THE PREPARATION OF A SALAD

Use only fresh greens. They must be cleaned and prepared with particular care. Discard the outside leaves, then remove each leaf separately with a knife until the heart is exposed. This is left whole. Wash the leaves quickly in several changes of water, or rinse them under the cold-water tap. Never soak salad leaves in water; soaking makes them limp. To drain, place them on a kitchen towel folded in two. Never shake salad greens in a wire salad basket; it bruises the tender leaves pitifully. Choose a bowl large enough to allow plenty of air to circulate among the leaves, and shallow enough for easy mixing. Some green salads, especially those that are garnished, can be made on a deep platter rather than a bowl.

DRESSING SALADS

The classic dressing for simple green salads is *sauce vinaigrette* (known as French dressing in the United States). But the composition of the dressing depends on the kind of salad greens used. Tender spring salad greens (various kinds of lettuce, romaine, or watercress) are seasoned differently from crisp winter ones—chicory (also known as curly endive), Belgian endive, and escarole—and these little variations in seasoning make an agreeable change in the taste of the daily salad.

Here are a few things to know before making French dressing: Salt blends more easily in oil than in vinegar. Poor-quality vinegar or too much vinegar is harmful to the salad. French dressing should not be made in too large quantity or too far ahead of time. Once the ingredients are assembled in a bowl, the dressing can stand for about ten minutes before being beaten. Just before it is poured on the salad, beat it for at least one minute. French dressing should never be placed in the bottom of the salad bowl with the salad piled on top. The leaves touching the oil and vinegar will come to the surface limp and faded when the salad is mixed.

Simple French Dressing   *Vinaigrette simple*

> 5–6 tablespoons peanut oil or olive oil
> salt
> 1½–2 tablespoons red wine vinegar
> freshly ground pepper

garnish (optional)

> 1 tablespoon finely minced chervil, or some finely cut (by scissors) fresh tarragon leaves (or a mixture of chervil and tarragon)

Put the oil and salt in a bowl and beat with a wire whisk. Add the vinegar, then the pepper. Beat for about 50 seconds, or until the mixture is well blended and smooth. Pour the dressing on the salad at the moment of serving. If you are garnishing the salad with herbs, sprinkle them on top. Mix the salad at the table, turning the leaves gently and not pressing on them, so the salad stays crisp and the leaves whole.

Lemon-Flavored French Dressing   *Vinaigrette au citron*

> 5 tablespoons peanut oil or olive oil
> 1 tablespoon red wine vinegar (Tarragon Vinegar* if possible)
> 2–2½ tablespoons freshly squeezed lemon juice
> salt
> freshly ground pepper

Use the same garnish (optional) as in the preceding recipe.

Cream and Lemon Dressing *Assaisonnement à la crème*

FOR 4–6 PEOPLE

3 tablespoons heavy cream
freshly squeezed juice of ½ lemon (about 2 tablespoons)
salt
1 tablespoon of chives finely cut with scissors

Beat the first 4 ingredients together and garnish with chives.

French Dressing with Hard-Boiled Egg *Vinaigrette mimosa*

Prepare 1 recipe of French Dressing with Mustard.* To this add a hard-boiled egg (or the hard-boiled yolk only), put through a small food mill. Beat the dressing thoroughly before adding it to the salad.

All the dressings listed in the preceding pages are particularly suitable for spring or summer salads.

Roquefort Cheese Dressing *Assaisonnement au roquefort*

The idea of making salad dressings with Roquefort cheese came to us from America about twenty years ago, and since then we have added our own little touches. Some people simply add crumbs of Roquefort cheese to the dressing. This is not a bad idea except that Roquefort does not harmonize very well with vinegar (unless it is sherry vinegar).

FOR 6 PEOPLE

3¼ tablespoons crumbled Roquefort cheese
5 tablespoons heavy cream
1–2 tablespoons cognac
freshly ground pepper
a very small amount of salt

Place the cheese in a bowl and mash it with a fork. Blend it with the cream until the mixture is smooth. Add the cognac (still blending with the fork), the pepper, and the merest pinch of salt. Spread the dressing over the salad, which has been put in a salad bowl, and mix at the table.

TENDER-LEAFED SPRING AND SUMMER SALADS
Salades de printemps et d'été, à feuilles tendres

Lettuce and romaine are among the finest of spring and summer salads. A medium-size head of lettuce will serve 2 people and a large head 4 people. Two medium-size heads of romaine will serve 4 people.

Heart of Lettuce and Heart of Romaine Salad
Coeur de laitue et coeur de romaine

FOR 4 PEOPLE

2 small heads lettuce or 2 small heads romaine
½ recipe of Simple French Dressing*
1 tablespoon finely minced mixed fresh chervil and tarragon

Remove all the outer leaves to get at the hearts. Cut each heart in half lengthwise and dress with French dressing. Sprinkle the hearts with the herbs before tossing.

Lettuce Salad with Orange   Salade de laitue à l'orange

FOR 6 PEOPLE

2 large heads lettuce
1 large healthy orange

dressing for the salad

4 tablespoons peanut oil or olive oil
juice of ½ orange
1–2 tablespoons lemon juice (amount of lemon juice depends on the
    acidity of the orange juice)
salt
freshly ground pepper

Wash, trim, and drain well the lettuce leaves, put them in a shallow salad bowl. With a lemon peeler remove the rind from the orange and cut the rind into slivers. Remove the pith from the orange with a sharp knife. Cut the orange into sections. Mix the dressing ingredients together, beat, and pour over the lettuce leaves. Garnish with orange sections and slivered peel.

*This salad goes wonderfully with cold duck or Chicken in Aspic.**

Lettuce Ribbons with Fruits   *Chiffonade de laitue aux fruits acidulés*

This salad is served on individual salad plates.

FOR 6 PEOPLE

2 large heads lettuce
2 oranges
1 small grapefruit
3 slices canned pineapple

Wash and drain the lettuce leaves. Peel the oranges and grapefruit with a knife, quarter them, remove the seeds and pith. Drain the pineapple slices. Cut the oranges, grapefruit, and pineapple into small pieces roughly the same size.

making the dressing

3 tablespoons cream cheese
3 tablespoons heavy cream, lightly beaten
3 tablespoons Mayonnaise,* made with lemon juice
2 tablespoons orange juice
1 tablespoon grapefruit juice
salt
freshly ground pepper (2 or 3 turns of the mill)
a dash of Cayenne pepper

Mix together the cream cheese and the lightly beaten cream. Beat in the mayonnaise by spoonfuls. Then add the orange juice, grapefruit juice, salt, pepper, and Cayenne pepper. The sauce will not be as thick as mayonnaise.

Cut the lettuce leaves *en chiffonade.* To do this, roll each leaf into the shape of a cigar. Then, with a stainless steel knife cut the "cigars" into slices that will look like ribbons when unfolded. Place these in the middle of large individual salad plates. Arrange the fruit garnish on one side of the plate, and the dressing on the other.

Watercress Salad   *Salade de cresson*

FOR 4 PEOPLE

1 bunch watercress
for 6–8 people
2 bunches watercress

Remove the tough ends and all the white threads from the stems of the watercress. Wash the watercress rapidly and thoroughly and drain on a folded kitchen towel. Dress the watercress with French Dressing with Mustard* (see below under Winter Salads) or with *Vinaigrette mimosa.**

WINTER SALADS

Chicory, escarole, and Belgian endive form the base of most winter salads. They are less delicate than spring or summer salad greens and can take a thicker, more highly seasoned dressing, such as the following:

French Dressing with Mustard *Vinaigrette moutardée*

FOR 6 PEOPLE

> 1 teaspoon strong Dijon mustard
> 1 teaspoon mild mustard
> 1 scant tablespoon red wine vinegar
> 5 tablespoons peanut oil or olive oil
> salt
> freshly ground pepper

Mix the two mustards together, then add to the rest of the ingredients, beaten together as in Simple French Dressing.*

Chicory with Garlic Crusts *Chicorée frisée aux chapons*

FOR 4 PEOPLE

making the garlic crusts (chapons a l'ail)

> 3–4 crusts of slightly stale French bread
> 1 clove garlic
> olive oil (optional) to brush on the crusts

Cut the crusts from the outside of stale French bread. Rub them with the cut side of the garlic. If you wish, brush the crusts lightly with olive oil. (I personally find this makes them too oily and does not improve the taste.)

making the salad

> 1 recipe of French Dressing with Mustard*
> 2 large heads chicory, washed carefully, drained, and cut

Pour the dressing over the chicory, place the *chapons* on top, toss the salad, and remove the *chapons.*

NOTE: *Usually only one* chapon *is made for a salad, but they are such a hit that I make more—sometimes one for each guest! This avoids arguments as to who is to win this succulent prize.*

Chicory Salad with Walnut Oil *Salade de chicorée à l'huile de noix*

FOR 4–6 PEOPLE

2 heads chicory

dressing for the salad

3 tablespoons walnut oil and 2 tablespoons peanut oil
1½ tablespoons wine vinegar
salt
freshly ground pepper
1 teaspoon strong Dijon mustard

garnish for the salad

10–12 walnuts, halved

Pick over, wash, and drain the chicory. Place it in a shallow salad bowl. Prepare the dressing and pour it over the chicory. Garnish with walnut halves.

Belgian Endive Salad *Salade d'endives*

Crisp and tasty, this is one of the most popular winter salads.

FOR 6 PEOPLE

2 pounds Belgian endives
1 recipe French Dressing with Mustard*

garnish for the salad

2 hard-boiled eggs, sliced or quartered
1 beet, cooked, peeled, diced or sliced, and dipped in a little French dressing
juice of 1–2 lemons
2 slices celery root, cut in thin strips and dipped in lemon juice; or 2 stalks celery, diced
1 eating apple, peeled, cut in thin strips, and dipped in lemon juice
10–12 walnuts, halved

Wash each endive separately. Discard the outer leaves and with the point of a knife remove the bitter-tasting cone-shaped core at the root end. Drain the endives on a kitchen towel. Served in leaves, endives are limp, unattractive, and insipid-tasting. The best way to prepare them is to cut them in half lengthwise just before serving, then cut these halves in half (also lengthwise). Then cut the halves into quarters. Do not let endives stand around too long after they have been washed, for they will turn brown. Add the mustard dressing to the endives and mix lightly. Then add the garnish.

This garnished endive salad goes well with Chicken in Aspic, cold roast veal or pork.*

Field Salad[1]   *Salade de mâche*

A delicious fall or early winter salad said to have a soothing effect on the nerves.

FOR 4 PEOPLE

    1 pound field salad
    1 recipe of French Dressing with Mustard*
    1 large beet, cooked, peeled, and diced
    a few pieces of celery root, cut in thin strips
    10 walnuts, quartered

Discard the outer leaves and remove the tough ends of the field salad stems but do not pick apart the head. Wash and drain thoroughly. Something to remember: this rather delicate salad green suffers in cold water. So in washing it, or refreshing it, take the chill off the water. Dress the salad with the French dressing, then garnish with the remaining ingredients.

DANDELION GREENS   *Le pissenlit, ou dent de lion*

This jagged-leaved (whence its alternative French name, *dent de lion*), pleasantly bitter plant is known for its diuretic and depurative qualities. From the end of November until the end of March country roadsides teem with dandelion hunters armed with sharp knives. When the ground is frozen hard, they dig in deep with their sharp little knives and unearth the delicious plants with their tender white hearts. Dandelions are also cultivated and sold in markets all over France.

Dandelion Salad with Shallots and Croutons
Salade de pissenlit à l'échalote et aux croûtons dorés

FOR 4–6 PEOPLE

    1 pound dandelion greens
    1 clove garlic or 1 tablespoon Garlic Oil*

dressing ingredients

    6 tablespoons red wine vinegar
    1 tablespoon minced shallot
    freshly ground pepper (3 turns of the mill)
    4 tablespoons peanut oil
    salt

---

[1] Field (or corn) salad is a rarity in most markets in the United States. It grows wild, however, in many parts of the country.

SALADS

4 or 5 slices slightly stale bread, crusts removed
margarine or peanut oil for sautéing.
salt

Cut off the root ends of the dandelions and remove the large, tough leaves, keeping only the small green leaves that surround the hearts. Depending on the size of the hearts, quarter or halve them (if very tiny, leave them whole). Wash the greens thoroughly, paying special attention to all the jagged, crinkly parts. Drain them on a folded towel, then place them in a salad bowl that has been rubbed with garlic or brushed with garlic oil.

preparing the dressing

Put the vinegar, shallot, and pepper in a saucepan, heat, and reduce to 2 tablespoons. Strain into another saucepan, add the oil, salt, a little more pepper, and heat but do not boil. Put into a small bowl, beat thoroughly, and while it is still warm pour it over the greens.

preparing the croutons

Cut the stale bread into cubes. Sauté them quickly in margarine or peanut oil. Drain them on paper towels and sprinkle with a little salt. Place the croutons on top of the greens and mix.

Dandelion Salad with Bacon   *Salade de pissenlit au lard*

A traditional way of preparing dandelion salad.

FOR 4–6 PEOPLE

    1 pound dandelion greens
    a little butter for frying bacon
    about ⅔ cup bacon (¼ inch thick) cut into pieces
    3 tablespoons red wine vinegar
    1 hard-boiled egg yolk, crumbled

Prepare the dandelion greens as in the preceding recipe and place them in a salad bowl that has been rubbed with garlic. Lightly butter a skillet, heat it, and fry the bacon until golden brown and crisp. Remove the bacon with a slotted spoon, drain on paper towels, and sprinkle over the dandelion greens.

Deglaze* the skillet in which the bacon was cooked by pouring in the vinegar and heating, taking care to scrape the bottom of the pan with a wooden spatula. Pour the contents of the pan over the greens. Toss the salad and garnish with the crumbled egg yolk.

This method may be used with chicory.

Soups

For centuries soup was the mainstay of all French meals. In times past it was served every day, and in some places, particularly in the country, twice a day. These country soups (*potées*) were a complete meal in themselves. How practical to combine vegetables, almost always including cabbage and meat, poultry, or some regional specialty—preserved goose, for example—in a single pot! Sometimes the soup was made of vegetables only and enriched with pork fat or goose fat. Slices of bread were laid in the bottom of the tureen and the soup poured over them, or pieces of bread were placed in individual soup bowls. Today our diet is so varied that the importance of soup has diminished. Even so, it is pleasant both in summer and winter to begin the evening meal with soup.

THICKENING AND ENRICHING SOUP

To vary the consistency and taste of soups, a thickening or enrichment can be added after the soup has finished cooking. The following groups of ingredients may each be added to 6¾ cups to 9 cups of soup.

milk thickening

> 1 cup milk brought to a boil then simmered until slightly reduced

Add the milk to the soup in a kettle and cook for 7–8 minutes. Adjust seasoning.

butter enrichment

> 1 tablespoon butter
> 1 tablespoon mixed minced fresh chervil, tarragon, and parsley

Put the butter and the herbs in a tureen, pour the soup over them, and serve.

egg and cream thickening (also called suprême)

> 1 very fresh egg yolk
> 2 tablespoons heavy cream
> a little extra salt and freshly ground pepper

Put the ingredients in the bottom of a tureen. Heat them by beating in gradually a ladleful of hot soup. Then beat in the remaining soup.

GARNISHES FOR SOUPS

Garnishes can be used not only to improve the fragrance and flavor of soups but also to enrich them.

HERB GARNISH

> 1 tablespoon chervil, or chives, or fresh tarragon, each finely cut with scissors

TOMATO GARNISH

> 2 medium-sized tomatoes, peeled and cut in thin strips

Place the strips of tomato in a tureen and pour hot soup over them. Decorate the surface of the soup with a tablespoon of any of the finely minced herbs cited above.

The same can be done with leftover string beans, cut on the bias, or a few tablespoons of cooked green peas or of cooked asparagus tips.

*Lettuce Ribbons** (chiffonade de laitue) *make an excellent garnish for vegetable soups. To make lettuce ribbons, see the preparation of the lettuce in the recipe Lettuce Ribbons with Fruits*

CROUTONS

A bowl of hot, diced Croutons* is a classical accompaniment to almost all soups.

BOUILLONS, CONSOMMÉS, AND VARIATIONS

Nothing is more pleasant for beginning a meal than a cup of bouillon or consommé served steaming hot in winter and ice cold in summer. They can be garnished or not, according to your taste. Consommé is beef or chicken bouillon made more full-bodied by the addition of minced raw meat and raw chicken giblets.

When making these bouillons or consommés count on ¾ or 1 cup per person.

Beef Bouillon *Bouillon de viande*

Always make a large quantity of bouillon, since it can be frozen or stored in the refrigerator. Cool the bouillon before placing it in a storage jar. It is wise to bring bouillon stored in the refrigerator to a boil after 3 days, in order to prevent its spoiling.

FOR 10–12 PEOPLE

6 quarts water, which will yield about 2½ quarts bouillon)
3 pounds *Pot-au-feu** meat (short ribs of beef, bottom round, or chuck pot roast)
3 carrots, washed, scraped, and quartered lengthwise
2 or 3 leeks with about 2 inches of stalk
2 onions (1 stuck with a clove)
1 turnip, peeled and cut in half
1 stalk celery
1 *Bouquet garni classique** (with fresh chervil and fresh tarragon if possible)

*For the cooking procedure and for straining the bouillon, see Pot-au-feu.**

Beef Consommé *Consommé de viande*

2½–3 quarts beef bouillon (see preceding recipe)
raw giblets of 2 chickens
½ pound ground round steak
a small piece of celery
the white of 1 leek

Simmer all these ingredients, uncovered, for 30–35 minutes. Degrease* and pour through a sieve lined with dampened cheesecloth.

Double Consommé *Consommé double*

In the old days a double consommé was one in which the proportion of meat was doubled. Today we have shortened the procedure. To a completed Beef Consommé (see the preceding recipe) or Chicken Consommé* add the following ingredients:

½ pound ground round steak
raw giblets of 1 chicken (optional but desirable)

Simmer slowly for 30–35 minutes. Degrease* and pour through a strainer lined with dampened cheesecloth.

Chicken Bouillon *Bouillon de volaille*

Use 3½ quarts of water to obtain 2¼ quarts of finished bouillon.

FOR 6 PEOPLE

    1 4-pound stewing hen, cleaned and dressed
    3½ quarts warm water
    1 *Bouquet garni classique**
    1 onion, peeled and quartered
    1 carrot, peeled, scraped, and cut in 2 lengthwise
    salt
    freshly ground pepper

Place the hen in a large, heavy-bottomed enameled kettle, pour in the water and gradually bring to a boil. Add the *bouquet garni* and all the rest of the ingredients. Simmer for 2 to 2½ hours. Adjust for seasoning. Remove chicken. Degrease* and strain the broth through a sieve lined with dampened cheesecloth.

Chicken Consommé *Consommé de volaille*

    2½ quarts chicken bouillon (see preceding recipe)
    raw giblets of 2 chickens
    1 *Bouquet garni classique** (with fresh chervil and fresh tarragon if possible)
    the white of half a leek

Simmer these ingredients slowly for 35–40 minutes, degrease,* and put through a sieve lined with dampened cheesecloth.

Clarifying Consommé

This method of clarification is astonishing and may be called a triumph of kitchen chemistry. It is always a good idea to clarify consommés, and when these are to be served jellied, the method is indispensable.

    1¾–2¼ quarts cold consommé
    2 or 3 egg whites (to which a crushed eggshell may be added)
    1 small stalk celery or some green from a leek, chopped
    2 or 3 sprigs of fresh chervil, minced fine
    2 or 3 sprigs of fresh tarragon, minced fine

Pour 2 ladlefuls of cold consommé into a bowl. Add the egg whites and beat vigorously until frothy. Then, using a fork, beat in the vegetable and herbs. Pour the remaining cold consommé into a large, heavy-bottomed enameled kettle and set over moderate heat. Beat in the contents of the bowl. Continue beating until the liquid begins to boil. During this procedure you will be aghast to see (if you are a novice) that the liquid has become cloudy and full of impurities. But as the heat intensifies, all these impurities will rise and form a layer of scum on top of the consommé. Continue beating. At a certain point a crack will appear in the scum, and it is at this moment that you stop beating. Boil for one minute to solidify the scum. Remove the kettle from heat.

Dampen a piece of cheesecloth, wring it out, and line a large strainer with it. Place the strainer over a large bowl. Remove part of the solidified scum with a skimmer and strain the consommé into the bowl. The crystal-clear result will astonish the cook who has performed this operation for the first time.

If you wish to improve the bouquet of the consommé, add ½ cup Madeira or ½ cup dry sherry to each quart of soup. Serve hot or cold.

Chicken Velouté   *Velouté de volaille*

A chicken consommé based on a Blond Roux* with egg yolks and heavy cream (*liaison suprême*) as a final enrichment.

    2½ tablespoons butter
    4 tablespoons flour
    9 cups lukewarm Chicken Consommé*
    freshly ground pepper
    a little freshly grated nutmeg

NOTE: *Add salt only after tasting. The consommé may be salty enough.*

Melt the butter in a heavy-bottomed enameled kettle and add the flour. Stir together with a wooden spatula until the *roux* foams and turns ivory-colored. Beat in a ladleful of consommé and cook gently for a minute or two. Off heat, beat in the rest of the consommé. Add the seasonings.

liaison suprême

    2 egg yolks
    3 tablespoons heavy cream
    a small pinch of salt
    a small amount of freshly ground pepper

Beat these ingredients together in the bottom of a soup tureen and add a ladleful of hot *velouté.* When the mixture is smooth and creamy, beat in the rest of the velouté.

Consommé suprême

A beef or chicken consommé thickened with egg yolks and cream. For a note of color, add one of the suggested garnishes.

FOR 6 PEOPLE

- 2 egg yolks
- 2–3 tablespoons heavy cream
- 7–8 cups hot Beef Consommé* or Chicken Consommé,* thoroughly degreased*
- a little freshly ground pepper

NOTE: *Taste before adding salt.*

garnishes for beef consommé

- 2 canned pimentos, drained, dried, and sliced thin, or
- 18 cooked asparagus tips, or
- 1/4 pound Sorrel Ribbons,* or
- 2 tablespoons finely scissored chives

garnishes for chicken consommé

- 2 peeled tomatoes, diced then mixed with 2 tablespoons minced tarragon leaves, or
- 1 recipe of lettuce ribbons (see the procedure under Lettuce Ribbons with Fruits)

Beat the egg yolks and cream together in the bottom of a soup tureen. Add a ladleful of hot consommé, mix thoroughly, and beat in the rest of the consommé.

Put the garnish in a small saucepan, pour a ladleful of hot consommé over it, and heat for a few seconds. Stir into the tureen of hot consommé.

Jellied Consommé   *Consommé en gelée*

FOR 7–8 PEOPLE

- 9 cups Chicken Consommé or Beef Consommé*
- 6–8 chicken's feet, scalded, skinned, and nails severed
- 1 *Bouquet garni classique** or the green part of a leek

Simmer these ingredients for 30 minutes. Strain through a double thickness of dampened cheesecloth. Test the consommé's ability to jell by placing a few tablespoons in a saucer and setting it on the top shelf of the refrigerator for 6 minutes. At the end of this time, it should be firm to the touch but soft enough to melt on the tongue. If the jelly is not firm enough, bring the consommé to a boil and add 1/2 envelope of unflavored gelatin that has been dissolved in a little cold water and allowed to soften for 3 minutes.

Serve the consommé ice cold.

Chopped Aspic for Garnishing

Place jellied consommé in a square dish or pan. (The jelly should be about ½ inch thick.) Leave in the refrigerator until completely set. Just before using it as a decoration, chop it into small pieces with a sharp knife.

Jellied Consommé with Tomato Balls
Consommé madrilene aux perles niçoises

FOR 6 PEOPLE

> 7 cups unclarified Beef Bouillon*
> ½ pound ripe tomatoes, peeled, seeded, and coarsely chopped
> a small piece of leek green
> 1 envelope unflavored gelatin

Place the first 3 ingredients in a kettle and proceed with the clarification (see Clarifying Consommé*). Dissolve 1 envelope unflavored gelatin in ¼ cup of cold water and allow it to soften for a few minutes. Add to the hot, clarified consommé, stirring well. Fill 6 bowls with the consommé and place in the refrigerator until slightly set.

perles niçoises

> about 3 firm tomatoes, peeled

With a *cuillère parisienne*[1] cut little balls out of the tomatoes. Make a hollow in the center of each bowl of jellied consommé and garnish with the balls. Garnish the edge of each bowl with a half slice of fluted lemon.

Iced Caviar-Flavored Consommé   *Consommé Volga, glacé*

FOR 6 PEOPLE

> 6¾ cups Jellied Consommé Madrilene* (recipe preceding)
> 12 teaspoons red caviar
> minced raw onion (about ½ teaspoon per person)
> 6 half slices fluted lemon

Make a hollow in the center of each bowl of jellied consommé and fill it with 2 teaspoons of red caviar. Sprinkle with the minced onion. Decorate the rim of each bowl with a half slice of fluted lemon. Serve ice cold with slices of buttered pumpernickel.

---

[1] A *cuillère parisienne* is a sharp, small round spoon. You probably do not possess one, so cut the tomatoes into tiny pieces with a knife.

Onion Soup, Paris Style *Soupe à l'oignon, gratinée parisienne*

A friend of mine who lives mostly at night maintains that onion soup is easy to digest and takes the place of sleep! Do not overcook the onions, as this will make them bitter.

FOR 6 PEOPLE

  3 tablespoons butter plus 2–3 tablespoons kept in reserve, or 6 tablespoons margarine plus 2–3 tablespoons kept in reserve
  3 tablespoons peanut oil
  2 pounds onions, minced fine
  2 heaping tablespoons flour
  3 quarts Beef Bouillon,* degreased.* Use more rather than less bouillon, as the bread garnish absorbs a good deal of liquid
  toasted bread garnish

Melt the butter or margarine in a heavy soup kettle and add the oil. Place the onions in the kettle and cook gently over low heat for 10 minutes, stirring with a wooden spatula. From time to time add bits of the reserved butter or margarine. The onions should be tender, transparent, and just slightly golden. Sprinkle in the flour, stirring, until it is completely absorbed. Add the heated bouillon and beat vigorously with a wire whisk. Pour the soup into a large, heavy enameled casserole. Cover and simmer for 15 minutes. (Some cooks strain the soup into the casserole, but I prefer not to. The soup can be prepared in advance up to this point.

garnish for the onion soup

  1 cup freshly grated Swiss cheese
  18 slices French bread, toasted and buttered
  freshly ground pepper
  freshly grated nutmeg
  1 small onion, cut into small pieces and squeezed through a garlic press
  Preheat oven to 375° F.

Fifteen minutes before serving, heat the soup thoroughly. Then off heat sprinkle in one third of the grated cheese. Put the casserole on the oven rack and, working quickly, place the toasted bread slices over the surface of the soup, as close together as they can possibly be. Sprinkle the toast with the rest of the cheese. Top each slice with a little pepper, nutmeg, and onion purée. Brown the soup in the oven for 10 minutes. Serve in warmed, large soup bowls.

Onion Soup with Soufflé *Soupe à l'oignon avec soufflé*

This may sound mysterious, but if you try it you will see there is no mystery at all. The secret is to pour the soufflé mixture very quickly on top of the toasted bread slices before they have become impregnated with soup.

FOR 6 PEOPLE

1 recipe of Onion Soup, Paris Style* (preceding recipe) poured
   into a flameproof tureen
enough toasted French bread to cover the surface of soup, butter for
   spreading on the toast
2 tablespoons grated Swiss cheese

making the soufflé mixture

2 egg yolks
1 cup thick Béchamel Sauce*
salt
freshly grated nutmeg
freshly ground pepper
2½ tablespoons freshly grated Swiss cheese
3 egg whites, stiffly beaten with a pinch of salt
Preheat oven to 390° F.

Beat the egg yolks one by one into the *béchamel* sauce. Add the seasonings and cheese. Beat a good tablespoon of stiffly beaten egg white into the mixture. Fold this into the remaining beaten whites. Place the heated soup on the oven rack and cover with buttered toast. Sprinkle with grated cheese. Working very quickly, spread the soufflé mixture evenly over the surface. Bake for 8–10 minutes, or until the soufflé is puffed and golden. Serve immediately in warmed bowls.

VEGETABLE SOUPS

One of the most popular of all French soups is vegetable soup, which consists of a variety of fresh vegetables, depending on the season, cut into pieces and simmered in water for 35 to 45 minutes. The soup is salted in the process of cooking. Use a good heavy kettle, the size depending upon how much soup you are making.

A vegetable soup serving 4–6 people should contain 9–11 cups of water. (Remember that about one person's portion will be lost through evaporation.) When the vegetables are cooked, crush them against the sides of the kettle with a fork. Stir well. This is the simplest way of thickening vegetable soup. Another way of thickening vegetable soup is to put the vegetables through a food mill. The soup can then be served as is, or it can be enriched and thickened (with cream or butter, for example), in which case it is called "cream soup" or *velouté*.

NOTE: *In France, thickened and enriched soups are sometimes distinguished from* soupes *and are called* potages.

Cooking Vegetable Soups

Start the soup on high heat and boil vigorously for 10 minutes (this allows the vegetables to release their juices into the water). Lower the heat and simmer until the vegetables are tender (35–45 minutes).

Cream of Watercress Soup   *Crème de cresson*

This is a very attractive soup. The watercress leaves that are used to garnish it rather resemble lily pads.

FOR 6 PEOPLE

> 1 large bunch watercress (choose a bunch with big leaves), about ½ pound after picking over
> 30 large watercress leaves for garnish
> 3 tablespoons butter
> 3 tablespoons flour
> 9 cups boiling water
> salt
> freshly ground pepper
> 2 cups milk reduced by half
> 3 tablespoons heavy cream
> 1 tablespoon butter

Pick over the watercress, discarding the tough stems and white threads. Wash thoroughly and drain on a folded kitchen towel. Set aside the leaves to be used as a garnish. Coarsely chop the rest of the watercress on a board.

cooking the soup

Melt the butter in a large, heavy-bottomed enameled kettle and add the watercress. Cook and stir for 5 or 6 minutes until soft. Sprinkle the flour on the watercress and cook, stirring with a wooden spatula, for a few minutes, without browning. Remove the kettle from heat and beat in the boiling water with a wire whisk. Add salt and pepper, lower heat, and simmer, half covered, for 25 minutes. Put the soup through a food mill (using the finest disk), return to the kettle, and pour in milk. Heat for a minute or two, add the cream, and adjust seasoning.

garnishing the soup

Prepare the garnish while the soup is simmering. Place the watercress leaves in a soup plate containing water a little hotter than lukewarm. Set the plate over a saucepan containing hot water, bring this water to a boil. In just a few minutes the watercress leaves will be made tender (though they will remain firm and green) and ready to use.

serving the soup

Add 1–2 tablespoons of butter to the hot soup, then ladle it into warmed soup bowls. Garnish each bowl with 5 watercress leaves.

Cream of Chervil Soup *Crème de cerfeuil*

3 tablespoons butter

2 onions, coarsely chopped

½ pound chervil, picked over, washed, dried, and minced

6¾ cups water

2 cups milk, simmered and reduced by half

2 teaspoons or 1 tablespoon (depending on how thick you want the soup) arrowroot, diluted in a little cold water

salt

freshly ground pepper

Heat the butter in a kettle, add the onion, and cook until transparent. Add the chervil, stir until it disintegrates, and cook, stirring, for about 3 minutes. Add the water and seasonings. Beat well with a whisk and simmer, uncovered, for about 25 minutes. Adjust seasoning. Put the soup through a food mill and return to heat. Add the milk. When the soup begins to simmer, add the diluted arrowroot, stirring well.

While the soup is simmering prepare the egg and cream mixture:

egg and cream enrichment

1 or 2 egg yolks, depending on size

3 tablespoons heavy cream

a pinch of salt

freshly ground pepper (1 turn of the mill)

1 tablespoon minced chervil for garnish

Beat the egg yolk (or yolks) and cream together. Add the salt and pepper. Warm the mixture with a ladleful of hot soup and beat it, off heat, into the soup. Heat for 2 or 3 minutes and pour into the tureen. Sprinkle with chopped chervil before bringing it to the table. Serve the soup in warmed soup plates or bowls.

Velouté of Asparagus Soup *Velouté d'asperges*

Begin a springtime dinner with this delicate soup.

2½–3 pounds fresh green asparagus

ingredients for the velouté

3 tablespoons butter

4 tablespoons flour

2 cups of the water in which the asparagus has been cooked (reheated at time of using)

4½ cups Chicken Consommé,* degreased*

ingredients for enriching

    3 egg yolks

    3 tablespoons heavy cream

    salt

    freshly ground pepper

ingredients for the garnish

    the cooked asparagus tips

    3 tablespoons butter

    a tiny pinch of salt

    freshly ground pepper

    a few drops of lemon juice

Prepare and cook the Asparagus.* For this recipe cook the asparagus for 10–15 minutes only (the stalks will finish cooking in the soup, and the tips should remain firm for the garnish). Remove the asparagus from the water with a slotted spoon and place on a board. Cut off the tips (1½–2 inches long) and set them aside. Cut the stalks into small pieces.

cooking the velouté

In a large, heavy-bottomed enameled kettle make a *roux** by cooking the butter and flour together for about 1½ minutes (do not allow it to color). Off heat, beat the reheated asparagus water into the *roux,* using a wire whisk. Place on heat, cook for 1 minute, then pour in the chicken consommé. Add the asparagus pieces and cook over medium heat for 15–20 minutes. Put the *velouté* through a food mill, using the finest disk. Replace in kettle and set over low heat.

enriching the velouté

While the *velouté* is heating, beat the egg yolks and cream together in a bowl. Heat these ingredients with a ladleful of hot *velouté.* Off heat, beat the egg and cream mixture into the *velouté.* Add salt and pepper, heat slowly, stirring. Adjust seasoning.

garnishing the velouté

Stew the asparagus tips gently in the butter (using a no-stick pan if possible), turning them carefully so as not to break them. Add very little salt and pepper and a few drops of lemon juice. Remove the pan from heat and cut each tip in two lengthwise. Pour a ladleful of hot *velouté* over them to keep them warm. Serve the asparagus *velouté* in warmed bowls. Garnish each bowl with asparagus tips.

Velouté of Mushrooms   *Velouté de champignons*

A fine soup that owes its characteristic flavor and fragrance to the fact that the mushrooms are puréed raw. The resulting soup tastes like the very essence of mushroom.

FOR 6 PEOPLE

3 tablespoons butter
3 tablespoons flour
6¾ cups of Chicken Consommé,* degreased*
salt
freshly ground pepper
a small amount of freshly grated nutmeg
1½ pound firm, fresh mushrooms
juice of ½ lemon
½ cup cold chicken consommé
1 small onion, cut into small pieces and squeezed through a garlic press
3 egg yolks
3 tablespoons heavy cream

making the velouté

In a heavy-bottomed enameled kettle make a *roux** by heating the butter and flour together and cooking it for 1 minute, without letting it color. Off heat, beat in the 6¾ cups of chicken consommé. Place on low heat, add salt, pepper, and grated nutmeg. Cook, stirring, for 1–2 minutes, or until the *velouté* comes to a boil.

preparing the mushrooms

Remove the sandy tips of the stems. Wash the mushrooms thoroughly, using half the lemon juice in the last two rinsing waters. Pat dry with a kitchen towel and sprinkle with the remaining lemon juice. Mince caps and stems and put through a food mill directly into the simmering *velouté*. Cook, stirring with a wooden spatula, for about 15 minutes.

Divide the cold chicken consommé into 3 portions and add it, portion by portion, to the *velouté*. This will cause the impurities to rise to the surface, where they can be skimmed off. During the last 5 minutes of cooking add the onion purée.

Beat the egg yolks and cream together. Add a ladleful of hot *velouté,* then, off heat, beat the mixture into the *velouté,* using a wire whisk. Place the kettle over medium heat and simmer for 3 minutes. Adjust for seasoning. Serve the mushroom *velouté* in warmed soup bowls.

NOTE: *Do not overcook this soup; it will lose its delicious fresh mushroom taste.*

Fresh Tomato Soup   *Potage de tomates fraîches*

A delicious summer soup made with juicy garden-fresh tomatoes. The added tomato juice provides a natural thickening.

FOR 6 PEOPLE

about 2½ pounds ripe tomatoes
1 pound onions
4 tablespoons olive oil
5½ cups boiling water
a sprig of thyme
1 bay leaf
a pinch of oregano
a pinch of sugar
salt
freshly ground pepper
a *Bouquet garni** of thyme, parsley with stems, chervil, a sprig of tarragon, and a sprig of rosemary
2 cups tomato juice
2–3 rounded teaspoons butter

ingredients for the garnish

6 tablespoons heavy cream
1 tablespoon finely cut fresh basil, or
1 tablespoon finely cut chervil and tarragon, mixed together

Wash the tomatoes under the cold water tap and dry them. Do not peel. Cut them in quarters or in chunks, remove the seeds, and put the tomatoes in a strainer set over a bowl to catch the juice. Peel the onions and slice thin.

cooking the soup

Put the olive oil and the onions in a heavy-bottomed enameled kettle. Stirring with a wooden spatula, cook until the onions begin to soften and turn yellow. Add 1 cup of boiling water, cover the kettle, and cook over medium heat for 7 or 8 minutes.

Stir in the tomatoes and their juice, add the thyme, bay leaf, oregano, sugar, salt, pepper, and the *bouquet garni,* and cook, half covered, for 10 minutes. Pour in the remaining 4½ cups of boiling water, raise heat, and boil for about 10 minutes. Stir in the 2 cups of tomato juice, bring to a boil again, and cook for another 7 or 8 minutes. Remove the *bouquet garni,* put the soup through a food mill, and pour back into the kettle. Lower heat and, stirring with a wooden spatula, simmer the soup until it is slightly reduced and has a good consistency. Add the butter and adjust seasoning. Serve the soup in warmed bowls, garnishing each bowl with a tablespoon of cream topped by a pinch of herbs.

NOTE: *If you wish a thicker soup, stir in* Beurre manié* *(using measurements given in that recipe) or a teaspoon of arrowroot dissolved in a teaspoon of cold water.*

You can turn this summer soup into a light meal by placing a poached egg in each warmed soup bowl and adding 2 ladlefuls of hot soup and a few diced Croutons. *Sprinkle each egg with a pinch of minced chervil or chives or tarragon and parsley.*

Vegetable Soup Ideas to Develop

Leftover cooked dried legumes (whole or puréed) such as white beans, split peas, or lentils can be used as a base for soup. Simply add to whatever vegetables you have on hand:

> 2–3 tablespoons finely minced onion, or 2 tomatoes, peeled, seeded, and
> cut in thin strips or diced

Add water (or half milk and half water) to the vegetables.[1] Cook for 10 minutes. If the dried vegetables are whole, put them through a food mill, using the finest disk. Place the kettle over low heat, and when the soup is hot add 1–2 tablespoons heavy cream and adjust seasoning. Beat with a wire whisk before serving.

REGIONAL SOUPS—*POTÉES*

Potées are complete meals in themselves. They are made of a great variety of vegetables, usually including cabbage and some member of the bean family. To a sensitive palate, vegetables from one region have a different taste from those of another region, resulting from climatic factors and the nature of the soil.

---

[1] The amount of water or milk and water depends on the amount of leftovers you have. The soup should be fairly thick.

All *potées* contain bacon or lean salt pork, which serves to enrich the broth. The other meats used vary with the region. In Alsace, pork and pork products are used; in Normandy it is not unusual to find chicken and goose in the same pot; the truffled poultry that is used in the Périgord region (sometimes accompanied by stuffed cabbage leaves) gives the broth the unforgettable aroma of truffles; the Rhone Valley *potée* is made with a truffled hen and vegetables, and in southwestern France preserved goose adds its succulent richness. The best and most famous of these southwestern soups is *la garbure.*

Garbure

A thick vegetable soup cooked with country-cured bacon. A piece of *confit d'oie* (preserved goose)[1] is added a half hour before the soup is done. Garlic is an essential seasoning for this soup.

FOR 6–8 PEOPLE

- 1 smooth green cabbage
- 3–4 tablespoons goose fat
- 3–4 carrots, washed, scraped, and cut into pieces
- 1–2 turnips, washed, peeled, and cut into pieces
- 2 onions, whole or sliced, or 2 whites of leek, chopped
- 1½ cups partially cooked navy beans
- 1 pound lean country-cured bacon, simmered for 10 minutes then refreshed in cold water
- 4½ quarts boiling water
- 4 large potatoes, diced or sliced thin
- ½ cup fresh or frozen green beans
- 2–4 cloves garlic, peeled and crushed
- 1 *Bouquet garni classique**
- the wing of a preserved goose (optional), fat melted off in a moderate oven for a few minutes

First prepare the cabbage. Strip away the tough outer leaves, trim the core, and make a gash in it so the blanching water can penetrate the heart. Blanch in a large quantity of boiling water for 10 minutes. Drain. Cut the leaves in pieces and the heart in quarters, and set aside.

Melt the goose fat in a large, heavy-bottomed enameled kettle. Add all the vegetables except the potatoes and green beans. Stir them gently in the fat, without browning, for 5 minutes. Remove the vegetables temporarily with a slotted spoon. Heat the slab of bacon in the fat, then pour in the boiling water. When the water is again boiling strongly, add the vegetables you have set aside, and the potatoes, green beans, garlic, and *bouquet garni.* Keep the soup at a boil

---

[1] *Confit d'oie* (preserved goose) may be very hard to come by in the United States. If it exists at all, you would find it only in specialty shops that feature French gourmet products. It is not absolutely essential to the soup, but *do* use goose fat instead.

and skim until the broth is perfectly clear. Turn down heat and simmer for 2½–3 hours. Do not salt. During the last half hour of cooking, remove the bacon, set it in a warm place covered with a little of the broth. If you have the preserved goose, add it now. (If you are planning to gratiné the soup, preheat the oven to 350° F.)

serving the garbure

Cut the bacon in slices; bone and fillet the preserved goose. Arrange the meats and vegetables in a flameproof earthenware casserole and cover with broth. Pour the leftover broth into a warmed, covered tureen.

If you wish to gratiné the soup, arrange on the surface slices of white bread that have been dried in the oven. Sprinkle the top of the soup with a layer of grated Swiss cheese. Top with a garlic clove that has been pounded to a paste with a little goose fat. Brown for 10 minutes.

Vegetable Soup with Basil and Garlic *Pistou*

Pistou originated in Genoa but years ago made its way to Nice and the surrounding countryside. Not so long ago the best *pistou* of the region was served in the Old City of Nice.

The soup contains such a variety of vegetables that you might almost think they were tossed in haphazardly. It is a delicious summer soup in which the taste and aroma of fresh basil predominate—in fact, it is sometimes called "basil soup."

The *pistou,* which forms the liaison of the soup, is made of fresh basil leaves pounded to a paste with olive oil. Into this is blended a reduced fresh *Fondue de tomates.** The hot soup is poured over the *pistou,* and the result is breathtakingly aromatic and very special. A bowl of grated cheese is served with the soup.

FOR 6–8 PEOPLE

4 tablespoons olive oil

3 medium-size onions or 3 leek whites, coarsely chopped

2 carrots, washed, scraped, and sliced

3½–4 quarts boiling water

3 potatoes, peeled and sliced thin

2–3 zucchini, peeled and diced

coarse salt

freshly ground pepper

a pinch of powdered saffron

2–3 cloves garlic, squeezed through a garlic press directly into the soup

¾ pound raw green beans, slivered

1 cup cooked navy beans, or ½ large can navy beans (drained, rinsed under hot water)

1 pound ripe tomatoes, peeled, seeded, and cut in small chunks

3 tablespoons vermicelli or ⅓ pound spaghettini (optional)

4 cloves garlic, squeezed through a garlic press

4 tablespoons fresh basil leaves[1]
2–3 tablespoons olive oil plus 4 tablespoons in reserve
a half piece of stale bread, finely crumbled
6 tablespoons tomato *Fondue de tomates** (optional)

cooking the soup

Heat the oil in a large heavy-bottomed enameled kettle, add the onions or leeks, carrots, and stir-cook for 2 minutes. Add the boiling water, stir, and cook, covered, for 2–3 minutes. Add the potatoes, zucchini, salt, pepper, saffron, and garlic, bring to a brisk boil and cook for 10 minutes. Lower heat and cook for another 15 minutes, adding the green beans. Cook the beans until they are just barely tender–about 12 minutes. Ten minutes before the end of cooking time, add the cooked navy beans, tomato, and vermicelli or spaghettini. Simmer, covered, for 10 minutes.

making the pistou

This can be prepared while the soup is cooking. Place all the remaining ingredients, except the 4 tablespoons of reserved olive oil and the *fondue,* in a mortar and pound into a paste. Put this fragrant base in the bottom of a tureen and add, drop by drop then gradually increasing the amount, the reserved olive oil. Work with a wooden spatula until the mixture is thick and whitish in color. Then, if you wish, add the 6 tablespoons of tomato fondue.

serving the soup

Mix well—do not beat—a ladleful of hot soup into the *pistou*. Then slowly pour in the remaining soup, stirring constantly. Serve a bowl of grated cheese with the soup—2 tablespoons of Parmesan and 4 tablespoons of Swiss cheese mixed together.

Pot-au-feu

This was originally a product of farm and village cooking, and the recipe I have chosen follows closely this simple, harmonious style of cooking.

The meat is placed in lukewarm water so that its juices flow freely and quickly into the liquid. The taste of no one vegetable should prevail over that of another, although the kinds of vegetables used may vary. As a rule they include large carrots, leeks, one or two onions, one stuck with a clove, a turnip or two, and a piece of celery root. If you like, include a head of smooth green cabbage blanched separately in some of the bouillon, then finished in the *pot-au-feu* itself. In winter a warm peppery taste is added if you use half of a kohlrabi. In summer one or two peeled, seeded garden fresh ripe tomatoes can be added just before the soup has finished cooking.

---

[1] You can use freshly dried basil but soak the leaves in a bowl of cold water for a few minutes, drain, and pat dry.

A small stewing chicken will give body to the broth. If you include a chicken, add it to the kettle after the other meats have cooked for a good hour. Before adding the chicken, place it in a preheated 350° oven for a few minutes to sweat.* Wipe off the fat with a paper towel before adding the chicken to the broth.

Country sausages, cooked separately then sliced, are often placed on the platter of meats and vegetables.

Always make a large amount of *pot-au-feu.* The leftover broth and meats can be used in a multitude of ways (see the end of this recipe).

FOR 6–8 PEOPLE

1 pound large carrots
1 pound leeks
2 medium-size onions, 1 stuck with a clove
1 celery stalk or 1 slice celeriac
3 medium-size yellow turnips
1 knucklebone, blanched separately in boiling water for a few minutes
7 quarts warm water
2 pounds chuck roast
2 pounds bottom round
2 pounds short ribs of beef
4–5 tablespoons cold water
1 *Bouquet garni classique**
salt
freshly ground pepper, added at the end of cooking

Wash and prepare the vegetables. Cut the carrots in half lengthwise, then cut these lengths in half crosswise. Leave about 2 inches of green on each leek and tie the leeks together. Cut the turnips in two.

Put the blanched knucklebone in a heavy soup kettle, pour in the warm water, and add all the meats. Bring to a boil over moderate heat, skimming off the impurities as they rise to the surface, adding a tablespoon of the cold water from time to time. This skimming process may take from 20 to 30 minutes. When the broth is clear, turn up heat, add the *bouquet garni,* vegetables, and salt. Boil briskly for 10 minutes. Then lower heat and simmer until the vegetables are tender. Remove them with a slotted spoon and place them in a large shallow serving dish, cover with a few ladlefuls of broth. Place a sheet of aluminum foil over the dish and set in a warm place. Continue cooking the *pot-au-feu* until the meats are tender. The whole cooking process may take as long as 3 hours. Remove the meat, place on a large platter, cover, and keep in a warm place. Remove and discard the knucklebone and the *bouquet garni.*

Line a strainer with dampened cheesecloth and pour the broth through it into a large pan. If the broth seems very fat, put an ice cube in the bottom of the cheesecloth and pour the broth over it all at once. The particles of fat will collect on the ice cube. Add freshly grated pepper, and adjust for salt seasoning. If the broth seems a little thin, place the pan over high heat and reduce it (just a few minutes will do). If globules of fat form on the surface of the broth, blot them up, working rapidly, with a paper towel.

serving the pot-au-feu

Pour the hot broth into a warmed tureen. Slice the meat neatly with a very sharp knife and arrange on a warmed metal platter. Bring the tureen, the platter of meat, and the dish of vegetables (leeks untied) to the table—and enjoy yourselves!

A bowl of coarse salt is always served with pot-au-feu. *Pickled onions, gherkins, and, if you're lucky enough to have this in your larder, a jar of preserved-cherry vinegar* make piquant accompaniments. Some people like to add grated Swiss cheese to the broth. I prefer substituting cheese* croûtes *(given below) because I find that grated cheese adds too strong a taste to the broth, besides clouding it.*

Cheese croûtes

FOR 6 PEOPLE (24 *croûtes*)

> 1 long loaf of French bread
> about ½ cup grated Swiss cheese
> butter
> freshly grated nutmeg

Cut the bread in 24 slices, dry them lightly under the broiler, and immediately butter them. Press a teaspoon of grated cheese in the center of each slice and grate a little nutmeg on top. Brown in a hot oven for a few seconds. Serve very hot on a plate covered with a napkin. Each person adds a few of the *croûtes* to his broth. These can be made in advance and reheated before serving.

Still another accompaniment for pot-au-feu *broth:*

Canapés with Beef Marrow   *Canapés à la moelle de boeuf*

FOR 6 PEOPLE (12 CANAPÉS)

> 12 slices, ¼ inch thick, of homemade (if possible) bread, crusts removed
> butter
> salt
> 2 beef marrowbones
> enough *pot-au-feu* broth to cover marrowbones
> coarse salt

Toast the bread slices and spread them lightly with butter. Salt them and set aside in a warm place. Lay the marrowbones flat on the bottom of a heavy pan, cover them with *pot-au-feu* broth, and cook very slowly for about 45 minutes. Using a slotted spoon, carefully lift the bones out of the pan, place them on a platter, and scoop out the marrow, using a marrow spoon (or ice-tea spoon). Spread the warm canapés with the marrow. Sprinkle each canapé with a few grains of coarse salt and serve with the broth.

Leftover *pot-au-feu* meat can be used to make Shepherd's Pie,* Beef Salad, Paris Style,* and many other delicious dishes. The leftover broth can be used in Borsch (see the following recipe) and Onion Soup.*

Île de France Meat and Vegetable Soup   *Potée de l'Île de France*

The best vegetables sold in the Paris markets are those grown in the marshy areas on the outskirts of the city. This springtime soup is garnished with such vegetables. Its broth is enriched by a chunk of country-cured bacon, a young chicken, and a few short ribs of beef.

FOR 6–8 PEOPLE

a 1-pound piece of country-cured bacon, placed in cold water to cover, simmered for 15 minutes, then refreshed in cold water

about 1½ pounds short ribs of beef

4½ quarts warm water

3 carrots, washed, scraped, and cut in half

3 onions, 2 stuck with a clove

1 white of a leek

2 *Bouquets garnis classiques**

aromatizing ingredients

salt

freshly ground pepper

a 3–3½ pound young chicken

the chicken liver

2 sprigs fresh tarragon

3–4 teaspoons butter

stuffing ingredients

2 chicken livers

3 tablespoons butter

3 tablespoons warmed cognac

salt

freshly ground pepper

4 tablespoons crumbled white bread

2 tablespoons fresh tarragon and 1 tablespoon fresh chervil finely cut with
    scissors and mixed together
1 egg, lightly beaten
Preheat oven to 350° F.

Cook the bacon separately in cold water to cover, along with one of the carrots
and an onion stuck with a clove. Simmer for about 45 minutes, until tender,
replenishing water if necessary. Set aside in a warm place in its liquid. Place the
short ribs in a soup kettle and pour in the 4½ quarts of warm water. Bring to a
boil and skim until the broth is clear. Add the remaining carrots and onions, the
leek, and a *bouquet garni.* Lower heat and simmer for about 1½ hours.

aromatizing the chicken

Salt and pepper the chicken and the liver. Push the liver inside the chicken
along with the tarragon and butter. Sew up opening and truss the chicken.

stuffing the chicken

Sauté the chicken livers in the butter for 2 minutes. It is important not to
overcook them. Pour in the cognac, set it aflame, shaking the pan. Sprinkle the
liver with salt, grind in a little pepper, and add the crumbled bread. Put this
mixture through a food mill into a bowl. Work in the herbs and egg with a
wooden spatula. Stuff the chicken, sew up the opening, truss, and sweat* in the
oven for about 15 minutes, until the chicken is ivory colored. Wipe the chicken
with a paper towel and set aside until you are ready to add to soup.

final preparation

Add the aromatized, stuffed chicken to the short rib broth, bring to a boil
and add the second *bouquet garni.* Lower the heat and simmer for 1 hour to 1
hour 20 minutes. Remove the short ribs and the chicken from the broth and set
aside in a warm place. Discard the 2 *bouquets garnis,* carrots, onions, and leek.
Carefully degrease* the broth and adjust for seasoning. Reheat and slightly
reduce the broth before serving. While the meats are cooking, prepare the
following fresh vegetable garnish: 1 pound fresh or frozen Green Peas, English
Style,* 1 pound young Glazed Carrots,* ⅔ pound young Glazed Turnips,*
10–12 Small White Glazed Onions.

Reheat the bacon in its liquid and slice. Cut the short ribs into pieces.
Arrange these on one side of a warmed large serving platter and cover with a
little hot broth.

Cut the chicken into 8 pieces and place on the other side of the platter.
Arrange the stuffing on top of the chicken pieces. Place the vegetable garnish in
little piles between the meat and chicken pieces. Cover the platter with 2–3
ladlefuls of hot broth, and serve the rest of the broth in a heated tureen.

Borsch *Bortsch*

A Russian *pot-au-feu* that, if accompanied by piroshki,[1] will make a complete meal that will overjoy your guests. The soup is always accompanied by a bowl of sour cream. To contribute to the Russian mood, serve small glasses of Russian or Polish vodka. This recipe uses *pot-au-feu* broth from which all the vegetables have been strained.

FOR 6–8 PEOPLE

2 beets, cooked, diced, for the infusion of beets given below

2 tablespoons wine vinegar for the infusion of beets

1 large green cabbage (about 2 pounds)

2 cups degreased* *Pot-au-feu** broth plus 1 cup water for cooking the cabbage

2 sprigs dried or fresh thyme

1 bay leaf

9 cups *pot-au-feu* broth, degreased

tomato *coulis* (procedure given below)
>   1 pound ripe tomatoes
>
>   1 cup water
>
>   1 clove garlic, squeezed through a garlic press
>
>   1 sprig dried or fresh thyme
>
>   a small piece of bay leaf

1 cup cooked navy beans

1 *Bouquet garni,** with thyme, parsley, bay leaf, and a sprig of dill or small piece of fennel

2 beets, cooked, diced, for the soup

1 fennel heart, sliced thin

1 onion, sliced thin

salt

freshly ground pepper

sour cream

preparing the infusion of beets

This can be done well in advance, even the day before. Place the beets in a small saucepan, add a little water, and simmer for 10 minutes. Remove from heat, add the vinegar, and steep for 10–15 minutes. Strain the infusion into a bowl. Discard the beets.

preparing the cabbage

Strip off the tough outer leaves and trim the core. Blanch for 10 minutes in a large kettle of boiling water. Drain, cut in slices or chunks, and cook for 7 minutes in the 2 cups of broth and 1 cup of water, along with the thyme and bay leaf. Set aside in its liquid.

---

[1] *Piroshki* are Russian delicacies consisting of flaky small rolls filled with highly seasoned ground meat or cabbage.

preparing the tomato coulis

Wash, peel, and seed the tomatoes, cut them in small pieces, and place in a saucepan along with the water, garlic, thyme, and bay leaf. Simmer until reduced and thick. Strain into a bowl and set aside.

preparing the soup

Heat the broth in a large soup kettle. Stir in the infusion of beets. Add the cabbage and its liquid, tomato *coulis,* and cooked navy beans. Bring to a boil and add the *bouquet garni.* Reduce heat, add the 2 diced beets, fennel, and onion. Simmer for 15–20 minutes. Add salt and pepper to taste and a few more drops of vinegar if you think the soup not sharp enough. Serve the soup boiling hot, as the sour cream added to each soup bowl will cool it slightly.

FISH SOUPS

Fish Pot-au-Feu   *Pot-au-feu de poissons*

A comforting soup, as hearty as the fisherman who invented it . . . casting their nets into the sea, starting some vegetables boiling, and adding a variety of fish straight from the deep! The dish is usually cooked in a large, flameproof earthenware stewing pot, but any heavy soup kettle will do.

FOR 6–8 PEOPLE

4½ quarts water, salted with sea salt if possible
4 leeks, tied together
2 onions, 1 stuck with a clove
1 stalk celery, cut in pieces
2 cloves garlic, cut in quarters
1 *Bouquet garni classique**
about 2 pounds conger or sea eel, cut in pieces
about 2 pounds fresh cod, cut in pieces
6 medium-size potatoes
the following selection of small fish, scaled and cleaned:
    4–5 whitings
    4–5 mackerel
    5–6 rockfish, or any small firm red fish
    3–4 flounders
freshly ground pepper

Bring the water to a boil and add some salt. Add the leeks, onions, celery, garlic, and *bouquet garni,* cook briskly for 35 minutes. Lower heat, add the eel, cod, and potatoes, and cook for 15–20 minutes. Then add the small fish and simmer for 10–12 minutes. These small fish must remain whole.

serving the soup

Remove and discard the *bouquet garni*. Snip the strings from the bunch of leeks. With a slotted spoon, arrange the vegetables and pieces of eel and cod on a warmed metal platter. Distribute the small whole fish on top. Cover with a few ladlefuls of hot bouillon and set in a warm place. Add pepper (2–3 turns of the mill) and taste the bouillon for seasoning. If necessary reduce it a little. Strain into a tureen and serve, along with the platter of vegetables and fish. The broth is ladled into soup plates, and your guests helps themselves to vegetables and fish.

Optional accompaniment: bowls of shrimp, mussels, or clams, cooked separately.

Basque Fish Soup   *Soupe de poissons basque*

Called *ttoro* in the Basque country, this rich soup is garnished with mussels and shrimp and served with croutons.

Choose a good variety from among the following kinds of fish: halibut, bluefish, haddock, whiting, mullet, hake, scrod, porgy. Have your fish dealer prepare them and cut them in pieces. Ask for the trimmings and one or two fish heads to make the stock more full-bodied.

FOR 6 PEOPLE

fish stock

    4 tablespoons olive oil
    1 carrot, coarsely cut
    2 onions, sliced
    1 stalk celery with leaves, cut in small pieces
    heads and trimmings of the fish called for below
    2–4 cloves garlic, squeezed through a garlic press
    1 *Bouquet garni classique** with extra thyme
    2 cups dry white wine
    2 quarts boiling water
    1 large green pepper, scalded, cored, seeded, and diced
    1 small chili pepper, scalded, seeded, and diced, then lightly pounded with
        2 tablespoons olive oil
    2 fresh tomatoes, peeled, seeded, and cut in pieces
    salt
    4–5 peppercorns, crushed

Heat the olive oil in a heavy kettle, add the carrot, onions, and celery, stir-cook for about 5 minutes. Add the fish heads and trimmings, garlic, *bouquet garni* and cook, covered, for 5 minutes. Pour in the wine, reduce, uncovered, to one half. Then add the boiling water gradually. Bring to a boil, add the green pepper, pounded chili pepper, tomatoes, salt, and peppercorns, simmer, covered, for 35–40 minutes, stirring up from the bottom from time to time. Strain the stock into a pan, pressing down on the fish heads with the back of a spoon to extract all their juices.

the fish

>   6½ pounds assorted fish, cut in pieces
>   salt
>   freshly ground pepper
>   flour for dredging fish
>   8 tablespoons olive oil for browning fish
>   12 raw jumbo shrimp
>   1 quart raw mussels
>   *Preheat oven to 350° F.*

Salt and pepper the pieces of fish and dredge in flour, place on a rack until ready to brown. Heat the 8 tablespoons of olive oil in a skillet. Brown the fish pieces for 2–3 minutes on each side. They should not be completely cooked. Place the browned fish in a large, deep metal or flameproof earthenware dish. Distribute the shrimp and mussels among the fish pieces. Cover with stock, place in the oven, and simmer gently for 15 minutes.

crouton garnish

>   2–3 tablespoons olive oil
>   6 slices French bread[1]
>   1 garlic clove, cut in half
>   salt

Heat the olive oil, brown the bread slices, and place on paper towels to drain. Rub the slices with the cut sides of garlic and sprinkle with salt. These croutons may be made in advance and reheated before serving.

serving the soup

Remove the earthenware dish from the oven. Just before serving, put the croutons among the pieces of fish, arranging them so they do not push all the way into the soup.

---

[1] Slightly stale homemade white bread may be substituted.

Provençal Fish Soup   *Soupe de poissons provençale*

The fish that make up Mediterranean fish soups, especially the darting small rockfish that swim near the shores, are not obtainable in the United States. But you can make a perfectly adequate Mediterranean soup by choosing from the following selection of fish: rock or sea bass, cod, eel, flounder, hake, halibut, bluefish, red or gray snapper, whiting, ocean perch. Have your fish dealer prepare them for you, cutting the large fish in pieces and leaving the small ones whole. Ask for the fish trimmings and one of the heads for the stock.

FOR 6 PEOPLE

4–4½ pounds assorted fish

fish stock

½ cup olive oil
2 pounds ocean perch
2 carrots, coarsely cut
3 onions, sliced thin
2 leek whites, sliced
1 stalk celery, cut in pieces
2 pieces fennel heart
2 large pinches of saffron
4 tomatoes, peeled, seeded, and cut into chunks
4 cloves garlic, squeezed through a garlic press and pounded with 2
    tablespoons olive oil
2½ cups dry white wine
7 cups boiling water
fish trimmings and 1 head
1 *Bouquet garni provencal**
salt
freshly ground pepper
a sprig of fresh basil (optional)
a handful of spaghettini broken in pieces and cooked in 2 cups fish stock

making the stock

Heat the olive oil in a large, heavy kettle and add the perch, carrots, onions, leeks, celery, fennel, saffron, tomatoes, garlic, wine, boiling water, trimmings and head of fish. Stir and bring slowly to a boil. Add the *bouquet garni,* salt, and pepper. Cook, covered, over low heat for about 25 minutes. Let the stock stand for about 5 minutes, then strain it through a sieve lined with dampened cheesecloth into a large saucepan, pressing with the back of a spoon against the ingredients to extract their juices. Adjust for seasoning. Reduce the stock a little and add the fresh basil. Set aside 2 cups of stock to be used in cooking the spaghettini.

Put the fish—with the small whole fish placed on top of the fish pieces—into a large, heavy-bottomed enameled casserole and slowly pour the cooled fish stock over them. The fish should be completely covered by the stock. Place over medium heat, bring to a boil, reduce heat, and simmer for about 20 minutes, or until the fish is tender. Remove it from the stock with a slotted spoon. Skin and bone it and place in a large flameproof tureen. Pour the stock over the fish and heat through very slowly without boiling. While the soup is heating, cook the spaghettini for about 8 minutes in the reserved strained stock. Add to the casserole and serve immediately.

Accompany the soup with 12 round Croutons,* made in advance and reheated, and a bowl of grated Swiss and Parmesan cheeses mixed together (about ⅔ Swiss and ⅓ Parmesan). Serve the soup in hot soup plates or bowls.

Provençal Fish Stew   *Bourride*

A succulent fish stew thickened and enriched with *aioli*.[1] For this dish choose four or five varieties from firm-fleshed fish such as cod, halibut, haddock, ocean whitefish, bluefish, or whiting. Have your fish dealer clean, scale, and cut the fish into chunks.

FOR 6 PEOPLE

    2 large onions, sliced
    2 leek whites, minced
    about 4 pounds fish (see those given above)
    1 pint mussels (optional), steamed open and removed from their shells
    3 potatoes, peeled and sliced fairly thick
    about 2 quarts cold water
    1 *Bouquet garni provençal**
    2–4 cloves garlic, peeled
    1 piece of dried orange peel
    salt
    freshly ground pepper

ingredients for the aioli

MAKES ABOUT 2 CUPS

    2 cloves garlic, squeezed through a garlic press
    a small piece of bread the size of a hazelnut, dipped in a little stock and
        squeezed out
    2 tablespoons olive oil
    3 egg yolks
    1½–2 cups olive oil

[1] This *aioli* is not the same as Garlic Mayonnaise* (*Sauce Aioli*).

preparing the fish

Place the onions and leeks in a large, heavy kettle. Arrange the fish chunks and mussels on top. Cover with the potatoes. Pour in the cold water and slowly bring to a boil. Add the *bouquet garni,* garlic, orange peel, salt, and pepper, simmer for 15 minutes. Remove the fish to a heated platter, cover with a little stock, and keep it warm. Skim out the vegetables and place in a warmed, covered dish.

preparing the aioli

Pound the garlic and bread together with the 2 tablespoons of olive oil. When a smooth paste has been obtained, beat in the egg yolks one by one, mixing well after each addition. Beat in the remaining olive oil as in Mayonnaise.* Place the *aioli* in a large bowl. Using a fine wire strainer, strain the soup over it, beating constantly with a whisk. Wash out the soup kettle, pour in the *aioli*-thickened soup, and then the reserved vegetables. Heat very slowly, never boiling, stirring constantly with a wooden spatula and scraping the bottom of the kettle from time to time. When the soup is hot and thick, pour it into a warmed tureen. Serve the soup and platter of fish at the same time; they are eaten together in the same soup plates.

Accompany the soup with round Croutons reheated and rubbed with garlic.*

Provençal Fish Stew with Poached Eggs   *Bourride aux oeufs pochés*

A more aromatic version of the preceding recipe. Tomatoes and green pepper are added to the list of vegetables, and each soup plate contains a poached egg placed on a crouton over which a ladle or two of soup is poured. The fish is not served with the soup as in *bourride.* Refrigerate it and serve it cold with Mayonnaise* the next day. Garnish the platter with lettuce leaves and black olives.

FOR 6 PEOPLE

2 large onions, sliced
2 leek whites, minced
about 4 pounds fish (refer to those given in the preceding recipe)
3 potatoes, peeled and sliced fairly thick
about 2 quarts cold water
1 *Bouquet garni provençal**
1 piece of dried orange peel
2–4 cloves garlic, peeled
1½ pounds ripe tomatoes, peeled, seeded, and mashed
1–2 green pepper, scalded, seeded, and diced
salt
freshly ground pepper

1 cup *aioli* (see the preceding recipe)
6 fresh eggs, poached* and kept warm in a little broth
6 round Croutons,* made in advance and reheated before using
1 tablespoon finely minced fresh basil or fresh tarragon, for garnishing the
   soup

Make the soup as in the preceding recipe. When it is done, remove the fish, place it in a covered dish, and refrigerate.

Prepare the *aioli* while the soup is cooking.

Reheat the croutons and poached eggs. Put an egg on each crouton, place in a well-warmed soup plate, and cover with one or two ladlefuls of the hot *bourride.* Top with a small pinch of scissored herbs.

La Rouille

This fiery red sauce often accompanies fish soups. It is served in a bowl and added to the individual soup plates. Take only an infinitesimal amount to begin with.

MAKES ABOUT 1¼ CUPS

2–4 cloves garlic, peeled and cut in small pieces
2 small red chili peppers, scalded, seeded, and minced
½ slice white bread, crust removed, dipped into fish bouillon then pressed
   out
2 tablespoons olive oil
1 scant cup fish bouillon

Put the garlic and chili pepper into a mortar or other heavy bowl. Pound them until they are completely crushed and blended together. Add the pressed-out bread and continue to pound and mash until a smooth paste has formed. With a wooden spatula slowly work in the oil, a mere thread at a time. Stir in the fish bouillon gradually. The sauce should not be too thin, so if you do not need the whole cup of bouillon, do not use it.

NOTE: *If the* rouille *is not red enough, add 1 teaspoon tomato paste diluted with 1 teaspoon olive oil.*

Eggs

How could we get along without eggs? The egg is one of the most important elements of human nourishment. What other foods can be prepared in such a variety of ways? Soft-, medium-, or hard-boiled in its shell, poached, grilled over an open fire (for this a special utensil is needed), shirred, cooked in cream, fried in oil, fried as an omelet if you are in a hurry, scrambled if you have the patience, in a soufflé if you have a taste for mystery, or *à la neige* (stiffly beaten whites) in desserts. . . . I cannot begin to list all the uses of the egg. If it didn't exist, how could we make our custards, sauces, thickenings, pancakes, cream puffs? How feeble our cuisine would be! And how would a bachelor—male or female—ever manage?

For satisfactory results eggs must be fresh. There is a world of difference between a fresh egg and one that is less than fresh. Above all, do not attempt to poach eggs that are not perfectly fresh.

BOILED EGGS

I have often wondered why we say of someone who is helpless in the kitchen, "She can't even boil an egg." It doesn't make sense, for cooking eggs involves a great deal of subtlety.

Soft-Boiled Eggs   Oeufs à la coque

An egg in its natural state is a rich food. To cook an egg seems so simple. . . . Always use eggs at room temperature. To warm them, dip them rapidly into lukewarm water. Wipe them dry. Then dip them in hot water.

An egg cooked for 2½ minutes is a liquid egg. Cooked for 3 minutes, it is a soft-boiled egg. Cooked for 4 minutes, it is a medium-boiled egg.

preparing 3-minute eggs

Lower the eggs into a pan of gently boiling water one by one, using a tablespoon or a skimmer. It is always a good idea to add a pinch of salt. Stir the water for a few seconds after adding the eggs, so the whites and the yolks are well-balanced inside the shell; this advice is particularly important for hard-boiled eggs.

The only difficulty in making a number of soft-boiled eggs is being sure that they are all done at the same time. Here is a practical solution: place the eggs in a small wire basket used for deep-fat frying. This way they can all be put in the water at once, and all removed at once.

The ideal accompaniment for soft-boiled eggs is thin fingers of bread either toasted or not. Butter is not necessary because soft-boiled eggs are a rich food. If you are really a devotee of them, I hope you will avoid peppering them. A little salt is all that is needed.

5- or 6- Minute Boiled Eggs   *Oeufs mollets*

This is a soft-boiled egg with a solidly set white and a soft, almost runny yolk. To achieve this effect, cook a small egg for 5 minutes and a large egg for 6 minutes. When you remove the egg from the water, plunge it into cold water immediately to stop the cooking, otherwise you will end up with a hard-boiled egg. For the proper way to shell eggs, see Hard-Boiled Eggs (the following recipe).

ideas for serving eggs mollets

Place the eggs on round Croutons* or canapés and coat them with Béchamel Sauce* or Béchamel Sauce with Cream.* The sauce should be very hot, as the eggs, after being plunged into cold water, will be lukewarm. Eggs served with the cream sauce may be garnished with a small pinch of fresh tarragon finely cut with scissors.

Eggs *mollet* may also be coated with Mornay Sauce.* Arrange them on round croutons or canapés, spoon the hot Mornay Sauce over them, and top with freshly grated Swiss cheese. Add a little freshly grated nutmeg and place under the broiler until they are very lightly browned.

Hard-Boiled Eggs   *Oeufs durs*

This egg is a friend. Many people who find eggs cooked in other ways indigestible are able to digest them hard-boiled. It is not true that a hard-boiled egg can be cooked for any length of time. The whites of such overcooked eggs are tough, rubbery, and are ringed with grayish green. They also tend to give off an unpleasant odor, as if they were not fresh. A hard-boiled egg that is started in cold water will have an unevenly cooked yolk and a "lumpy" white—it will be very hard to stuff.

cooking hard-boiled eggs

Put the eggs in a wire basket and lower it into a pan of simmering water. Medium-size eggs should cook (always gently simmering) for 10 minutes and large eggs for 12 minutes.

peeling the eggs

Plunge the eggs in cold water and allow them to stand for several minutes. Then tap them lightly all over with the back of a knife until the shell is covered with cracks. Remove a piece of the shell with the point of a knife to allow air to penetrate. The egg will now peel neatly and easily.

Gratin of Hard-Boiled Eggs   *Gratin d'oeufs à l'indienne*

Slices of hard-boiled eggs in a highly spiced curry sauce with shrimp and slices of onion.

FOR 6 PEOPLE

2 large onions, sliced thin
6 tablespoons butter
a pinch of curry powder
a pinch of sugar
salt
freshly ground pepper
½ pound unpeeled raw small, shrimp
1 sprig thyme
1 small piece bay leaf
4 tablespoons warmed cognac
1 double recipe of Béchamel Sauce with Curry*
9 or 10 hard-boiled eggs, cut in even slices
grated Swiss cheese
Preheat oven to 350° F.

Place the onion slices in a saucepan, cover with water, add 2 tablespoons of butter, the curry powder, sugar, salt, and pepper, cook without stirring for about 10 minutes. The onion slices should be tender but intact. Place them in a bowl and set aside. Heat 3 tablespoons of butter in a small skillet. Add the unpeeled shrimp and sauté gently, stirring, for about 2 minutes. Add thyme and bay leaf. Pour in the warmed cognac, set it aflame, and shake the pan back and forth. Put out the flame by covering the pan. Add a pinch of salt, a little pepper, the remaining tablespoon of butter and cook, covered, for 3 minutes, shaking the pan from time to time. Peel and clean the shrimp, put them in the bowl with the onions. Place the shrimp shells in a food mill, and with a backward and forward movement of the blade handle, extract all the juices and add to the onions and shrimp.

to make the curry sauce

Place the double recipe of *béchamel* sauce with curry in a small, heavy-bottomed saucepan. Add the onion and shrimp mixture, place over low heat, stirring gently with a wooden spatula, until hot. Do not boil.

Place a layer of sauce on the bottom of a buttered flameproof oven dish. Add a layer of hard-boiled egg slices, then a layer of sauce, etc., ending with a layer of sauce. Sprinkle with grated Swiss cheese and place in the oven until golden brown.

STUFFED EGGS *Les oeufs farcis*

Stuffed hard-boiled eggs are a favorite standby of cooks, for they are not only delicious but are quickly and easily prepared and, for the most part, can be made in advance.

Preparing the Eggs for Stuffing (Basic Method)

The same procedure is used in all recipes for stuffed eggs. Hard-boil* the eggs, peel them, and cut them in half lengthwise. Remove the yolks and mash them. If necessary, scoop out a little of the white so the hollow is large enough to hold the filling.

HOT STUFFED EGGS *Oeufs farcis chauds*

Stuffed Eggs with Mixed Herbs *Oeufs farcis aux fines herbes*

A deliciously fresh springtime hors-d'oeuvre, and so simple to make. Once stuffed, the eggs may be covered with a light white sauce such as Mornay Sauce* or Béchamel Sauce with Cream* or simply melted butter. In this recipe the eggs are very lightly browned in the oven. They are served with a bowl of Cream with Chives (recipe given below).

FOR 6 PEOPLE

9–10 hard-boiled eggs,* prepared as in the basic method for stuffing eggs
1 tablespoon finely minced fresh chervil
2 tablespoons finely scissored chives
1 tablespoon finely minced fresh tarragon
salt
freshly ground pepper
3 rounded tablespoons heavy cream
¼ teaspoon onion squeezed through a garlic press (optional)
1 recipe of Mornay Sauce* or Béchamel Sauce with Cream*
Preheat oven to 350° F.

Work the egg yolks and herbs together. Season with salt and pepper. Blend in a tablespoon of cream with a wooden spatula. Work in the rest of the cream until a smooth mixture has been obtained. Stir in the onion. Stuff the hard-boiled egg whites with domes of filling, place them close together in a buttered heatproof oven dish.

Prepare either of the two sauces called for above, or if you have opted for melted butter, melt 6 tablespoons in a saucepan and add a very small pinch of salt and a little white pepper. Pour the sauce or butter over the eggs and place the dish in the oven until the eggs are heated and a light glaze has formed on top. Serve Cream with Chives (recipe follows).

Cream with Chives *Crème à la ciboulette*

  1¼ cups heavy cream
  salt and freshly ground pepper to taste
  2 tablespoons finely scissored chives

In a small saucepan, boil the cream for 2 minutes, stirring constantly with a wooden spatula. Remove from fire, add salt and pepper, and adjust for seasoning. Pour into a warmed metal bowl and stir in the chives.

Eggs Stuffed with Mushrooms *Oeufs farcis duxelles*

These hard-boiled eggs are filled with mushrooms prepared as in Dry Mushroom Duxelles,* then covered with reduced heavy cream, topped with grated cheese, and lightly browned in the oven.

FOR 6 PEOPLE

  9–10 hard-boiled eggs, prepared as in basic method for stuffing eggs*

ingredients for the filling

  3 tablespoons butter
  ½ pound mushrooms, prepared as in Dry Mushroom Duxelles*
  1½ tablespoons finely minced shallot
  salt
  freshly ground pepper
  mashed yolks of the eggs, placed in a bowl
  1 tablespoon heavy cream, for binding the stuffing
  Preheat oven to 350° F.

preparing the filling

  Heat the butter in a small skillet and lightly sauté the minced mushrooms and shallot over moderate heat, stirring constantly. Remove from heat, add salt and pepper to taste, and mix into the mashed egg yolks. Stir in the cream. Spoon the filling into the whites in dome shapes and place the eggs very closely together in a buttered flameproof oven dish.

making the sauce of reduced cream

  2 cups heavy cream
  a few drops of lemon juice
  salt
  freshly ground pepper
  3 tablespoons grated Swiss cheese

Place the cream in a saucepan over moderate heat for 2 minutes, stirring constantly. Remove from heat, add the lemon juice, salt, and pepper to taste. Beat and pour over the eggs. Dot each egg with a good pinch of grated cheese, place the dish in the oven until a light-colored glaze is obtained.

COLD STUFFED EGGS *Oeufs farcis froids*

Spread on canapés,* both these fillings make delicious hors-d'oeuvre.

Eggs Stuffed with Anchovies *Oeufs farcis aux anchois*

FOR 6 PEOPLE

3 tablespoons Anchovy Mayonnaise*
1 tablespoon anchovy paste stirred into 1 tablespoon heavy cream
9–10 hard-boiled eggs,* prepared as in basic method for stuffing eggs
1 small can anchovies rolled around capers

Work the anchovy mayonnaise and anchovy paste into the mashed egg yolks to obtain a creamy mixture. Spoon the filling into the hard-boiled whites in dome shapes. Cut each rolled anchovy into 2 thin rounds and place a round on top of each egg.

Eggs Stuffed with Pimento *Oeufs farcis aux poivrons rouges*

FOR 6 PEOPLE

4 large canned pimentos, well drained and wiped dry
9–10 hard-boiled eggs,* prepared as in basic method for stuffing eggs
3–4 tablespoons *Sauce Françoise** or *Sauce Perrine**

Cut one of the pimentos into narrow strips 1¼ inches long, set aside. Cut the 3 others in pieces and grind through the coarsest disk of a food mill or put them through a blender. Stir into the mashed egg yolks and beat in whichever sauce you have chosen (*sauce Perrine* is less highly spiced than *sauce Françoise*). Taste for seasoning. A touch of mild mustard might appeal to you. Spoon the filling into the hard-boiled whites in dome shapes and decorate the top of each egg with 2 strips of pimento in the form of an X.

SHIRRED EGGS *Oeufs au plat*

There are two methods of preparing shirred eggs. In one, the cooked yolk is plainly visible. In the other, it is covered with a translucent film. These are called "veiled" or "mirrored" eggs. I once found "oriental eggs" on a menu. With oriental mystery in mind, I ordered them and was thoroughly disappointed when they turned out to be nothing more than veiled shirred eggs—delicious but not very oriental.

Shirred Eggs with Visible Yolks (basic recipe)

To prepare this recipe, you will need a small copper or flameproof porcelain dish 4–5 inches in diameter.

FOR 1 SERVING

    3 tablespoons butter
    2 very fresh eggs
    freshly ground white pepper
    salt

Place the dish over moderate heat, add the butter, and allow it to melt. Crack the eggs and slide them gently into the dish, one after the other. Cook them for 2 or 3 minutes. Add the pepper in the middle of the cooking and the salt at the end. Serve the eggs immediately in the same dish for they will continue to cook for a minute or so after they are taken off the heat, especially if the dish is of copper.

Veiled Eggs *Oeufs voilés*

FOR 1 SERVING

    2 very fresh eggs
    5 tablespoons butter (2 are melted in a small saucepan and kept warm)
    salt
    freshly ground white pepper

Begin cooking the eggs as in the preceding recipe, using 3 tablespoons of the butter. After about 1½ minutes, when the whites have begun to set, pour the 2 tablespoons of melted butter on top of the eggs. Cover the dish with a double thickness of aluminum foil, glossy side facing the eggs, and cook for 2 minutes. When the yolks are "veiled," season them with salt and pepper and serve immediately.

NOTE: *Shirred eggs can also be cooked in an oven preheated to 350° F., then turned off.*

Shirred Eggs with Pork Sausages   *Oeufs au plat à la chipolata*

This dish is prettier if the egg yolks are visible rather than "veiled."

FOR 1 SERVING

> 2 small pork sausages, cooked separately and kept warm
> 2 tablespoons butter
> 2 very fresh eggs
> ½ cup Tomato Sauce*

Cut each sausage in half. Melt the butter in a skillet, arrange the sausage halves around the edge, slide in the eggs, and cook for 2 minutes. Ring the dish with hot tomato sauce and serve immediately.

Other dishes based on the same principle: shirred eggs with cooked asparagus tips; shirred eggs with Ratatouille; and one of the best of all, Shirred Eggs, Provençal Style (recipe follows).*

Shirred Eggs, Provençal Style   *Oeufs au plat à la provençale*

FOR 6 PEOPLE

> the oil from the stuffed tomatoes (below)
> 10 small Stuffed Tomatoes, Provencal Style,* already cooked
> 6 very fresh eggs
> salt
> freshly ground pepper
> 1 tablespoon finely scissored basil leaves
> *Preheat oven to 375° F., turn it off just before putting in the pan.*

Grease a large, shallow oven pan with oil and set over moderate heat. Arrange the tomatoes in the pan, leaving enough space between them for the eggs. Crack the eggs and slide them between the tomatoes. Heat until the egg whites have begun to set, then place the pan in the turned-off oven until the eggs have finished cooking—about 2 minutes. Lightly salt and pepper them. Garnish with the basil.

Eggs in Ramekins with Cream   *Oeufs en cocotte à la crème*

These are eggs cooked in boiling hot cream. If the cream is not hot enough, the eggs will be both tough and sticky. The ramekins may be made of flameproof porcelain or Pyrex. For this recipe you will need 6.

FOR 6 PEOPLE

15 tablespoons heavy cream
salt
freshly ground white pepper
6 very fresh eggs

Have a shallow pan of boiling water ready. There should be just enough water in the pan to reach halfway up the ramekins. Boil the cream in a saucepan for 2 minutes, stirring with a wooden spatula. Lightly salt and pepper it. Put 1 tablespoon of hot cream into each ramekin and set them in the pan of water. Crack the eggs one by one and slide one gently into each ramekin. Cover each egg with a tablespoon of hot cream. Cook in the simmering water for 4–6 minutes. To test for doneness, touch an egg with your finger: it should be firm but supple. Place the ramekins on a napkin-covered platter and serve immediately.

Eggs in Ramekins with Tarragon Cream
Oeufs en cocotte à la crème d'estragon

This recipe is the same as the preceding one except for the addition of:

3 tablespoons minced tarragon[1] (reserve 1 tablespoon for decorating the eggs)

Mix 2 tablespoons of the tarragon into the cream before boiling it. Place a pinch of tarragon on each egg before serving.

Fried Eggs, French Style   *Oeufs frits*

Frying eggs properly is such a rapid affair—about 1½ minutes—that you must have all your utensils and ingredients at hand: a skimmer, 6 small cups, and a heated oven tray covered with a double thickness of paper towels. Use a small, heavy skillet.

FOR 6 PEOPLE

6 medium-size very fresh eggs
1 cup peanut oil or olive oil, keeping the oil bottle near at hand
salt
freshly ground pepper

[1] Use fresh tarragon for this recipe if possible.

Crack the eggs into the cups. Heat the oil in the skillet. When the surface of the oil begins to wrinkle, tilt the skillet with the left hand so that the oil flows to one side. With the right hand pick up one of the cups and slide the egg into the oil. With the skimmer push the egg white around the yolk so as to cover it. Turn the egg and after 3 seconds remove with the skimmer and place on paper towels. Remove the skillet from the heat. Add salt and pepper. Cook the rest of the eggs the same way, adding a little fresh oil from the bottle for each egg.

Fried eggs may be served on Croutons* or on Broiled Tomatoes.* They are sometimes used as a garnish for various purées—for example, Onion Purée,* Sorrel Purée*—or for ratatouille*. They can also be used to accompany broiled sausages or crisply fried bacon and onion rings.

For an original as well as substantial dish, prepare a recipe of Rice with Saffron and Curry.* Place it in the middle of a warmed round platter with fried eggs on top and crisp pieces of bacon and broiled tomato halves around the rice.

POACHED EGGS   *Oeufs pochés*

Poached eggs—eggs cooked in varely simmering water—are simplicity itself. For this reason they lend themselves to a greater variety of combinations than eggs cooked in any other way. They can be served with almost any sauce—white sauces, all sauces of the hollandaise family, and others. They are marvelously suited to tomato sauce. Placed on round croutons, they go well with Cream-Puréed Spinach or Sorrel Purée* and can also be used to garnish artichoke hearts. The eggs used in poaching must, of course, be very fresh.

Poached Eggs, Basic Recipe   *Oeufs pochés*

Making poached eggs is a delicate affair, and cooking them in an egg poacher does not produce the same result as dropping them into simmering water. It does give perfectly round eggs, but they are too solid and have a "machine made" look. A shallow saucepan or a skillet about 3 inches deep, large enough to hold 3 or 4 eggs at a time and with enough in which to manipulate the skimmer, is ideal. As in making fried eggs, it is essential to have all the utensils at hand. The following recipe is for 4 eggs.

ingredients and utensils

    4 very fresh eggs
    4 tablespoons wine vinegar
    a shallow saucepan or skillet
    1 bowl of warm water (if the eggs are to be served hot)
    1 bowl cold water (if the eggs are to be served cold)
    1 skimmer
    1 tablespoon or wooden spatula
    4 small cups
    1 oven tray warmed and covered with a double thickness of paper towels

poaching the eggs

Begin by placing the eggs, in their shells, in almost boiling water (off heat) for 40–50 seconds. Then crack the eggs into the cups. Pour about 2 inches of warm water into the pan and place over moderate heat. Just before the water begins to simmer, add the vinegar. When the water is just simmering (and you must keep it at a simmer—do not let it boil), slide in an egg. With the spoon or spatula push the egg white over the yolk from all sides. Do this as evenly as possible so as to give the egg a round shape. Add the three other eggs, one at a time, and repeat the process. Remove the eggs after 3–3½ minutes (3 minutes for medium-sized eggs, 3½ minutes for large ones) with the skimmer in the order in which you have put them into the water, rinse them in one of the two bowls of water (mentioned above)—this will rid them of the taste of vinegar. Place them on the paper towels to drain.

Poached Eggs in Aspic   *Oeufs pochés en gelée*

A delicious beginning for a springtime or summer meal. It can be kept, covered, in the refrigerator up to 24 hours. This recipe uses unflavored gelatin, which, if you follow package instructions as to seasonings (above all, do NOT add salt!), will be just as good as homemade jellied consommé.

FOR 12 POACHED EGGS

2 envelopes unflavored gelatin
½ cup red port wine, dry sherry, or dry vermouth
1 *Bouquet garni classique,** including chervil and tarragon
4½ cups homemade or canned beef consommé (add ½ cup water to the canned consommé, making 5 cups)
12 trimmed poached eggs on paper towels to drain

Dissolve the gelatin in the wine you have chosen. Let it soften for 2–3 minutes, then blend it into warm consommé over moderate heat, bring to a boil. Add the *bouquet garni,* lower heat, and simmer for 5 minutes. Turn off heat and let the liquid stand for another 5 minutes. Strain, taste for seasoning. You might want to add a little pepper, a few drops of lemon juice, or a little more of one of the wines. Cool in the refrigerator until it has a syrupy consistency.

preparing the molds

12 tarragon leaves plunged into nearly boiling water when immediately removed and dried between paper towels
12 small rounds of cooked carrot, or canned pimento, drained, dried, and cut into 12 small rounds

Set 12 porcelain or Pyrex ramekins on a platter. Place 1 tablespoon of the thickened aspic in each, and on top of this a round of carrot or pimento, and finally 2 tarragon leaves formed into an X. Set a poached egg is each ramekin, attractive side down, cover with aspic. Place a clean towel over the top of the ramekins, set in the center of the refrigerator, where they can be kept for at least 2 days.

unmolding and serving the eggs

Spread a layer of crisp, trimmed lettuce leaves on a round platter. Run a knife around the inside edge of each ramekin, being careful to reach all the way to the bottom. Unmold the ramekins on the bed of lettuce. Garnish the edges of the platter with red radishes, black olives or tomato quarters.

If you are using the eggs for a buffet, do not unmold them—serve them in their ramekins, providing small spoons.

Poached Eggs in Croustades with Choron Sauce
Oeufs pochés en croustades, sauce Choron

An attractive first course for a dinner party, the eggs can be prepared in advance, and both the puff pastry dough and *croustades* can be made the day before and kept, well covered, in the refrigerator. For baking the pastry dough you will need 12 rather deep small molds about 3 inches in diameter.

FOR 12 PEOPLE

12 very fresh Poached Eggs, Basic Recipe,* rinsed in warm water and kept warm or reheated; trim the eggs of any dangling wisps of cooked white
12 Croustades* (if you bake the *croustades* the day before, unmold them before you place them in the refrigerator)
2 recipes of Choron Sauce*
minced fresh or dried tarragon for garnish

assembling the dish

Warm a metal platter and arrange the reheated *croustades* on it. Place a warm poached egg in each *croustade,* cover with lukewarm Choron Sauce, and decorate the top of each egg with a pinch of minced fresh or dried tarragon. Serve immediately.

Poached Eggs with Burgundy Sauce   *Oeufs pochés à la bourguignonne*

Poached eggs served warm on croutons and covered with a delicious Burgundy sauce made from red and white Burgundy wines, herbs, and a touch of cognac. This fragrant sauce, tasting faintly of wine, has many other uses.

FOR 6 PEOPLE

6–9 warm, unrinsed Poached Eggs, Basic Recipe*
6–9 Croutons,* reheated just before the eggs are placed on them

Burgundy Sauce (recipe follows)

Burgundy Sauce   *Sauce bourguignonne*

This rich, aromatic sauce can also be served with poached fish fillets, particularly freshwater fish such as carp. It goes well with Sautéed Chicken* or Casseroled Chicken.* It is added after the fish or meat has been arranged on the platter. It can be garnished with Mushroom Caps Sautéed in Butter* and Glazed Small White Onions.*

MAKES ABOUT 3 CUPS

    3 cups red Burgundy wine
    1½ cups fruity dry white Burgundy wine
    1 medium-size onion, chopped
    3 shallots, minced
    1 clove garlic, squeezed through a garlic press
    a few sprigs of parsley with stems
    2 small sprigs of thyme
    half of a bay leaf
    freshly ground pepper
    *Beurre manié,** using 1 tablespoon flour and 1 tablespoon butter
    3–4 tablespoons cognac warmed in a ladle
    salt
    lemon juice (optional)
    3 tablespoons butter
    1 tablespoon minced fresh tarragon for garnish

Pour the wines into a heavy-bottomed enameled saucepan along with the herbs and condiments. Do not salt at this time. Over fairly high heat, reduce the wine to about 2½ cups. Strain into another saucepan. Using a whisk, beat the *beurre manié* into the reduced wine over very low heat. Flame the warmed cognac, pour into the wine sauce. Add salt, taste for seasoning, add more pepper or a few drops of lemon juice if necessary. Heat the sauce to the boiling point, remove from heat, and swirl in the 3 tablespoons of butter.

serving and decorating the eggs

Place the warmed poached eggs on the heated croutons and arrange on a platter. Give the Burgundy sauce a final beating, pour it over the eggs. Decorate each egg with a pinch of minced tarragon.

OMELETS   *Omelettes*

No question about it—it is not so easy to make a proper French omelet—one that is nice and runny inside and dry and golden yellow outside. Any trouble you encounter can be overcome by practice. And remember: the nerve-racking part of omelet-making occurs only in the 3-minute cooking period! How can it be possible not to master the technique?

A Few Recommendations

An omelet may be plain or garnished. If you are making a garnished omelet, prepare the garnish first and keep it near.

Warm the oval metal omelet platter and keep it warm. It should be just large enough to hold the omelets. After cooking, place the omelets with the folded sides next to each other on the platter.

Crack the eggs into a bowl, add salt and pepper and a few drops of cold water.

Just before cooking the eggs, beat them for about 30 seconds with a large fork, raising the fork in the air from time to time while beating.

The Omelet Pan

Use an iron pan with 2-inch-high sloping sides. The size of the pan depends upon how many eggs you are cooking.

Taking Care of the Omelet Pan

The omelet pan should be cleaned with soap and water. If you *must* scrape it, use a plastic scouring pad, but never scouring powder, otherwise you will scratch the smooth bottom of the pan and the omelet will stick when being slid off. After washing the pan, rub the inside with oil and place between two sheets of brown paper. This will prevent it from rusting. Wipe it out with paper towels before using.

Small omelets are easier to make and taste better than large ones. Therefore, for six people, it is best to make two omelets of six eggs each, rather than one omelet of ten to twelve eggs.

For plain omelets make a border of diced Croutons* or an edging of Tomato Sauce.*

Plain Omelet, Basic Recipe

FOR 3 PEOPLE (*if used as a first course*)

FOR 2 PEOPLE (*if used as a main luncheon dish*)

4 tablespoons butter plus 3–4 pats in reserve
6 fresh large eggs
salt
freshly ground pepper
a few drops of cold water

Place the 4 tablespoons of butter in the omelet pan. Crack the eggs into a bowl, add salt, pepper, and the drops of water. Beat the eggs with rapid and regular strokes, using a fork and lifting the egg mixture, until it is slightly frothy. Put the pan over high heat, turning it back and forth so that the sides are coated with melted butter. When the butter is sizzling hot but not browned, pour the eggs in all at once, and let them set for a second or two. For the next 2½–3 minutes you must work fast and expertly. With one hand, move the pan back and forth over the heat, and with the other (using the back of a fork) make one swirling movement as though to scramble the eggs. Turn down heat and place the reserved butter under the omelet. Shake the pan before you fold the omelet.

folding the omelet

Tilt the pan and let the omelet slide to the far end, pushing it a little with the fork. Fold the half nearer you over the other half. Turn off heat.

transferring the omelet to the serving platter

Hold the heated platter in your left hand and with the right hand grasp the omelet pan under the handle. Hold the pan at an angle, bring it to the platter, and let the omelet slide onto it.

Omelet with Croutons   *Omelette aux croûtons*

FOR 3 PEOPLE

1 cup diced Croutons*
6 very fresh eggs

Prepare the croutons and keep them warm. Make a Plain Omelet, Basic Recipe.* When it has set, sprinkle ⅓ of the croutons over it. Fold it and slide it onto a warmed platter. Arrange the rest of the croutons along the open side. The omelet will look as if the croutons had just tumbled out of it.

Potato Omelet   *Omelette aux pommes de terre*

FOR 3 PEOPLE

1 cup diced Sautéed Potatoes*
6 very fresh eggs

Prepare the potatoes and keep them warm. Proceed as in the recipe above, substituting the potatoes for the croutons. Either of these omelets will provide a delicious, quickly made meal if accompanied by a green salad.

Cheese Omelet   *Omelette au fromage*

FOR 3 PEOPLE

6 very fresh eggs
⅓ cup finely diced Swiss cheese

Prepare a Plain Omelet, Basic Recipe,* and when it begins to set, sprinkle it with the cheese. Fold, slide onto a heated platter, and serve immediately.

The following two omelets make excellent entrees:

Gratin of Fresh Tomato Omelet
Omelette aux tomates fraîches, gratinée

This wonderfully delicious omelet might seem very complicated, but nothing could be simpler once you have mastered the art of omelet-making.

FOR 2 6-EGG OMELETS (ENOUGH TO SERVE 8 PEOPLE)

12 very fresh eggs
8 tablespoons butter
2 cups Tomato Coulis*
salt
freshly ground pepper
1⅓ cups heavy cream
½ cup grated Swiss cheese
a little freshly grated nutmeg
Preheat oven to 375° F.

Prepare 2 Plain Omelets, Basic Recipe.* Spread each one with 1 cup of warm tomato *coulis.* Fold the omelets and slide them onto a flameproof oval or rectangular dish with folds touching. Spread the cream very lightly over them, sprinkle with grated cheese and a little grated nutmeg. Place in the oven to glaze for 1–2 minutes. Serve immediately.

Sorrel Omelet with Ham
Omelette à l'oseille et au jambon de campagne

FOR 3–4 PEOPLE

a good handful of fresh sorrel, picked over, washed, and drained
7 tablespoons butter
¼ pound prosciutto or raw country ham, diced
6 very fresh eggs
3 tablespoons heavy cream
salt, after tasting ham for saltiness
a little freshly grated nutmeg
freshly ground pepper
Preheat oven to 375° F.

Prepare Sorrel Ribbons* with 2 tablespoons of the butter. In a skillet sauté the diced prosciutto or ham in 2 more tablespoons of the butter. Mix the sorrel and ham together and keep warm. Prepare a Plain Omelet, Basic Recipe,* using the remaining 3 tablespoons of butter. When the eggs have begun to set, fill the center with the sorrel and ham mixture. Fold the omelet and slide onto a warmed flameproof dish. Heat the cream, salt it if necessary, and sprinkle with nutmeg and pepper. Make a slit 2–2½ inches long in the center of the folded omelet, gently pour 2 tablespoons of the cream into this opening. Spread the remaining cream over the omelet, lightly glaze for just a few seconds in the oven, and serve immediately.

SCRAMBLED EGGS *Les oeufs brouillés*

Scrambled eggs, unlike omelets, must be cooked slowly over low heat. At the end of cooking they should look creamy and slightly lumpy. The most foolproof way to cook them is over a pan of simmering water or in a double boiler. If you are really expert, you may cook them without setting them over hot water, but by using a heavy-bottomed enameled saucepan set on an asbestos mat. Eggs have an odd way of shrinking when scrambled, so you must allow three or four eggs per person. For six people make two separate batches. Have your utensils near at hand: a fork, a wooden spatula, and a wire whisk.

Scrambled Eggs, Basic Recipe

FOR 3 PEOPLE

> 3 tablespoons butter plus 2–3 pats of cold butter
> 10 very fresh eggs
> a few drops of water (no more than a teaspoon)
> salt
> freshly ground white pepper

Melt the butter in the saucepan or in the top of a double boiler. Crack the eggs into a large bowl, add the water, salt, and pepper. Beat the eggs rapidly with a fork until the yolks and whites are just blended. Pour the eggs into the sauce-pan, place on top of the simmering water over moderate heat. With a wooden spatula stir the eggs with a smooth, wide, regular, circular motion, the spatula touching the bottom of the pan. For one or two minutes nothing will seem to happen, the mixture will not seem to be thickening. With patience, continue to work with the spatula without increasing speed, and suddenly the eggs will start to thicken and a few lumps will appear. Stir a little faster, scraping down the bits of egg on the sides of the pan. Remove it from the heat, and with the whisk beat in the pats of cold butter one after the other. This will stop the cooking and make the eggs shine. Place the eggs immediately onto a warmed metal dish, then serve on warmed plates.

For a more elaborate presentation, scrambled eggs may be served on Canapés* or in *Croustades.* If you serve them on canapés, accompany them with a few slices of crisply fried bacon or a bowl of Tomato Sauce.*

Scrambled Eggs on Canapés with Asparagus Tips
Canapés d'oeufs brouillés aux pointes d'asperges

A delicate hot hors-d'oeuvre.

FOR 6 CANAPÉS

6 canapes made of 6 slices homemade white bread and 4–5 tablespoons
  margarine
1½ pounds slender green asparagus
2–3 tablespoons butter
salt
freshly ground pepper
Scrambled Eggs, Basic Recipe*

Prepare the canapés in advance. Cut the crusts from the bread and discard them, sauté the slices in the margarine until they are very lightly browned. Set on paper towels to drain, sprinkle lightly with salt.

Wash, peel, and cut off the tips of the asparagus to a length of 1½ inches (the stalks can be used in soup). Stew the tips in the butter, turning them carefully with a fork, until they are tender. Salt and pepper them, keep them warm.

Cook the eggs, distribute them on the reheated canapés, and garnish with the asparagus tips.

Croustades with Scrambled Eggs and Truffles
Croustades d'oeufs brouillés aux truffes

One canned small truffle gives this elegant first course its magic touch. Make the *croustades* the day before, cover them, and store in the refrigerator.

FOR 6 PEOPLE

Scrambled Eggs, Basic Recipe* (10–12 eggs)
1 small truffle, sliced fine
truffle juice
6 *Croustades**

Prepare the scrambled eggs. Add the truffle juice along with the reserved pats of butter (in basic recipe) at the end of cooking. Fill the reheated *croustades* with the eggs and garnish each one with a thin slice of truffle.

Molded Rice Pilaf with Scrambled Eggs and Tomato Sauce
Couronne de riz aux oeufs brouillés accompagnée de sauce tomate

You will need a ring mold for preparing this delicious, colorful dish.

FOR 6 PEOPLE (*if served as a first course*)
FOR 4 PEOPLE (*if served as a light meal*)

5 cups cooked Rice Pilaf* (a little underdone, as it will cook more in the mold)
Scrambled Eggs, Basic Recipe*
2 cups well-seasoned Tomato Sauce*

Put the pilaf in a buttered ring mold, place the mold over a pan of boiling water on medium heat for 10 minutes. While the rice is cooking, prepare the scrambled eggs. Heat the tomato sauce. Unmold the rice on a warmed round plate and fill the center with the hot scrambled eggs. Serve the tomato sauce in a bowl.

First Courses

CRÊPES

In France crêpes are traditionally eaten on Candlemas Day,[1] when they are sold in bakery shops and when a good many people make them at home and have crêpe parties. Nevertheless they are eaten all year round.

Crêpes salées (Unsweetened Crêpes)

There are many ways of preparing unsweetened crêpes. They can be filled with leftover cooked chicken or other white meat, with Cream-Puréed Spinach* or Sorrel Purée* or Mushrooms Duxelles.* They can be garnished with shellfish (small shrimp, mussels, and crab meat, for example). If necessary, garnished crêpes can stand, before being served. Cook them, garnish them, and put them on a buttered flameproof platter until time to reheat them.

Crêpes, Basic Recipe

Unsweetened crêpe batter (*pâte à crêpe salée*) is a good, reliable batter. It spreads out easily and is not difficult to turn. To make the crêpes, you will need a crêpe pan or cast-iron skillet with a bottom diameter of five to six inches.

FOR ABOUT 12 CRÊPES

1½ cups all-purpose flour
a pinch salt taken by 3 fingers
2 eggs
½ cup milk and ½ cup water mixed together
5 tablespoons melted butter
3 tablespoons light beer for leavening
1 tablespoon rum to neutralize the taste of the beer
peanut oil for greasing the pan

---

[1] Candlemas Day (*Chandeleur*) is a church festival celebrated on February 2. All over France crêpes are eaten on this day.

Sift the flour into a bowl. Make a well in the center and add the salt, eggs, and 3–4 tablespoons of the milk and water mixture. With a wooden spatula push the flour from around the edges of the bowl over these ingredients, stir, adding little by little the rest of the liquid. Beat with a whisk or electric beater until the batter is smooth and creamy. Beat in the melted butter, beer, and rum. Let the batter rest for 1 hour.

cooking the crepes

Coat the pan with a thin layer of oil, then wipe with a paper towel. Place a good tablespoon of peanut oil in the pan and heat until smoking hot. Beat the batter. Remove the pan from heat and pour in ⅓ ladleful (about 3 tablespoons) of batter and, working rapidly, turn the pan in all directions so the batter spreads out evenly and smoothly and completely covers the bottom of the pan. Return it to heat for about 60 seconds, move it briskly back and forth and around in a circle. This will loosen the crêpe from the bottom of the pan.

Turn the crêpe over, either with a metal spatula or, if you are expert enough, by flipping it in the air. Lower heat and cook for 25–30 seconds. After turning the crêpe push a little butter under it to prevent it from browning too much.

Slip the crêpe onto a round flameproof platter, place the platter over a pan of boiling water. Pile the next cooked crêpe on top, and so on until all have been cooked. If they must stand before serving, they should be covered. You might turn a large saucepan upside down over them.

NOTE: *Remove scraps of batter from the pan after cooking each crêpe, rub the pan with fresh oil.*

Here are a few of my favorite recipes for garnished crêpes. . . .

Crêpes with Crème de Fromage   *Crêpes à la crème de fromage*

FOR 6 PEOPLE

12 Crêpes, Basic Recipe,* cooked and kept warm
1½ cups *Crème de fromage* (recipe given below)
4 tablespoons grated Swiss cheese
a little freshly grated nutmeg
Preheat oven to 350° F.

In the middle of each crêpe heap 2 good tablespoons of *crème de fromage*. Fold two edges inward until they meet, then fold in the ends over the cheese filling; the result will be a small rectangular package. Arrange the crêpes closely together in a buttered oven dish. Sprinkle the grated cheese and a little grated nutmeg over each crêpe, bake for 6–8 minutes, or until lightly browned.

For a more substantial crêpe, place a thin slice of boiled ham on each one before garnishing.

Crème de fromage may also be used as a garnish for Cheese Puffs.*

Crème de fromage

    1 cup milk
    2 tablespoons flour
    2 eggs
    1½ cups finely diced Swiss cheese
    a pinch of salt
    freshly ground pepper
    a little grated nutmeg

Pour the milk into an enameled saucepan, sprinkle in the flour, and whisk until it is completely absorbed. Beat the eggs and whisk them into the milk and flour. Place the saucepan over moderate heat and, continuing to whisk, bring the mixture to a boil. Immediately remove from heat, stir in the cheese, mix well, and add salt, pepper, and nutmeg.

Crêpes with Spinach *Crêpes aux épinards*

12 Crêpes, Basic Recipe*
1½ cups Cream-Puréed Spinach*
2–3 tablespoons heavy cream
2–3 tablespoons grated Swiss cheese
a little freshly grated nutmeg
Preheat oven to 375° F.

In the middle of each crêpe heap a good tablespoon of spinach, then fold the crêpes into rectangular packages. Place them closely together in a buttered oven dish. Lightly spread each crêpe with cream, sprinkle with grated cheese and grated nutmeg, and bake until golden brown.

NOTE: *Smaller spinach-garnished crêpes are lovely with roast veal. Cook them in a crêpe pan or cast-iron skillet about 4–5 inches in bottom diameter.*

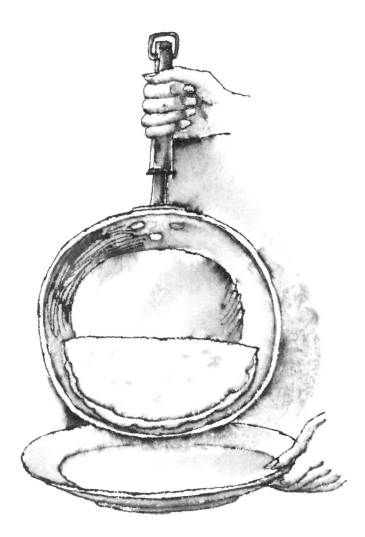

Crêpes with Red Caviar   *Crêpes au caviar de saumon*

> 1 crêpe for each person (see Crêpes, Basic Recipe)
> 1 tablespoon red caviar for each crêpe
> 2 or 3 drops lemon juice for each crêpe
> 1 quarter of a lemon for each person

In this recipe the crêpes are served very hot, and the caviar very cold. Place the caviar in the middle of each crêpe, squeeze 2 or 3 drops of lemon juice on top, fold the crêpes, and serve on a warmed platter decorated with the lemon quarters.

The crêpes are very good served with a bowl of sour cream.

Love Crêpes   *Crêpes d'amour*

What could be nicer for a late breakfast . . . for two?

> For this recipe you will need four small bowls and a crêpe pan.

FOR 2 PEOPLE

> 2 cooked crêpes, made the day before and refrigerated, or enough leftover
>   batter to make 2 crêpes (see Crêpes, Basic Recipe)
> 2 very fresh eggs
> a little oil for the crêpe pan
> 3 tablespoons hot melted butter
> salt
> freshly ground pepper
> *Preheat oven to 350° F.*

Remove the cooked crêpes or crêpe batter from the refrigerator and allow them to reach room temperature. Crack an egg and put the white in one bowl and the yolk in another. Repeat with the second egg. Beat the whites lightly with a fork so they spread easily.

procedure for the cooked crêpes

Lightly oil the crêpe pan, set it over medium heat, and lay the crêpe in it until it is heated through. Turn it and spread the white of one egg over it. Place the pan in the oven for a few seconds, just long enough for the egg white to set, leaving the oven door open. Remove the pan from the oven, slide an egg yolk on top, and place it over moderate heat. Pour half the hot melted butter over the yolk, add salt and pepper, and put the pan back in the oven, leaving the door open, until the yolk is "veiled." Fold two of the edges inward over the egg and return the pan to oven for a second or two. Place on a warmed plate.

Repeat for the second crêpe. The procedure is the same if you are using leftover batter, but the crêpes are cooked according to the basic recipe instead of being reheated.

Accompany the crêpes with a tender look.

Breton Crêpes *Crêpes bretonnes*

These crêpes, made with buckwheat flour, have a tendency to be a little drier than crêpes made with white flour, but this does not make them less tasty! Some people use a proportion of ⅔ buckwheat flour to ⅓ white flour, which is all right but it does not produce a true Breton crêpe.

FOR ABOUT 12 CRÊPES

2 cups buckwheat flour
4 very fresh eggs
3 scant cups cooled, scalded milk
a pinch of salt
4 tablespoons melted butter
¾ cup clarified butter* (this measure is before clarification)

Sift the flour into a bowl. Make a well in the center and place in it the eggs, half the milk, and salt. Blend with a wooden spatula, gradually stirring in the rest of the milk until the batter is smooth. Add the melted butter and beat for a minute or two with an electric beater. Set the batter aside to rest for 1 hour. Coat the pan with some of the clarified butter before making each crêpe, according to instructions in Crêpes, Basic Recipe.

They can be garnished with ham, fried or scrambled eggs, or small shellfish. If you want to be elegant, serve them with Mornay Sauce*. Jam, honey, or melted butter also go very well with them.

Blini

These little Russian crêpes are delicious, especially when served with smoked fish. Blini may be bought frozen or vacuum-packed, but how delightful to make one's own. They are cooked one at a time on a small cast-iron griddle. If you have three or four of these small griddles, so much the better.

MAKES 12–14 BLINI

1 package active dry yeast
½ teaspoon salt
1¼ cups lukewarm scalded milk
4½ cups all-purpose flour
5 eggs, separated
a pinch of salt
peanut oil for greasing the griddle

Put the yeast and ½ teaspoon of salt in a bowl, add a little of the lukewarm milk, and stir until dissolved. Sift the flour into a large bowl, make a well in the center, and add the egg yolks and yeast mixture. Mix well with a wooden spatula, gradually adding the rest of the lukewarm milk. Beat until completely smooth. Cover and let rise in a warm place for about 2 hours. When the batter has fully risen, beat the egg whites until stiff, after adding a pinch of salt. Fold into the batter. If the batter seems too rigid, add a little more milk.

Coat the griddle with oil, heat and drop about ¼ cup of batter onto it. When the underside of the blini is lightly colored, turn it, cook the other side, remove it, and keep it in a warm place while cooking the rest. Serve piping hot with a bowl of sour cream.

These are delicious with smoked salmon, smoked eel, or caviar.

MOUSSELINES AND MOUSSES

These elegant molded entrees are closely related to soufflés, but they have the advantage of being somewhat less fragile. If necessary, they can stand for a while in the mold, placed over a pan of hot water, heat turned off.

They are made of blended fish, shellfish, chicken, chicken livers, which are mixed with eggs and cream and are then molded. They are often accompanied by a sauce and can be served hot as a first course or cold for a buffet.

Fish Mousseline in a Ring Mold   *Mousseline de poisson en couronne*

A superb first course accompanied by shrimp sauce. For this recipe use fish that is rich in gelatin (such as whiting or cod) or fat fish (such as salmon or salmon trout) or a mixture of both.

FOR 6 PEOPLE

1 pound fish (see above), skinned, boned, and trimmed
3 eggs
1½ cups heavy cream
salt
freshly ground pepper
¼ pound shelled shrimp

Reserve the skin, bones, and trimmings of the fish and the shrimp shells for use in the sauce—Shrimp Bisque (recipe follows).

Butter a 1-quart ring mold thoroughly and place in the refrigerator to harden the butter. This makes it easier to unmold.

preparing the fish

Salt and pepper the fish and cut it in small pieces. Place in a blender and process at top speed for about 1 minute. You can also put the fish through a food mill twice, using the finest disk. Place the blended or puréed fish in a bowl. Put several ice cubes in a shallow dish and set the bowl of fish in the middle. Stir in the eggs one by one, beating the mixture thoroughly after each egg is added. Beat in the cream little by little to obtain a smooth, creamy texture. It is now ready to pour into the mold. Pour a layer of the *mousseline* mixture into the buttered mold and spread half the shrimp on it. Cover with another layer of the mixture, then the remaining shrimp, ending with the rest of the mixture.

cooking the mousseline

Place the mold in a pan of lukewarm water set over moderate heat. Bring the water to a gentle boil and cook the mixture for 20 minutes from the time the water boils. Let the *mousseline* stand for a few minutes, then unmold it on a warmed round platter. Drain off any juice that has collected in the mold. It will be used in the following sauce:

Shrimp Bisque   *Bisque de crevettes*

MAKES ABOUT 1½ CUPS OF SAUCE

skin, bones, and trimmings of fish used in the *mousseline* mixture
2 cups water
fish juice from the *mousseline* mold
1 sprig thyme
a small piece of bay leaf
a pinch of salt
freshly ground pepper
4 tablespoons butter
shells of the shrimp
a dash of Cayenne pepper or pinch of curry powder
4 tablespoons cognac, warmed
a few drops of lemon juice (optional)
2 tablespoons heavy cream (optional)

Place the skin, bones, and trimmings of the fish in a saucepan. Add the 2 cups of water, fish juice, herbs, salt, and pepper. Simmer gently, covered, for 20 minutes.

During this cooking heat 2 tablespoons of the butter in a small skillet. Add the shrimp shells and the Cayenne pepper or curry powder, cook gently, stirring, for 3–4 minutes. Add the warmed cognac and set it aflame, shaking the pan back and forth. Put all these ingredients in a food mill placed over a bowl. Move the blade back and forth, exerting as much pressure as possible to extract all the juices and creamy matter. Stir in the remaining 2 tablespoons of softened butter.

Strain the fish stock into a saucepan and heat it slowly, then beat in the buttery juice of the shrimp shells. Adjust for seasoning. Stir in the lemon juice and heavy cream.

Cold Salmon Mousse *Mousse de saumon froide*

Another fine first course that is practical as well, since it can be made in advance. The salmon gives the mousse its lovely pinkish color. Leftover poached fish can also be used to make a cold mousse, but it is not nearly as delicate. You will need a 1-quart ring mold for the dish.

FOR 6 PEOPLE

butter for greasing the mold
1 pound uncooked salmon
3 eggs
1¼ cups heavy cream
salt
freshly ground pepper

Butter the ring mold thoroughly and place in the refrigerator until ready to use. Cut the salmon in small pieces, place in a blender, and process at top speed for about 1 minute, or put through a food mill twice, using the finest disk. Spoon the blended or puréed salmon into a bowl. Put several ice cubes in a shallow dish and set the bowl of salmon in the middle. Stir in the eggs one by one, working the mixture thoroughly with a wooden spatula after each egg is added. Add the cream little by little and work until a smooth mixture is obtained. Add a small amount of salt and pepper and mix. Fill the mold.

Place the mold in a pan of lukewarm water, bring the water to a gentle boil, and cook over moderate heat for 20 minutes from the time the water boils. Let the mousse cool in its mold. Unmold the mousse just before serving.

For a simple garnish, decorate the hollow in the mousse with a bouquet of fresh small lettuce leaves. For a more elaborate garnish decorate the top of the mold with peeled cooked shrimp, allowing 2 or 3 per person.

Suggestions for accompanying sauces: Sauce Françoise,* *Watercress Sauce* (for a color contrast),* or a very lemony Mayonnaise.*

Chicken Liver Loaf, Bresse Style   *Pain de foies de volaille à la bressane*

A wonderfully light *mousseline* originating in the region of Bresse. It makes a superb first course, especially when served with cream of mushroom sauce. The dish may be molded in a large round cake pan measuring 9 inches in diameter and 2½ inches in depth.

FOR 6–8 PEOPLE

butter for greasing the mold
2¼ pounds raw chicken livers
4 eggs
2 cups heavy cream
salt
freshly ground pepper
¼ teaspoon freshly grated nutmeg
1 recipe of Cream of Mushroom Sauce*
Preheat oven to 375° F.

Butter the mold thoroughly and place in the refrigerator. Put the livers through a food mill, using the finest disk, into a large bowl. Work in the eggs one by one, beating after each addition. Stir in the cream and seasonings and beat the mixture with a whisk for 5 minutes.

Fill the cake pan and place in a pan of lukewarm water. Set over moderate heat, bring the water to a boil, then place both the pan of water and the mold in the oven. Bake for 10 minutes, reduce heat to 325°, and continue baking for about 20 minutes. Test for doneness with a larding needle. If it comes out clean but slightly moist, the loaf is done. It is essential to make this test, for if the loaf is underdone it will not unmold. Remove the pan from the oven and let it settle for several minutes before unmolding onto a round serving platter. Spoon a little cream of mushroom sauce over it and serve the rest in a warmed sauce bowl.

Ham Mousseline *Mousseline de jambon*

This *mousseline* is similar to an unmolded soufflé, for it has a thick *béchamel* sauce as a base. It is baked over a pan of hot water in a soufflé mold and served with a sauce (see the end of this recipe).

FOR 6–8 PEOPLE

Béchamel Sauce* made with

>   3 tablespoons butter
>   3½ tablespoons flour
>   2 cups heated milk
>   salt
>   freshly ground pepper
>   freshly grated nutmeg

1 pound cooked ham, cut in small pieces
¼ cup Madeira, dry sherry, or dry vermouth
4 egg yolks
4 tablespoons heavy cream
6 egg whites, stiffly beaten with a pinch of salt
4 tablespoons grated Swiss cheese
Preheat oven to 360° F.

Before you begin, butter a soufflé mold thoroughly and place in the refrigerator.

Make the *béchamel* sauce and set aside to cool.

Put the ham through a food mill, using the finest disk. Add the Madeira, sherry, or vermouth, then stir in the cooled *béchamel* sauce little by little. Add the egg yolks one by one, working them in with a wooden spatula. Add the cream a tablespoon at a time, continuing to work with the spatula until it has been entirely absorbed. Beat the egg whites with a pinch of salt until stiff and stir 3 tablespoons into the ham mixture. Fold in the rest of the egg whites, along with the grated cheese.

Pour into the cold buttered mold and place in a shallow pan of warm water. Bring to a boil on top of the stove, then transfer to the oven. Cook for about 1 hour, adding more boiling water to the bottom pan if necessary. When the edges have slightly shrunk away from the sides of the mold, the *mousseline* is done. Remove it from the pan of water and let stand for a few minutes before unmolding on a warmed round serving platter.

Accompany the ham mousseline *with Béchamel Sauce with Cream,* Aurora Sauce,* or Cream of Mushroom Sauce.* Spoon a little sauce over the* mousseline *and serve the rest in a warmed sauce bowl.*

SOUFFLÉS

These wonderfully light first courses taste as appetizing as they look. Unfortunately they have a tendency to fall as easily and quickly as they rise. A soufflé does not wait until the guests arrive—the guests must wait for *it.* And what if one of the guests is late? This kind of emotional situation is almost too much for the hostess, who is thinking, as she chats away with her guests, not only of the latecomer, but also of her soufflé slowly sinking in the kitchen. No, better not plan on a soufflé as a first course when you are having guests. Wait until your family are all together, for a weekend, for example, and surprise them with a soufflé! How does one make a successful soufflé?

The Copper Bowl and the Balloon Whip

If you have strong wrists and good strong muscles in your arms, you will be able to beat your egg whites by hand in a copper bowl with a balloon whip. The copper bowl for beating eggs is a thing of beauty in itself. Hanging on the wall beside the whip, it will add a professional look to your kitchen. With these two utensils, plus your strong wrists and arms, you will be able to beat egg whites into a mass stiff enough to support an egg in its shell! If you beat your egg whites in this way, your soufflés will be less fragile, less likely to fall. If, like me, you do not have the muscular equipment to perform this feat, use an electric beater. But remember: never let the beater remain in one place; move it around the bowl, always in the same direction. And always start by adding a pinch of salt to the egg whites. One last thing: do not stop beating, keep going until a lump of white stands in a stiff peak at the end of your whip or beater.

Soufflés are usually baked in metal charlotte molds, which usually come in various sizes: 3, 6, or 9 cups. If you cannot find one, a flameproof earthenware soufflé dish will serve, or, if all else fails, a Pyrex mold.

Basic Recipe for a Soufflé

FOR 4 PEOPLE

2 tablespoons butter
2 tablespoons flour
1 cup scalded milk
salt
freshly ground pepper
a little freshly grated nutmeg
3 large or 4 medium-size egg yolks
5 egg whites, stiffly beaten
Preheat oven to 375° F.

Make a Béchamel Sauce* with the butter, flour, milk, and seasonings. Add the egg yolks one by one, beating well after each addition. Whisk in 2 tablespoons of stiffly beaten egg whites, then fold the egg yolk mixture gradually into the rest of the beaten whites. Put the soufflé mixture into the lightly buttered mold and place on a rack in the middle of the oven. Bake for about 35 minutes, until the soufflé has risen and is nicely browned. Halfway through the cooking, lower oven heat to 350°. Serve immediately in the mold.

Unmolded Crab Soufflé   *Soufflé démoulé au crabe*

This soufflé is baked in a 9-cup soufflé mold over a pan of water, like a *mousseline*. Apart from being delicious, it has a great advantage: you can let it stand in the hot water for 10–15 minutes before unmolding and serving.

Crab meat and grated Swiss cheese are added to the soufflé base, and the bottom and sides of the mold are sprinkled with a little grated cheese. This dish is delicious served with Crab Sauce à l'Américaine.*

FOR 4–6 PEOPLE

butter for greasing the mold
2 tablespoons grated Swiss cheese
1 6-ounce can crab meat
3 tablespoons cognac in a heated ladle
2½ tablespoons butter
2½ tablespoons flour
1 cup scalded milk
freshly ground pepper
a little freshly ground nutmeg
4 egg yolks
6 egg whites, stiffly beaten with a pinch of salt
¾ cup grated Swiss cheese
Preheat oven to 365° F.

Lightly butter a soufflé mold and sprinkle both bottom and sides with the 2 tablespoons of grated Swiss cheese. Place the mold in the refrigerator.

preparing the crab meat

Drain the liquid from the crab meat and set the liquid aside for adding to the sauce. Remove all cartilage from the crab meat. Flake it with a fork and grind a little pepper over it. Flame the cognac and douse the crabs with it, set aside. When you are ready to use the crab meat, press it gently to squeeze out any remaining liquid and reserve it for the sauce.

making the soufflé base

Make a *béchamel* sauce with the 2½ tablespoons of butter, the flour, milk, and seasonings. Let it cool a little, then add the egg yolks one by one, beating well after each addition. Stir 2 tablespoons of stiffly beaten egg whites into the egg yolk mixture. Fold the egg yolk mixture into the rest of the beaten whites, at the same time sprinkling in the grated cheese. The folding procedure should be done with a wooden spatula as gently as possible, otherwise the beaten whites will lose their stiffness as well as their lightness.

Fill the mold with ⅓ of the soufflé mixture. Sprinkle half the crab meat on top. Add another third of the soufflé mixture, then the rest of the crab meat, and top with the remaining soufflé mixture. Put the mold in a pan of warm water, heat for a minute or two on top of the stove, until the water is just simmering. Place the mold in the oven. After 15 minutes reduce the heat to 350°, or even a little lower if the water shows a tendency to boil. Bake for 55 minutes to 1 hour, until it has risen about 2 inches above the mold and is golden brown. As noted above, if necessary this soufflé can stay in the oven, heat turned off, for 10–15 minutes without damage.

With great care unmold the soufflé onto a warmed plate. Top with a few tablespoons of Crab Sauce à l'Américaine,* and serve the rest of the sauce in a warmed sauce bowl.

NOTE: *Never press down into a soufflé with a spoon when you serve the first piece. This is likely to cause the soufflé to fall. Instead, make a little tear or crack in the surface with two forks—a kind of gentle pulling apart. You can then proceed to portion out servings.*

Fish

POACHED FISH *Les poissons pochés*

Fish may be poached in a court bouillon (see below) or *au naturel,* that is, in salted water to which the juice of a half lemon and a little crushed black or white pepper have been added. In either case the water should not boil, or the flesh of the fish will disintegrate.

Poached Salt Cod with Garlic Mayonnaise *Morue pochée, à l'aioli*

Aïoli sauce is a Provençal garlic mayonnaise that goes wonderfully with poached salt cod. The fish is accompanied by steaming hot vegetables.

FOR 5–6 PEOPLE

1 recipe of Garlic Mayonnaise* (*Sauce Aïoli*)
3–3½ pounds salt cod
11 cups water
2 cups dry white wine
2 medium-size carrots
2 onions, each stuck with a clove
2 shallots
1 garlic clove
1 bay leaf
1 fennel shoot
2 sprigs of thyme
1 stalk celery, cut in pieces
1 lemon, sliced, seeded, and pith removed
1 piece dried orange peel
7–8 coriander seeds
4–5 white peppercorns

NOTE: *Do not add salt.*

desalting the salt cod

Soak the fish in cold water for 12–14 hours. If you do this overnight, leave the cold water tap dripping; if in the daytime, change the water several times. Combine the remaining ingredients in a large kettle to make the court bouillon. Boil, covered, for 20 minutes. Cool completely.

---

poaching the cod

Place the fish in the cold court bouillon and set over moderate heat. When the liquid just begins to simmer, reduce heat and poach for 10 minutes. Remove the kettle from the heat and let the fish remain, covered, in the court bouillon for 20 minutes. Transfer the cod to a large platter and surround it with the following: boiled small potatoes, blanched medium-size carrots, blanched green beans, fennel hearts, cut in half and blanched, hard-boiled eggs, cut in half.

Accompany with the garlic mayonnaise and a napkin-covered dish containing ½ cup vinegar capers; 1 finely minced onion; 1 finely minced shallot; and 3–4 tablespoons finely minced parsley, chives, and chervil mixed together.

Salt Cod with Garlic and Cream   *Brandade de morue*

Another garlic-fragrant dish from Provence. The cod is poached and flaked, then blended with garlic paste and cream until light and fluffy. Accompany the dish with Steamed Potatoes* dotted with parsley.

FOR 6 PEOPLE

3–4 pounds salt cod, desalted and poached (see the preceding recipe)
5–6 cloves garlic, squeezed through a garlic press, then pounded to a paste with 3 tablespoons olive oil
1 cup olive oil
1 cup heavy cream
4–5 tablespoons thick Béchamel Sauce* with very little seasoning
freshly ground white pepper (2 turns of the mill)
½ tablespoon lemon juice
10–12 triangular Croutons* for garnish

Skin, bone, and flake the poached cod while still hot, put in a blender. Add the garlic paste and 3 tablespoons each of oil and heavy cream. Blend at low speed for 1 minute. Blend in the remaining oil and cream a tablespoon at a time. Transfer to a saucepan placed over hot water and set on low heat. Using a wooden spatula, gradually stir in the *béchamel* sauce. If you see oil rising to the top of the saucepan, stir more vigorously with the spatula. When the *brandade* is thick, grind in the pepper and add the lemon juice. Adjust for seasoning.

serving the brandade

Heap the *brandade* on a warmed round platter and shape it into a dome. Stripe the top of the dome with the tines of a fork. Stick with croutons. Decorate the edge of the platter with the carrots cooked in the court bouillon, cut in slices.

Cod Croquettes   *Croquettes de morue*

These croquettes are made from leftover *brandade de morue* (see the preceding recipe—Salt Cod with Garlic and Cream). But do not make them the very next day. You will appreciate them even more if you let two days go by. Your *brandade* will keep perfectly this long if covered and refrigerated. Remove it from the refrigerator two hours before making the croquettes.

MAKES ABOUT 8–10 CROQUETTES (ENOUGH FOR 3 OR 4 PEOPLE)

about 2 cups leftover *brandade de morue*
1 egg
.1 egg white
a little freshly ground white pepper
½–1 cup flour
2–3 egg whites, lightly beaten with a fork
½–1 cup bread crumbs
2 cups peanut oil
1 recipe of Fried Parsley*
lemon quarters for garnishing the croquette platter

Put the *brandade* in a bowl and work in egg with a wooden spatula. When it is well mixed, beat in the egg white, working vigorously with the spatula. Add the pepper. Let the mixture rest for a few minutes. Form the *brandade* into sausage shapes about the thickness of a wine cork. Roll each first in the flour, then in the beaten egg whites, then in the bread crumbs. Set them on a wire rack to dry for 10 minutes or more.

Pour the peanut oil into a deep-fat fryer and heat it to 375° F., using a deep-fat thermometer. Lower the rolls of *brandade* into the pan and cook them until they are golden brown, turning them with a skimmer or slotted spoon. Remove and drain on paper towels. Place on a warmed metal platter and garnish with lemon quarters and fried parsley.

Sauce suggestions for the croquettes: Mayonnaise* made with lemon and a little crushed garlic is an excellent choice. I also recommend Béchamel Sauce with Cream,* garnished with capers, or a bowl of boiling hot heavy cream salted and peppered and mixed with a tablespoon of finely scissored chives.

Poached Salmon Trout with Sorrel Butter
Truite saumonée pochée au beurre d'oseille

A simple but sumptuous dish recommended for a springtime dinner party. Bass, halibut, or any fairly large fine-grained saltwater fish may be substituted. Make the fish in a fish poacher equipped with a poaching rack or in a shallow pan large enough to hold the fish easily. In the second case, line the pan with a piece of muslin, letting it drape over the ends of the pan, so as to be able to lift the fish out. The fish is poached *au naturel,* that is, in water seasoned only with salt, pepper, and lemon.

FOR 6 PEOPLE

1 4-pound salmon trout
handful of sea salt or coarse salt
½ lemon, seeded
½ tablespoon white peppercorns, crushed
½ tablespoon black peppercorns, crushed
1–2 sprigs of parsley
1 small round of carrot or a piece of black olive
6 half slices lemon, fluted
sorrel butter (given below)

Place the fish on a poaching rack or muslin. Just barely cover with water and add the salt. Squeeze in the juice from the lemon and place the squeezed half lemon beside the fish. Fit a piece of aluminum foil securely over the pan and set on low heat. After 8 minutes of the merest simmering, remove the foil and add the peppercorns. Cover again and simmer as slowly as possible for 5 minutes. Turn off heat and let fish remain in its liquid 15 minutes.

Transfer the fish to a board covered with paper towels. Let it drain for a minute or so, then remove the skin, being careful not to penetrate the flesh. Place the fish on a warmed oval platter with a folded napkin or four layers of paper towels laid along its length. Arrange the napkin or paper so that it cannot be seen when the fish is lying on it.

Stick a sprig or two of parsley in the fish's gill and a small round of carrot or piece of black olive in its eye. Garnish the edges of the platter with half slices of fluted lemon. Serve the fish warm with sorrel butter and, if you wish, a few Steamed Potatoes.*

Sorrel Butter   *Beurre d'oseille*

1 pound fresh sorrel
2 tablespoons butter (a little more if necessary)
3 egg yolks
1 scant tablespoon butter
2 pinches of salt
freshly ground pepper
a few drops of lemon juice
¾ cup butter, cut in small pieces

Wash and pick over the sorrel. Drain and cut into Sorrel Ribbons.* In a heavy-bottomed enameled saucepan stew the sorrel in the 2 tablespoons of butter for 6–8 minutes, stirring constantly with a wooden spatula and adding more butter if the sorrel begins to stick to the pan. The sorrel should be limp but not fully cooked. Put the sorrel through a food mill, using the finest disk. Replace in the saucepan. (The recipe can be made in advance up to this point.) Stir the sorrel purée over low heat until heated through. Work in the egg yolks one by one, add the tablespoon of butter, salt, pepper, and lemon juice. Beat in the pieces of butter as for Hollandiase Sauce* over very low heat, until completely absorbed. Remove from heat, taste, and adjust seasoning. Beat and pour into a sauce bowl. Sorrel butter can stand for a short time if you place the covered saucepan over moderately hot water, off heat, then beat it well before pouring it into the sauce bowl.

FROZEN FISH

Many people buy frozen fish these days because it tends to be cheaper than fresh fish. The flesh of frozen fish may be somewhat drier than that of fresh fish, but if proper care is taken in thawing and cooking, succulent dishes can be made with it.

Poached Salmon   *Saumon congelé poché*

I strongly recommend this recipe for frozen salmon poached in a special court bouillon.

FOR 8 PEOPLE

    1 4–5 pound salmon with head cut off
    salt (coarse salt if possible)
    Special Court Bouillon for Frozen Fish (recipe given below)
    1 large bunch of parsley for garnish
    8 quarters seeded lemon for garnish
    4 hard-boiled eggs cut in half for garnish
    8 peeled tomatoes (optional), quartered, for garnish

Place the salmon on a kitchen towel and let it thaw at room temperature. (Never thaw a frozen fish by placing it in warm water or in a warmed oven, and never put a thawed frozen fish back in the refrigerator before it has been cooked. When the fish is thawed, wipe it with a towel and salt it. Examine it carefully to make sure that no pieces of ice remain inside. Wipe out the inside and salt it.

Place the fish in the court bouillon, adding water if necessary, so that the fish is just barely covered. Seal the pan hermetically with aluminum foil. Bring the liquid to a boil, turn down heat, and simmer for 15 minutes. Remove from heat. If serving the salmon warm, let it stand in the court bouillon for 30 minutes. If serving cold, let it stand until the court bouillon is completely cool. Transfer the fish to a board covered with paper towels to drain. Peel away the skin, being careful not to penetrate the flesh.

serving the fish

Place the fish on an oval platter covered by a napkin or 4 thicknesses of paper towels folded in such a way as to be invisible under the fish. Arrange the parsley at the head end of the fish and garnish the edges of the platter with lemon quarters, egg halves, and tomatoes.

Special Court Bouillon for Frozen Fish

> 6¾–9 cups milk
> 3 heaping tablespoons butter
> 1 bay leaf
> 1 fennel shoot (optional), split
> 1 teaspoon coriander seeds
> 2 cloves
> 1 tablespoon salt (sea salt or coarse salt if possible)
> freshly ground white pepper
> water if necessary

Place these ingredients in an enameled pan and simmer for 12–15 minutes. Cool completely and strain into a fish poacher equipped with a poaching rack, or in a shallow pan lined with muslin (see Poached Salmon Trout with Sorrel Butter*).

Fish in Aspic   *Poisson en gelée*

Any fairly large freshwater or saltwater fish, such as lake or river trout, bass, pike, carp, salmon, can be used for this recipe. The fish is poached in a highly seasoned, peppery court bouillon. The taste and quality of the aspic depend a good deal on the excellence of the white wine used in the poaching liquid. A full-bodied dry white wine such as Chablis, Côte-de-Beaune or Gewürztraminer is recommended.

FOR 8–10 PEOPLE

> a 5–6 pound fish (see those given above)
> 2–2½ cups court bouillon (see Poached Salt Cod with Garlic
>   Mayonnaise*), with a little extra pepper added
> 1 bottle dry white wine
> 1 tablespoon meat jelly
> 1½ envelopes unflavored gelatin, dissolved in a little warmed court
>   bouillon

1 small pinch of sugar (optional)
2 tablespoons cognac (optional)
2 sprigs of tarragon
1 sprig of chervil
a handful of fresh tarragon leaves, scalded then refreshed in cold water
the carrots from the court bouillon, cut in thin slices
a small bunch of parsley

Place the fish on the rack of a fish poacher or oval pan lined with muslin. Pour in the bottle of wine, minus 1 cup, then the court bouillon, and bring gently to a boil. Cover with aluminum foil, reduce heat, and simmer for 30 minutes. Remove the foil cover and let the fish cool in the liquid. Set the fish on a board covered with paper towels to drain. Peel off the skin, being careful not to penetrate the flesh. Trim the fish and place it on an oval serving platter. The fish will continue to give off a certain amount of moisture, so it is very important to drain off any liquid and to pat the fish dry before applying the jelly, otherwise it will not set.

To make the aspic, strain the court bouillon through a strainer lined with dampened cheesecloth into a saucepan. Stir in the meat jelly, dissolved in the reserved cup of wine. Bring to a boil and stir in the dissolved gelatin. Remove from heat and taste, adding the sugar if the mixture seems too acid and the cognac if you want this extra taste. Place the pan on moderate heat, add the sprigs tarragon and chervil, and clarify.* Strain into a bowl and refrigerate until the jelly has the consistency of a thick syrup.

Arrange the scalded tarragon leaves in a herringbone pattern along the length of the fish. Place a slice of carrot in the middle of each point formed by the leaves. Push the parsley into the fish's gill and a small round of carrot in its eye. Spoon 2 or 3 layers of the syrupy jelly over the fish, smoothing it with a pastry brush. Refrigerate until set. Repeat this process 2 more times to obtain a shiny coating of aspic.

For a more elaborate garnish, use half slices of fluted lemon; peeled, quartered tomatoes; and hard-boiled eggs cut in half lengthwise. Serve with a cold sauce such as Mayonnaise* and Tartar Sauce.*

GRILLED OR BROILED FISH

Grilled or Broiled Fresh Sardines *Sardines fraîches grillées*

In French ports where sardines are fished, you can buy a dozen grilled sardines in a paper container and eat them with your fingers right there. You can also prepare them at home, either grilling them on an iron grill on top of the stove, or broiling them in the oven. Fresh sardines are excellent grilled over an open fire or barbecued.

FOR 6 PEOPLE

24 fresh, medium-size sardines
peanut oil
salt
slices of buttered rye bread
lemon quarters
1 recipe of Lemon Butter*

Wipe off the sardines (don't wash them). Scale them. Then empty them through their gills, making as small an opening as possible so they do not disintegrate in cooking.

If you are grilling them on top of the stove, heat the grill to the smoking point. Brush the sardines with peanut oil and place them on the grill. Cook over high heat for 7–10 minutes, turning them once only. Remove from heat and sprinkle with salt.

If you are broiling them, preheat the broiler. Brush the sardines with oil and place them on the rack about 3½ inches under the broiler. Broil for 7–10 minutes, turning them once only. Remove from the oven and sprinkle with salt.

Serve with the slices of buttered rye bread and lemon quarters. The sardines are delicious with the lemon butter.

Grilled or Broiled Fresh Herring with Mustard Sauce
Harengs frais grillés, sauce moutarde

Never buy herring that have been split open and cleaned. Cleaning a herring is no more difficult than cleaning a sardine. Choose fairly small herrings and be sure that you have 2 or 3 males in the group. Male herrings contain milt (also known as soft roe), an indispensable element of the mustard sauce. You can tell a male herring by pinching the stomach. If it is soft, it is a male.

FOR 6 PEOPLE

12 fairly small herrings
peanut oil
salt
lemon quarters
Mustard Sauce (recipe given below)

Clean and prepare the herrings following the procedure for fresh sardines given in the preceding recipe. Grill them on top of the stove or under the broiler. Grill or broil each side for 10 minutes before turning. Transfer the herrings to a heated metal dish. Salt them and keep warm.

Mustard Sauce *Sauce moutarde*

Béchamel Sauce* with 2 tablespoons butter, 2½ tablespoons flour, 2 cups
    scalded milk, and no seasoning
2–3 tablespoons strong Dijon mustard
2–3 herring milts, put through a food mill
2 egg yolks
4 tablespoons heavy cream
salt
a little freshly ground pepper
juice of ½ lemon

Start the *béchamel* sauce while the fish are broiling. Add the mustard and puréed milts, stir well. Whisk the egg yolks and cream together in a bowl, add to the sauce, and place over very low heat, beating constantly. Add a pinch of salt, a tiny amount of pepper, and the lemon juice. Remove from heat. Taste and adjust for seasoning. Beat the sauce thoroughly for a minute and pour into a warmed sauce bowl.

A suggestion: for a lighter, frothier sauce, beat the whites of 2 eggs (adding a pinch of salt) until stiff, fold them into the mustard sauce in the saucepan. Place over very low heat, still beating, for about 1 minute. This makes the sauce milder.

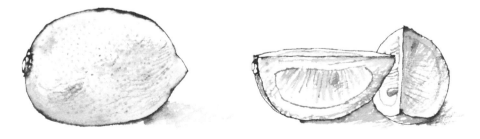

Broiled Red Mullet with Anchovy Butter
Rougets grillés au beurre d'anchois

A delicious dish . . . the fish are stuffed with a little anchovy butter and a small sprig of dried thyme.

FOR 6 PEOPLE

6½ pounds red mullets with heads
salt
1 recipe of Anchovy Butter*
6 small sprigs of dried thyme
peanut oil
6 slices fluted lemon
3 anchovies rolled with capers, cut horizontally through the middle to
    make 6 flat rolled anchovies
1 tablespoon finely minced parsley
Preheat broiler.

Clean the fish through the gills. Wipe carefully and rub with salt. Place ½ tablespoon anchovy butter and a sprig of thyme inside each fish. Brush the fish with oil, place in an oval flameproof dish, and set on the broiler rack about 3 inches from heat. Broil for 10–12 minutes or until skin browns and blisters. Slide the rack a little out of the oven, turn off the broiler, and dot each fish with anchovy butter. Broil the fish for about 3 minutes more, or until the butter is almost completely melted. Baste once, remove the dish from the oven, and garnish the fish with the remaining anchovy butter. Place a lemon slice garnished with a rolled anchovy just under the head of each fish. Sprinkle with parsley and serve immediately in the dish in which it was broiled.

Broiled Sea Bass with Fennel   *Bar grillé au fenouil*

A renowned Mediterranean dish. The garnish of fennel hearts gives it an inimitable flavor. For this dish you will need a long, well-oiled flameproof oven dish.

FOR 6 PEOPLE

herb marinade
    3–4 sprigs of dried thyme
    2 bay leaves
    5–6 peppercorns, crushed
    5–6 coriander seeds, crushed
    4 tablespoons olive oil
    2 tablespoons lemon juice
a 6-pound sea bass, cleaned and ready to cook
olive oil for oiling the oven dish

salt

1 recipe of Fennel Hearts Braised in Butter*
Preheat broiler.

Marinate the herbs and condiments in the oil and lemon juice for a few minutes.

Wipe the fish and rub it with salt inside and out. Cut short shallow slits on the back. Strain the marinade and place half the herbs and condiments inside the fish, brush it with the marinade and place it in the well-oiled oven dish. Set the dish in the middle of the oven under the broiler and broil for 30–35 minutes, until the fish is tender and brown, basting at least twice. Strew the herbs and condiments from the marinade around the fish after 20 minutes of broiling.

Prepare the fennel hearts while the fish is cooking. Serve it in the dish in which it was cooked, garnished with the fennel.

Accompany the fish with two sauces: Mayonnaise* made with olive oil and a small piece of crushed garlic, and a bowl of Lemon Butter* into which a few minced raw fennel shoots have been stirred.

BAKED FISH

Firm-fleshed fish such as sea bass, salmon trout, striped bass, small salmon, and bluefish are best for baking. In the recipe below, sea bass is stuffed with salmon *mousseline,* a company dish if there ever was one. A recipe for a less elaborate stuffing consisting of bread crumbs, mushrooms, and herbs is also included if you care to use stuffing instead.

Baked Sea Bass Stuffed with Salmon Mousseline
Bar farci d'une mousseline de saumon et rôti

FOR 6 PEOPLE

salmon mousseline ingredients

1 pound fresh salmon
1 cup heavy cream
1 egg white, unbeaten
salt
freshly ground pepper
a little freshly grated nutmeg

fish ingredients

      a 4–5 pound sea bass, cleaned and scaled
      1 recipe of Salmon Mousseline (see above)
      2 strips aluminum foil 2½–3 inches wide and as long as the fish
      string for tying the fish
      peanut oil for oiling the roasting pan and fish
      salt
      freshly ground pepper
      1 bay leaf
      1 sprig of dried thyme
      1 bottle white Burgundy wine, either Chablis or Côte-de-Beaune

sauce ingredients

      liquid from the baking pan
      ½ cup butter cut in small pieces
      juice of ¼ lemon
      a small pinch of salt
      freshly ground pepper
      Preheat oven to 365° F.

preparing the mousseline

Cut the salmon into small pieces, place in a blender, and process at high speed for 1 minute. The salmon may also be puréed by putting it through a food mill twice, using the finest disk. Place the blended or puréed salmon in a bowl and set in a shallow dish containing several ice cubes. Add the heavy cream, a tablespoonful at a time, beating vigorously with a wooden spatula until all the cream has been used. Beat in the egg white until it is absorbed. Season with salt, pepper, and nutmeg to taste. Beat the mixture for a few seconds. Let the *mousseline* stand in the dish of ice cubes until you are ready to use it (adding ice cubes when necessary).

preparing the fish

Beginning at the tail, insert a sharp knife under flesh close to the backbone, being careful not to pierce the skin on either side of the body. Making as clean an incision as possible, follow the backbone to the head with the knife, loosening the flesh from the entire side of the fish in one piece. Loosen the flesh from other side in the same way. Remove the backbone in one piece and any small bones.

Stuff the fish with the mousseline. Seal the sides with the strips of foil, tie it loosely with string around the middle.

baking the fish

Place the fish in a well-oiled roasting pan. Brush it lightly with oil, and season with salt and pepper. Set the bay leaf and thyme beside the fish. Bake in the preheated 365° oven for 20 minutes, basting once. Pour the wine around the edges of the pan (not over the fish), reduce oven heat to 325–40°, and bake for 30–35 minutes, basting three or four times. Add more wine if necessary. With great care transfer the fish to a heated metal platter. Discard the foil. Cover the fish and keep it warm.

making the sauce

Strain the liquid in the baking pan into an enameled saucepan, place over medium-low heat, and reduce to about 6 tablespoons. Lower heat and whisk in the pieces of butter one after the other. The sauce should not boil, or it will lose its opacity. As soon as the butter is absorbed, remove the pan from heat, stir in the lemon juice, salt, and pepper, adjust for seasoning. Serve in a warmed sauce bowl.

When sorrel is in season, substitute Sorrel Butter* for the sauce. Fennel Hearts Braised in Butter* go admirably with this dish. Another delicious accompaniment is Small Tomatoes Stuffed with Fish Mousseline.*

Simple Stuffing for Baked Fish

3 tablespoons butter
1 small shallot, squeezed through a garlic press
enough onion squeezed through a garlic press to make 1 tablespoon
3 tablespoons Dry Mushroom Duxelles*
1 large egg (or 2 small ones)
1 tablespoon minced chervil
1 tablespoon minced parsley
a good pinch of dried thyme
1 hard-boiled egg,* minced as finely as possible
2 tablespoons fine white bread crumbs
salt
freshly ground pepper

Heat the butter and stir-cook the shallot, onion, and mushrooms for 2 minutes. Place the egg in a bowl and work in the rest of the ingredients, including the mushroom mixture, with a wooden spatula. Adjust for seasoning. Fill the fish, seal with aluminum foil, tie, and bake as above.

Baked Tuna with Ratatouille   *Rôti de thon à la ratatouille*

This succulent oven-braised fish served on a bed of *ratatouille* can be served hot or cold. For braising the fish you will need a large, heavy-bottomed enameled casserole.

FOR 6 PEOPLE

a 3½–4 pound chunk of fresh tuna
salt
pepper
a 2-inch strip pork fat for barding the fish
5–6 tablespoons olive oil
1 medium-size onion, sliced
1 carrot, sliced
1¼ cups dry white wine
1 slice lemon
5–6 peppercorns
5–6 coriander seeds
1 *Bouquet garni classique** with added rosemary and savory
1 dried fennel shoot (optional)
3 tablespoons water
1 tablespoon butter
juice of ½ lemon
3 large cups cooked *Ratatouille** (this can be made the day before)
Preheat oven to 350° F.

Salt and pepper the fish and tie the barding fat around it.

Heat 2–3 tablespoons olive oil in a skillet and stir-cook the slices of onion and carrot for a minute or so. Spread them, along with the oil, on the bottom of the casserole and place the fish on top. Pour the wine carefully around the fish, add the lemon slice, peppercorns, and coriander seeds. Heat on top of stove until the liquid bubbles, add the *bouquet garni* and fennel shoot, and place the casserole in the oven. Bake for about 30 minutes, basting with pan juices, the rest of the olive oil, and the 3 tablespoons of water. Lower oven heat to 300°, cover the casserole with aluminum foil, and bake for another 10 minutes, for a total baking time of 40 minutes. Remove from the oven.

Transfer the fish to a heated platter and keep warm. Strain the cooking liquid into a saucepan, pressing the vegetables and herbs with the back of a spoon to extract their juices. Heat, stir in a tablespoon of butter and the lemon juice. Taste and adjust for seasoning.

Heat the *ratatouille* thoroughly in a covered pan and spread it out on a shallow platter.

Remove the barding and central bone from the fish. Slice the fish, lay the slices over the bed of *ratatouille* and pour the reheated cooking juices over them.

This dish is very good served cold, garnished with a handful of black olives.

Baked Whiting *Merlans au plat*

For this dish you will need an oval fireproof serving dish, preferably in earthenware.

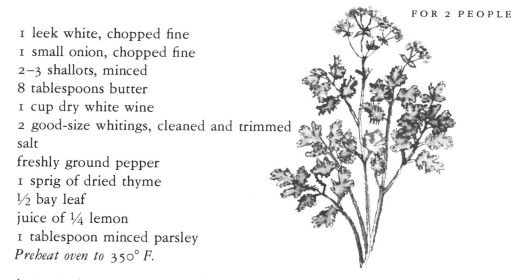

FOR 2 PEOPLE

1 leek white, chopped fine
1 small onion, chopped fine
2–3 shallots, minced
8 tablespoons butter
1 cup dry white wine
2 good-size whitings, cleaned and trimmed
salt
freshly ground pepper
1 sprig of dried thyme
½ bay leaf
juice of ¼ lemon
1 tablespoon minced parsley
Preheat oven to 350° F.

Sauté the leek, onion, and shallots in 2 tablespoons of the butter, stirring constantly. After about 5 minutes, add another tablespoon of butter to make more juice and keep the vegetables from coloring. When they are soft and slightly transparent, place them, along with their juices, in the flameproof dish, which has been oiled with 2 tablespoons butter. Pour in the wine.

Salt and pepper the whitings and lay them in the dish. Pour 3 tablespoons of melted butter over them and set the sprig of thyme and piece of bay leaf beside the fish. Place in the oven and bake for about 15 minutes, basting at least 3 times. When the fish are cooked but still firm, remove them from the oven, sprinkle with the lemon juice and parsley, and serve in the dish in which they were baked.

Baked Stuffed Carp, Oriental Style *Carpe farcie à l'orientale*

A delicious summer dish that can be served hot for a dinner party or cold for a buffet. It will have a more interesting taste if you substitute Limes Preserved in Olive Oil* for the lemons.

For this recipe you will need an oval flameproof dish large enough to hold the fish and the braising ingredients.

FOR 6–8 PEOPLE

a 4½-pound carp prepared for stuffing as in Baked Sea Bass Stuffed
    with Salmon Mousseline*
salt
freshly ground pepper

stuffing (given below)

2 strips aluminum foil 2½–3 inches wide and as long as the fish

string for tying the fish

ingredients for stuffing

1¼ cups fresh white bread crumbs

⅓ cup seedless white raisins, macerated in cup boiling hot tea until plump, then strained

1 small onion and 1–2 garlic cloves squeezed through a garlic press and pounded with 1 tablespoon olive oil

the carp liver, finely minced, salted, peppered, and sprinkled with a few drops lemon juice

1 hard-boiled egg, minced

2 pinches of dried oregano

2 pinches of dried thyme

2 pinches of curry powder

1 tablespoon minced parsley

1 fresh mint leaf, finely scissored, or 1 dried mint leaf pulverized between the fingers

salt

freshly ground pepper

1 egg for binding

ingredients for braising

2 small onions, sliced thin

2–3 ripe tomatoes, peeled, and sliced

1 canned pimento, drained, patted dry, and sliced

3 Limes Preserved in Olive Oil,* cloves removed, seeded and sliced, or 2 lemons, seeded and sliced thin

2 sprigs of dried thyme

2 bay leaves

1 sprig of dried rosemary

1 fennel shoot, split in half

1 teaspoon coriander seeds

1¾ cups dry white wine

3 tablespoons olive oil

Preheat oven to 350° F.

Salt and pepper the fish inside and out. Put the stuffing ingredients in a bowl and mix by kneading or by using a wooden spatula. Spoon the stuffing into the fish, fit the foil strips along the sides, with the string tie the fish loosely around its middle section. Place the fish in an oval flameproof baking dish.

Arrange the braising ingredients (except the wine and olive oil) around the fish, then pour in the wine and olive oil. Place the dish in the oven and bake for 40–45 minutes, basting frequently, especially toward end of cooking. Serve in the dish in which it was baked.

*An excellent accompaniment is Rice with Saffron and Curry.**

FISH FILLETS

Fillets of fish have a practical as well as an elegant side. It is easy to apportion them: ordinarily one allows two fillets per person. They can be cooked in advance and kept warm until the sauce, the base of which is made in advance, is finished. They can also be served with Savory Butters,* which can be made in advance and refrigerated.

Flat fish such as flounder are best for filleting.

For this recipe you will need an oval flameproof dish and a piece of aluminum foil for covering the fish.

Fish Fillets in Fish Stock (*Classical Method*)

The backbones and trimmings of the fish give the stock its fine flavor.

FOR 5–6 PEOPLE

ingredients for fish stock

> the backbones and trimmings of 2 of the flounders
> 2 cups cold water
> 1 cup good dry white wine
> 1 small carrot, sliced thin
> 1 small onion, sliced thin
> 1 *Bouquet garni classique**
> ½ tablespoon coarse salt
> 4–5 peppercorns, crushed

other ingredients

> 10—12 medium-size fillets of flounder
> salt
> freshly ground pepper
> 1 cup dry white wine
> butter for the baking dish
> *Preheat oven to 350° F.*

Put the fish stock ingredients in a heavy-bottomed enameled saucepan, cover, and simmer slowly for 20 minutes. Cool to lukewarm, then strain. The stock may be used as is or slightly reduced to concentrate the flavor.

preparing the fish

Salt and pepper the fillets and arrange them in the buttered oven dish flat side down. Pour in the 1 cup of white wine and 1 cup of stock. The fillets should be just barely covered with liquid. Fit a piece of aluminum foil, glossy side down, over the fillets.

Set the dish over low heat and bring the liquid to a simmer. Place in the oven and bake for about 8 minutes. Do not overcook the fillets, especially if they are to be gratinéed or sauced. Test for doneness with the wooden end of a match. If the match enters the flesh easily, the fillets are done.

Keeping the fillets in place by pressing gently on the foil with one hand, drain the liquid into a bowl. Set the dish, still covered, in a warm place. The fillets will release still more liquid while standing, and this too must be drained off before they are sauced.

Fish Fillets Modern Method au Naturel

In this recipe each fillet is wrapped in a piece of aluminum foil along with some butter and herbs, then baked and served with a buttery fish sauce. What could be simpler!

FOR 4–5 PEOPLE

8–10 medium-size fillets of flounder
salt
freshly ground pepper
2–3 teaspoons butter for each fillet
1 piece dried sage leaf or a small piece dried thyme for each fillet
1 small bunch parsley for garnish

sauce for the fish

½ cup of the fish liquid
4 tablespoons cold butter, cut in small pieces
salt
freshly ground pepper
juice of ½ lemon (optional)
Preheat oven to 350° F.

Salt and pepper the fillets and place each one on a piece of aluminum foil large enough to envelop it completely. Dot the fillets with butter and the dried sage leaf or thyme. Fold the foil around them drugstore style and place in an oven pan. Bake for 8 minutes, then open one of the packages and test for doneness as in the preceding recipe.

preparing the sauce

Remove from the oven, open the packages one by one. Pour the juice that has collected inside into an enameled saucepan, keep the fillets warm while making the sauce. Cook the fish liquid over low heat until it has slightly reduced. Whisk in the pieces of butter, two at a time, until thoroughly absorbed. Add salt and pepper to taste and the lemon juice.

serving the fillets

Arrange the fillets on a warmed oval platter garnished at one end with the bunch of parsley. Serve the sauce in a separate bowl.

A dish of small Steamed Potatoes* is a good accompaniment.

You may replace the butter sauce with some of the Savory Butters*: Herb Butter,* Tarragon Butter,* or Shallot Butter.* Or if you wish a more elaborate dish, serve the fillets with Hollandaise Sauce,* Béarnaise Sauce,* Crab Sauce à l'Américaine,* or White Butter Sauce.* Almost any sauce, hot or cold, can accompany these simple but tasty fish fillets.

Fish Fillets, Florentine Style *Filets de poisson à la florentine*

FOR 2 PEOPLE

1½–2 cups cooked spinach
4 small fish fillets, Modern Method*
1 recipe of Mornay Sauce*
1 tablespoon grated Swiss cheese
Preheat oven to 350° F.

Spread the spinach on the bottom of a small flameproof dish and place the fillets on top. Spoon the Mornay sauce over them, sprinkle with grated cheese, and cook in the oven for 8–10 minutes, until the top is golden brown.

Flounder or Halibut Fillets with Sorrel
Filets de turbot à l'oseille

Since turbot does not exist in the United States (except in certain fine restaurants on the Eastern seaboard, where it is flown in for special menus), substitute flounder or halibut. The baked fillets are set on a bed of puréed sorrel, covered with hollandaise sauce, sprinkled with ground almonds and glazed. Can you think of anything more elegant for a springtime dinner?

For this recipe you will need a flameproof oven dish.

FOR 6 PEOPLE

6–8 ½-pound fillets of flounder or halibut
salt
3 pieces of aluminum foil
3 pounds fresh sorrel for making Sorrel Purée*
1 recipe of Hollandaise Sauce*
½ cup ground almonds
Preheat oven to 350° F.

Salt the fillets and place them two by two (one on top of the other) on the glossy side of the pieces of foil. Wrap as in the preceding recipe, place in the dish, and bake for about 20 minutes. Test for doneness by opening one of the packages and inserting the wooden end of a match in a fillet. If the match enters the flesh easily, they are done.

Prepare the sorrel purée. Taste, and if it seems too sour, beat in an egg yolk. Butter a warmed metal serving dish and spread the purée on the bottom. Remove the fillets from the foil wrappings, drain them, and place on top of the sorrel. Cover with foil and keep warm.

Turn over to broil heat.

Make the hollandaise sauce. Spoon it over the fish fillets, sprinkle with ground almonds, and glaze for 1–2 minutes under the broiler.

The fillets may be accompanied by a dish of small Steamed Potatoes, preferably new potatoes.

Fillets of Flounder with Champagne *Délices de soles au champagne*

A dish for a special occasion . . . the truffles are poached in sherry and champagne and the fillets are served with a very fine sauce.

FOR 6 PEOPLE

2 canned truffles
½ bottle extra-dry champagne (¼ cup for poaching the truffles)
½ cup dry sherry
12 medium-size fillets of flounder
salt
freshly ground pepper
1 shallot, squeezed through a garlic press
butter for the baking dish

sauce for the fish MAKES ABOUT 1 CUP

fish liquid from the saucepan
3 egg yolks
6 tablespoons heavy cream
6–8 tablespoons Hollandaise Sauce* made with a moderate amount of
    lemon juice so as not to overpower the aroma of truffle
salt and freshly ground pepper if necessary

fish liquid from the saucepan

3 egg yolks

1 pinch of arrowroot, diluted in a little cooled fish liquid

6 tablespoons heavy cream

2 tomatoes, peeled, seeded, and cut into fine strips

12 mushrooms caps, sliced thin and cooked in 2 tablespoons butter, 3 tablespoons water, a few drops of lemon juice, then salted and peppered

Preheat oven to 350° F.

preparing the truffles

Drain, pat dry, and peel the truffles. Mince the peelings and set them aside. Poach the truffles in ¼ cup champagne and ½ cup sherry for 10–15 minutes. Turn off heat and let the truffles steep and cool in the liquid. Remove them with a slotted spoon and set aside. Reserve liquid.

preparing and cooking the fillets

Place the fillets on a board and make small slits around the edges to prevent them from curling up. Salt and pepper them lightly. Place them, inside-face down, in a well-buttered flameproof oven dish. Add the rest of the champagne, the shallot, and the cooled liquid in which the truffles have been poached and steeped. Fit a piece of parchment paper over the fillets. Place the dish on moderate heat, and when the liquid begins to simmer, put the dish in the oven and bake for 6–8 minutes.

Remove the dish from the oven, let the fillets stand in the liquid for 3–4 minutes. Then, pressing lightly with one hand against the paper, strain the liquid, using a fine sieve, into a saucepan. Place the dish of fillets, covered, over boiling water, heat off.

making the sauce

Over moderate heat reduce the fish liquid to 6–8 tablespoons. Remove the pan from heat, cool, and add the egg yolks, stirring with a whisk. Place the pan over very low heat and whisk vigorously until thickened. Then whisk in the cream by tablespoons and finally the hollandaise sauce, 2 tablespoons at a time, beating constantly. Adjust for seasoning, adding salt and pepper if necessary.

decorating and serving the fish

Cut the ends of each truffle, mince finely, and set aside. Cut each truffle into 6 slices. Place the well-drained fillets on a warm metal platter. Reheat the sauce and spoon it over the fillets. Sprinkle the minced truffle ends and peelings on each side of the platter.

preparing the alternate sauce

Reduce the fish liquid to 6–8 tablespoons and cool. Stir in the egg yolks. Add the diluted arrowroot and place over low heat, beating until slightly thickened. Whisk in the cream. When the sauce is heated through, remove it from heat and add the tomato strips and mushrooms, mixing carefully with a wooden spatula. Spoon the sauce gently over the fillets.

Fish Fillets Gratiné   *Filets de daurade gratinée*

Bluefish or any firm-fleshed ocean fish can be substituted for *daurade.*

Fish fillets sprinkled with a layer of mushrooms *lié,* then sprinkled with grated cheese and breadcrumbs and gratinéed . . . what could be more delicious?

FOR 6 PEOPLE

1 pound raw mushrooms, carefully washed, patted dry, then finely minced or put through a food mill

2 tablespoons peanut oil

3 tablespoons butter

1 garlic clove and 2 shallots, squeezed through a garlic press and pounded to a paste with 1 tablespoon peanut oil

about 3 pounds bluefish or other firm-fleshed fish, cut into 6 fillets

salt

freshly ground pepper

butter for oiling the baking dish plus 6 pats of butter

1 cup dry white wine

liquid from the baked fish

a few drops of lemon juice (optional)

2 tablespoons grated Swiss cheese and 2 tablespoons breadcrumbs for the gratin

Preheat oven to 365° F.

making the mushrooms lié

Mince the mushrooms or put them (cut in pieces) through a food mill, using the coarsest disk. Heat half the peanut oil and half the butter in a saucepan and add the mushrooms. Stir-cook for a minute or so and add the rest of the oil and butter. When the mushrooms begin to give off their juices, stir in the garlic and shallot paste. Mix well, remove from heat, and set aside.

preparing the fish

Salt and pepper the fillets arrange them in a buttered flameproof dish. Pour in the wine, heat to a simmer on top of the stove. Remove from heat, place a pat of butter on each fillet, cover the dish with aluminum foil, and set in the oven. Bake for 8 minutes. The fillets will finish cooking when they are gratinéed.

Remove the dish from the oven and, holding the paper against the fish with one hand, strain the liquid into a saucepan. Set the dish of fillets in a warm place.

Raise the oven setting to broil.

Reduce the fish liquid to about 3 tablespoons, add to the mushrooms, mixing thoroughly. Taste for seasoning, add a few drops of lemon juice if you wish.

Spoon the mushroom mixture over the top of the fillets after draining off any liquid in the dish. Sprinkle the top with the grated cheese, then the bread crumbs. Place the dish under the broiler until the top is golden brown (about 3 minutes). Serve immediately in the dish in which they have been baked.

Two excellent garnishes are halves of Broiled Tomatoes* or Braised Lettuce.* For a more elaborate garnish, prepare Small Tomatoes Stuffed with Fish Mousseline,* a special garnish for fish dishes.

Fillets of Mackerel, Normandy Style
Filets de maquereaux à la normande

For this recipe you will need an oval heavy-bottomed enameled (or stainless steel) pan, not too deep, for scalding the fish, and a buttered flameproof earthenware oven dish in which you can serve the fish.

FOR 6 PEOPLE

6 very fresh, cleaned, whole mackerel
hot water to cover fish
butter for the baking dish
salt
freshly ground pepper
a few drops of lemon juice
1¾ cups heavy cream
2 tablespoons finely minced chervil and tarragon mixed together
lemon quarters (optional)
Preheat oven to 365° F.

Put the mackerel in the pan, pour the hot water over them, barely covering. Place over moderate heat. When the water begins to bubble, remove the pan from heat and transfer the fish to a board. Skin them, cut off the heads, remove the backbones, and divide each fish into 2 fillets. Remove any small bones and trim the outer edges of the fillets.

Arrange the fillets (outside down) in the buttered dish and season with salt and pepper. Squeeze a little lemon juice on them. Spoon the cream over the fillets and top with the herbs. Place the dish somewhat above the middle of oven and bake the fish for 7–8 minutes.

Raise the oven setting to broil.

Place dish about 3 inches from the broiler and broil for 3–4 minutes, until the cream begins to turn golden brown. Serve the fish immediately. If you wish, have a plate of quartered lemons available for squeezing over the fish.

Small Steamed Potatoes* are a good accompaniment.

Flounder Fillets with Sage   *Filets de sole à la sauge*

A simple dish sure to be a great success.

FOR 6 PEOPLE

4–5 tablespoons butter
4 tablespoons dry white wine
salt
freshly ground pepper
12 medium-size fillets of flounder
12 dried sage leaves
a few quartered lemons (optional)
Preheat oven to 370° F.

Grease a large oval baking dish with half the butter. Add the wine. Salt and pepper the fish fillets and arrange them in the dish, inside down. Distribute the sage leaves between the fillets. Cream the remaining butter and brush a little on each fillet. Bake for 12–15 minutes, basting 3 times.

Serve the golden-brown fillets in the dish in which they were baked, along with their delicious, savory sauce.

If you wish, have a plate of quartered lemons available for squeezing over the fish.

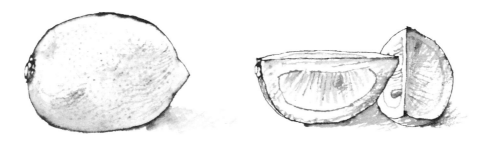

ROLLED FISH FILLETS   *Paupiettes de poisson*

Fish *paupiettes* are a delicious first course. The fillets are spread with Savory Butter* (Shrimp Butter,* Smoked Salmon Butter,* Tarragon Butter*) or with Dry Mushrooms Duxelles.* They are then rolled, but not too tightly, secured with a wooden toothpick or two, baked, and served covered with a sauce.

Cold Rolled Fillets of Whiting   *Paupiettes de merlan froides*

An attractive supper or luncheon dish that can be prepared entirely in advance. Although the flesh of whiting is more fragile than that of flounder, it becomes firm after cooking. That is why it is safer to garnish whiting *paupiettes* after cooking and cooling. In this recipe the fillets are garnished with Tuna Mousse.*

FOR 6 PEOPLE

6 fillets cut from 3 pounds whiting (have your fish dealer flatten the fillets to a uniform thickness)
salt
freshly ground pepper
butter for the oven dish
1¼ cups white wine
1 sprig of dried thyme
1 bay leaf
1 recipe of Tuna Mousse* (this can be prepared well in advance and refrigerated until ready for use)
Preheat oven to 350° F.

Trim the edges of the fillets and cut a piece from the head end (about as thick as a finger) of each one. Salt and pepper the fillets. Roll each fillet around the piece that has been cut off. Secure the rolls with a toothpick or two.

Place the rolled fillets in a well-buttered flameproof dish and pour in the wine, which should reach about halfway up the fillets. Place the thyme and bay leaf in the dish. Cover the dish with a piece of aluminum foil and bring to a simmer on top of the stove, then place it in the oven and bake for about 10 minutes, basting once.

Remove the *paupiettes* from the oven and let them cool in their juices, then place them on a board covered with paper towels to drain. Discard the toothpicks. Remove the pieces of fish around which the fillets were rolled. This will leave a space for the garnish. Transfer the *paupiettes* to a shallow dish.

serving the paupiettes

If any *paupiette* liquid has collected in the serving dish, drain it off, sponge the dish dry. Garnish the *paupiettes* with the tuna mousse, top each with a tablespoon of sauce, and serve the rest in a sauce bowl.

Suggested sauces: Béatrice Sauce, Pimento Mayonnaise,* or Anchovy Mayonnaise.*
For a more elegant presentation, place each paupiette *on a round Crouton.**

Rolled Flounder Fillets with Shrimp Butter and Normandy Sauce

Paupiettes de soles aux crevettes, sauce normande

1 double recipe of Shrimp Butter*

2 1-pound flounders, cut into 8 fillets (have your fish dealer flatten the
   fillets to a uniform thickness)

salt

freshly ground pepper

a little butter for the baking dish

½ cup dry white wine

Normandy Sauce (recipe given below)

Preheat oven to 350° F.

Make the shrimp butter and divide it into two parts, setting one part aside. Wipe the fillets and lay them on a flat work space. Salt and pepper them lightly. Spread the outer side of each fillet with a layer of shrimp butter. Roll the fillets and secure them with a wooden toothpick or two.

Butter an oval baking dish and arrange the rolls of fish in it. Pour the wine around the sides of the dish. Cover with aluminum foil and bring to a simmer on top of the stove, then place the dish in oven and bake for 10 minutes.

Remove the dish from the oven and, holding down the foil with one hand, drain the cooking juices into a bowl. Set the *paupiettes* in a warm place.

Prepare the Normandy Sauce.

serving the paupiettes

Arrange the warm, well-drained puapiettes on a heated round serving dish. Place about 1 teaspoon of reserved shrimp butter on each *paupiette*. Surround the dish with the mussels called for in the Normandy sauce. Beat the sauce and spoon it over the *paupiettes* and their garnish.

Normandy Sauce   *Sauce normande*

1 quart Mussels Marinière, Paris Style,* cooked in double the amount of
   liquid

¾ cup mussel liquid

1¼ cups Fish Velouté*

cooking juices from the *paupiettes*

3 tablespoons heavy cream

3 egg yolks

salt

freshly ground pepper

3–4 tablespoons butter

1 tablespoon lemon juice

Prepare the mussels mariniere. Remove the mussels from their shells and set in a warm place. Pour the mussel liquid into a saucepan and stir in the fish *velouté* and *paupiette* juices.

In a bowl whisk the cream and egg yolks together, along with a little salt and pepper. Beat in 2–3 tablespoons of the hot liquid. Beat the egg and cream mixture into the saucepan, off heat. Place over moderate heat and continue to beat until the sauce is slightly thickened.

Remove the pan from heat and stir in the butter and lemon juice. Taste and adjust seasoning.

Eel Stew with Glazed Onions
Matelote d'anguilles aux petits oignons glacés

This dish originated in Lyons. The best *matelote* in France is made in the region of the Ain River, between the Rhône and the Saône. Both red and white wines are used, and this combination gives the dish a more delicate taste and a lighter color than similar dishes made entirely with red wine.

For this recipe you will need a large cast-iron skillet and a large, heavy-bottomed enameled saucepan.

FOR 6 PEOPLE

4–5 pounds fresh eels[1]
salt
freshly ground pepper
about 1½ cups flour for dredging eels
5 tablespoons peanut oil
4 tablespoons butter
1 onion, stuck with a clove
⅓ pound fat bacon simmered for 10 minutes, refreshed in cold water, and cut into pieces ¼ inch thick and 1½ inches long
½ cup warmed cognac
3 cups full-bodied red wine
1¼ cups dry white wine
1 *Bouquet garni classique**
1 clove garlic, squeezed through a garlic press
1 recipe of *Beurre manié**
2 shallots, chopped, squeezed through a garlic press
12–15 Mushrooms Sautéed in Butter*
18–20 Small White Glazed Onions*
12 round or triangular Croutons,* made in advance and reheated before serving
1 tablespoon mixed finely minced parsley, tarragon, and chives

---

[1] If possible buy eels live from a tank. Have your fish dealer skin, clean, and cut off the heads, tails, and fins.

Cut the eels into 2-inch chunks. Wash them in cold water and pat dry. Salt and pepper the chunks, dredge in flour, shaking off excess, and place on a board to allow the flour to dry.

Heat 2 tablespoons of the oil and 1 tablespoon of the butter in a large skillet. Add the onion and pieces of bacon. Stir-cook for 3–4 minutes, remove from pan, and set aside. Add 1 tablespoon of oil and 1 tablespoon of butter to the skillet, turn heat fairly high, and sauté the chunks of eel, turning them with a wooden spatula. When they begin to color, pour in the warmed cognac, set it aflame, shaking the skillet back and forth. Turn off heat, remove eel chunks to a side dish, cover, and keep warm.

making the matelote sauce

Pour the red wine into the skillet and place it over moderate heat, scraping the bottom of the pan with a wooden spatula. Cook for 3–4 minutes until wine is slightly reduced. Add the white wine and bring to a boil. Then add the *bouquet garni,* garlic, onion, and bacon pieces. Reduce heat slightly and simmer for about 15 minutes, or until the liquid has been reduced by a good third.

Strain the liquid into a heavy-bottomed enameled saucepan. Remove the pieces of bacon from the strainer and add them to the liquid in the saucepan. Press against the solid matter remaining in the strainer with the back of a spoon to extract juices and flavors. Place the saucepan over medium heat, bring to a boil, reduce heat, and bind with the *beurre manié.*

Put the eel chunks back in the skillet along with the 2 tablespoons of oil and 2 tablespoons butter. Add the pressed shallot, heat, and turn the eel chunks in the hot fat for a few seconds. Pour in the sauce and let the eel reheat in the barely simmering sauce, adding the mushrooms and their cooking juices.

serving the matelote

With a slotted spoon transfer the eel to a heated round metal serving dish. Cover with sauce (setting ½ cup aside), spooning the mushrooms out of the sauce so they are visible on top. Garnish the dish with the glazed onions, spoon the reserved sauce over them, garnish with herbs, and arrange the reheated croutons around the edge of the dish.

Lotte with Crab Sauce à l'Américaine   Lotte à l'américaine

NOTE: *There is no exact equivalent of* lotte *in the United States. The fish most resembling it in taste and texture is goosefish, also known as monkfish.*

The crab sauce accompanying the fish can be made hours ahead or even the day before; reheating improves it.

To prepare this dish you will need a deep, heavy skillet and a heavy sauté pan.

FOR 6 PEOPLE

3½ pounds goosefish, cut in pieces
salt
freshly ground pepper
flour for dredging fish
1½ cups peanut oil
2 tablespoons olive oil
3 shallots, chopped and squeezed through a garlic press
2 cloves garlic, squeezed through a garlic press
½ cup warmed cognac
1 *Bouquet garni classique** with fresh or dried tarragon
1 recipe of Crab Sauce à l'Américaine (recipe given below)
1 tablespoon finely minced fresh or dried tarragon
12 round Croutons,* made in advance and reheated before serving

Salt and pepper the fish pieces, dredge in flour, shaking off excess, and place on a board to allow the flour to dry. Heat the peanut oil in the skillet until smoking hot. Carefully lower the fish pieces into the oil and cook for 3 minutes, turning each piece once. Remove the browned pieces with a slotted spoon and place on paper towels to drain.

Heat the olive oil in the sauté pan and add the fish pieces. When they are hot, add the pressed shallots and garlic. Pour in the warmed cognac and set aflame, shaking the pan back and forth and turning the fish. Add the *bouquet garni,* cover the pan, and cook over low heat for 2–3 minutes. Transfer the fish pieces to a heated shallow serving dish and keep warm.

serving the fish

Pour the reheated crab sauce over the fish and top with the pieces of crab meat from legs and claws. Sprinkle with tarragon. Place the reheated croutons around the edges of the dish.

*Accompany the dish with a bowl of Creole Rice.**

Crab Sauce à l'Américaine   *Sauce à l'américaine au crabe*

This is a delicious, highly seasoned sauce not at all complicated to make.

A 1½-POUND LIVE CRAB

sauce base

2 tablespoons butter
2 tablespoons flour
1¼ cups dry white wine
1¼ cups hot beef bouillon, made from a cube or cubes

tomato fondue

> 3 tablespoons olive oil
> 1 pound ripe tomatoes, peeled, seeded, and coarsely chopped
> 1 *Bouquet garni classique** with a sprig of fresh or dried tarragon
> ½ small onion and 2 cloves garlic, squeezed through a garlic press
> a pinch of sugar
> salt
> freshly ground pepper

ingredients for finishing sauce

> crab meat from the body
> 1 tablespoon butter
> creamy matter of the crab
> 1 jigger red port wine
> a dash of Cayenne pepper
> 5 tablespoons cognac[1]
> salt only after tasting

Plunge the live crab into a kettle of salted boiling water, cook for 15–20 minutes. Remove from the water and set aside to cool.

To make the sauce base, in a fairly large heavy-bottomed enameled saucepan blend the butter and flour together for a few minutes over low heat. Stir in the wine and reduce to about ½ cup. Off heat, beat in the hot bouillon. Set aside.

To make the tomato fondue, heat the olive oil and tomatoes in another enameled saucepan. Add the *bouquet garni.* Stir in the onion, garlic, sugar, salt, and pepper to taste, simmer over low heat for 10 minutes, stirring occasionally. Add the tomato mixture to the sauce base and simmer for 15 minutes, stirring from time to time. Set aside.

preparing the crab

Break off the claws and legs and carefully extract the meat, keeping the pieces as whole as possible, for they will be used to garnish the finished sauce. Place in a bowl, cover, and refrigerate. With a small spoon remove the creamy matter in the carapace and place in a bowl. Using a thin knife or nutpick, get all the meat you can out of the body, not worrying if it comes out in uneven bits. Discard the pieces of shell and cartilage. Add the crab meat removed from the body to the sauce and simmer gently for 10 minutes. Put the sauce in a blender and process at low speed for 1 minute. Transfer to a heavy-bottomed enameled saucepan. Set it over low heat and stir in the butter and creamy matter of the crab, port wine, and Cayenne pepper. Heat through, stirring constantly. Remove from heat and taste for seasoning. If the sauce is to wait for any length of time, cover and refrigerate.

[1] If this sauce is to accompany a dish that has been flamed in cognac, omit it here.

Shellfish

Mussels Marinière, Paris Style
Moules marinière à la parisienne

You don't have to live near the ocean to be able to eat delicious mussels. Many Paris restaurants, for example, serve them as a specialty. You too can make a specialty of mussels in your own home, where they will be just as good as, or better than, any served in restaurants.

FOR 6 PEOPLE

½ cup water
4 quarts fresh mussels
1 onion, sliced thin
a few sprigs of parsley
1 sprig of thyme
a small piece of bay leaf
freshly ground pepper
½ cup dry white wine
1 heaping tablespoon finely minced shallot
5 tablespoons butter, divided in two parts
1 heaping tablespoon finely scissored parsley
2 tablespoons finely crumbled fresh white bread
salt only after tasting

Sort over the mussels, discarding any broken or open ones. Beard them (that is, cut off all the hairy fibers) and with a good strong knife scrape off barnacles and other foreign matter clinging to the shells. Then, using a stiff brush, scrub them thoroughly, rinse several times in cold water until the water is free of sand or grit. Drain well.

Put the ½ cup of water in an 8–10 quart kettle. Add the mussels, onion slices, parsley, thyme, bay leaf, and pepper. Cover. Put the kettle over high heat. Grasping the handles of the pan and holding down the lid with your thumbs, toss the mussels about in the kettle by moving it with an up-and-down motion for about 2 minutes. Let the mussels settle for a minute, then repeat the operation. When all the mussels are open, remove them with a skimmer to a large platter.

Strain the mussel juice into a bowl, using a sieve lined with a double thickness of dampened cheesecloth. It is important that not a grain of sand remains in the juice.

Wash out the kettle, add the wine, and shallot. Place over moderate heat and reduce almost completely.

Remove the half of each shell that is not attached to the mussel, and place the mussels in their half shells on top of the reduced wine and shallot. Distribute half the butter, cut into pieces, over the mussels, pour in the strained mussel juice. Put the kettle over very low heat, stir the mussels so they will be coated with butter. Sprinkle with the parsley, bread, and the rest of the butter, also cut in pieces. Add more pepper (2 or 3 turns of the mill), cover, and reheat the mussels, taking care not to let them boil, as this would toughen them. Shake the kettle up and down twice, remove from heat, and pour the contents into a hot metal tureen. Ladle into warmed soup bowls.

Serve with rye bread and butter and good dry white wine.

Mussels with Snail Butter   *Moules au beurre d'escargot*

A delicious hot hor-d'oeuvre for a festive luncheon.

FOR 6 PEOPLE

8–12 fresh mussels per person
1 recipe of Snail Butter,* prepared ahead and refrigerated
Preheat oven to 375° F.

Clean the mussels as in the preceding recipe. Pry them open by inserting the point of a paring knife between the shells where they are attached at the hinge.[1] Discard the empty shells. With a knife, smooth the snail butter over the mussels in their half shells. Arrange them in an oven pan, making sure that each shell is level so the butter does not drip to the bottom of the pan. Bake the mussels for 6–8 minutes, or until brown and bubbling hot.

Serve with French bread and good dry white wine. The mussels are usually eaten with oyster forks.

Mussel Pilaf with Saffron and Curry
Pilaf de moules au safran et au curry

A highly seasoned dish with a rich sauce . . . perfect as the main course of a festive luncheon.

To make the dish, you will need a large kettle for steaming open the mussels and a ring mold about 8 inches in diameter for molding the rice.

FOR 6 PEOPLE

---

[1] A quicker way to open mussels is to place them in a covered large kettle for 2 minutes only—just until they "yawn." A quick method—but the mussels won't be quite as juicy.

---

3 quarts fresh mussels
butter for the mold
1 recipe of Rice with Saffron and Curry,* made ahead

sauce ingredients   MAKES ABOUT 1½ CUPS

2 tablespoons butter
2 scant tablespoons flour
strained mussel juice
2 egg yolks
1 cup heavy cream
salt
freshly ground pepper
a few drops of lemon juice
1–2 good pinches of curry powder

Prepare the mussels as in Mussels Marinière, Paris Style,* using 1 cup of water instead of ½ cup and omitting the crumbled white bread.

Strain the mussel juice into a saucepan through a strainer lined with a double thickness of dampened cheesecloth. Set aside. Remove the mussels from their shells and place in a saucepan.

Butter the inside of the mold generously. Place about 10 mussels at regular intervals on the bottom of the mold. Lightly pack the cooked rice in the mold, cover the mold with aluminum foil, and place over a pan of hot water set on very low heat. The rice will be ready to unmold when you have finished making the sauce.

making the sauce

Over low heat, stir the butter and flour together until smooth and ivory colored. Remove from heat and whisk in the strained mussel juice.

Beat the egg yolks and cream together and add to the mussel juice mixture. Place over low heat and beat until the sauce is slightly thickened. Add salt, pepper, lemon juice, and curry powder. Taste and adjust seasoning.

Add 3 tablespoons of sauce to the mussels in the saucepan and place over very low heat on top of an asbestos pad to keep the mussels from toughening.

Unmold the rice onto a warmed round metal serving dish. Put the mussels in the hollow, spoon a little sauce over the rice. Place the remaining sauce in a warmed sauce bowl.

Mussel Salad   *Salade de moules*

An original salad that can be served along with other cold hors-d'oeuvre. This is delicious with black bread and butter and a glass of good dry white wine.

FOR 6 PEOPLE

4 quarts fresh mussels

2 tablespoons mussel juice

1 recipe of Cold Sauce with Curry Powder,* prepared ahead

1 tablespoon finely scissored parsley

Prepare the mussels as in Mussels marinière, Paris Style.* Remove them from their shells and place in a bowl.

Strain the mussel juice into a small saucepan through a sieve lined with a double thickness of dampened cheesecloth. Put over medium-low heat and reduce to about 2 tablespoons. Stir the reduced mussel juice into the cold curry sauce. Add the sauce to the mussels by spoonfuls, mixing gently after each addition. Add just enough sauce to coat the mussels.

Place the salad in a shallow bowl and sprinkle with minced parsley, or garnish halved avocadoes with some of the salad.

Small Lobsters in Aromatic Bouillon
Petits homards à la nage d'écrevisses

Some people claim that there is no better way to cook live lobsters than to plunge them into boiling water to which a little salt and pepper have been added, and then serve them warm with seasoned melted butter. For small lobsters, here is something a little different, a little festive. The *nage d'écrevisse* is the aromatic bouillon in which crayfish are usually cooked.

You will need a large, heavy-bottomed enameled or stainless steel kettle for making this recipe.

FOR 4–6 PEOPLE

9 cups water

1 bottle good dry white wine (Chablis, Mâcon, Sancerre, or Pouilly)

2 carrots, sliced thin

2 onions, sliced thin

6 cloves garlic, peeled

1 tablespoon salt (coarse salt if possible)

1½ tablespoons black peppercorns

1½ tablespoons allspice

1 *Bouquet garni classique** with 8 spearmint leaves and 5 fresh or dried sage leaves

4–6 live lobsters, each weighing 1–1½ pounds

For the bouillon put all the ingredients except the lobsters into the kettle and bring to a boil. Cook for 10 minutes. Plunge the live lobsters into the bouillon, cover, and boil for 20 minutes. Remove them from the bouillon and keep in a warm place. Reduce the bouillon by half. Discard the *bouquet garni*. Strain the bouillon into a large shallow serving dish and add the lobsters. Serve immediately.

Accompany the lobsters with the same wine you have used for the aromatic bouillon.

The dish may be cooked ahead. To reheat: bring the bouillon almost to the boiling point. Remove from heat and add the cooked lobsters just long enough to warm them. Serve as above.

The dish may also be served lukewarm. But never put the lobsters in the refrigerator to cool.

Crab in the Shell, au Gratin   *Crabe en coquille gratiné*

In this elegant recipe the cooked crab meat is mixed with a specially seasoned Mornay Sauce,* put back in the shells, and gratinéed just before serving.

Use a large enameled or stainless-steel kettle for cooking the crabs.

FOR 4 PEOPLE

bouillon for cooking the crabs

10–12 cups water
1 tablespoon salt
7 or 8 black peppercorns
1 *Bouquet garni classique**

other ingredients

4 live hard-shell blue crabs
2 tablespoons butter
2 tablespoons cognac
salt
freshly ground pepper
1 double recipe of Mornay Sauce,* moistened with half milk and half reduced crab bouillon
2 tablespoons heavy cream
3 tablespoons grated Swiss cheese
4 small pinches of Cayenne pepper
Preheat oven to 350° F.

Bring the water to a boil, add the seasonings, and plunge in the live crabs. Cook, covered, for 18–20 minutes. Remove the crabs and set them on a board on their backs to cool. Reduce the bouillon about two thirds.

Break off the claws and legs of the crabs as close to the body as possible. Pull off and discard the top shell. Remove the digestive tract and all spongy material from the center of the body and discard. Then, with a good strong knife, cut under the crab meat and take it out of the shell. Pour the juice and creamy matter into a bowl and reserve. Remove any cartilage from the crab meat. Crack the claws and remove the meat as neatly as possible, set aside.

Melt the butter in a small sauté pan, add the crab meat, and sauté quickly, turning once, and not allowing the meat to color. Place it in a bowl, douse with cognac, season with salt and pepper, and knead the mixture until it is smooth.

Make the Mornay sauce, stir in the cream and the liquid and creamy matter from the crabs. Set aside 8 tablespoons of sauce. Beat the remaining sauce and add the crab meat. Adjust seasoning.

Wash and dry the crab shells and fill them three quarters full with the crab and sauce mixture. Garnish the top of each shell with the claw meat and cover with 2 tablespoons of reserved sauce. Top each shell with grated cheese and a pinch of Cayenne pepper. The recipe may be made ahead up to this point.

Just before serving, place the filled crab shells in the oven and gratiné for 8–10 minutes, until the top is golden brown and the sauce is bubbling.

An interesting variation of this recipe: fill the crab shells with Crab Sauce à l'Américaine* and accompany it with Creole Rice.*

Crab Meat with Spicy Sauce, Served Cold
Coquille de crabe, sauce épicée, servi froid

An ideal dish for a summer evening . . . especially if you have it outside on the terrace.

FOR 4 PEOPLE

bouillon for cooking the crabs (see the preceding recipe)
4 live hard-shell blue crabs
1 small head lettuce cut into ribbons
1 double recipe of *Sauce Françoise** or 1 double recipe of Pimento Mayonnaise* (*Bayonnaise*)
4 pinches of Cayenne pepper

Cook, shell, and prepare the crabs as in the preceding recipe, setting aside the pieces of claw meat.

Wash and dry the bottom crab shells, line each one with lettuce ribbons.

Mix the crab meat with whichever sauce you have chosen and top with pieces of claw meat. Add a pinch of Cayenne pepper. Refrigerate until time to serve.

A simple and highly original version of this recipe can be made by using 2 large cans of crab meat mixed with one of the sauces. Stuff empty avocado halves with the mixture.

Shellfish Cocktail *Cocktail de crustacés*

12–16 sea scallops, carefully cleaned
12–16 jumbo shrimp, peeled and deveined
boiling water
1 cup dry white wine
1 *Bouquet garni classique**
salt (sea salt if possible)
freshly ground pepper
1 celery heart, minced
1 recipe of *Sauce Françoise**
6–8 trimmed lettuce leaves
2 tablespoons finely scissored fresh chervil

Plunge the scallops and shrimp into a kettle of boiling water to which have been added the wine, *bouquet garni,* salt, and pepper. Lower heat and poach for 5–8 minutes. Remove from heat and let the shellfish cool in the liquid.

Using a slotted spoon, transfer the cooled shellfish to a bowl and stir in the minced celery heart. Mix in half the *sauce Françoise.*

Line each cocktail cup with a lettuce leaf, fill with the sauced shellfish, top with a spoonful of reserved sauce and a small pinch of chervil. Serve very cold.

Poultry

BROILED CHICKEN

Broiled Squab Chickens with Sauce Diablesse
Coquelets grillés, sauce diablesse

NOTE: *A squab chicken is an infant weighing about one pound.*
An elegant and original dish—and not much more expensive than a large roasting chicken for two. The marinating and first baking of the chickens can be done two or three hours in advance.

FOR 6 PEOPLE

3 1¼-pound squab chickens
marinade ingredients
     ¼ cup peanut oil
     juice of ½ lemon
     1–2 tablespoons pulverized dried tarragon leaves
     freshly ground pepper
salt
butter for the dripping pan
2 egg whites, lightly beaten with a fork
2 cups dry white bread crumbs
4–5 tablespoons melted butter, kept warm in a saucepan
6–8 lemon quarters and a small bunch of watercress for garnish
Preheat oven to 370° F.

preparing and marinating the squab chickens

With a sharp knife make a *lengthwise* incision in each chicken, starting at the back and continuing all around the chicken. Cut along this line with poultry scissors, dividing the chicken in half. Remove the backbone and breast cartilage and cut through the small breast bones after loosening the flesh. Place the marinade ingredients in a shallow dish and beat with a fork. Put the chicken halves in it, turning them until they are well coated. Marinate for about 10 minutes, turning the pieces once or twice.

first baking of the chickens

Remove the halved chickens from the marinade, shape them into rounded bundles, and season lightly with salt. Butter the dripping pan and arrange the chicken bundles on it close together. Place the pan about 5 inches from the bottom of the oven and bake the chicken halves, without turning or basting, for about 15 minutes, until they are ivory colored.

Remove the dripping pan and carefully pour the juices into a bowl. Cover the chicken bundles with aluminum foil. The recipe can be prepared ahead to this point.

finishing the cooking

Brush the chicken pieces with beaten egg white, sprinkle with bread crumbs, and set them on a board or rack to dry for a few minutes. Replace in the dripping pan and heat through in the oven.

Turn the oven to broil position.

Brown the chickens under the broiler, not too close to the heat, for 10–12 minutes, basting twice with the melted butter, until the chickens are golden brown.

Remove the dripping pan and pour the cooking juices into the bowl of juices from the first baking.

Place the chickens on a heated oval platter, preferably a metal one, and keep warm. Just before serving, garnish the platter with the quartered lemons and watercress. Serve with the sauce given below.

Sauce Diablesse

The base of this sauce is a reduced chicken stock made with the bones of the squab chickens. It can be prepared well ahead. The sauce has a "sweet and pungent" flavor, heightened by the taste and aroma of fresh tarragon.

½ cup Chicken Stock*
juices from the chickens
2–3 tablespoons hot barbecue sauce
1 tablespoon ketchup
a few drops of lemon juice
4 tablespoons red port wine or 2 tablespoons warmed cognac flamed in a
    ladle
a generous amount of freshly ground white pepper
2 tablespoons butter, cut in small pieces
1 tablespoon finely scissored fresh tarragon leaves

In an enameled saucepan, heat the chicken stock and the squab chicken cooking juices. Remove the saucepan from heat, add the condiments, lemon juice, wine or cognac, and pepper. Place over low heat and slowly stir in the pieces of butter. When all the butter has been absorbed, pour the sauce into a heated metal sauce bowl and garnish with the tarragon.

Suggested accompaniments: Corn Croquettes,* Zucchini Fritters,* Broiled Tomatoes,* or Stuffed Mushrooms.*

SAUTÉED CHICKEN

Minute Chicken with Tarragon   Poulet minute à l'estragon

A practical method for cooking a cut-up chicken in less than half an hour. I once watched a restaurant chef prepare this dish, and since then I have often made it myself. It is an excellent quick dish, but one requiring your constant attention.

You will need an oven pan, just large enough to hold the chicken, and a heavy sauté pan.

FOR 3 PEOPLE

marinade ingredients

> 5 tablespoons peanut oil
> 2 good tablespoons lemon juice
> 1 tablespoon dried tarragon
> 4–5 peppercorns, crushed
> 4–5 coriander seeds, crushed

for making the chicken

> 1 young 2-pound chicken, cut in 6 pieces
> 1 tablespoon peanut oil
> 2 tablespoons butter, cut in tiny pieces, plus 1 tablespoon butter
> 1–2 sprigs of fresh tarragon
> 4–6 tablespoons boiling water
> 1 small bunch watercress for garnish
> 1 tablespoon finely scissored fresh tarragon
> *Preheat oven to 380° F.*

Beat the marinade ingredients together in a shallow dish, add the chicken pieces, turning them until they are well coated with the marinade. Remove the pieces after 10 minutes and place on paper towels to drain.

Oil the oven pan with the tablespoon of peanut oil. Distribute the tiny pieces of butter on top of the oil, add the chicken, and bake for 8 minutes, until the chicken is slightly colored and has shrunk a little. Transfer the chicken pieces to a buttered sauté pan and place over low heat. Add the tarragon sprigs and cover the pan.

Rapidly deglaze* the oven pan with 2–3 tablespoons of the boiling water and place in a saucepan. Add the remaining tablespoon of butter, heat, then pour over the chicken pieces.

Fit a piece of parchment paper over the sauté pan, cover, and heat without boiling for a few minutes on top of the stove. Transfer to the oven and bake for 15–16 minutes. Remove the sauté pan from the oven, being careful to grasp the handle with a well-padded pot holder.

Salt the chicken pieces and place on a warmed platter garnished at one end with the bunch of watercress. Sprinkle the chicken with the minced tarragon.

Pour the cooking juices into a warmed sauce bowl. Deglaze the sauté pan with the remaining 2–3 tablespoons of boiling water, and stir into the sauce bowl. Degrease the surface of the sauce and adjust for seasoning.

A good accompaniment for this dish is Rice Pilaf* garnished with Broiled Tomatoes* or Stuffed Tomatoes, Provençal Style.* A green salad is very good too.

This recipe may also be used for domestic rabbit; it needs 2–3 minutes less cooking time.

Chicken Marengo *Poulet sauté Marengo*

This dish was served for the first time in Marengo, a small village in the Piedmont region of Northern Italy, after the famous Battle of Marengo, on June 14, 1800. Legend has it that Bonaparte's cook cut a chicken in pieces, sautéed it, added an onion, two or three tomatoes, a fistful of olives, a hefty pinch of *Mignonnette,** and flamed it with some cognac filched from the general's flask. A savory dish to present on the night of such a hard-won battle! Since that time, the recipe has become more elaborate.

For cooking the chicken you will need a large sauté pan with a cover.

FOR 6 PEOPLE

a 4-pound chicken, cut in 8 pieces
salt
freshly ground pepper
4 tablespoons butter
4 tablespoons olive oil
1 sprig of fresh or dried thyme
1 bay leaf
the sauce (ingredients and preparation given below)
15–18 small mushroom caps, sautéed in 2 tablespoons butter, salted, and
    sprinkled with a few drops of lemon juice (these can be made
    ahead)
10–12 Small White Glazed Onions,* made ahead and set aside in their
    liquid
1 heaping tablespoon finely scissored tarragon and chervil mixed together
12 triangular Croutons,* made ahead and reheated before using
    the sauce (ingredients and preparation given below)

sautéing and baking the chicken

Salt and pepper the chicken pieces. Heat 2 tablespoons each of the olive oil and butter in the sauté pan. Add the chicken pieces and brown them, turning. After 5–6 minutes, remove the wings and other white meat. Continue browning the dark meat for another 2–3 minutes.

Replace the white meat in the pan, add the remaining 2 tablespoons each of olive oil and butter and the herbs. Fit a piece of parchment paper over the sauté pan, cover, and cook for 2–3 minutes. Place the pan in the oven and bake for about 1 hour, turning and basting the pieces once. To test for doneness, prick the drumstick with the point of a knife. If the juice runs a clear amber color, the chicken is done. Transfer the chicken pieces to a warmed dish, cover with parchment paper, and keep warm. Set the sauté pan aside.

the sauce (based on a tomato fondue)

2 tablespoons olive oil
2 shallots, minced
1 pound tomatoes, peeled, seeded, and cut into small pieces
1 tablespoon tomato paste
1 clove garlic, squeezed through a garlic press
a large pinch of oregano
1 *Bouquet garni classique**
salt
freshly ground pepper
1 heaping tablespoon flour
3 tablespoons warmed cognac flamed in a ladle
½ cup dry white wine
1 cup warmed chicken Bouillon*
*Beurre manié** made of 1 tablespoon butter and 1 tablespoon flour (to be used only if necessary)
Preheat oven to 350° F.

making the sauce

The first part of this recipe can be made ahead.

Heat the olive oil in a saucepan, add the shallots, and stir-cook for a minute. Stir in the tomatoes and cook for 3–4 minutes, until the mixture begins to boil. Add the tomato paste, garlic, oregano, *bouquet garni,* salt, and pepper. Cover, lower heat, and simmer, for 20–30 minutes, stirring from time to time, until the tomatoes have disintegrated. Adjust seasoning.

finishing the sauce

Place the chicken sauté pan along with its juices over low heat, stir in the flour, and brown it. Remove the pan from heat and beat in the flamed cognac and the wine, place over medium-high heat, boil for 2 minutes. Add the bouillon and reduce to about 1 cup.

After discarding the *bouquet garni,* stir the tomato mixture into the sauté pan. Bring to a boil, stirring with a wooden spatula. If the sauce seems too thin, beat in the *beurre manié.* Lower heat, add the chicken pieces and the garnish of mushrooms and onions, heat through.

Remove the sauté pan from heat and let it stand a minute or two until the fat has risen to the top, then degrease.*

to complete the recipe

With a slotted spoon transfer the chicken pieces to a warmed metal serving dish and pour the sauce over them, the onion and mushroom garnish well in evidence. Sprinkle with the minced tarragon and chervil, stick the reheated croutons among the pieces of chicken, and serve.

An excellent accompanying dish is Creole Rice.

CASSEROLED CHICKEN

Casseroled Chicken *Poulet cocotte*

A classical method of preparing a tender, juicy chicken. Some cooks prefer to leave the chicken whole, but in this recipe it is cut in pieces to avoid carving. The entire dish may be made in advance and reheated just before serving.

FOR 6 PEOPLE

½ pound lean salt pork or bacon, cut in pieces ¼ inch by 1½ inches
1 tablespoon butter and 1 tablespoon oil
6 small artichoke hearts
½ lemon
½ pound Mushroom Caps Sautéed in Butter*
20 Small White Glazed Onions*
20 small new potatoes (see Potatoes*) blanched and sautéed
a 4-pound chicken, cut in 8 pieces
salt
freshly ground pepper
6 tablespoons butter
6 tablespoons peanut oil
2 tablespoons finely minced shallot
¾ cup dry white wine
¾ cup chicken bouillon or bouillon made from a cube
1 sprig of fresh or dried tarragon
1 sprig of fresh or dried chervil
1 tablespoon finely minced fresh tarragon and chervil mixed together for
    garnish

preparing the salt pork or bacon

Scald the salt pork or bacon for 2 minutes. Drain on paper towels. Heat the butter and oil in a skillet and quickly sauté the pieces over high heat. Remove, drain on paper towels, and set aside.

preparing the garnishes

Remove the leaves from the artichokes by breaking them off at the base until you can get to the hearts. Cut away the chokes (the hairy parts). Trim the hearts neatly and quarter them. Rub each quarter with the cut side of the ½ lemon. Blanch in boiling salted water for 8–10 minutes. Drain, pat dry, and set aside.

Prepare the sautéed mushrooms, glazed onions, and sautéed potatoes, set aside. Do not cook the potatoes completely.

cooking the chicken

Salt and pepper the pieces of chicken. Heat 3 tablespoons each of butter and oil in a heavy-bottomed enameled casserole. Turn the chicken pieces in it until they are lightly browned, adding 3 tablespoons each of butter and oil while they are browning.

Place the salt pork or bacon pieces in the casserole, sprinkle in the shallot, and stir together. Pour in the wine and bouillon, add the sprigs of tarragon and chervil, cover, and cook over moderate heat for 10 minutes. Lower heat and simmer for 20–25 minutes. Add the artichoke hearts, mushrooms, onions and their juice, and the potatoes. Cover and simmer for 10 minutes. Taste the juice and adjust seasoning.

serving the chicken

Transfer the contents of the casserole to a flameproof porcelain dish with a cover. Sprinkle the chicken with the mixed herbs.

reheating the dish

Preheat the oven to 325° F. Turn off heat and place the covered casserole inside for about 15 minutes, or until heated through.

Chicken in Wine   *Coq au vin*

A dish that well deserves its reputation . . . many people prefer it to game meats cooked in the same kind of sauce. The choice of wine used in cooking the dish is particularly important. It should be a young wine—not more than five years old. Burgundy and Côtes-du-Rhône are both recommended.

FOR 6 PEOPLE

2 tablespoons butter

2 tablespoons peanut oil

2 onions, minced

⅓ pound lean salt pork, simmered for 10 minutes, refreshed in cold water, and diced

a young 3–3½ pound chicken, cut in 8 pieces

salt

freshly ground pepper

3 heaping tablespoons flour

3 cups good red wine

2 cups hot Chicken Bouillon*

1 tablespoon tomato paste

1 clove garlic, squeezed through a garlic press

1 *Bouquet garni classique**

¼ cup warmed cognac flamed in a ladle

*Beurre manié** made with 1 tablespoon flour and 1 tablespoon butter

15–20 Mushrooms Caps Sautéed in Butter* *p 348*

15–20 Small White Glazed Onions*

1 tablespoon minced parsley

12 triangular Croutons,* reheated before using

cooking the chicken

Heat 1 tablespoon of butter and 1 tablespoon of oil in a large, heavy-bottomed enameled casserole. Add the minced onions and pieces of salt pork, stir-cook until lightly colored. Transfer to a side dish.

Add 1 tablespoon each of butter and oil to the casserole and sauté the chicken pieces, starting with the dark meat, seasoning the pieces with salt and pepper as they brown. Set the pieces on a platter after they are browned, being careful not to pierce them.

If necessary heat a little more fat in the casserole before you put back the onions, pieces of salt pork, and the chicken. Sprinkle with flour and turn the pieces until the flour is golden brown. (A quick way to do this is to put the casserole under a hot broiler for a few minutes, turning the chicken pieces once.)

Pour in the wine, bring to a boil, cook for 1–2 minutes, then add the bouillon and bring to a boil. Add the tomato paste, garlic, and the *bouquet garni*. Cover and cook gently for 30–35 minutes, until the chicken pieces are tender. Transfer the chicken and salt pork to a heated dish, cover with aluminum foil, and keep warm. Strain the sauce into a bowl. Wash the casserole.

finishing the coq au vin

Pour the strained sauce into the casserole, let the fat rise to the surface, and degrease* with a spoon. Place over low heat, add the flamed cognac, and increase heat. When the sauce begins to bubble, stir in the *beurre manié*. Place the chicken pieces and salt pork in the casserole along with the sautéed mushrooms and glazed onions and their juices. Simmer until heated through.

serving the coq au vin

Transfer the contents of the casserole into a heated dish, the onion and mushroom garnish well in evidence. Sprinkle on the minced parsley and stick the croutons among the chicken pieces near the edges of the dish.

Suggested accompaniments: Celery Root Purée,* Chestnut Purée,* Noisette Potatoes,* or Potatoes Dauphine.*

SAUCED CHICKEN

Chicken and Sweetbreads with Dried Morels and Cream
Poulet et ris de veau aux morilles, à la crème

Except for the sauce, this sumptuous dish can be made entirely in advance.

Two simplified versions you might like to try another time: chicken with dried morels without sweetbreads, or sweetbreads and dried morels without chicken.

For cooking the dish, you will need a heavy sauté pan, a large heavy-bottomed enameled casserole, and a no-stick skillet.

FOR 6–7 PEOPLE

chicken

3 tablespoons butter
3 tablespoons peanut oil
2 2½-pound roasting chickens, each cut into 8 pieces
salt
1 cup hot Chicken Stock*
½ cup boiling water
1 *Bouquet garni classique** with added fresh or dried tarragon

sweetbreads

4 sweetbreads
1 tablespoon distilled vinegar
2 tablespoons peanut oil
3 tablespoons butter plus 3–4 pats kept in reserve
salt
freshly ground pepper
½ cup Madeira or red port wine
½ cup dry sherry or dry vermouth
4 tablespoons cognac

dried morels

> 2 ounces dried morels
> 2 tablespoons peanut oil
> 2 tablespoons butter plus 1 tablespoon in reserve
> 2 shallots, squeezed through a garlic press
> salt
> 2 teaspoons lemon juice

sauce

> 1 ½ cups heavy cream
> *Beurre manié,** using 2 teaspoons butter and 2 teaspoons flour, or 1 scant
>   teaspoon arrowroot dissolved in 2 teaspoons cold water (both to be
>   used if a thicker sauce is desired)

preparing the chicken

Put the butter and oil in the sauté pan and place over moderate heat. When the fat begins to foam, add as many chicken pieces as the pan will hold, sauté them until lightly browned. Sprinkle the pieces with salt, transfer to a casserole, and brown the rest of the chicken. Pour the hot chicken stock over the chicken pieces and set the casserole over moderate heat.

Degrease* the fat in the sauté pan, deglaze* with the ½ cup of boiling water, and add the resulting juice to the casserole along with the *bouquet garni.* Reduce heat, cover, and simmer for 25–30 minutes. Remove the chicken pieces to a side dish and set aside in a warm place, covered.

Pour the casserole juices into a bowl and degrease. Wash and dry the casserole.

preparing the sweetbreads

Wash the sweetbreads, place in a bowl, and cover with cold water. Add the vinegar and soak for 1 hour. Strain, rinse, place in a saucepan of cold water, and blanch for 7–8 minutes, adding a pinch of salt when the water begins to boil. Strain and rinse thoroughly under the cold-water tap. Pat dry. Then, working delicately, strip off the outer membranes. In each pair pull out the tube that separates the two lobes.

In a small heavy skillet, heat the 2 tablespoons of butter and the peanut oil. Add the sweetbreads and cook on one side for 10 minutes, lifting them up from time to time with a metal spatula. Turn them, add the reserved butter pats, cover, and cook slowly, using an asbestos mat, for about 20 minutes. The sweetbreads should be lightly browned and soft when pricked with a fork. Season with salt and pepper and transfer to the dish containing the chicken pieces.

Deglaze* the pan with the wines and cognac. Degrease* and strain the juices into the clean casserole.

preparing the dried morels

Soak the morels as indicated on the package, pat dry. Heat the 2 tablespoons each of oil and butter in a no-stick skillet, add the morels and shallots. Sauté over fairly high heat for 5–7 minutes, adding the reserved butter. Sprinkle with salt and transfer with a skimmer to a bowl. Stir the lemon juice into the skillet, strain the liquid through a strainer lined with dampened cheesecloth, and add to the casserole containing the juices. The recipe can be made ahead to this point.

preparing the sauce

Bring the juices in the casserole to a boil over moderate heat and cook for 2–3 minutes. Stir in the heavy cream and boil gently until the sauce has a light consistency. If you would like a thicker sauce, add the *beurre manié* or arrowroot binding. Taste the sauce for seasoning: it may need more salt.

Transfer the chicken pieces and sweetbreads (cut in thick slices) to a warmed metal serving dish. Garnish the dish with the morels and spoon on the sauce, reheated if necessary.

Accompany the dish with Creole Rice* and Buttered Green Beans.*

Roast Chicken with Sauce Financière   *Poulet en terrine financière*

An elegant and extremely practical dish—it can be prepared entirely in advance. The chicken is spit- or oven-roasted, then cut in pieces and partially boned. The chicken pieces are added to the *Sauce Financière* and at serving time reheated in a flameproof porcelain or earthenware terrine—the kind you make pâtés in.

If you want to be sublimely elegant, make a cover of Pastry.*

FOR 6–7 PEOPLE

a 3½-pound roasting chicken
1 recipe of *Sauce financière,** using the larger quantity of chicken Velouté
    Sauce*
Preheat oven to 425° F.

Roast the chicken for 15 minutes at 425°, then turn down the oven to 350°, roast for 2¼ hours more. Place on a board and cut in pieces, removing bones from drumsticks and second joints, discarding the wishbone and the cartilage surrounding the breast and ribs. Degrease* the cooking juices and strain into a bowl.

Prepare the *sauce financière* in a saucepan, stir in the degreased chicken juices. Add the pieces of chicken to the sauce, cover the saucepan, and refrigerate. The dish will keep for 24 hours.

reheating the chicken and sauce

Preheat oven to 375° F.

Transfer the saucepan of chicken and sauce to a flameproof porcelain or earthenware terrine. Turn off the oven, place the terrine in it, setting the cover slightly askew so as to let the steam escape. Leave the terrine in the oven for about 20 minutes. It is a good idea to place the terrine on an electric hot tray once you have brought it to the table.

POACHED CHICKEN

Périgord Stuffed Chicken with Stuffed Cabbage "Sausage"
Poularde farcie périgourdine, au saucisson de chou

In the Périgord region poultry is almost always stuffed. It makes a more substantial dish, and the "Périgourdins" are hearty eaters. This dish is made more substantial by stuffed cabbage.

FOR 6–7 PEOPLE

a 3–4 pound roasting chicken, prepared for stuffing
salt
freshly ground pepper
1½ cups white bread (no crusts used)
½ cup milk
¼ small onion and 1 clove garlic, squeezed through a garlic press
2 chicken livers, cut in pieces and ground
1 fairly thick slice prosciutto, cut in pieces and ground
3 tablespoons finely scissored parsley
2 eggs
7 large cabgage leaves of uniform size
2 *Bouquets garnis classiques**
4 quarts (16 cups) Chicken Bouillon* or Beef Bouillon,* degreased*
1 small onion, stuck with a clove
1 carrot
1 tablespoon butter
Preheat oven to 350° F.

Salt and pepper the inside of the chicken, set aside.

preparing the stuffing

Crumble the bread into a bowl, pour the milk over it, and let it soak for a few minutes. Press it out and place in a large bowl. Add the onion and garlic, chicken livers, prosciutto, parsley and eggs (one after the other), working vigorously with a wooden spatula and adding a little salt and pepper.

Place 2 big tablespoons of the stuffing inside the chicken, sew up or skewer the opening, and truss.

preparing and cooking the cabbage "sausage"

Wash the cabbage leaves, plunge them into a kettle of boiling salted water, and blanch* for 10 minutes. Drain the leaves and trim the edges neatly.

Spread a tablespoon of the stuffing on a leaf of cabbage. Place another leaf on top and fold in the ends of the leaves to enclose the stuffing. Roll the 2 leaves together in an oblong shape. Repeat this process with the third and fourth leaves, adding them to the oblong "package." Then arrange the remaining 3 leaves around the package, taking care to fold in the ends. The whole thing will look like a miniature football. Tie the package firmly, but not too tightly, at each end and in the middle.

Pour 7 cups of bouillon in a kettle, bring to a boil, and add the stuffed cabbage and 1 *bouquet garni.* The cabbage should be covered with liquid, so add the necessary amount of boiling water. Cover the kettle, turn down heat, and simmer until the cabbage is tender (about 1 hour). Set aside in its liquid.

poaching the chicken

Place the chicken in a buttered oven pan and sweat* for about 15 minutes or until ivory colored. Remove from the oven and wipe off the fat with a paper towel. Leave the oven on.

Heat the remaining 9 cups of bouillon in an oval, heavy-bottomed enameled casserole. When the liquid begins to simmer, put in the chicken, turning it on its side. Add boiling water if necessary, so that chicken is just covered with liquid. Slip in the onion, carrot, and remaining *bouquet garni.* Cover, simmer for a few minutes, then place in the oven for about 1 hour and 15 minutes.

Remove the chicken from the casserole, pierce the flesh near the neck, and drain the interior juices into casserole. Let the chicken rest on a board while you reheat the cabbage in its bouillon.

carving and serving the chicken

Remove the legs, separating the drumsticks from the second joints, and cut off the wings. Remove the breast meat, including the 2 fillets lying next to the breastbone. With poultry scissors, cut around the entire chest area in such a way that you will have a boat-shaped structure filled with stuffing. Place this in the middle of a heated metal platter and arrange the chicken pieces around it.

Drain the cabbage and cut in slices. Garnish each slice with a round of the cooked carrot and place around the edges of the platter. Keep warm.

Reduce the bouillon in the casserole to about 2 cups. Strain into a saucepan, taste for seasoning, and stir in the 1 tablespoon of butter. Spoon some of the reduced bouillon over the contents of the platter and serve the rest in a warmed metal sauce bowl.

In Périgord, poached chicken is often accompanied with Soft-Boiled Egg Sauce* (Sauce de Sorges).

SUPRÊMES OF CHICKEN   *Suprêmes de volaille*

Chicken *suprêmes* (boned breasts) can be made into lovely, delicate dishes that are perfect for entrees or light meals.

Cutting the *suprêmes* into *aiguillettes* (very thin strips) is one of the most elegant ways of preparing them. The *suprêmes* can be sliced raw, then sautéed or deep-fried and served hot with a sauce, or they can be cooked first, then sliced and served cold with *chaud-froid* sauce or an egg- and butter-thickened sauce.

Chicken Strips on Canapés   *Blancs de volaille sur canapés*

This dish makes a delicious entree or a charming addition to a buffet. It can be served with a *chaud-froid* sauce or a cold *sabayon* sauce (recipes for both given below).

    2 large, cooked chicken breasts, including wings
    8 rectangular Canapés,* 2½ by 3½ inches, made ahead and reheated

Remove the breasts and wings from the cooked chicken. Skin, bone, and cut into 32 thin strips (*aiguillettes*).

chaud-froid sauce

A substantial, rich sauce that has a *roux** base and that makes a good coating for the chicken strips.

    2½ tablespoons butter
    3 tablespoons flour
    salt
    freshly ground pepper
    a little freshly grated nutmeg
    2¼ cups hot Chicken Consommé*
    3 egg yolks
    1 cup heavy cream
    3 tablespoons jellied Chicken Consomme,* clarified,* plus a little in
        reserve
    2 tablespoons minced tarragon leaves (optional)

to prepare the chaud-froid sauce

In a heavy-bottomed enameled saucepan make a *roux** of the butter, flour, salt, pepper, and nutmeg. Off heat, beat in the hot consommé. Set the saucepan over low heat and stir for 4–5 minutes. Remove from heat.

Beat the egg yolks and cream together in a bowl. Stir them gradually into the saucepan, along with spoonfuls of jellied consommé. Place the saucepan over low heat, cook for a minute or so until the mixture has a good consistency. Do not allow the sauce to boil. Remove from heat, stir for a second or two with a wooden spatula, and adjust seasoning. Let the sauce cool, stirring from time to time to prevent it from thickening too quickly and forming lumps.

to prepare the chicken

Beat the sauce and dip each chicken strip in it until coated with sauce. Place a grate over a large rectangular dish and lay the coated chicken strips on it to drain and set. With a spoon, spread another layer of the sauce on the strips and allow to set. Finish with a light coating of the reserved jellied consommé to make the strips glisten. Garnish each canapé with 4 chicken strips. Top each strip with a pinch of minced tarragon.

cold sabayon sauce

This sauce makes a lighter, finer coating for the chicken strips.

1¼ cups Chicken Stock* reduced to ½ cup
¾ cup dry white wine or ½ cup dry sherry, dry vermouth, or red port wine
a sprig of tarragon
a small piece of shallot, squeezed through a garlic press
salt
freshly ground pepper
4 egg yolks
4 tablespoons heavy cream placed in a bowl and refrigerated until ready for use
few drops of lemon juice (optional)

to prepare the cold sabayon sauce

Boil the first 6 ingredients together for 2 minutes. Taste and adjust seasoning.

Place the egg yolks in a heavy-bottomed enameled saucepan. Slowly pour the hot liquid over them, beating vigorously with a whisk. When all the liquid has been incorporated, continue to beat for 2 minutes. Place the saucepan over very low heat and continue to beat until the sauce has slightly thickened. Place the saucepan in a bowl containing cold water and a few ice cubes, and continue to beat until the sauce is somewhat cooler than lukewarm.

Remove the bowl of cream from the refrigerator, set it in a dish containing a few ice cubes. Beat the cream until it begins to thicken, add by spoonfuls to the sauce, beating after each addition. Taste and adjust for seasoning. You might wish to add a few drops of lemon juice, though not if you have used red port wine.

When the sauce is cold, dip the chicken strips in it, following the method in the preceding recipe. *Sabayon* sauce thickens as it cools, but it will never attain the thickness of *chaud-froid* sauce, since it has no *roux* base. Place the coated chicken strips on the canapés and refrigerate until time to serve.

Delicious with a crisp green salad.

Chicken Strips à la Meunière *Aiguillettes de volaille à la meunière*

FOR 6 PEOPLE

2 raw chicken breasts, cut so as to include wings
flour for dredging chicken
⅔ cup butter
salt
freshly ground pepper
juice of ½ lemon
6 Canapés,* 2½ by 3½ inches, made ahead and reheated before serving
1 tablespoon mixed finely scissored chervil and tarragon

Remove the breast meat from each side of the wishbone, leaving the wing attached. Skin it. Bone the wings and remove the cartilage from breasts. Following the grain of the meat, cut it into very thin strips. In all, you should have 24–26 strips. Lightly dredge the strips in flour, shaking off the excess: they should be just barely coated with flour.

Heat one third of the butter in a cast-iron or no-stick skillet. Put in the chicken strips. Cook over moderate heat for 10–12 minutes, turning them after 5 minutes. From time to time add a little butter to prevent the strips from burning. When they are lightly browned, season with salt and pepper and distribute them on top of the canapés, which have been placed on a heated metal platter.

Off heat, quickly deglaze* the skillet with lemon juice and pour the resulting sauce over the chicken. Garnish the strips with the mixed herbs and serve.

The platter may be garnished with halves of broiled tomatoes and diced sautéed potatoes set on cooked artichoke hearts.

Breaded Deep-fried Chicken Strips
Aiguillettes de volaille panées-frites, à l'anglaise

2 raw chicken breasts, cut so as to include wings
flour for dredging chicken
a soup plate containing 1 egg beaten with 1 egg white and 2 drops of water
a soup plate containing bread crumbs
2 cups peanut oil
salt

Prepare the chicken breasts and wings as in the preceding recipe. Dredge the chicken strips in flour, shaking off the excess. Dip each strip first in the beaten egg mixture, then in the bread crumbs. Place on a board to dry.

In a heavy pan heat the oil until the surface begins to wrinkle. Lower the strips into the fat and deep-fry for a few minutes until golden brown. Drain on paper towels, sprinkle with salt, and serve in a heated metal dish.

Accompany the aiguillettes *with* Sauce Françoise* *or the highly seasoned* Sauce diablesse.*

CHICKEN IN ASPIC *Poulet en gelée*

Because it can be prepared ahead, chicken in aspic is excellent for a late dinner—after a movie or play or during a pause in an evening bridge foursome.

Chicken in Tarragon Aspic *Poulet rôti à la gelée d'estragon*

a 2½–3 pound roasting chicken
salt
freshly ground pepper
1–2 sprigs of fresh or dried tarragon
2–3 pats of butter
butter for the roasting pan
3 cups clarified* jellied Chicken Consommé* (set ½ cup aside for chopped
    aspic garnish)
½ cup red port wine or dry sherry
4 tablespoons warmed cognac flamed in a ladle
12 fresh tarragon leaves, scalded, refreshed, and patted dry, for decoration
Preheat oven to 365° F.

Salt and pepper the inside of the chicken. Slip the sprigs of tarragon and pats of butter in the cavity. Truss the chicken and set it breast side up in a well-buttered roasting pan. Brown the breast and both sides, seasoning lightly with salt and pepper each time you turn it. Place the chicken on its back and roast for about 1 hour, or until juices run a clear amber color when the thick part of a leg is pricked. Prepare the aspic while the chicken is roasting.

to prepare the aspic

Heat the consommé, stir in one of the wines, add the flamed cognac, and adjust seasoning. The jelly should be very well seasoned, as it loses some of its aromatic taste as it turns to jelly. Cool and place in the refrigerator until it has the consistency of thick syrup.

to prepare the chopped aspic for garnishing

Put the reserved ½ cup of jellied consommé in a square pan (the jelly should be about ½ inch thick). Place in the refrigerator until completely set. Just before using it as decoration, chop it into small pieces with a sharp knife.

to prepare the chicken

Cut the legs and wings from the roast chicken. Remove the breast, trimming away the cartilage, cut it in half with poultry shears. Place the chicken back side up on an oval platter. Using this as a base, reconstruct the chicken as far as possible in its original form, using wooden toothpicks for holding the pieces together until the first coating of jelly has set. Decorate the chicken with a herringbone pattern of tarragon leaves, pushing them into the skin so they stick.

When the chicken is completely cool, brush it with a layer of jelly, refrigerate until the jelly has set. Remove the toothpicks, brush the chicken with another coating of jelly, and replace in the refrigerator. Repeat the process 2 more times, refrigerating after each layer of jelly has been added. Keep the chicken in the refrigerator until ready to serve.

Just before serving, ring the platter with the ice-cold chopped aspic.

Patchwork Chicken *Poulet en patchwork*

An attractive and amusing dish that will add a note of charm and gaiety to a buffet dinner.

After being cooked, the chicken flesh is removed and cut into tiny irregularly shaped pieces, then replaced on the carcass along with small bits of ham, prunes, and pickles—thus achieving the patchwork effect. As a final touch, the patchwork bird is painted with clear jelly, which makes the dish sparkling and lustrous.

You can make patchwork duck as well—indeed, for a large buffet why not serve a patchwork chicken *and* a patchwork duck?

Have at hand a few sheets of tissue paper, some aluminum foil, and a few toothpicks.

---

3 cups clarified* Jellied Consommé* (set ½ cup aside for chopped aspic garnish)

4 tablespoons red port wine, dry sherry, or dry vermouth

a 3–4 pound roast chicken, made ahead

⅓ pound boiled ham, cut in small rectangular pieces

24 "tenderized" prunes, macerated in a bowl of hot tea until plump and soft, then pitted (12 of the prunes cut in small pieces and used for the patchwork, the other 12 used whole for garnish)

3 sweet pickles, cut in small pieces

Make the consommé, stirring in one of the wines after cooking. Place in the refrigerator until it has the consistency of a thick syrup. Put the reserved jellied consommé in a small square pan, for making a chopped aspic garnish. Place in the refrigerator.

Remove the legs from the chicken. Then with poultry shears cut around the chicken in such a way that the breast and wings are detached and only the boat-shaped portion of the carcass and the bony extremities of the wings remain. Place the carcass, cavity up, on a serving platter.

Skin and bone the legs, cut the meat into small pieces, and place on a dish. Repeat the process for the breast and wings, placing these pieces in another dish.

Make a "cushion" of tissue paper large enough to fit into the cavity and rise slightly above it. Cover the cushion with aluminum foil, glossy side up. Cover the foil with a layer of pieces of dark meat placed closely together. Using toothpicks, fasten pieces of white meat to this layer. Remove the toothpicks and make a patchwork layer of pieces of ham, prunes, pickles, and white meat. Over this, brush on the thickened jelly, use enough to penetrate all three layers of patchwork ingredients. Place the chicken in the refrigerator until the jelly has set, then repeat the operation, replacing the chicken in the refrigerator. Brush it with jelly two or three more times, allowing it to set after each new layer has been added. Keep the chicken in the refrigerator until ready to use. Just before serving, ring the platter with chopped aspic. (see the preceding recipe). Place 6 prunes at each end of the platter.

Provide a glass of toothpicks for the guests to use in picking off pieces of patchwork and a plate for holding discarded toothpicks.

The procedure is the same for a patchwork duck. To make a more colorful patchwork, since duck meat is dark, alternate the bits of duck meat with small triangles cut from orange slices or halved pitted cherries. Pieces of black olive and pimento may also be used as color contrasts.

Chicken Livers in Aspic   *Petits aspics de foies de volaille*

These chicken livers are sautéed, flamed, and molded in jelly . . . a delicious garnish for Chicken in Aspic.* They are unmolded on rounds of lightly toasted white bread and placed around the edge of the platter.

FOR 12 METAL MOLDS *(each holding ½ cup)*

12 fresh chicken livers
3 tablespoons butter plus 2 tablespoons cut in pieces and kept in reserve
2 shallots, squeezed through a garlic press
4 tablespoons warmed cognac
3 tablespoons red port wine or Madeira wine
salt
freshly ground pepper
1½ cups Jellied Consommé,* clarified*
2 tablespoons Madeira wine
12 rounds toasted white bread

Look the livers over carefully and cut out any greenish-looking spots. Separate the livers into 2 parts.

Heat the 3 tablespoons of butter in a cast-iron skillet, add the chicken livers and the shallots. Turn the livers in the butter, add the warmed cognac, and set it aflame, shaking the pan back and forth. Add the port wine or Madeira, the reserved pieces of butter, a little salt and pepper, cook for 2–3 minutes. The livers should be rosy pink inside; otherwise they will be tough. Transfer the livers to a shallow bowl. Strain the cooking juice, slightly reduced if necessary, into a bowl and let it stand until lukewarm, then spoon it over the livers and allow to cool completely.

Heat the jellied consommé, add the 2 tablespoons of Madeira, and taste for seasoning. Place in the refrigerator until the jelly has the consistency of thick syrup.

Place a tablespoon of the thickened jelly into each of the molds. On top of each mold place 2 halves of liver, arranged to look whole. Cover with jelly (though not quite to the top of the mold). Keep in the refrigerator until set. Unmold and serve on the rounds of toast.

Suggestions for other dishes using chicken livers: Chicken Liver Mousse with Port Wine and Chicken Liver Butter.**

Seashell Macaroni with Madeira   *Coquillettes au Madère*

A delicious and simple pasta dish for your leftover chicken. It can be prepared quickly on a day when you haven't time to go marketing. You can give this dish an elegant air by serving it in a timbale. In fact, this is a shorter version of an old dish called "macaroni timbale," which was garnished with *Sauce financière** enriched with brains, kidneys, sweetbreads, and—yes—cockscombs! But we are not going that far. . . .

FOR 6 PEOPLE

½ pound seashell macaroni
3–4 pats butter
¼ pound mushrooms with their Concentrated Essence*
¼ pound cooked ham, diced
⅔–1 cup diced leftover cooked chicken
10 pitted green olives
½ cup Madeira wine
3 tablespoons heavy cream
salt
freshly ground pepper

Cook the macaroni *al dente* ("to the tooth"—meaning that the macaroni offers a little resistance when bitten into). Drain and place in a heavy-bottomed enameled casserole along with the pats of butter. Place the casserole over low heat on top of an asbestos mat. Add the rest of the ingredients, mixing them into the macaroni with two forks. Heat for 3–4 minutes, pour into a warmed timbale or bowl, and serve.

This dish is delicious with veal roast. Add 5–6 tablespoons of veal pan juice to the macaroni while reheating it.

Chicken Bouillon   *Bouillon de volaille*

This excellent bouillon is generally used as the liquid ingredient in sauces served with chicken. But there is no reason why a cup of this rich nourishing broth should not be served at the beginning of a meal for two or three people.

FOR 2–3 CUPS OF BOUILLON

1 chicken neck, washed, skinned, and trimmed
2 chicken feet, scalded for 30–40 seconds, skinned, and nails severed
1 chicken gizzard, well cleaned and cut into 4 pieces
1 chicken heart, washed, skinned, and trimmed of fat
2 chicken wing ends, flamed and split
4½ cups water
1 carrot
1 onion stuck with a clove
1 small stalk celery or a celery leaf
a cracked veal bone scalded for 5 minutes before adding to water, or ½ chicken bouillon cube (optional). Either of these makes a fuller-bodied bouillon.

1 small tomato, peeled and seeded (optional)
1 *Bouquet garni classique** with added fresh tarragon
salt
freshly ground pepper

Place all these ingredients, with the exception of the *bouquet garni,* salt, and pepper, in a soup kettle and bring to a boil, skimming if necessary. Add the *bouquet garni* and simmer for 30–40 minutes, uncovered or partially covered, depending on how concentrated you want the bouillon. Add salt and pepper to taste, and strain.

If you wish to serve this in cups as a broth, add the tomato and cook for an additional 10 minutes before straining.

Chicken Stock   *Jus de volaille*

A rich, highly concentrated stock made with the neck, wing ends, feet and giblets of a chicken and, if possible, a few chopped pieces of the raw or cooked chicken carcass.

MAKES ABOUT 1½ CUPS

2 tablespoons butter
2 tablespoons peanut oil
the neck, feet, wing ends, and giblets of a chicken, prepared as in the
    preceding recipe
a few chopped pieces of raw or cooked chicken carcass (optional)
½ carrot, sliced
½ onion, sliced
2½ cups water
1 *Bouquet garni classique**
salt
freshly ground pepper

Heat the butter and oil in a deep sauté pan or heavy saucepan and brown the chicken parts with the carrot and onion. Stir-cook for 10–15 minutes, turning the pieces with a wooden spatula. Pour in the water, bring to a boil, and add the *bouquet garni.* Reduce heat and simmer for 25–30 minutes or until reduced by about half. Add salt and pepper and taste for seasoning. Strain and degrease* before using.

This stock provides an excellent liquid ingredient for sauces served with poultry. In modern cooking it is used to enrich sauces based on *jus lié,** particularly sauces that accompany duck, guinea hen, and other poultry. It is highly recommended for spit-roasted poultry. In this case, the stock should be reduced even further and stirred into the juices that run out of the chicken while cooking and after carving.

GUINEA HEN

Casserole-Roasted Guinea Hen with Fruit Sauce
Pintade rôti en cocotte, sauce fruitée

All gourmets appreciate the slightly gamey taste of this fowl, and many find it comparable to the choicest of game birds. The meat of guinea hen is drier than that of chicken, so it is a good idea to bard it to keep it moist while cooking.

A heavy-bottomed enameled casserole just large enough to hold the hens is needed for this dish.

FOR 6 PEOPLE

ingredients for guinea hen

> 2 2–2½ pound guinea hens, with the necks cut off and reserved
> salt
> freshly ground pepper
> livers of the hens
> 4 tablespoons cognac
> 5 tablespoons butter
> 2 strips barding fat, each 3 fingers wide
> 3 tablespoons peanut oil
> 3 shallots, squeezed through a garlic press
> 8 rectangular Canapés,* 2½ by 3½ inches, made of homemade white
>   bread, reheated before using
> 1 small bunch watercress
> 2 lemons, cut in quarters

jus lié—a sauce or base for a sauce　　　　　MAKES ABOUT 1½ CUPS

> 1 tablespoon butter
> the necks of the guinea hens, cut in 3 pieces
> bone trimmings, left over from quartering, of the guinea hens
> a small sprig of fresh or dried thyme
> a small piece of bay leaf
> 1 tablespoon flour
> 1 cup Chicken Bouillon* or 1 cup boiling water
> salt
> 12 small shallots

Fruit Sauce

2 tablespoons currant jelly

2 tablespoons lemon juice

3 tablespoons orange juice

½ cup red port wine

thinly peeled rind of 1 orange and 1 lemon, finely shredded, scalded for 5 minutes, refreshed in cold water, and patted dry

1 teaspoon strong Dijon mustard

a small dash of Cayenne pepper

a small pinch of ginger

NOTE: *Add salt only after tasting.*
Preheat oven to 360° F.

preparing the hens for roasting

Salt and pepper the insides of the hens. Marinate the livers in 2 tablespoons of cognac for 10 minutes. Remove and pat dry. Slip a liver and 1 tablespoon of the butter inside each bird. Sew up or skewer the openings. Bard and truss the hens.

roasting the hens

Grease the casserole with half the peanut oil and 1½ tablespoons of butter. Put the guinea hens, breast sides up, in the casserole, one against the other. Place in the oven and brown for 15 minutes. Turn the hens on their sides, season with salt and pepper, add the shallots, the remaining 2 tablespoons of cognac, and the remaining butter and oil. Cook for 15 minutes, turn them on the other side, and cook for another 15 minutes—a total of 45 minutes. Test for doneness by pricking the fleshy part of one of the legs with the point of a knife—the juice should run pale pink. (If you prefer the birds a little less rare, add another 10–15 minutes to the cooking time.)

Transfer the hens to a board and cut each one in quarters, using poultry shears. Arrange the reheated canapés on a warm metal platter and place a quartered hen on top of each. Keep warm.

Degrease* the cooking juices in the casserole and reserve.

preparing the jus lié[1]

This can be served as is, or used as the base for the fruit sauce.

Heat the tablespoon of butter in a sauté pan. Add the neck pieces, bone trimmings, and herbs. Sauté, covered, shaking the pan from time to time, for about 10 minutes or until the ingredients are brown. Sprinkle in the flour, stir-cook for a minute or two, then add the bouillon or boiling water and cook

---

[1] If you are using the *jus lié* as a sauce rather than as a base for a sauce, add 2 tablespoons of lemon juice with the shallots.

gently for 15 minutes. Strain into a saucepan, pressing with the back of a spoon to extract all the juices.

Using a garlic press, squeeze all 12 shallots into the degreased juices in the casserole. Cook gently, not allowing the shallots to color, for about 5 minutes. Strain this liquid into the saucepan of *jus lié,* pressing against the shallots with the back of a spoon. Degrease, taste and adjust seasoning.

preparing the sauce fruitée

Stir the ingredients into the *jus lié* and simmer, uncovered, for 15 minutes. Whisk the sauce every 5 minutes. Taste and adjust seasoning. Pour into a saucepan in which it can be reheated and served.

serving the hens

Place the bunch of watercress at one end of the warmed platter containing the quartered hens, and arrange the quarters of lemon around the edges of the platter.

In winter, chestnut,* lentil,* or celery purée* goes excellently with this dish.

In spring or summer, serve with Dauphine Potatoes* or various light purées such as Green Pea Purée* or Mushroom Purée.*

TURKEY *Dinde*

TRANSLATOR'S NOTE: *In France Turkeys are much smaller than in the United States. Big 15–20 pound turkeys are almost nonexistent. You can choose your turkey from a vast selection of hens and Toms coming from different regions of the country, and your poultry dealer will prepare it for you with loving care. According to Mme. Bertholle the traditional turkey stuffing contains truffles, but she is of the opinion that the fine savor of turkey tends to be lost when it is mingled with the wonderful but overpowering taste and aroma of truffles. She also admits that truffles in the stuffing these days are a wild extravagance, and one we can easily live without. She very kindly supplies us with a recipe* sans truffes *that is as delicious and original as it is thrifty.*

Roast Turkey with Prune and Pork Sausage Stuffing
Dinde rôtie aux pruneaux et aux chipolatas

A wonderfully savory dish to set before your guests on Christmas Day! If it comes as a disappointment that the truffle-colored prunes are not really truffles, just taste— you will find they are a delicious disappointment.

Remember that turkeys must be basted frequently, not with the pan juices, but with melted butter kept warm in a small saucepan.

For cooking the turkey, you will need a large roasting pan equipped with a rack and a large oval heavy-bottomed enameled casserole.

1 pound "tenderized" prunes
1 bowl hot tea
butter for the skillet
1 pound small link pork sausages plus a little butter for browning them
the turkey liver
1½ tablespoons cognac
1 ready-to-cook, young 7-pound turkey, neck cut off and set aside
salt
freshly ground pepper
3 strips barding fat each 3 fingers wide, for tying on drumsticks and breast
oil for the roasting pan
3–4 tablespoons margarine, cut in small pieces
4 tablespoons hot water placed in with turkey (optional)
5–8 tablespoons butter, kept warm in a small pan
½ cup hot water for deglazing the roasting pan
Preheat oven to 350° F.

Macerate the prunes in the hot tea flavored with ½ tablespoon of the cognac until they are plump and soft. Drain, pit, and pat dry.

Butter a skillet and lightly brown the sausages. They should not be completely cooked, just relieved of some of their fat. Drain on paper towels and allow to cool completely.

Cut the turkey liver into 4–6 pieces and marinate for a few minutes in the 1 tablespoon of cognac, remove, and pat dry.

Salt and pepper the inside of the turkey and stuff it with the prunes, sausages, and liver. Sew up or skewer the opening. Tie the barding fat around the drumsticks and breast. Truss the turkey.

Grease the roasting pan with oil and distribute the pieces of margarine. Place the turkey, breast side up, on the rack. The hot water may be added at this time.

Melt the butter and keep it warm. Roast the turkey for 20 minutes, basting frequently with melted butter. Turn the turkey on its side, roast for another 20 minutes, continuing to baste. Repeat the process for the other side.

Transfer the turkey to the casserole. Remove the barding fat. Deglaze* the cooking juices in the roasting pan with the ½ cup of hot water, strain into the casserole. Cover the turkey loosely with aluminum foil. Set the cover on slightly askew, cook the turkey either over moderate heat on top of the stove or in the oven turned down to 300° for at least 1 hour, or until the juices run a clear amber color when the fleshy part of the leg is pricked.

Turkey Stock Served as a Sauce *Jus de dinde*

This can be made in advance or prepared while the turkey is cooking.

MAKES ABOUT 1½–2 CUPS

Follow the recipe for Chicken Stock,* using the turkey neck cut in 3 pieces and the giblets, which have been marinated in 1 tablespoon of cognac for 10 minutes. Strain the stock into a small saucepan and degrease.* Taste and adjust seasoning.

serving the turkey

Transfer the turkey to a board and let it rest for 10 minutes before carving it. Cut the breast meat into thin slices and arrange on a warmed large metal platter with the rest of the pieces. Garnish the platter with the prunes and sausages. Heat the sauce and pour it into a warmed sauce bowl.

Accompany the turkey with Corn Croquettes, Chestnut Purée,* or Braised Chestnuts.**

November Goose with Fall Apples
Oie de novembre aux pommes d'automne

Nothing goes better with goose than tart, juicy apples impregnated with goose fat.

TRANSLATOR'S NOTE: *You may be using a frozen goose. To thaw, follow Mme. Bertholle's instructions for frozen duck (for best results see the introductory note in the duck section, just following this recipe).*

A large roasting pan equipped with a rack will be needed for roasting the goose.

FOR 8–10 PEOPLE

2 pounds (about 6–7) tart, juicy apples
juice of ½ lemon
3 tablespoons butter
1 jigger warmed Calvados, armagnac, or rum
2 pinches of salt
2 pinches of sugar
2 teaspoons grated lemon rind
freshly ground pepper
a 6½–7 pound goose
peanut oil for oiling the roasting pan
1 recipe of Chicken Liver Butter,* using 3 chicken livers and the goose
    liver, made ahead, remove from the refrigerator ½ hour before
    using
8–10 3-inch-square Canapés,* made ahead and reheated before using
Preheat oven to 340° F.

making the stuffing

Peel and core the apples. Cut each into quarters, then cut the quarters in half. Stir in the lemon juice.

Heat the butter in a skillet and sauté the apples, turning them with a wooden spatula, for 2 minutes. Add the warmed Calvados, armagnac, or rum, set aflame, shaking the pan back and forth. Remove from heat, add the salt, sugar, lemon rind, and pepper, allow to cool completely.

preparing and roasting the goose

Salt and pepper the inside of the goose, spoon in the cooled stuffing, and sew up or skewer the opening. Truss.

Spread a thin layer of oil on the bottom of the roasting pan to prevent the goose fat from burning. Place the goose breast side up on the rack of the pan. Do not baste for the first hour. During this time spoon out the fat that accumulates, place it in a saucepan, and keep warm. This is the fat you will baste with.

When the breast is golden brown and the skin crisp, turn the goose on its side, salt and pepper it, and let it brown, basting once or twice. Turn the goose on the other side and repeat the process. It is a good idea to lower heat slightly when you turn the goose for the first time, and to cover it loosely with a piece of aluminum foil to keep it from drying out.

After 2 hours, test the goose for doneness by pricking the fleshy part of one of the legs with a fork. If the juice runs a clear amber color, the bird is done.

carving and serving the goose

Using poultry shears, cut around the breast, then remove it. Scoop out the apple stuffing and place in a warmed bowl. Cut off the legs, separating the drumsticks from the second joints. Slice the breast meat as well as the meat from the second joints. Arrange the slices and drumsticks on a heated metal platter.

Spread the chicken liver butter on the reheated canapés and top with spoonfuls of apple stuffing. Place the canapés around the platter.

Thoroughly degrease* the cooking juices. Taste and adjust seasoning, strain into a heated metal sauce bowl.

Suggested accompaniments:
Chestnut Purée,* Mushroom Purée,* or Sorrel Purée* followed by a salad of curly endive or escarole.

DUCK *Canard*

TRANSLATOR'S NOTE: *In the United States there is only one kind of commercially raised duck—the white Peking. These ducks, or ducklings, as they are commonly called, may be cooked in the same manner as the famous French ducks: the Rouen duck, the Nantais duck, and the larger Barbarie duck. Unless you live near a duck farm, your duck will undoubtedly be frozen and ready to cook. To thaw, place the duck on a board in the kitchen. Cover it with a quadruple thickness of paper towels, patting and turning it around from time to time. When the duck is supple, rub it dry with a kitchen towel inside and out.*

French people prefer ducks a little on the rare side; they like the juices to run very slightly pink when the fleshy part of a leg is pricked, and consequently allow about 15 minutes of cooking time to the pound for a roasted or casseroled duck. Most Americans prefer a well-done bird, one whose juices run a clear amber color. To achieve this, you must allow at least 25 minutes of cooking time to the pound. But beware of overcooking: an overdone duck is a pathetic, dry thing. Whether you cook a duck the "French" way or the "American" way, always begin testing for doneness a little before estimated cooking time.

In the following recipe we have adhered to Mme. Bertholle's French timing. It is only a matter of simple arithmetic to increase the time. Her method does tend to produce a juicier duck (and not the least bit "bloody"), so why not try her way?—you might become a devotee!

Since ducks raised in the United States come ready-to-cook, there is not much to be done to prepare them for cooking. If there are any hairs or pinfeathers, singe them off. Check to see that all loose fat has been removed from the body cavity, and that the fat glands from the base of the tail have been cut out.

The French method of carving a duck is different from the usual American way. After the legs—both drumsticks and second joints—have been cut off, the breast meat is removed, first on one side of the wishbone, then on the other, and cut diagonally into thin slices (escalopes) or thin strips (aiguillettes). If the duck must wait for any length of time before serving, it is better to remove the breast meat, cover it with hot cooking juices, and keep in a warm place before slicing.

Roast Duck with Glazed Turnips and Glazed Onions
Canard rôti aux navets et aux oignons

This is the basic recipe for roast duck.

FOR 4 PEOPLE

1 3-pound ready-to-cook duck
salt
freshly ground pepper
the duck liver (optional)
2 tablespoons butter plus 1 tablespoon for buttering the roasting pan
¼ cup hot water for deglazing
1 recipe Glazed Turnips,* made ahead
1 recipe Small White Glazed Onions,* made ahead
Preheat oven to 350° F.

Salt and pepper the inside of the duck. Put the liver and 1½ tablespoons of the butter, cut in pieces, in the body cavity. Soften ½ tablespoon of butter and rub it on the outside of the duck. Truss. Place in a buttered roasting pan, breast side up.

Brown the breast for 15–20 minutes.[1] Turn the duck on its side, season with salt and pepper, and brown for 10–15 minutes more, basting with the pan juices. Reduce oven heat to 300°, turn the duck, add a little salt and pepper, and brown for another 10–15 minutes. If more cooking is required, turn the duck breast side up, cover with aluminum foil, and continue cooking until done.

Deglaze* the cooking juices with the ¼ cup of hot water. Strain, degrease,* adjust seasoning, and pour into a warmed sauce bowl.

Carve the duck (see the note at the beginning of the duck section), place on a warmed platter, and garnish with the reheated glazed turnips and glazed onions.

*An excellent accompaniment for the duck is a dish of Green Peas, French style.**

Casserole-Roasted Duck   *Canard poêlé*

For this recipe you will need an oval heavy-bottomed enameled casserole.

FOR 6 PEOPLE

a 3½–4 pound ready-to-cook duck
salt
freshly ground pepper
peanut oil and butter for the casserole plus a little in reserve
¼ cup hot water (more if necessary)
1 small bunch watercress for garnish
Preheat oven to 345° F.

Salt and pepper the inside of the duck. Truss. Place in a well-oiled and buttered casserole, breast side up, for about 10–15 minutes[1] or until golden brown. Turn the duck on its side, baste with pan juices, season with salt and pepper, and brown for another 10–15 minutes. Turn and repeat the process, adding a little oil and butter if necessary. Add the boiling water, turn the duck on its back, salt and pepper the breast, and fit a piece of aluminum foil loosely on top. Cover the casserole, lower heat to 325°, and let the duck cook in its own steam for 15–20 minutes. Check from time to time to see if there is enough liquid in the casserole, adding more hot water if necessary.

---

[1] Remember, this is French cooking time.

When the duck is done, carve (see the note at the beginning of the duck section), and arrange on a warmed platter. Decorate one end with the watercress.

Accompany the duck with Sautéed (new) Potatoes* or Stuffed Mushrooms* and with Glazed Turnips.*

Braised Duck   *Canard braisé*

Older, and usually tougher, ducks always used to be braised. Braising was also the most common way of cooking fruit-garnished ducks. The method is rarely used today because it takes so much longer than roasting. But it is still the best way to cook a large duck.

FOR 8 PEOPLE

braising ingredients

Make this stock the day before.

3 tablespoons lard or 3 tablespoons peanut oil
2 carrots, cut in pieces
2 medium-size onions, quartered
1 leek white, coarsely chopped
1 stalk celery, coarsely chopped
2½–3 tablespoons flour
salt
freshly ground pepper
2 pinches of sugar
¼ pound cooked ham, diced
the neck of the duck, cut in 3 pieces
1 double recipe of Chicken Bouillon,* using 9–11 cups water

duck and ingredients for cooking it

a 4½–6 pound ready-to-cook duck, with neck cut off
a coating of butter and 2 tablespoons peanut oil for the braising pan
1½–2 tablespoons softened butter
salt
freshly ground pepper

final ingredients

4½ cups braising liquid (6 tablespoons set aside)
1 tablespoon tomato paste
1 clove garlic or 2 shallots, squeezed through a garlic press
1 *Bouquet garni classique**
Preheat oven to 350° F.

preparing the braising ingredients

Turn oven to broil position.

Heat the fat in a large cast-iron sauté pan, add the vegetables, and stir-cook until they begin to color. Sprinkle with flour, mix with a wooden spatula, and place under the broiler for 1 minute. Remove from the broiler, season with salt and pepper, sprinkle on the sugar, and replace under the broiler for 3 minutes, by which time the mixture will be nicely browned.

Remove the sauté pan from the oven, add the ham and pieces of duck neck, and beat in the heated chicken bouillon. Set the sauté pan over medium heat until it begins to bubble, then transfer the ingredients to a large heavy-bottomed enameled casserole and simmer, uncovered, for 45–60 minutes. Strain into another heavy casserole, using a fine strainer and pressing the solid matter with the back of a spoon in order to extract all the juices. When the fat rises to the surface, degrease* carefully with a spoon.

braising the duck

Butter a heavy casserole with a tight-fitting cover, add a coating of butter and 2 tablespoons of oil. Daub the breast and wings of the duck with the softened butter, place in a casserole breast side up. Brown the breast, basting at least once with pan juices, and season with salt and pepper. Turn the duck on its side, basting once or twice, until brown, add a little salt and pepper, turn the duck on its other side, and repeat the process. The browning process should take 30–40 minutes.

Remove the casserole from the oven, tilt it and spoon off fat. Add the hot braising liquid, tomato paste, and garlic or shallots. The duck should be about half covered with liquid. Bring to a simmer on top of the stove, add the *bouquet garni,* fit a piece of aluminum foil on top, cover, and place in the oven. Cook for at least 45–50 minutes, testing for doneness as in the note at the beginning of the duck section.

Transfer the duck to a board, let it rest for a few minutes, then carve (see the note in the duck section). Place the carved duck on a heated metal platter.

Strain the braising liquid into a large saucepan and degrease.* Taste and adjust seasoning. If you want to add a little "dash" to the sauce, stir in 3–4 tablespoons of heated cognac flamed in a ladle.

Place the pieces of duck, breast meat thinly sliced, in the sauce, heat through, and replace on the metal platter.

suggested garnishes for this dish

    20–24 small Glazed Turnips,* made ahead
    18–20 Small White Glazed Onions,* also made ahead

Reheat the garnishes (along with their cooking juices) in the reserved 6 tablespoons of braising liquid.

In winter, Braised Chestnuts or Chestnut Purée* can be used as accompaniments.*

The following recipe is my simplified version of a much more complicated one. I believe it will please all those who prefer the modern, lighter style of cooking. It is particularly adaptable to all fruit-garnished ducks.

Roast Duck with Jus Lié   *Canard rôti avec un jus lié*

Both the duck and the fruit garnish can be prepared entirely in advance. See recipes that follow for possible fruit garnishes and their preparation. The duck is roasted whole, then carved; the *jus lié* is added to the cooking juices and bound with *beurre manié*.

The fruit garnish can be prepared while the duck is roasting. Refrigerated, both duck and garnish will keep for at least 24 hours.

After roasting the duck as in the basic recipe, cut off the wings and legs, separating the drumsticks and second joints. Remove the breast meat on both sides of the wishbone, but do not slice at this time. Place the duck pieces in a heavy-bottomed enameled casserole, spoon a little of the deglazed pan juices over them, cover, and refrigerate.

making the jus lié   MAKES ABOUT 1½ CUPS

> the cooked carcass of the duck (after carving), cut in pieces with poultry shears
>
> butter for greasing the sauté pan
>
> the raw neck of the duck, cut in 3 pieces
>
> 1 sprig of fresh or dried thyme
>
> a small piece of bay leaf
>
> 2 cups Chicken Bouillon* or 2 cups hot water in which a chicken bouillon cube has been dissolved
>
> ¼ cup hot water for deglazing roasting pan juices
>
> 1 recipe *Beurre manié** made of 1 heaping tablespoon flour and 1 tablespoon butter
>
> 2 tablespoons warmed cognac flamed in a ladle (optional), or 4 tablespoons red port wine or Madeira (optional)

Put the cut-up carcass and pieces of duck neck in a well-buttered sauté pan. Add the herbs and stir-cook until brown. Pour in the chicken bouillon and simmer gently, covered, for about 25 minutes.

Strain the stock into a heavy saucepan. Deglaze* the pan juices in the roasting pan, add to the liquid in the saucepan. Cook gently for a few minutes until slightly reduced, then beat in the *beurre manié* little by little until it has been completely absorbed.

Taste and adjust for seasoning. Now is the time to add the flamed cognac or one of the two wines. If you use either of these additions, reduce the *jus lié* a minute or so to concentrate the flavors.

Pour some of the *jus lié* over whatever fruits you have prepared for garnishing the duck, and spoon the rest over the duck in the casserole.

serving the duck

Place the duck in the casserole over low heat for about 10 minutes (until heated through), leaving the cover off for the last 5 minutes.

Cut the breast meat into thin slices or strips, arrange on a warmed platter along with the rest of the duck pieces. Surround with the fruit garnish. Spoon a little *jus lié* sauce over both the garnish and duck and serve the rest in a small sauce bowl.

Duck with Olives *Canard aux olives*

In this delicious, well-balanced dish, which needs only the simplest of accompaniments, the duck can be roasted ahead (see Roast Duck with glazed Turnips and glazed Onions*) or casseroled (Casserole-Roasted Duck*). Just before serving, it is heated in the olive-garnished sauce.

FOR 5–6 PEOPLE

a 4½ pound ready-to-cook duck, neck cut off
¼ cup hot water for deglazing pan juices
1 recipe of *jus lié* (from Roast Duck with Jus Lié*)
1½ cups green lives
2 tablespoons butter for cooking mushrooms
⅓ pound mushrooms, washed, patted dry, and cut in quarters
a few drops of lemon juice
2 thin slices cooked smoked tongue cut in small pieces
2–3 tomatoes, peeled, seeded, and cut in fine strips
1 cup tomato juice, reduced to about ½ cup
1 sprig of fresh or dried thyme, added to tomato juice while it is reducing
1 shallot, squeezed through a garlic press
a small pinch of curry powder
a pinch of sugar
freshly ground pepper
1 jigger red port wine
3 tablespoons warmed cognac flamed in a ladle
salt if needed

Roast or casserole the duck. When done, transfer to a board and let it rest for 10 minutes. Degrease* the pan juices and deglaze* with the ¼ cup of hot water. Strain and set aside. Carve the duck (see the note in the duck section) and place the pieces in a clean casserole. As soon as the *jus lié* sauce is made, pour a ladleful over the duck pieces to prevent them from drying out. Cover the casserole.

Blanch* the olives in a small enameled saucepan for 5–7 minutes to rid them of excess salt. Do not refresh them in cold water, as this would harden them.

Heat the butter in a small skillet add the mushrooms, sprinkle with a few drops of lemon juice, and sauté rapidly for 5–6 minutes, turning the pieces with a wooden spatula. Add ½ tablespoon of hot water if the mushrooms seem dry, place them in a bowl, and set aside.

Heat the *jus lié* sauce, add the olives, tongue, tomato, reduced tomato juice, thyme, shallot, curry powder, sugar, and pepper. Stir in the port wine and flamed cognac, simmer, stirring, for 5 minutes. Add the mushrooms and their juice and simmer for another 5 minutes, stirring gently. Taste and adjust seasoning. Now is the time to add salt if necessary.

serving the duck

Pour the sauce over the pieces of duck in the casserole and heat through slowly. Taste again for seasoning. Transfer to a warmed deep serving dish and serve immediately.

Accompany the duck with Creole Rice* or buttered noodles.

Roast Duck with Pineapple   *Canard à l'ananas*

The slightly tart flavor of pineapple goes very well with duck. In this recipe, the *jus lié* is flavored with dark rum.

FOR 4–5 PEOPLE

a 4–4½ pound Roast Duck*
roasting pan juices, deglazed* with ¼ cup hot water
1 cup *jus lié* of duck (see Roast Duck with Jus Lié*)
1 teaspoon arrowroot dissolved in 2 teaspoons water
4 tablespoons warmed dark rum to be flamed in a ladle
1 cup pineapple juice
2 tablespoons lemon juice
1 rounded tablespoon butter
8–10 slices canned pineapple, each slice cut in half
1 tablespoon brown sugar

Turn oven to broil position.

Prepare the roast duck.

(NOTE: *If the duck is cooked ahead, do not slice the breast meat; place the two breast sections, along with the other duck pieces, in a casserole, spoon a little juice over them, and cover the casserole.*)

Deglaze* the pan juices with the hot water and strain into a bowl.

Prepare the *jus lié* and strain the stock into a heavy saucepan. Add the deglazed pan juices. Stir in the arrowroot binding, flame the rum, and add it to the saucepan. Simmer, stirring, for 5 minutes. Remove from heat.

making the pineapple garnish

Pour the pineapple juice into an enameled saucepan and reduce to ½ cup. Stir in the lemon juice and set aside.

Heat the butter in a large sauté pan, add the pineapple slices and sauté them, turning, for 2–3 minutes. Sprinkle the slices with the brown sugar, place under a hot broiler (not too close to the heat) until sugar is slightly caramelized. Remove the pan, transfer the pineapple slices to a side dish, and keep warm.

Deglaze* the sauté pan with the pineapple and lemon juice and pour into the saucepan of *jus lié* sauce.

serving the duck

Slice the breast meat, arrange on a heated platter along with the other pieces of duck. Surround with the pineapole slices. Spoon a little reheated sauce over the duck and serve the rest in a warmed sauce bowl.

*Accompany the dish with steamed rice or Creole Rice.**

Duck with Peaches   *Canard aux pêches*

Of all the duck and fruit combinations, this one is my favorite. Big yellow peaches add an inimitable flavor; the sauce is heightened with lemon peel and seasoned with pepper and coriander seeds. Good quality canned peaches may be substituted when fresh ones are unobtainable.

FOR 6–7 PEOPLE

2 3½-pound Roast Ducks,* carved and placed in a covered casserole for
    reheating

sauce ingredients

MAKES ABOUT 2 CUPS

6–8 firm large yellow peaches
2 thin strips lemon rind, each about 2 inches long
2 tablespoons sugar
12 peppercorns
12 coriander seeds
degreased* roasting pan juices (using ¼ cup hot water)
1 teaspoon arrowroot dissolved in 2 teaspoons water

making the sauce

Wash and dry the peaches. Place them whole and unpeeled in an enameled saucepan. Cover with water, add the lemon rind, sugar, peppercorns, and coriander seeds, poach for 15–20 minutes. The peaches should remain whole and firm. Let them cool in the liquid, then strip away the skin and cut them in half, discarding the stones. Place in another saucepan and set aside.

Strain the poaching liquid into a saucepan and reduce to about 1 cup. Add the degreased roasting pan juices, stir in the dissolved arrowroot, place over low heat, and simmer until the sauce is slightly bound.

Pour a little sauce over the saucepan of peaches and the rest over the casserole of duck. Reheat just before serving.

serving the duck

Arrange the duck pieces and sliced breast meat on a warmed platter and place the peach halves around the edge. Spoon a little sauce over both peaches and duck, serve the rest in a heated sauce bowl.

Accompany with Creole Rice* or wild rice, along with Green Peas, French Style* garnished with small Braised Lettuce.*

Roast Duck with Preserved Limes
Canard rôti aux citrons verts confits

Remove the cloves from 2 Limes preserved in Olive Oil.* Slice the fruit with a fluting knife and take out the seeds and membranes.

Place the Roast Duck* on a platter and arrange the lime slices on both sides of it. While you are roasting the duck, baste it from time to time with the aromatic lime oil.

Duck with Lemon   *Canard au citron*

The flavor of lemon makes a pleasant change from orange-flavored duck.

FOR 6 PEOPLE

3 lemons
salt
freshly ground pepper
1 3¾–4½ pound ready-to-cook duck
1 tablespoon butter
the liver of the duck, salted, peppered, and doused with a few drops of
    cognac (optional)

    2 lumps sugar
    2 tablespoons wine vinegar
    1 cup *jus lié* (see Roast Duck with Jus Lié*)
    the reserved lemon juice and blanched lemon rind
    3 tablespoons red port wine or dry sherry
    2–3 tablespoons warmed armagnac or cognac
    Preheat oven to 350° F.

preparing the lemons and duck

Cut the rind from 2 of the lemons as thinly as possible. Cut into narrow strips 1 inch long with scissors and blanch in boiling water for 5 minutes. Refresh in cold water and pat dry.

Salt and pepper the inside of the duck. Push in half the lemon rind, the butter, and the liver if you are using it. Truss.

Remove the pith from the peeled lemons, cut them into thin segments, seed, and set aside. Squeeze the juice from the third lemon and set aside.

Roast and carve duck as in the basic recipe, cover with a little pan juice, and keep warm.

making the sauce

In a stainless steel or copper saucepan, cook the lumps of sugar and vinegar together, stirring, until caramel has formed. Dilute with a little heated *jus lié*, scraping the bottom of the saucepan with a spatula. Add the rest of the *jus lié,* the reserved lemon juice, and strips of rind. Stir in one of the wines. Flame the armagnac or cognac and add to the contents of the saucepan. Remove from heat and degrease* thoroughly. Add the lemon segments and place over low heat for a minute or so, stirring carefully so as not to cause them to disintegrate.

Arrange the sliced breast meat and pieces on a heated metal platter. Spoon some of the sauce on top and pour the rest in a warmed sauce bowl.

Accompany the duck with Creole Rice and Corn Croquettes,* or with Creole rice and Zucchini Fritters.**

Duck with Orange Glaze   *Canard glacé à l'orange*

A cold dish consisting of partially boned roast duck painted with glaze that tastes of the very essence of orange.

This delicate dish can be served after a hot first course or as part of a buffet dinner . . .

FOR 8 PEOPLE

2 4½-pound Roast Ducks,* set aside whole to cool (chop off the necks before roasting the ducks, for making chicken stock)

ingredients for the glaze

4½ cups Chicken Stock* made with necks of ducks cut in 3 pieces and 2 chicken giblets (may be done ahead)
¼ chicken bouillon cube
¼ cup Madeira wine
2 envelopes unflavored gelatin dissolved in a little chicken stock

orange peel addition to glaze

6 medium-size oranges with perfect skins
2 cups liquid glaze
½ cup orange juice
2–3 lumps sugar
2 tablespoons wine vinegar

making the glaze

Heat the chicken stock, adding the piece of bouillon cube. Stir in the Madeira and dissolved gelatin. Test for glaze consistency by putting 3 tablespoons of the liquid on a saucer and placing on the top shelf of the refrigerator for 6 minutes. If the glaze does not set, reheat the stock and add a little more gelatin. Remove 2 cups of the liquid glaze and set aside.

preparing the orange addition to the glaze

Using a vegetable peeler, peel the oranges as thinly as possible. Avoid cutting into the white of the peel. Cut the peels into fine strips about 1 inch long with scissors. Squeeze the juice out of as many of the peeled oranges as it will make ½ cup orange juice.

To rid the strips of orange peel of any bitterness, place them in a saucepan, cover with cold water, bring to a boil, and strain. Refresh the peel with cold water.

Place the orange peel in a heavy-bottomed enameled saucepan, add the reserved liquid glaze and the orange juice. Simmer, covered, stirring frequently, for 40–45 minutes until the peels are tender and have a frosty, candied appearance.

In another saucepan stir-cook the lumps of sugar and vinegar until a caramel has formed. Dilute the caramel immediately with a little reheated liquid glaze, scraping the bottom of the pan with a spatula. Pour this mixture into the orange peel and syrup, stir, and add to the liquid glaze. Taste to see if the glaze is too sour or too sweet. It may be necessary to add a pinch of sugar or a few drops of lemon juice. A tablespoon of Madeira and a little pepper may also be added, depending on your taste. Place the glaze in the refrigerator until it has the consistency of thick syrup.

preparing the duck

Cut the legs and wings from the ducks. Divide the legs into drumsticks and second joints. With poultry shears cut around each duck and remove the entire breast along with the breastbone. Trim the carcass and place it, hollow side down, on an oval platter.

Bone the second joints and wings and cut the meat into slices. Leave the drumsticks intact. Remove the bones and cartilage from the breast meat and cut into strips (*aiguillettes*) or slices (*escalopes*). Arrange the slices on the carcass of the duck and place two drumsticks at each end of the platter. Brush the duck slices on the carcass and the drumsticks with a layer of glaze and refrigerate. Repeat this process two or three times, refrigerating after each coating of glaze.

The platter may be garnished with Chicken Livers in Aspic* made with orange glaze or chicken liver mousse with port wine* molded in small ramekins with orange glaze.

Salmis of Duck *Salmis de canard*

The principle of *salmis* is this: poultry (duck in the present recipe) or game birds are oven- or spit-roasted until just barely tender, so they retain all their juices. The small bones of the carcass and the neck, cut in pieces, are used in making the salmis sauce.

FOR 6 PEOPLE

a 4½-pound ready-to-cook duck, neck cut off
salt
freshly ground pepper
2–3 tablespoons peanut oil
1 tablespoon softened butter
oil for the roasting pan
¼ cup warmed cognac, flamed in a ladle

ingredients for finishing the salmis sauce

1 tablespoon butter
1 tablespoon peanut oil
1 recipe of Brown Sauce with *Mirepoix** with the following changes in
    proportions:
    2 tablespoons butter and 1 tablespoon peanut oil
    3½ tablespoons flour
    3 cups red Burgundy wine
    3 cups Chicken Bouillon,* degreased*
8–10 triangular Croutons,* reheated, for garnish
Preheat oven to 340° F.

preparing and roasting the duck

Salt and pepper the inside of the duck, coat the outside with oil and rub the breast with the softened butter. Place the duck, breast-side up in an oiled oven dish. Brown the breast for 15 minutes, turn the duck on its side, season with salt, and brown for 10–12 minutes. Repeat the process for the other side. Total roasting time should be between 35 and 40 minutes, or until the juice runs pale pink when the fleshy part of a leg is pricked.

Remove and bone the wings, legs, and breast. Do not slice at this time. Place the duck pieces in a heavy-bottomed enameled casserole and pour the flamed cognac over them. Grind a little pepper over the duck. Cover the casserole with parchment paper and set aside.

making the salmis sauce

Using poultry shears, cut all the small carcass bones and the neck into small pieces, place in a food mill set over a bowl. Work the blades backward and forward in order to extract all the juices and to crush the bones a little.

Heat the butter and oil in a large, heavy saucepan and add the bones, turning them with a wooden spatula until they begin to color. Stir in the bowl of duck juices from the bones, then the strained brown sauce. Simmer slowly, uncovered, for 30 minutes.

Strain the sauce through a fine strainer into a large, heavy-bottomed enameled saucepan. Let the fat rise to the surface and degrease.*

finishing the dish

Thinly slice the boned wings, legs, and breast. Heat the slices in the sauce, adding the juices from the casserole in which the duck pieces were waiting. Taste the sauce and adjust seasoning.

serving the salmis

Spread some sauce over the bottom of a heated, fairly deep metal platter. Place the sliced duck meat on top and spoon on the rest of the sauce. Put the reheated croutons around the edge of the dish.

This rich dish is best served with something simple such as Creole Rice* followed by a green salad.

Game

Different people hunt for different reasons. A nature lover may hunt as an excuse for spending an autumn day in the woods. A dog lover may hunt more for his dog's pleasure than his own. Some people go on hunting expeditions for the companionship they offer. And some, quite simply, hunt in the hope of bringing home some game for dinner. Perhaps the happiest of hunters is the one who combines all these pleasures.

Suggested pâtés, marinades, and sauces for game are given at the end of the section.

GAME BIRDS

Partridge (Perdreau)

TRANSLATOR'S NOTE: *The only true partridge in the United States is the rock partridge, sometimes known as the gray chukar* (Alectoris graeca chukar). *The name "partridge," however, is sometimes given to certain species of grouse and quail that are admirably suited to the two following recipes.*

Young partridges shot at the beginning of the hunting season do not have to be hung. There is almost nothing more delicious that a partridge shot on a sunny autumn morning and eaten, spit- or oven-roasted, the same evening.

Roast Partridge for Two on Canapés
Perdreau rôti pour deux sur canapés

For two people you really need two partridges—the season is too short for one to be miserly! But just supposing you had only one bird for two people . . . roast it, cut it in half with poultry shears, and serve each half on a canapé as an entrée.

For cooking the birds you will need a small round flameproof dish, preferably earthenware, just large enough to hold them. If you can, place a small rack on the bottom of the dish.

An alcohol lamp for singeing is also necessary. Singeing over a gas flame gives game birds a very unpleasant taste.

FOR 2 PEOPLE

1 recipe of Chicken Stock,* made of the heads and necks of the partridges, made ahead

2 young partridges, heads and necks cut off

the livers of the partridges

1 tablespoon cognac for moistening the livers

salt

freshly ground pepper

2 tablespoons butter plus 1–2 pats for the grape leaves

2 grape leaves

2 strips pork fat for barding, each no wider than 3 fingers

a little peanut oil and butter for greasing the roasting dish

4 rectangular Canapés,* sautéed in butter, made ahead, and reheated

1 recipe Wild Fowl Liver Butter* made from the partridge livers (may be made ahead and refrigerated until 15 minutes before using)

4 lemon quarters for garnish

2–3 tablespoons boiling water for deglazing the baking dish

Preheat oven to 370° F.

Make the chicken stock with the heads and necks of the partridges, set aside until ready to prepare the juice.

Pluck the partridges just before you are ready to cook them. If you pluck them before this, they will lose some of their juices and become dry. Draw the birds. Wipe off the livers, cut away and discard any greenish spots, and moisten with the cognac. Set aside.

Wipe out the cavity of each bird with a clean cloth. Singe birds over an alcohol lamp. Salt and pepper the insides of the partridges. Place a tablespoon of butter in each, sew up the opening. Lightly salt, pepper, and butter the grape leaves, place one over the breast of each bird. Wrap the barding fat around the birds over the leaves. Truss the partridges by tying two strings crosswise around each bird and knotting firmly.

roasting the partridges

Grease the roasting dish with oil and butter and place the birds on top of the rack, breast side up. Roast the partridges for about 25 minutes, turning the birds first on one side then on the other after about 10 minutes. Do not overcook them, for they will become dry and tough. Remember that the juices should run a pale pink when the partridges are cut.

Transfer the birds to a board. Do not remove the grape leaves and barding fat until just before cutting the partridges in half. Many people are extremely fond of the golden-brown grape leaves impregnated with partridge juices, so if you like, place them on the platter along with the birds.

serving the partridges

Spread the reheated canapés with the wild fowl liver butter and arrange them on a heated platter. Keep warm in oven, heat off, door open.

Remove the leaves and barding from the birds. Cut partridges in two with poultry scissors. Place half a partridge on each canapé, garnish the platter with lemon quarters (to be squeezed over the partridges) and the two vine leaves.

making the juice

Degrease* the cooking juices in the roasting dish. Deglaze* the dish with the boiling water. Bring to a boil, stirring and scraping the bottom of the dish. Strain into a small metal saucepan, then strain in the stock made from the heads and necks of partridges. Stir well, heat through, and pour into a warmed sauce bowl.

No accompaniment is necessary, though the partridges may be served with shoestring potatoes or potato chips, followed by a green salad.

Partridge with Cabbage   *Perdrix au chou*

TRANSLATOR'S NOTE: *The French word* perdrix *refers to an older bird, not a bird of the year, as is a* perdreau. Perdrix *may be mothers or fathers of* perdreaux (*young partridges*). Perdrix *are usually about fifteen months old and should be stewed or braised, since they tend to be relatively tough.*

In this recipe the *perdrix* and the cabbage are cooked separately, then reunited for a final assembling and cooking in a covered casserole.

FOR 6 PEOPLE

ingredients for braising the cabbage

> 1 large green cabbage
> butter for greasing the casserole
> 1 thick slice (about ¼ pound) fat bacon, simmered for 10 minutes then refreshed in cold water; cut half the bacon into thin strips for lining the casserole, dice the rest for adding to the cabbage
> 2 carrots, sliced
> 2 onions, minced
> 3–4 coriander seeds
> 3–4 juniper berries
> freshly ground pepper
> 4¼ cups heated Beef Bouillon* (set 3–4 tablespoons aside)
> 1 *Bouquet garni classique**
> ¼ pound Polish sausage cut in 2-inch pieces

partridge ingredients

> 3 adult partridges, plucked, drawn, and singed over an alcohol lamp
> salt
> freshly ground pepper
> 12 coriander seeds
> 12 juniper berries
> 4 tablespoons butter plus a few pats
> 3 slices pork fat, each no wider than 3 fingers, for barding the birds
> butter for greasing the casserole
> ¾ cup warmed cognac, armagnac, or Calvados
> 1 sprig of dried thyme
> 1 bay leaf
> partridge cooking juices
> 3–4 tablespoons boiling water
> 3–4 tablespoons Beef Bouillon* (see beef bouillon in the braising ingredients)
> salt only after tasting
> *Preheat oven to 350° F.*

preparing and braising the cabbage

Strip off the tough outer leaves, remove the core, and cut the cabbage into chunks, quartering the hearts. Wash in cold water. Blanch for 10 minutes in a large kettle of boiling salted water. Drain the cabbage thoroughly, set it on a board, and chop fine.

Butter a casserole and line it with the bacon strips. Place over medium heat and sauté the bacon lightly, turning each strip once. Add the carrots, onions, coriander seeds, juniper berries, and pepper. Stir-cook for a minute or so, add the chopped cabbage and heated bouillon. Bring to a boil, add the *bouquet garni,* lower heat, and simmer slowly for about 1½ hours. After 1 hour, add the diced bacon, the sausage, and the partridges (see below), cook together over low heat for ½ hour.

cooking the partridges

Salt and pepper the insides of the birds. Push a tablespoon of butter, 4 coriander seeds, and 4 juniper berries into each cavity. Sew up the openings and bard and truss the birds. Place them in a lightly buttered casserole, breast side up. Place in the oven, uncovered, for about 15 minutes, turning each one first on one side then on the other and adding a little more butter (1–2 pats).

Transfer the casserole to the top of the stove over medium-low heat. Add the warmed cognac, armagnac, or Calvados and set aflame. When the flames have died down, add a little more butter (2–3 pats) and the herbs. Cover and cook over low heat for 45 minutes to 1 hour, adding a little bouillon if necessary.

final cooking

Place the partridges in the casserole containing the cabbage. Fit a piece of parchment paper over the top of the casserole, cover, and simmer for ½ hour.

While the partridges and cabbage are cooking, strain the partridge cooking juices into a saucepan and carefully degrease.* Deglaze* the casserole with the 3–4 tablespoons of boiling water, pour into the saucepan. Bring to a boil, stirring, remove from heat, taste, and adjust seasoning. Set aside.

Transfer the partridges to a side dish, cover with aluminum foil, and keep warm.

Remove the pieces of bacon and sausage from the casserole of cabbage and place them in a small saucepan. Pour the reserved heated beef bouillon over them.

Reduce the liquid in the casserole of cabbage if necessary and discard the *bouquet garni.* Stir in the remaining 1 tablespoon of butter, heat through, and transfer the braised cabbage to a warmed shallow dish, slices of carrot well in evidence.

serving the dish

Cut the partridges in half with poultry shears, place on top of the cabbage. Garnish the dish with the drained pieces of sausage and bacon. Pour the heated cooking juices over the partridges and garnish, serve immediately.

PHEASANT (*Faisan*)

These days, pheasants are hung only until cold, or at most 24 hours. They should be hung by their feet in a cool, well-ventilated, shady place and protected against insects by screening or cheesecloth.

Preparing a Pheasant Brought in from the Field

Pluck the feathers from around the anus. Make a slit to enlarge the opening and draw out the insides.

If the liver is whole and healthy, grind a little pepper over it, place it in a bowl, and sprinkle it with a few drops of cognac. Cover and refrigerate. The liver can be used in making Wild Fowl Liver Butter.*

Many people "hang" or age game birds by wrapping them (after eviscerating) in paper and storing them in the bottom of the refrigerator. A young bird may be aged for 3 days in the refrigerator, an older one for 4–5 days.

Like partridges, pheasants should be plucked just before cooking.

Hen pheasants are better for roasting than cocks, being more tender and having a finer taste. Unless they are very young, cocks are better casseroled.

A hen pheasant weighs about 1¾ pounds and will serve 3 people. A cock usually weighs about 2 pounds and will serve 4 people.

Roast Pheasant *Faisane rôtie*

For roasting the pheasants use a heavy-bottomed enameled oven dish or a flameproof earthenware dish about 3 inches high and just large enough to hold the birds. If possible, put a rack in the dish.

FOR 6 PEOPLE

2   1¾-pound hen pheasants, eviscerated but not plucked
salt
freshly ground pepper
2 tablespoons softened cream cheese
2 strips pork fat, each 3 fingers wide, for barding
peanut oil and butter for the oven dish
8 rectangular Canapés* made ahead and reheated before using
1 recipe Wild Fowl Liver Butter* made ahead, using the pheasants' livers
    (see the preceding note on pheasant)
8 lemon quarters for garnish
1 small bunch watercress (optional)
3–4 tablespoons boiling water for deglazing juices
Preheat oven to 350° F.

Pluck the birds and singe them over an alcohol lamp. Salt and pepper the cavities and push 1 tablespoon of cream cheese into each bird. This is an old trick: the cheese will impart mellowness to the meat and cause it to swell in cooking. But do not exaggerate the use of the cheese! An overzealous friend of mine stuffed 2 tablespoons into each bird and then came to me wailing, "Half the cheese just stayed there!" I was not surprised. The pheasants were only able to absorb a small quantity of cheese—the rest formed a lump and did no good whatsoever.

Sew up the openings, bard the birds, and truss them.

roasting the pheasants

Spread oil on bottom and sides of the oven dish and cover with a generous coating of butter. Set the pheasants in the dish, breast side up. Roast for about 40 minutes, turning the birds first on one side then on the other. Toward the end of cooking time, prick the thick part of a leg with the point of a knife. If the juice runs pale pink, it is time to take the pheasants out of the oven.

serving the pheasants

Remove the barding and cut the pheasants into quarters with poultry shears.

Spread the reheated canapés with wild fowl liver butter and place a pheasant quarter on top of each. Arrange on a heated platter garnished with lemon quarters, to be squeezed over the pheasant, and, if you wish, the watercress.

Serve with the degreased* cooking juices, have been deglazed* with the 3–4 tablespoons of boiling water and strained into a warmed sauce bowl.

The classical accompaniment for roast pheasant is Chestnut Purée,* followed by a crisp salad of escarole or Belgium endive.

Casseroled Pheasant *Faisan poêlé*

For this recipe you will need an oval heavy-bottomed enameled casserole, just large enough to hold the pheasant. If possible, place a rack in the casserole. Serve the pheasant quarters on a bed of cooked apples, Normandy style. Simple and delicious.

FOR 4 PEOPLE

> a 2-pound cock pheasant, eviscerated but not plucked
> salt
> freshly ground pepper
> 1 tablespoon softened cream cheese
> 1 strip pork fat, 4 fingers wide, for barding
> peanut oil and butter for greasing the casserole
> 4–5 coriander seeds
> 4–5 juniper berries
> ½ cup cognac
> 2–3 tablespoons boiling water for deglazing the casserole
> 1–2 pats of butter
> 4 Canapés* made ahead and reheated before using
> 1 recipe of Wild Fowl Liver Butter* made ahead, using the pheasant's liver
>   (see the note on pheasant)
> 1 lemon, cut in quarters, for garnish

cooked apples, Normandy style

> 4–5 golden apples
> 1 jigger warmed cognac
> 1 tablespoon Calvados
> 1 tablespoon heavy cream
> *Preheat oven to 350° F.*

Pluck the bird and singe it over an alcohol lamp. Wipe out the cavity with a clean cloth, salt and pepper it, and push in the cream cheese. Sew up the opening, tie on the barding fat, and truss the bird.

Spread peanut oil then a coating of butter over the bottom and sides of the casserole, put the bird in, breast side up. Place in the oven, uncovered, and brown for 10–12 minutes. Add the coriander seeds and juniper berries, pour the cognac around the edges of the casserole. Baste the pheasant, turn it on its side for about 10 minutes, baste again, turn on its other side for about 10 minutes, and salt lightly. Turn the pheasant breast side up, cover with parchment paper and a casserole cover, and cook slowly until the pheasant is fork-tender (total cooking time 45–60 minutes, including browning). After the first half hour, reduce oven heat to 300°.

Transfer the pheasant to a board, still covered with paper.

making the juice

Degrease* the cooking juices and strain into a small saucepan. Deglaze* the casserole with the 2–3 tablespoons of boiling water and strain into the saucepan. Stir in the butter, heat through, and pour into a warmed sauce bowl.

serving the pheasant

Cut the bird into quarters with poultry shears. Spread the heated canapés with wild fowl liver butter, arrange them on a heated platter. Place a pheasant quarter on top of each. Garnish the platter with lemon quarters, to be squeezed over the pheasant.

preparing the apples

Peel, core, and quarter the apples. Simmer in a little water until tender but not reduced to a pulp. Place the apples on a heated metal platter, pour on the warmed cognac and set aflame. When the flames have died down, set the quartered pheasants on top of the apples. Stir the Calvados and cream into the pheasant juice and heat. Serve in a warmed sauce bowl.

The pheasant may be accompanied by Chestnut Purée,* Celery Root Purée,* or Braised Chestnuts.* Spiced apple purée* is another good accompaniment.

Braised Savory Cabbage* and Sauerkraut, Alsatian Style,* are also good with pheasant. Always cook these accompaniments separately so their flavor does not overpower the fine taste of the pheasant or cause the meat to become too soft.

Another time, garnish the pheasant with Corn Croquettes* and Grapefruit Fritters.*

Roast Pheasant with Pig's Foot Stuffing
Faisan rôti farci d'un pied de cochon

The gelatinous quality of the pig's foot imparts the same mellowness to the pheasant meat that cream cheese does in the partridge recipes.

FOR 4 PEOPLE

    1 medium-size pig's foot, not too fat, cleaned and prepared for cooking
    1 *Bouquet garni classique**
    a pinch of powdered thyme
    salt
    freshly ground pepper
    a few drops of cognac
    a 2-pound pheasant, eviscerated but not plucked

1 strip pork fat, 3 fingers wide, for barding
4 rectangular Canapés,* made ahead and reheated before using

Place the pig's foot in a kettle of cold water. Bring the water to a boil, add the *bouquet garni,* lower heat, and simmer for 2½ hours or until fairly tender (it will finish cooking inside the pheasant). Drain thoroughly, bone, and dice. Season with the thyme, salt, and pepper, sprinkle with the cognac. Set in a warm place.

Pluck and singe the pheasant. Wipe out the cavity with a clean cloth, salt and pepper it. Stuff the bird with the diced pig's foot, sew up the opening, tie on the barding fat, and truss the bird.

Roast the pheasant (as in Roast Pheasant*), in this case prolonging the cooking time for 10–15 minutes.

serving the pheasants

Cut the bird in quarters with poultry shears. Scoop out the stuffing and spread it on the heated canapés. Arrange them on a heated metal platter and set a quarter of a pheasant on top.

FURRED GAME

Lapin de Garenne (Wild Rabbit)

Wild rabbit is one of the most popular of all furred game. Its meat is light, tender, and delicate-tasting. Though it is not necessary to marinate a rabbit, it is often done. See suggested marinades at the end of the game section, especially Special Light Marinade for Wild Rabbit.*

Sautéed Wild Rabbit Chasseur   *Lapin sauté chasseur*

In this classical recipe the rabbit pieces are first sautéed, then simmered in a fragrant sauce garnished with mushrooms and diced bacon.

For preparing the dish you will need a large cast-iron sauté pan and a large heavy-bottomed enameled casserole with a cover.

FOR 6 PEOPLE

3 tablespoons butter

3 tablespoons peanut oil

2   1½-pound rabbits, skinned, cleaned, dressed, and jointed

2 tablespoons flour

butter for greasing the casserole

1 tablespoon shallot or onion, squeezed through a garlic press

1–2 cloves garlic, squeezed through a garlic press

¼ pound chunk of lean bacon, simmered for 10 minutes, refreshed in cold
water, and diced

salt

freshly ground pepper

2¼ cups dry white wine

2¼ cups hot Beef Bouillon* or Chicken Bouillon*

1 *Bouquet garni classique** with extra thyme

⅓ pound mushrooms, prepared as in Concentrated Essence of
Mushrooms*

1 tablespoon minced parsley

12 small round Croutons* made, if possible, from a long French loaf[1]

Preheat the broiler. After browning the rabbit pieces, preheat oven to 350° F.

Heat half the butter and oil in the sauté pan. Add the rabbit pieces and sauté
for 15 minutes. Sprinkle the rabbit with the flour, place the sauté pan under the
broiler for a few minutes, turning the pieces occasionally, until they are lightly
colored.

Transfer the rabbit to a buttered casserole, add the shallot or onion, garlic,
bacon, salt, and pepper. Stir well with a wooden spatula. Pour in the wine and
reduce by half. Add the hot bouillon, bring to a boil, and put in the *bouquet
garni.* Cover the casserole and place in oven for 35–40 minutes until the rabbit
is tender. About 10 minutes before the end of cooking, add the mushrooms
and their essence.

Remove the casserole from the oven, discard the *bouquet garni,* and transfer the casserole ingredients to a warmed shallow round dish. Sprinkle with
parsley and garnish the edge of the dish with the reheated croutons. Serve
immediately.

Accompany the dish with Steamed Potatoes or Creole Rice.**

[1] Triangular croutons made from white bread may be substituted.

Rabbit Stew   *Gibelotte de lapin*

The *gibelotte* is a light rabbit stew. Use the same ingredients and procedure as in the preceding recipe, substituting red Burgundy wine for the white.

SEE ALSO: *Minute Chicken with Tarragon,* a recipe that works equally well with rabbit.*

Saddle of Rabbit, Vouzeron Style   *Râble de lapin à la Vouzeron*

An old Sologne recipe just as it used to be made.
    For making the dish you will need a large heavy oval casserole, not too high, with a cover.

FOR 6 PEOPLE

2   1½–2-pound rabbits, skinned, cleaned, and dressed
3 tablespoons butter plus 2 tablespoons in reserve
3 tablespoons peanut oil
salt
freshly ground pepper
½ cup hot water for deglazing casserole (two times)
4–5 tablespoons minced shallot
¼ cup wine vinegar
a sprig of fresh or dried thyme
a sprig of fresh or dried savory
2 cups heavy cream
6–8 Croutons* made ahead and reheated before using (optional)
Preheat oven to 350° F.

Cut off the heads of the rabbits at the base of the neck, level with the shoulders. Chop off the legs with one stroke of a cleaver.
    Heat half the butter and oil in the casserole. Put in the 2 saddles and legs and brown them, turning, then turning again in 15 minutes, adding the remaining butter and oil little by little. When the pieces are golden brown, season them with salt and pepper and transfer them to a platter.
    Deglaze* the casserole with ¼ cup of the hot water, strain the liquid into a saucepan. Wash out the casserole.
    Heat the 2 tablespoons of reserved butter in the casserole and add the saddles. Sprinkle the shallot on and around them. Pour in the vinegar and add the herbs. Bring to a gentle boil, remove from heat, and stir in half the cream. Cover the casserole, set over moderate heat, and bring to a boil. Place the casserole in the oven and bake for 1½–1¾ hours, until the rabbit meat is

tender. Baste frequently with the reheated deglazing juice and, if necessary, a few tablespoons of hot water.

Remove the saddles and legs from the oven, transfer them to a board, and cut into good-sized pieces after boning the legs. Place the pieces on a heated metal platter, cover with parchment paper, and keep warm.

Deglaze the casserole with the remaining ¼ cup of hot water, strain the juices into a saucepan. Stir in the rest of the heavy cream, place over low heat until slightly thickened, stirring constantly. Remove from heat, degrease* the surface of the sauce, taste and adjust seasoning. Whisk the sauce a second or so before pouring over the rabbit pieces.

If you are using croutons, garnish the edge of the platter with them.

Poacher's Pot-au-Feu *Pot-au-feu du braconnier*

A modest theft . . . just enough for the poacher and his wife.

FOR 2 PEOPLE

a small ham butt (about ½ pound) plus water for desalting ham
9 cups water
a 1½–2 pound rabbit, skinned, cleaned, and dressed
3 carrots, cut in half lengthwise
2 onions, 1 stuck with a clove
2 large leek whites
2 turnips
1 stalk celery
5–6 cloves garlic
1 *Bouquet garni classique** with a sprig of fresh or dried rosemary
freshly ground pepper
4 slices bread, dried out in the oven

NOTE: *Do not add salt.*

Cover the ham butt with cold water and bring to a boil. Boil for 15 minutes, drain, and refresh in cold water.

Pour the 9 cups of water into a good-size kettle, add the ham butt, bring to a boil, lower heat a little, and cook for 20 minutes. Fit the rabbit into the kettle and boil for about 20 minutes, skimming constantly. Add the vegetables, garlic, *bouquet garni,* and pepper. Reduce heat and simmer gently until the rabbit is nice and tender, 2½–3 hours. If necessary add hot water—the rabbit should be kept just covered.

Transfer the rabbit to a board and cut it in pieces. Slice the ham butt. Place the vegetables in a warmed deep serving dish, arrange the rabbit pieces and ham slices on top. Keep warm. Degrease* the broth, reduce a little if necessary, and strain into a tureen garnished with the slices of dried bread.

Serve the meat, vegetables, and broth in warmed soup plates.

HARE

[TRANSLATOR'S NOTE: *True hare* (Lepus timidus) *does not exist in the United States. But any large wild rabbit can be substituted for these European hare recipes, which we will persist in referring to as "hare."*]

Roast Saddle of Hare with Cream   *Râble de lièvre rôti à la crème*

A simple and delicious way to prepare a tender young hare. After being skinned, cleaned, and cut (as in Saddle of Rabbit, Vouzeron Style*)[1] it is marinated two or three days, then roasted and served with a rich sauce based on cream.

For this recipe you will need an oval, heavy-bottomed enameled casserole, not too deep.

FOR 6 PEOPLE

saddle of a 5–6 pound hare (weight after dressing)
1 recipe of Marinade for Furred Game* or Dry Marinade* (at the end of
    the game section)
1 strip pork fat, 4 fingers wide, for barding
freshly ground pepper
peanut oil and butter for the roasting pan
¼ cup hot water or Beef Bouillon*
2 cloves garlic
a sprig of fresh or dried thyme
1 cup heavy cream
salt
8 rectangular Canapés,* made ahead and reheated before using

---

[1] In this recipe the saddle does not include the hind legs.

2–3 tablespoons hot water
4 tablespoons Tarragon Vinegar* (or wine vinegar)
1 teaspoon arrowroot dissolved in 1 tablespoon cold water
1 cup heavy cream
a few drops of lemon juice (optional)
Preheat oven to 350° F.

After marinating the hare, sponge it dry, and tie on the barding fat. Grind some pepper on the saddle and place it, back side up, in the oiled and buttered casserole, put in the oven, and brown the meat for about 20 minutes. Pour the ¼ cup of hot water or bouillon around the edge of the pan, add the garlic and sprig of thyme, and continue to cook for another 10 minutes. Begin adding the cream, 2 tablespoons at a time at regular intervals, until it is used up. Salt the hare and cook, counting about 15 minutes to the pound after browning, until the meat is tender and has a tendency to detach from the bone. Baste regularly with the golden-brown juice throughout the cooking.

About 20 minutes before the end of cooking time, cover the hare with aluminum foil and reduce oven heat to 300°.

When the hare is done, remove from the oven and transfer, still covered with foil, to a heated covered dish.

making the sauce

Degrease* the cooking juices in the roasting pan and deglaze* with the hot water and tarragon vinegar. Strain into a heavy saucepan. Beat the dissolved arrowroot into the cream and whisk into the juice. The addition of the arrowroot binding prevents the cream and pan juices from separating. Bring these ingredients to a boil over moderate heat, whisking constantly. Remove from heat, taste and adjust seasoning. If you wish, add a few drops of lemon juice at this time. Keep the sauce warm by placing it over a pan of hot water, heat off.

carving the hare

A roast saddle of hare must be carved with a fork and spoon "made of silver," as the headwaiter of a restaurant near the Madeleine explained to me. "If the meat comes in contact with any other metal, it immediately turns black. And cutting the saddle with a knife causes the juices to run out."

So, using a silver fork and spoon, detach the fillets from each side of the backbone. Then, still "forking and spooning," divide each fillet into 4 rectangular pieces.

serving the hare

Arrange the reheated canapés on a warmed large platter and place a piece of hare on each. Spoon a little sauce on top and serve the rest of the sauce in a heated metal sauce bowl.

Accompany the dish with Chestnut Purée.* If you want to be more sumptuous, serve Mushroom Purée* and Celery Root Purée* as well.

Jugged Hare *Civet de lièvre*

What distinguishes jugged hare from other dishes using *Sauce Civet* (Game Sauce*) is the addition of the reduced marinade to the sauce and above all the blood of the hare, which is used for binding. For this, of course, you must have a freshly killed hare and you must gather as much blood as possible. The hare's liver (if undamaged) is also an important element in the sauce. If fresh hare's blood is unavailable, the blood from two freshly killed chickens may be substituted. If this proves impossible, make a simple binding of the hare's liver, cognac, and *beurre manié* (given below).

For cooking the dish, you will need a large, heavy-bottomed enameled casserole.

FOR 6–8 PEOPLE

a 7-pound hare, skinned, cleaned, dressed, and jointed
1 recipe of Cooked Marinade for Venison*
4 tablespoons butter
4 tablespoons peanut oil
2 onions, cut in quarters
¼ pound packaged bacon, simmered for 10 minutes, refreshed in cold water, and diced
salt
freshly ground pepper
4 tablespoons flour
1 bottle red Burgundy wine
3 cups hot Beef Bouillon,* degreased,* plus a little cold bouillon reserve
stems cut from the mushroom caps used in garnish
3 shallots, squeezed through a garlic press
2 cloves garlic, squeezed through a garlic press
1 *Bouquet garni classique*
a pinch of curry powder
1 recipe of Mushroom Caps Sautéed in Butter*
1 recipe of Small White Glazed Onions*
8 triangular Croutons,* made ahead and reheated before using

simple binding without hare's blood

½ cup warmed cognac, flamed in a ladle
1 recipe of *Beurre manié** made with 1 tablespoon butter and 1 tablespoon flour
the hare's liver, prepared as in hare's blood binding, below (optional)

hare's blood binding

> 2 tablespoons butter plus 1–2 pats of butter
> the liver of the hare, cut in 4 pieces
> 4 tablespoons warmed cognac
> the blood of the hare
> 2 tablespoons vinegar if necessary
> *Preheat oven to 350° F.*

Place the pieces of hare in the bowl of marinade, cover, refrigerate, and allow to marinate for 3–4 days. Turn the pieces twice a day. Remove from the marinade and wipe dry. Strain the marinade into a saucepan and reduce by half. Set aside.

Heat half the butter and oil in the casserole, add the onions and diced bacon, and stir-cook until they are very lightly browned. Transfer to a plate covered with paper towels add the rest of the butter and oil to the casserole, and brown the pieces of hare, turning, for about 10 minutes. Season with salt and pepper.

making the civet sauce

Sprinkle the flour on the pieces of hare (*Roux Brun Fin**). Pour in the wine, simmer, and slightly reduce. Add the bouillon to cover, then the re-heated reduced marinade. Bring to a boil and skim until the liquid is clear. Compensate for the liquid removed in skimming by adding about 2 table-spoons of cold bouillon at each skimming. Put the onions and bacon pieces back in the casserole, add the mushroom stems, shallots, garlic, *bouquet garni,* and curry powder.

Fit a piece of parchment paper over the top of the casserole, cover, and bring to a boil on top of the stove. Place in the oven for 2 hours, until the hare is tender, checking every 30 minutes. Add more wine and bouillon if the level of liquid becomes too low. Lower the oven heat slightly if the liquid is simmering too hard.

While the hare is cooking, prepare the garnishes of mushroom caps sautéed in butter and the small white glazed onions. Set them aside.

finishing the sauce (without hare's blood)

Remove the pieces of hare from the sauce and place on a side dish. Strain the sauce into a saucepan, degrease,* and put back in casserole. Stir in the flamed ½ cup of cognac, then the *beurre manié.* If you are using the hare's liver, prepare it as described below and add to the casserole of sauce.

finishing the sauce (with hare's blood)

Heat the 2 tablespoons of butter in a small sauté pan and sauté the liver for 1–2 minutes, no longer. Add the warmed 4 tablespoons of cognac, set aflame,

---

shaking the pan back and forth. When the flames have died down, stir in 1 or 2 pats of butter. Place the liver in a blender and process at high speed for ½ minute, or put through a food mill using the finest disk. Set the remaining purée aside.

preparing the blood

If clots have formed in the bowl of blood beat in the vinegar with a fork and continue beating until the clots have dissolved. Strain the blood through a fine sieve into a Pyrex bowl. Slowly beat in 2 ladlefuls of hot *sauce civet.* When perfectly blended, whisk this mixture into the casserole containing the rest of the *sauce civet.* Add the liver purée. A good way to do this is to gather as much of the purée as you can on the tip of the whisk and mix it into the sauce until all the purée has been used. If the sauce seems to lack body, beat in the *beurre manié,* made with 1 tablespoon of butter and 1 tablespoon of flour.

assembling the civet

Put the pieces of hare back into the sauce along with the mushroom and onion garnish and heat through, not allowing the liquid to boil.

Place the *civet* in a warmed shallow serving dish, mushroom and onion garnish well in evidence, and decorate the edge of the dish with reheated croutons.

Suggested accompaniments: Steamed Potatoes* and Chestnut Purée.* Spiced Apple Purée,* lukewarm or cold, may also be served.

Noisettes of Hare on Canapés
Noisettes de lièvre sautées sur canapés

A delicate dish for true gourmets.
You will need a large, heavy sauté pan for cooking it.

FOR 4–6 PEOPLE

a 5½–6 pound hare, skinned, cleaned, and dressed
1 recipe of Special Light Marinade for Wild Rabbit* (at the end of the game section)
5–6 tablespoons butter
salt
freshly ground pepper
6 large round or rectangular Canapés,* made ahead and reheated before using

sauce ingredients

> the strained marinade
> 2 tablespoons heavy cream
> 2 tablespoons currant jelly
> 1 tablespoon butter
> freshly ground pepper

preparing the noisettes

Cut the hare as in Saddle of Rabbit, Vouzeron Style.* Remove the 2 fillets from the saddle (one on each side of the backbone). Cut off the legs and bone them. Holding the knife on the bias, carve 4 thick oval slices from each fillet (these are the noisettes). Still cutting on the bias, carve 2 thick oval noisettes from each leg. Marinate the noisettes for 1–2 hours. Drain well and pat dry.

Heat half the butter in a sauté pan and sauté the noisettes for 10–12 minutes, turning them occasionally and adding the rest of the butter little by little. Season with salt and pepper. Do not cook the noisettes more than 12 minutes in all, as overcooking would make them tough. They should remain juicy and slightly pink inside.

Place the reheated canapés on a warmed metal platter and put 2 noisettes on each. Keep warm.

making the sauce

Deglaze* the sauté pan with the strained marinade, strain into a saucepan, and degrease.* Stir in the cream and currant jelly, heat slowly, adding the 1 tablespoon of butter and grinding in a little pepper. Do not let the sauce boil. When the sauce is heated through, remove from heat and taste for seasoning. Whisk the sauce and pour it over the noisettes.

*Accompany the dish with Chestnut Purée.**

Sauce poivrade* *or* Sauce venaison* (*Game Sauce**) *can substitute for the sauce above, though neither of these is quite as light, and both take a good deal longer to make.*

Hare in Aspic, Alsatian Style
Lièvre en gelée à l'alsacienne

Serve this delicious cold dish on a golden autumn day. It can be prepared one or even two days in advance and kept in the refrigerator. The hare is braised in a highly seasoned mixture of assorted vegetables, Alsatian wine, beef bouillon, lemon slices, and various herbs and condiments. After boning, the pieces of hare are molded in their natural jelly.

For making the dish you will need a large, heavy-bottomed enameled casserole and a large round, not too deep mold.

FOR 6–8 PEOPLE

a 5½–6 pound hare, skinned, cleaned, and dressed

1 pound pork or bacon rind, simmered for 10 minutes, refreshed in cold water, patted dry, and cut in 2½-inch strips

peanut oil for greasing the casserole

3 carrots, sliced neatly

2 onions, sliced

1 whole onion stuck with a clove

3 slices celery root, diced

salt

freshly ground pepper

1 *Bouquet garni classique** to which a celery leaf has been added

3–4 slices lemon

3–4 coriander seeds

1 bottle dry white Alsatian wine

2 cups hot Beef Bouillon*

a few sprigs of fresh chervil, scalded, refreshed in cold water, and patted dry

½ envelope unflavored gelatin dissolved in warm water

Preheat oven to 350° F.

Cut off the head of the hare at the base of the neck, level with the shoulders. Chop off the legs with one stroke of a cleaver. Cut the back in large pieces and leave the legs whole.

Oil the casserole lightly and spread half the pork rind, fat side down, on the bottom. Place half the vegetables on top, on these place the pieces of hare and the legs. Season with salt and pepper. Push in the *bouquet garni* and distribute the lemon slices and coriander seeds here and there. Cover with the rest of the vegetables and top with the pork rind.

Place the casserole over moderate heat until the ingredients begin to steam. Pour in the wine, bring to a boil, and cook for 5 minutes. Pour in the bouillon, bring to a boil, cover the casserole, and place in the oven for about 3 hours, until the meat is tender and separates easily from the bones.

Transfer the pieces of hare to a board to cool. Strain the bouillon into a saucepan through a sieve lined with dampened cheesecloth. Taste and adjust seasoning. Degrease* with care but do not clarify the bouillon. Remove carrot slices from the sieve, pat dry, set them on a plate, and reserve.

Cool the bouillon completely and test for jelly consistency by placing a few spoonfuls on the top shelf of the refrigerator for 10–15 minutes. If the bouillon does not thicken, place the saucepan of bouillon over a large pan of hot water and heat through. Stir in the dissolved gelatin, cool the bouillon, and place in the refrigerator.

Bone the legs and pieces of hare. Cut the leg meat into long slices. These will be used to line the sides and to place on top of the mold.

When the jelly has the consistency of thick syrup, spoon a layer onto the bottom of the mold. Garnish with the carrot slices and the chervil leaves. Put the pieces of hare in the mold and arrange the slices of leg around the sides and on top. Pour in the rest of the syrupy jelly and place in the refrigerator until set (about 2 hours). The dish will keep up to 48 hours, refrigerated.

Unmold the hare onto a round serving platter and accompany with Belgian endive salad.

VENISON

The best way to prepare large cuts of venison is to lard the meat, marinate it for two or three days, then roast it, avoiding overcooking. It may be served with *jus lié* sauce made from the pan juices, or with any of the sauces included in this section.

Roast Saddle of Venison   Selle de chevreuil rôtie

FOR 10–12 PEOPLE

a 5-pound saddle of venison, boned and trimmed

10 thin strips bacon, simmered for 10 minutes, refreshed in cold water, and patted dry, for larding

1 recipe of Cooked Marinade for Venison*

bones and trimmings of the saddle

1 carrot, cut in 4 pieces

2 onions, quartered

2 tablespoons butter

4½ cups Beef Bouillon* (or bouillon made from cubes)

1 *Bouquet garni classique*

1 stalk celery

oil and butter for the roasting pan

salt

freshly ground pepper

sauce ingredients:

    1 jigger armagnac or cognac

    1–2 tablespoons wine vinegar

    the strained marinade, reduced to ¼ cup

    the strained bouillon, reduced to ⅔ cup

    2 tablespoons heavy cream

10 Oval Tartlets* (*barquettes*) made ahead and reheated before using

currant jelly or cranberry sauce for garnishing the tartlets

Preheat oven to 350° F.

Remove the sinews from the saddle and lard it by weaving the blanched bacon strips through the meat with the aid of a larding needle. Place the meat, bones, and trimmings in the marinade for two or three days, refrigerated. Turn the meat once or twice a day.

Remove the ingredients from the marinade and pat dry. Set the venison aside. Place the bones and trimmings on a dripping pan along with the carrot, onions, and butter. Place the pan in the oven and brown the ingredients, turning and basting, for about 15 minutes. Remove the dripping pan from the oven.

Heat the bouillon, transfer the dripping pan ingredients to a large, heavy-bottomed enameled saucepan, and pour the bouillon over them. Bring to a boil, add the *bouquet garni* and celery stalk. Lower heat and simmer for about 45 minutes.

Strain the bouillon through a sieve lined with dampened cheesecloth into another heavy-bottomed saucepan. Degrease*. Set over low heat and reduce to ⅔ cup.

roasting the saddle of venison

Spread a layer of oil and butter over a large heavy roasting pan, add the meat, and place in the oven. Roast the meat, basting it every 10 minutes, for 45–50 minutes. Turn the meat after about 25 minutes, seasoning with salt and pepper before and after turning. Do not overcook the meat unless you want it to be abominably tough. The juices should run rosy pink when the meat is carved.

Transfer the roasted saddle to a board and let it rest for about 15 minutes before carving.

making the sauce

Deglaze* the roasting pan with armagnac or cognac, vinegar, and the reduced, strained marinade and bouillon, stirring and scraping the bottom of the pan with a wooden spatula. Strain into a saucepan, degrease, and stir in the heavy cream. Heat through and adjust seasoning. Serve in a warmed sauce bowl.

serving the saddle of venison

Carve the meat in slices and place them on a heated metal platter. Garnish with the reheated tartlets filled with currant jelly or cranberry sauce.

Accompany the meat with Chestnut Purée,* Celery Root Purée,* and Spiced Apple Purée.*

Haunch of Venison with Master of the Hunt Sauce
Gigue de chevreuil, sauce grand veneur

FOR 6–8 PEOPLE

1 Roast Saddle of Venison (the preceding recipe), using a 3½–4 pound haunch, boned and trimmed

master of the hunt sauce (Sauce grand veneur)

2 cups strained venison bouillon (see the preceding recipe)
2 cups strained Cooked Marinade for Venison*
1 recipe Brown Roux Sauce*
a scant ½ cup red port or Madeira wine
4 tablespoons warmed cognac, flamed in a ladle
1–2 tablespoons heavy cream
freshly ground pepper

Follow the procedure in the preceding recipe for marinating, browning the bones and vegetables, and roasting the meat. Reduce cooking time to 40–45 minutes. Do not reduce the bouillon before making the sauce.

Pour the bouillon and marinade into a saucepan and simmer until reduced by half.

Make the *roux brun* and, off heat, stir it slowly into the bouillon. Place on low heat and simmer for 10–15 minutes, stirring more or less constantly.

Strain the liquid into a saucepan through a sieve lined with dampened cheesecloth. Off heat, whisk in the wine, cognac, cream, and pepper. Place the saucepan over low heat and whisk for 3–4 minutes. Taste and adjust seasoning, adding more pepper if you think the sauce needs a little heightening.

Roast Loin of Young Wild Boar *Carré de marcassin rôti*

TRANSLATOR'S NOTE: *You will not find wily, bad-tempered (but only when attacked) Sus scrofa (wild boar) scuffing through the woods in the United States. But frozen loins and other cuts are shipped in from Europe and can be found in shops specializing in "exotic" frozen foods, or even in some well-stocked supermarkets. Thaw the boar according to directions on the package.*

FOR 6–8 PEOPLE

1 recipe of Dry Marinade*
1 4-pound boned loin of wild boar
peanut oil for the roasting pan

5–6 coriander seeds
5–6 juniper berries
freshly ground pepper
salt
1 tablespoon butter or 1 tablespoon heavy cream
Preheat oven to 380° F.

Marinate the meat for 4–5 days. When the marinating process is over, pour into a bowl all the liquid that has accumulated in the parchment paper, set aside.

Spread a coating of peanut oil on the bottom and sides of a heavy roasting pan. Place the oil-impregnated meat in the pan and distribute the coriander seeds and juniper berries around it. Pepper the meat. Roast the meat allowing about 30–35 minutes to the pound. Turn the meat halfway through the cooking, adding salt and pepper before and after turning and lowering oven heat to 350° F. When the meat juices run clear, transfer it to a heated platter and keep warm.

Deglaze* the roasting pan with the bowl of reserved liquid from the marinade. Stir in the butter or cream. Strain into a saucepan, heat through, and pour into a warmed sauce bowl. Carve the roast into slices and serve immediately.

Accompany the roast boar with Celery Root Purée* and Spiced Apple Purée.*

GAME PÂTÉS

These elegant creations have a practical side, since they can be stored in the refrigerator for as long as two weeks. There is no better between-meal snack than a slice of hare or pheasant pâté eaten with a piece or two of crusty French bread and accompanied with a glass of good wine.

Shimmering in aspic, a pâté may be served as an original first course or even, more originally, as a savory ending to a grand dinner.

Pâté of Hare   *Terrine de lièvre*

To make the pâté, you will need a 10-cup oval terrine of flameproof earthenware or porcelain with a cover. An electric meat grinder will facilitate the work.

FOR 10–12 PEOPLE

sheets and strips of pork fat about ⅛ inch thick for lining the bottom and
    sides of the terrine
salt
freshly ground pepper
the heart, lungs, and liver of the hare
1 thick slice pork liver, cut in pieces
½ cup cognac plus a few drops in reserve
1½ pounds saddle of hare, cut in pieces
¾ pound sausage meat
¾ pound fresh pork fat
⅓-pound chunk of smoked ham, cut in pieces
1 teaspoon crushed coriander seeds
a pinch of curry powder
a sprig of dried thyme pulverized between the fingers
1–2 eggs
½ bay leaf
6–7 peppercorns
a sprig of dried thyme
sheets of pork fat for covering the pâté ingredients
flour and water paste for sealing the terrine
Preheat oven to 365° F.

lining the terrine

Place the sheets of pork fat on the bottom of the terrine and cut them to fit with the point of a knife. Then line the sides with strips of it, using enough so that it hangs over the outside edge of the terrine (they will be tucked in later). Salt and pepper the fat.

Marinate the heart, lungs, and liver, along with the pieces of pork liver, in the cognac for 20–30 minutes.

Bone the pieces of hare. Remove the ingredients from the cognac marinade and pat dry. Grind these, using an electric grinder if possible, along with the pieces of hare, sausage meat, fresh pork fat, and smoked ham. Place in a large bowl and knead. Season generously with salt and pepper, add the curry powder, crushed coriander seeds, and pulverized thyme. Then add the egg and knead vigorously, using both hands, until a smooth mixture is obtained.

NOTE ON TASTING RAW GAME PÂTÉ INGREDIENTS: *All conscientious cooks taste whatever they are preparing, but in the case of pâtés made from raw meat of game it is not advisable to taste the raw ingredients because they may be toxic. Here is a little trick I use:*

Heat a small amount of water in a saucepan. Lightly flour your hands and form a small ball of the pâté mixture. When the water boils, drop in the ball and cook it for 2 minutes. Remove from the water, cool slightly, and taste. With this method you will be able to adjust the seasoning without any danger. Remember: a pâté should be highly seasoned.

Place the pâté mixture in the terrine and press it down with the flat of your fists. Fold the overhanging barding fat over the pâté. Cut the remaining sheets of barding fat to fit the top of the terrine and lay them on.

Make a vent by sticking the point of a knife through the barding fat and pâté until it touches the bottom of the terrine. Place the bay leaf, peppercorns, and the sprig of thyme on top of the fat and sprinkle with a few drops of cognac.

Seal the terrine by using the thick paste of flour and water and forming it into a strip about 1½ inches wide. Mold this around the top edge of the terrine and set the cover on it, pressing firmly.

cooking the pâté

Place the terrine in a pan of hot water. Bring to a boil on top of the stove, then place the pan of water and terrine in the oven and bake for 1 hour 45 minutes to 2 hours. Check from time to time to see that the water is not simmering too hard. If the level gets too low, add some boiling water.

When the paste sealing of the terrine is good and brown, remove the terrine from the oven and place it on a rack to cool. Then place it in the refrigerator.

The pâté may be eaten after 2 days, but it is preferable to wait 3 or 4 days or even a week.

Aspic for a Terrine of Hare   *Gelée pour une terrine de lièvre*

If the terrine is to be eaten soon after cooking, it can be covered with aspic made from the bones of the hare.

    1 cup dry white wine
    1 cup water
    the bones of the hare
    1 carrot, sliced
    1 onion, sliced
    1 *Bouquet garni classique,** including a celery leaf
    ½ tablespoon unflavored gelatin dissolved in a little cold water
    2 small bunches of parsley

Pour the wine and water in a saucepan, add all the other ingredients except the gelatin. Strain into a bowl and place in the refrigerator until the jelly has the consistency of thick syrup.

preparing the terrine

Cool the pâté and, using 2 metal spatulas or 2 forks, transfer it to a board. Working carefully, scrape off all the fat and paste sealing that surrounds it. Wash and dry the terrine. Set it in the refrigerator for a few minutes to cool, then pour a layer of thickened jelly on the bottom. Put the terrine back in the refrigerator until the jelly has set.

Put the pâté back into the terrine; it will have shrunk during cooking, thus leaving space for the jelly. Pour the thickened jelly around and on top of the pâté. Refrigerate for 1–2 hours until set.

serving the pâté

Unmold the pâté onto a platter and slice. Decorate each end of the platter with a bunch of parsley.

Rillettes of Rabbit[1] *Rillettes de lapin*

Delicious spread on bread for a snack during a hunt . . . or for a picnic . . . You can also serve small earthenware pots of rillettes along with other hors-d'oeuvre.

You will need a large, heavy-bottomed enameled or stainless steel stewing kettle to make this recipe.

THIS MAKES ABOUT 8 POTS, EACH HOLDING 1 CUP

2 1½-pound saddles of rabbit
a 1-pound chunk of lean bacon, rind removed, cut in 4 pieces, simmered
      for about 20 minutes, then refreshed in cold water
½ cup water or Beef Bouillon* or Chicken Bouillon*
1–2 cloves garlic
1 *Bouquet garni classique**
2 cloves
a little freshly grated nutmeg
3–4 coriander seeds
3–4 juniper berries
1 pound lard or goose fat
salt

Cut each saddle into 4 or 5 pieces and place in the kettle. Distribute the pieces of blanched bacon among them. Add the water or bouillon, garlic, *bouquet garni,* cloves, nutmeg, coriander seeds, and juniper berries. On top, place the lard or goose fat. Cover the kettle. Simmer over low heat, stirring from time to time, for 3½ hours, until the rabbit meat is completely detached from the bones.

---

[1] Rillettes are a kind of rich pâté, usually made of pork products. This recipe is a highly original one.

Turn off heat and with a skimmer transfer the rabbit pieces to a large platter. When they are cool enough to handle, shred them into a heavy earthenware terrine, discarding all the bones, including the tiny ones embedded in the flesh. Grind the bacon pieces and add it to the terrine. Discard the *bouquet garni* and strain into the terrine the fat left in the kettle through a sieve lined with dampened cheesecloth. Twist and squeeze the cheesecloth the extract every bit of fat.

Work all these ingredients together with a heavy wooden spatula, employing a pestle from time to time. Taste and add salt if necessary. When the mixture is smooth, spoon it into earthenware pots. Let the rillettes rest until cool. Cover each pot with a round of waxed paper fastened with a rubber band and store in the refrigerator. Before serving, remove the layer of fat that has risen to the surface.

NOTE: *If a fine mixture is desired, put the rillette mixture through a food mill after the ingredients are worked together.*

Pheasant Pâté *Pâté de faisan*

FOR 10–12 PEOPLE

sheets and strips of pork fat about ⅛ inch thick for lining the bottom and
    sides of a 10-cup flameproof terrine
¼ pound raw chicken livers
the pheasant liver (if in good condition)
¼ pound prosciutto cut in pieces
3 tablespoons Madeira or dry sherry or dry vermouth
2½ pounds raw pheasant meat
¾ pound fresh pork fat
salt
freshly ground pepper
1 teaspoon crushed coriander seeds
a pinch of curry powder
a sprig of dried thyme, pulverized between the fingers
1–2 eggs
½ bay leaf
6–7 peppercorns
a sprig of dried thyme
sheets of pork fat for covering the pâté ingredients
flour and water paste for sealing the terrine
Preheat oven to 365° F.

Prepare the terrine with the pork fat as in Pâté of Hare.*

Marinate the chicken and pheasant livers and pieces of ham in the Madeira, sherry, or vermouth for 20–30 minutes.

Bone the pheasant pieces. Remove the ingredients from marinade and pat dry. Grind these, using an electric grinder if possible, along with the pieces of pheasant and pork fat. Place in a large bowl and knead. Season generously with salt and pepper, add the coriander, curry powder, and thyme. Then add the egg and knead vigorously, using both hands, until a smooth mixture is obtained.

For tasting the pâté mixture, see the note in Pâté of Hare. *

For concluding the recipe, follow the procedure after the note in Pâté of Hare. *

Wild Fowl Liver Butter   *Beurre de foies de gibier à plume*

Since the livers of wild fowl tend to be small, it is necessary to add chicken livers to the ingredients.

FOR 4 LARGE CANAPÉS *

3 tablespoons butter for sautéing the livers
2 chicken livers
2–3 partridge livers or 1 pheasant liver
2–3 tablespoons butter added to livers when they are put through the food
   mill
salt
freshly ground pepper

Follow the procedure for Chicken Liver Butter.*

MARINADES

Marinating game meat makes it pungent and tender without destroying its gamey taste. Keep in mind, however, that not all game meat is marinated—feathered game, for instance. Cooks belonging to the modern school of cooking do not recommend marinating tender young game.

It is advisable to use white wine for making marinades. Red wine tends to darken both meat and sauce.

The meat should not be completely immersed in the marinade. Turn it twice a day, basting it each time, using a wooden spoon. Most game meats are marinated for three to five days. Keep the marinating meat, covered, in the lower part of the refrigerator to avoid any danger of bacterial activity.

Use a porcelain, Pyrex, or glazed earthenware dish or bowl for marinating. Metal has a corrosive effect on the wine as well as the other marinade ingredients and will cause them to darken and to have a metallic taste.

ONE LAST POINT: *Salt is never added to marinade ingredients. The flesh of the game would absorb too much of it.*

Special Light Marinade for Wild Rabbit

This marinade recipe is enough for 1 rabbit (cut in pieces) weighing about 1½ pounds after skinning and cleaning. A rabbit this size will serve 3 people. For 2 rabbits, each weighing 1½ pounds, double the marinade recipe.

    ½ cup peanut oil
    1 jigger cognac
    juice of 1 small lemon or ½ large one
    a few crushed peppercorns
    a sprig of dried thyme
    4–5 sprigs of parsley

Mix these ingredients together, add the rabbit, cut in 6 or 8 pieces, and marinate for 1–2 hours. Pat the pieces dry before proceeding with cooking.

Marinade for Furred Game *Marinade pour le gibier à poil*

This marinade admirably suits a whole or cut-up hare, saddle of hare, or a large wild rabbit.

    1¼–1¾ cups white Burgundy wine
    ¼ cup wine vinegar or sherry vinegar
    1 carrot, sliced
    1 medium-size onion, sliced
    a sprig of fresh or dried thyme
    1 bay leaf
    1 clove
    1 clove garlic
    2 shallots, minced
    5–6 coriander seeds
    5–6 juniper berries
    a few peppercorns, crushed
    2–3 tablespoons olive oil

Mix these ingredients together. The marinade may be used as is or simmered for 20 minutes; in the latter case add about ½ cup of white wine. Let the marinade cool completely before using. See the following recipe for the procedure in marinating.

Cooked Marinade for Venison   *Marinade cuite pour venaison*

  1 bottle white Burgundy wine
  1¼ cups wine vinegar
  3–4 tablespoons olive oil
  1 carrot, sliced
  1 onion, sliced
  1 stalk celery or 1 slice celery root, diced
  4 sprigs of dried thyme
  2 bay leaves
  2–3 dried sage leaves
  a sprig of dried rosemary
  a sprig of dried savory

Mix these ingredients together and cook slowly for about 20 minutes. Cool completely before using.

Place the game in a large porcelain, Pyrex, or glazed earthenware bowl or dish. Add the marinade, cover with wax paper or a kitchen towel, and refrigerate, basting and turning the meat twice a day.

Before using the marinade for a sauce, strain it and recook it for a few minutes in order to make sure that all bacteria are destroyed.

Dry Marinade   *Marinade sèche*

An original and excellent marinade for all kinds of furred game.

For this recipe you will need a double thickness of parchment paper large enough to fold around the meat to be marinated.

  a generous amount of olive oil to grease the top side of the paper
  4–5 sprigs of dried thyme
  4–5 sprigs of dried rosemary
  4–5 sprigs of dried savory
  2 bay leaves
  5–6 peppercorns, crushed
  a pinch of curry powder
  3–4 slices seeded lemon
  2 cloves garlic, unpeeled
  2 small shallots, unpeeled

Oil the paper and spread half of the mixed ingredients on it. Place the pieces of game on top. Arrange the rest of the mixed ingredients on top of the game. Form the paper into a package, cover with a kitchen towel, and place in the bottom part of refrigerator for 3 days. Open the package carefully when ready to use, pour the accumulated juices into a bowl. Cover and place in the refrigerator until time to make the sauce.

SAUCES FOR ACCOMPANYING VENISON, BOAR, AND OTHER LARGE GAME ANIMALS

Sauce poivrade

A sauce based on *Mirepoix** and heightened with vinegar and dry white wine.

MAKES ABOUT 2 CUPS

1 tablespoon butter and 1 tablespoon peanut oil
⅛ pound lean bacon or boiled ham, diced fine
1 carrot, minced
1 onion, minced
1 stalk celery, diced
2 tablespoons minced shallot
¼ cup wine vinegar
½ cup dry white wine
1 recipe of Simple Brown Roux Sauce,* using only the first 2 ingredients
2 cups hot beef bouillon

Heat the butter and oil in a sauté pan, add the bacon or ham, the carrot, onion, and celery, and stir-cook for 3–4 minutes. Stir in the shallot and cook for a minute or so, not allowing it to color. Add the vinegar and wine. Reduce the liquid by half.

Using the lard and flour of the Simple Brown Roux Sauce, make the *roux* in a heavy-bottomed enameled saucepan. Off heat, beat in the bouillon. Place over medium heat, bring to a boil and add the *mirepoix* ingredients from the sauté pan. Lower heat, cover, and simmer for 35–40 minutes, stirring occasionally, until reduced to about 2 cups. Strain through a sieve lined with dampened cheesecloth, pressing against the ingredients with the back of a spoon to extract all the juices and flavors. Heat through, adjust seasoning, and pour into a warmed sauce bowl.

Roman Sauce *Sauce romaine*

1 recipe of Simple Brown Roux Sauce* (about 3 cups)
4 lumps sugar
4 tablespoons vinegar
⅓ cup currants
2 tablespoons warmed cognac, flamed in a ladle
¼ cup candied orange peel, minced
½ cup pine nuts
2 squares bitter chocolate
2 tablespoons water

Prepare the brown sauce and while it is simmering stir the sugar lumps and vinegar together over a low flame for a few minutes, until a caramel forms. Do not allow the caramel to harden. Stir the brown sauce into it, turn heat low, and simmer, covered, for about 35 minutes, stirring occasionally.

During this time macerate the currants in the flamed cognac until they are plump and soft, 15–20 minutes. Add these, along with the candied orange peel and pine nuts, to the sauce after it has been simmering 20 minutes. Dissolve the chocolate in the water over low heat and stir into the sauce.

Game Sauce   *Sauce venaison*

  1 recipe of *Sauce poivrade**
  2 tablespoons currant jelly
  2 tablespoons heavy cream
  freshly ground pepper

Make the *sauce poivrade* and stir in the jelly and cream. Heat through, stirring, season with pepper, and pour into a heated sauce bowl.

Cold Game Sauce   *Sauce venaison froide*

This is a fresh-tasting, highly seasoned sauce used to accompany cold game, especially venison. It is also excellent served with cold duck and cold roast ham.

ABOUT 2½ CUPS

  rind of 1 orange, finely shredded, scalded for 5 minutes, refreshed in cold
    water, and patted dry
  1 tablespoon orange marmalade
  2 tablespoons currant jelly
  1 tablespoon mango chutney
  1 tablespoon Worcestershire sauce
  1 teaspoon ketchup
  2 tablespoons warmed cognac, flamed in a ladle, or 2 tablespoons red port
  deglazed* juice (about ¾ cup) of a Roast Saddle of Venison*[1]
  salt
  freshly ground pepper

Put all these ingredients except the deglazed juices and salt and pepper in the top of a double boiler. Place over hot water, set the double boiler on medium heat, and stir in the deglazed juices until all ingredients are well blended. Add salt and pepper to taste. Cool the sauce, place in a jar, and cover. Stored in the refrigerator, the sauce will keep for 2 weeks.

[1] Use the deglazed juices of whatever kind of game you are preparing.

Meat

VEAL

Mixed Grill of Veal Scallops *Minutes de veau en mixed grill*

Thin veal scallops are brushed with marinade, grilled on top of the stove in a heavy cast-iron skillet, topped with herb or shallot butter, and surrounded with delicious garnishes. All the garnishes can be made ahead and reheated in the oven just before serving.

FOR 6 PEOPLE

marinade ingredients

> ½ cup peanut oil or olive oil
> 2 tablespoons lemon juice
> salt
> freshly ground pepper
> a sprig of fresh or dried thyme
> a small bay leaf or half a large one

garnish ingredients

> 1 double recipe of Herb Butter* or Shallot Butter,* made ahead and
>   refrigerated until 15 minutes before using
> 9 large Mushrooms Caps Sautéed in Butter* (minus the lemon juice)
> 9 Broiled Tomatoes*
> 6 slices packaged bacon, crisply fried and drained on paper towels
> 6 small pork sausages, sautéed until golden brown

other ingredients

> 6 veal scallops, cut very thin
> salt
> freshly ground pepper
> *Preheat oven to 400° F.*

Beat the marinade ingredients together in a bowl. Using a brush, coat the veal scallops with the marinade, then set aside on a large platter for 15–20 minutes.
    Prepare the garnishes while the veal is marinating.

Holding a scallop between thumb and forefinger, shake off excess marinade.

Heat the skillet and cook the scallops 2 or 3 at a time, 5–6 minutes on one side and 4–5 minutes on the other, seasoning with salt and pepper before and after turning. Keep them warm. When all of them have been cooked, arrange them on a heated metal platter and top with herb or shallot butter. Place the tomatoes and mushrooms at each end of the platter and the bacon and sausages along the sides. Place the platter in the oven for 2–3 minutes, then serve immediately.

Fricandeau of Veal with Sorrel *Fricandeau à l'oseille*

A delicious, old-fashioned dish that deserves to be revived every now and then. The long, slow braising process produces a rich sauce, thick and amber-colored. This is a dish for a special occasion.

For cooking it you will need a large heavy-bottomed enameled casserole with a tightly fitting cover.

FOR 6–8 PEOPLE

3 tablespoons peanut oil
1 large carrot, cut in pieces
1 large onion, coarsely chopped
¼ pound fat pork rinds, simmered for 10 minutes, refreshed in cold water,
    and diced
2 tablespoons butter plus 1 tablespoon creamed butter
a 3½–4 pound boned rolled roast of veal cut from the leg, larded and
    barded by your butcher
salt
freshly ground pepper
1¼ cups dry white wine
2¼ cups hot Beef Bouillon*
1 *Bouquet garni classique**
1 recipe of Sorrel Purée*
Preheat oven to 340° F.

preparing the meat

Heat the oil in the casserole, add the carrot, onion, and pork rinds, stir-cook for 2 minutes. Stir in the 2 tablespoons of butter, add the veal, and cook, turning it on all sides, for 10 minutes. Season lightly with salt and pepper. Pour in the wine and cook until slightly reduced. Add the beef bouillon, bring to a boil, and add the *bouquet garni*. (The meat should not be completely covered with liquid.)

Cut out a piece of parchment paper and place it on top of the casserole. Set the cover on, bring to a boil, then place the pan in the oven and cook for about 2 hours. Baste every 20 minutes, adding a little of the 1 tablespoon of creamed butter each time.

When the meat is golden brown and tender in its fragrant, well-reduced sauce, transfer it to a heated metal platter and keep warm.

Degrease*—but only partially—the braising juices. (The rich, slightly fat sauce takes the edge off the tart flavor of sorrel.) Strain into a small saucepan.

preparing the sorrel

This can be done while the meat is cooking, or you might try this method: wash, pick over, and blanch the sorrel the day before. Press out the liquid with your hands, and place the sorrel in the refrigerator until you are ready to prepare it. Remember: count 1 pound of sorrel per person.

Prepare the sorrel purée, keep it hot by placing it in a metal vegetable dish and setting it, covered, over a pan of gently simmering water.

Slice the veal and place the slices on top of the sorrel. Spoon a little sauce over the meat and serve the rest of the sauce in a warmed bowl.

Sautéed Veal Chops with Mushrooms
Côtes de veau poêlées aux champignons

A delicious combination of flavors: the savor of mushrooms is enhanced by the delicacy of the veal and its succulent juice.

Have your butcher level the bone at the top of each chop so the meat will lie flat in the pan. Take the bones with you (along with two or three more sawed-up veal bones), for these will be the basis of the succulent sauce.

A large (preferably cast-iron) sauté pan will be necessary for preparing both bones and sauce.

FOR 6 PEOPLE

6 rib or loin chops veal, 1 inch–1¼ inches thick
a little flour for dusting the chops
2 tablespoons lard, or 1 tablespoon peanut oil and 1 tablespoon butter for
    browning the bones
the pieces of veal bones
a sprig of fresh or dried thyme
1 bay leaf
1¾ cups boiling water
salt
freshly ground pepper
peanut oil and 2–3 pats of butter for cooking the chops (keep the oil bottle
    and extra butter at hand)
juice of ¼ lemon and ½ cup boiling water for deglazing the sauté pan

mushroom ingredients

> 2 tablespoons butter
> ¾ pound mushroom caps, washed, patted dry and cut in quarters
> 1 shallot, squeezed through a garlic press
> a few drops of lemon juice

ingredients for finishing the sauce

> strained juice from the browned bones
> veal chop deglazing juice
> mushroom juices
> 1 tablespoon butter
> 2 tablespoons minced parsley for garnishing chops

Dust the chops with flour, shake off the excess, and place on a board to dry.

Heat the lard, or the oil and butter, in the sauté pan. Begin browning the bones, turning them and shaking the pan. Add the herbs. When the bones are good and brown, pour in the boiling water. Cover the pan, reduce heat, and simmer for 20–25 minutes. Strain the liquid into a saucepan and season lightly with salt and pepper. Set aside. Wash and dry the sauté pan.

Spread a thin coating of oil over the sauté pan and distribute 2–3 pats of butter. Heat the fat, add the veal chops, and cook them for 8–10 minutes on one side, raising them from the pan with a metal spatula from time to time. When the chops show signs of browning, turn them, adding a little more oil and 1–2 pats of butter. Cover the pan and cook the chops for 6–8 minutes, checking frequently to see that they are not sticking, adding a little oil if they are. Transfer the cooked chops to a heated metal platter, cover, and keep warm.

If there is an excess of oil and butter floating in the pan, remove it with a spoon. Then deglaze* it (off heat) with the lemon juice and boiling water, scraping the bottom with a wooden spatula. Place over heat and allow to boil for a minute or so, strain into the saucepan containing the juices from the bones.

preparing the mushrooms

Heat the 2 tablespoons of butter in a small skillet, put in the mushroom caps, and cook as in Mushroom Caps Sautéed in Butter* (but here add a little shallot while they are cooking). Using a skimmer, transfer the mushrooms to a heated dish. Add a few drops of lemon juice, cover, and keep warm. Strain the juices into the saucepan containing the bone and chop juices.

finishing the sauce

Bring the liquid in the saucepan to a boil, then turn down heat and simmer for a minute or two. Remove from heat, add a tablespoon of butter, shaking the pan until it has melted. Taste and adjust seasoning.

Put a few spoonfuls of the sauce on the chops and serve the rest in a warmed sauce bowl. Arrange the mushrooms at each end of the platter.

The following accompaniments may take the place of the mushrooms: Fresh Green Pea Purée,* Mushroom Purée,* or Green Bean Purée.*

Veal Grenadins with Three Purées
Grenadins de veau aux trois purées

True *grenadins* are the veal equivalents of beef tournedos—small, round, fairly thick pieces cut from the fillet. Since these will not be easy to get hold of, you may substitute a boned and larded veal loin roast cut into the number of pieces required.

The veal pieces are braised, served on round croutons and covered with *jus lié* sauce. The height of elegance is achieved if you serve the *grenadins* with three purées, but if this is too daunting, make Sorrel Purée,* which goes perfectly with the delicate taste of veal.

You will need a large, heavy-bottomed enameled casserole for braising the veal.

FOR 6–8 PEOPLE

1–2 tablespoons butter for greasing the casserole
¼ pound fat pork rinds, simmered for 10 minutes, refreshed in cold water, and diced
1 carrot, coarsely, chopped
1 onion, chopped
a 2½-pound veal loin roast cut into 10–12 ½" pieces
salt
freshly ground pepper
½ cup dry white wine (slightly reduced before adding)
2–2½ cups hot Beef Bouillon*
1 *Bouquet garni classique**
10–12 round Croutons,* made ahead and reheated before using
2 tablespoons minced mixed herbs (parsley, chives, tarragon, and chervil) for garnish

ingredients for the jus lié sauce

the strained braising juice
¼ cup Madeira, red port wine, or dry sherry
2 tablespoons heavy cream

braising the grenadins

Butter the casserole generously, place over medium heat, put in the pork rinds, carrot, and onion. Stir-cook for a few minutes. Raise heat, add the veal pieces, and cook them for 5 minutes, turning each piece once. Season lightly with salt and pepper. Add the wine, bouillon, and *bouquet garni.* Cover the casserole, lower heat, and braise for about 40 minutes, stirring and checking the amount of liquid from time to time (if necessary add a little more bouillon).

When the *grenadins* are tender, remove them carefully with a slotted spoon and place on top of the reheated croutons, which have been arranged on a warmed metal platter. Keep warm.

making the jus lié sauce

Strain the braising liquid into a heavy saucepan, pressing against the ingredients in the strainer with the back of a spoon. Stir in the Madeira or one of the other wines, heat to the boiling point, lower heat, and reduce slightly. Off heat, slowly stir in the cream, place over low heat, and cook, stirring and lifting the pan off the heat now and then, until the sauce is lightly bound. Remove from heat, taste, and adjust seasoning. Beat the sauce and spoon it over the *grenadins*. Dot each one with the minced mixed herbs.

Suggested purée accompaniments: purées for wintertime, Chestnut,* Celery Root,* Spiced Apples;* purées for spring and summertime, Sorrel,* Fresh Green Peas,* Mushrooms,* Spinach.*

Blanquette de Veau

Almost all cooks agree that *blanquette* sauce is finer and lighter when moistened with water rather than with bouillon.

FOR 6 PEOPLE

salt
freshly ground pepper
a 1¼-pound veal breast, cut into 6 pieces
a 1¼-pound veal shoulder, cut into 6 pieces
6¾–7 cups cold water plus a little cold water in reserve
2 carrots, cut in quarters
2 onions, 1 stuck with a clove
a small stalk celery
20 mushroom stems
1 *Bouquet garni classique**

garnishes

These can be prepared while the meat is cooking.

10 Small White Glazed Onions*
20 small Mushroom Caps Sautéed in Butter* (set both of these garnishes aside in their juices)

sauce for the blanquette

ABOUT 3½–4 CUPS

the blanquette cooking liquid
3 tablespoons butter
3 tablespoons flour
2 egg yolks

4 tablespoons heavy cream
a little salt
freshly ground pepper
1 tablespoon minced parsley for sprinkling over sauce

cooking the veal

Salt and pepper the veal pieces, arrange them in a heavy-bottomed enameled casserole, and cover with cold water. Have the reserved cold water at hand. Place the casserole over medium heat and bring slowly to a boil, skimming until broth is clear, 15–20 minutes. During the skimming process add a spoonful of reserved cold water for every spoonful of liquid you remove. This helps the impurities to rise to the surface.

Add the carrot, onions, celery, and mushroom stems, bring to a boil. Add the *bouquet garni*. Lower heat and simmer for 1 hour to 1 hour 15 minutes. The meat will not be absolutely tender, but this is how it should be; it will finish cooking in the sauce. Remove the meat to a side dish.

sauce for the blanquette

Strain the veal cooking liquid into a saucepan. Discard the onions and *bouquet garni*. Remove the carrot pieces and with a knife shape them to resemble miniature carrots.

Make a blond *roux** of the butter and flour, stirring and cooking it over moderate heat. Off heat, pour in the *blanquette* cooking liquid, place in casserole in which the *blanquette* has been cooked. Cook and whisk for a few minutes over low heat. Remove from heat and continue to whisk until the sauce is smooth and thick. Add the pieces of veal, place over low heat, and simmer for 10–15 minutes until the meat is tender. Then add the mushroom caps and their juice. Add a few tablespoons of the hot sauce to the pan containing the glazed onions to warm them.

binding the sauce

Five minutes before serving, beat the egg yolks and cream together in a bowl. Add a little salt and pepper. Stir this mixture into the *blanquette* along with the glazed onions and their juice. Heat through, stirring with a wooden spatula. Nothing bad will happen if the sauce boils for a minute. It has been made stable by the flour in the *roux.*

serving the blanquette

Transfer the pieces of veal to a fairly deep serving dish. Arrange the carrots, onions, and mushrooms on top and spoon the sauce over all. Sprinkle with minced parsley.

Accompany the dish with Creole Rice or buttered noodles.*
To make a fresh-tasting springtime blanquette, *add some fresh tarragon to the* bouquet garni. *Then with scissors finely cut enough tarragon leaves to make a tablespoon, garnish the dish with it.*

Sweetbreads Colbert on Artichoke Hearts with Béarnaise Sauce
Ris de veau Colbert sur fonds d'artichauts, sauce béarnaise

An elegant entree that has the advantage of being easy to make.

FOR 6 PEOPLE

> 2 fresh veal sweetbreads[1]
> cold water for soaking, blanching, etc., the sweetbreads
> a few drops of wine vinegar
> salt
> freshly ground pepper
> a small sprig of fresh or dried thyme
> a piece of bay leaf
> breading ingredients consisting of a plate of flour, a bowl containing 1
>   lightly beaten egg white, and a plate of fine bread crumbs
> 1 tablespoon melted butter plus butter for the baking dish
> a few drops of lemon juice
> 2 tablespoons butter for heating sweetbreads

ingredients for the artichoke hearts

> 8 canned artichoke hearts
> 2 tablespoons butter
> salt
> freshly ground pepper
> a few drops of lemon juice

sauce

> 1 double recipe of Béarnaise Sauce*
> *Preheat oven to 350° F.*

preparing the sweetbreads

Wash the sweetbreads and soak for 1 hour in cold water to which a few drops of vinegar have been added. Rinse well and place in a pan of cold water, set over moderate heat. When the water boils, add salt, pepper, and herbs. Blanch the sweetbreads for 14–16 minutes. Strain and rinse under cold water. Strip off the outer membrane, remove fatty pieces and bits of cartilage. In each pair pull out the tube that separates the two lobes.

Holding the knife at a slant, cut each sweetbread into 8 slices. Coat each slice lightly with flour, then with egg white, and finally with bread crumbs. Put the slices in a well-buttered oven dish and bake for about 12 minutes or until they are a light golden color. Remove from the oven, add the melted butter, a little salt and pepper and lemon juice. Cover with parchment paper and keep warm.

---

[1] Sweetbreads should be served the day they are bought, unless they are blanched, in which case they may be kept for 24 hours.

---

preparing the artichoke hearts

Drain and rinse under cold water. Pat dry and trim the edges neatly. Melt the 2 tablespoons of butter in a sauté pan and heat the artichokes hearts, turning them, until they begin to color. Season with salt and pepper. Add the lemon juice. Remove from heat, place on a heated, round platter, cover with parchment paper and keep warm.

preparing the sauce

Make the *béarnaise* sauce. Keep it warm by letting it stand over not too hot water (heat off), beating it now and then.

serving the sweetbreads

Melt the 2 tablespoons of butter in a sauté pan and heat the sweetbreads through. Place a slice on each artichoke heart. Whisk the *béarnaise* sauce and top each slice of sweetbread with about 1½ tablespoons of it, not letting the sauce drip outside the artichoke hearts.

Veal Kidneys Sautéed with Sherry *Rognons de veau sautés au Xérès*

A delicious dish appreciated by all gourmets.

FOR 3 PEOPLE

4 veal kidneys
the fat from the kidneys
2 tablespoons butter (a little more if necessary)
salt
freshly ground pepper
½ cup dry sherry
4 tablespoons heavy cream
a few drops of lemon juice
1 tablespoon mixed minced chervil and parsley

Strip the membranes from the kidneys, remove and discard the nerves. Cut off the kidney fat and let it melt over low heat in a heavy or no-stick skillet. Cut the kidneys into rather large pieces; if the pieces are too small, they will dry out and toughen when cooked.

Remove any solid kidney fat from the skillet, add the butter and heat. Sauté the kidneys, turning them constantly and not allowing them to brown, for about 6 minutes. Add more butter if necessary. Transfer the kidneys and juices to a side dish, season with salt and pepper, cover, and keep warm.

Deglaze* the skillet with the sherry. Off heat, whisk in the cream. Put the skillet back on heat and boil the ingredients, beating constantly, for 2–3 minutes. Stir in the kidneys and their juices and heat for about 2 minutes. Transfer the kidneys to a heated metal serving dish, using a slotted spoon. Taste the sauce and adjust seasoning. Stir in the lemon juice and strain the sauce over the kidneys. Sprinkle with the minced herbs.

*Accompany the dish with a bowl of Creole Rice.**

Casserole-Roasted Loin of Veal   *Carré de veau rôti en cocotte*

Your veal roast will be juicy and succulent if you roast it in a casserole with fairly high sides, rather than in a flat roasting pan. Have your butcher give you the chopped-up bones. They will make the juice rich and savory.

FOR 6 PEOPLE

3 tablespoons peanut oil plus a few pats of butter, or 2 tablespoons lard
a 2½-pound loin of veal, boned, rolled, and barded
the chopped raw veal bones
1 onion
salt
2–3 tablespoons boiling water to put in with the meat if necessary
¼ cup boiling water for deglazing the casserole
1 tablespoon butter
Preheat oven to 350° F.

Grease the casserole with the oil and distribute the pats of butter on top, or use lard alone for greasing.

Put the veal in the casserole along with the bones and the onion, place in the oven. Brown the meat for a good 15 minutes, turn, and brown for another 15 minutes. Salt the meat before and after turning. Remove the onion and bones.

Reduce oven heat to 325°. Add the 2–3 tablespoons of boiling water if the bottom of the casserole seems too dry. Roast, basting frequently, allowing about 20 minutes to the pound. The meat should be tender and the juice should run amber clear. If the meat seems to be cooking too fast, fit a piece of aluminum foil over the top. This is usually done toward the end of the cooking.

Transfer the meat to a board and cover with parchment paper. Strain the cooking juices into a saucepan. When the fat rises to the surface, degrease* with care. Deglaze* the casserole with the ¼ cup boiling water and add to the saucepan. Place over low heat, stir, adjust seasoning, and swirl in the tablespoon of butter.

serving the roast

Slice the meat and place on a warmed metal platter. Serve the sauce in a heated sauce bowl and accompany the roast with the vegetables listed below.

Fresh Green Peas, English Style* or Sautéed Potatoes* served on artichoke hearts,* small Braised Lettuces,* a small amount of Green Beans,* and some large Stuffed Mushrooms.* Place these decoratively on the platter around the meat slices, or arrange on another warmed platter.

A simpler accompaniment could be Small White Glazed Onions,* Glazed Turnips,* Glazed Carrots* and a dish of Fresh Green Peas, English Style.*

Oven-Casseroled Veal *Pièce de veau poêlée*

A simple but delicious way of cooking a top or bottom round of veal.

For this recipe you will need a large, heavy-bottomed enameled casserole with a cover.

FOR 10 PEOPLE

2 tablespoons each of oil and butter plus 2 tablespoons of each in reserve
the cut-up raw veal bones from the boned meat
a 3½–4 pound top or bottom round of veal, boned and larded
salt
freshly ground pepper
2 carrots, coarsely chopped
2 onions, cut in small chunks
1 *Bouquet garni classique**
2 ¼-inch-thick slices fat bacon, simmered for 10 minutes, refreshed in cold
  water, patted dry, and diced
⅓ cup dry white wine
1 tablespoon butter
Turn oven to broiler position. After browning the veal bones, preheat oven to 340° F.

Grease the casserole with the 2 tablespoons each of oil and butter, arrange the bones in it. Place under the broiler for 10–15 minutes, turning and basting the bones until they are golden brown.

Transfer the bones to a side dish, add the reserved oil and butter to the casserole, and put in the meat. Still using the broiler, brown the meat for about 12 minutes on each side. Remove the casserole. Preheat the oven.

Salt and pepper the meat, surround it with the browned bones, vegetables, *bouquet garni,* and bacon pieces. Pour the wine around the edges of the casserole. Fit a piece of aluminum foil over the top of the meat, glossy side down, cover, and place in the preheated oven. Cook for about 1½ hours or until the meat is tender and the juice runs amber clear. It is a good idea to lower the oven heat to 300° about halfway through the cooking to let the roast cook even more slowly in its fragrant juice and vapor.

Transfer the foil-covered roast to a board and let it rest for about 10 minutes before slicing.

Remove and discard the bones from the cooking juice, then strain the liquid into a saucepan, pressing against the vegetables and *bouquet garni* with the back of a spoon. Taste and adjust seasoning and swirl in the 1 tablespoon of butter. Heat and strain into a warmed sauce bowl.

Cut the meat into thin slices and arrange on a warmed oval metal platter.

In winter the veal may be accompanied by Belgian Endives Steamed in Butter,* Oven-Braised Belgian Endives,* or Potatoes, Morvan Style.* Garnish the platter with a small bunch of watercress.

In spring and summer accompany the veal with tartlets filled with Ratatouille,* Zucchini Fritters,* or Corn Croquettes.*

Purées also go well with veal cooked in this manner, especially Celery Root Purée* or Split Pea Purée.*

Braised Veal with Curry Powder *Noix de veau braisée au curry*

A sumptuous dish for a large dinner party. Either of the sauces has a highly seasoned base that mingles with the delicacy of the veal and sets it off.

You will need a large, heavy-bottomed enameled casserole for cooking the dish.

FOR 10–12 PEOPLE

2 tablespoons peanut oil
2 tablespoons butter plus 2 tablespoons butter in reserve
a 4-pound rolled top round of veal
½ cup warmed cognac
salt
freshly ground pepper
1 tablespoon curry powder
½ pound prosciutto, diced
3 carrots, sliced
3 onions, sliced thin
1 bottle California champagne or 1 bottle dry white Alsatian wine
1 cup heated Beef Bouillon*
3 sprigs of fresh or dried tarragon, tied together
1 *Bouquet garni classique**
1 small bunch watercress for garnish

sauce with a simple binding
the strained cooking juices of the meat
⅓ cup butter
1 cup heavy cream

sauce with a rich binding
the strained cooking juices of the meat
1 cup heavy cream
3 egg yolks
Turn the oven to broil position for browning the meat, then preheat the oven to 340° F.

preparing the meat

Heat the 2 tablespoons each of oil and butter in the casserole, put in the meat. Place the casserole under the broiler, brown the meat for about 20 minutes, turning it once or twice during the process. Turn off the broiler and preheat the oven.

Set the casserole on top of the stove over low heat, pour in the warmed cognac, and set aflame. When the flames have died down, baste the meat and season it—sides, top, and bottom—with salt, pepper, and curry powder. Transfer the meat to a board.

Heat the reserved 2 tablespoons of butter in the casserole, add the prosciutto, carrot, and onion, and stir-cook for a few minutes over moderate heat. Put the meat back in the casserole, pour in the champagne or wine, raise heat, and cook briskly for 4–5 minutes. Add the bouillon, bring to a boil, and add the tarragon and *bouquet garni.*

Fit a piece of aluminum foil over the top of the meat, glossy side down, cover, and place the casserole in the oven for a slow braising of 1 hour 50 minutes to 2 hours. Check from time to time to see if the liquid is maintaining a slow simmer. During the cooking, lift the cover three or four times to let the condensed steam that has formed drop into the casserole and become part of the redolent sauce. After about 1 hour, remove the foil, turn the meat, replace the foil and cover. Reduce oven heat to 300° for the last hour of braising.

Transfer the veal to a covered side dish and keep warm.

making the sauce with a simple binding

Strain the veal cooking juices into a heavy-bottomed enameled saucepan, pressing against the braising ingredients with the back of a spoon. Taste for seasoning.

Place the juice over low heat, add the butter, and allow it to melt. Do not boil. Add the cream gradually, stirring constantly, until the sauce is lightly bound. Pour into a warmed sauce bowl and keep warm while slicing the meat.

making the sauce with a rich binding

Strain the veal juice as above.

Whisk the cream and egg yolks together and gradually stir into the meat juices, off heat, until well blended. Place the sauce over low heat and allow to thicken, stirring constantly with a wooden spatula. Pour into a warmed sauce bowl.

serving the meat

Cut the veal into thin slices and arrange on a warmed oval platter. Place the bunch of watercress at one end of the platter.

A dish of Creole Rice* served in a vegetable dish is one of the best accompaniments for this dish. For an added touch of elegance, garnish the platter with large Stuffed Mushrooms.* Various purées, depending on the season, also go very well with braised veal.

PORC (PORK)

Lacquered Roast Pork   *Rôti de porc laqué*

Roast pork studded with cloves and basted with a rich marinade sauce gives the meat its lacquered look and slightly Oriental taste. The meat platter is garnished with caramelized pineapple slices.

Ask your butcher to give you the chopped-up bones from the roast. With these you can make a rich, concentrated bouillon that, when the pork pan juices are added, is served as a sauce.

The marinade sauce can be made well in advance.

marinade basting sauce

MAKES ABOUT 3 CUPS

- ½ cup soy sauce
- ½ cup clear liquid honey
- ½ cup wine or sherry vinegar
- 1 cup canned crushed pineapple
- ½ cup pineapple juice
- 1 washed lemon, sliced thin
- 2 cloves garlic, crushed
- freshly ground pepper
- 2 teaspoons powdered ginger

bouillon ingredients

- a little peanut oil and 2–3 pats of butter for greasing the pan used for browning the bones
- the chopped-up pork bones
- 1 onion
- a sprig of fresh or dried thyme
- 1 bay leaf
- 2 cups boiling water

pork ingredients

- peanut oil and 2–3 pats of butter for greasing the roasting pan
- a 3½–4 pound loin of pork, boned, rolled, and tied
- 12–15 whole cloves
- 1 clove garlic, cut in half
- salt
- 2–3 large pinches of dark brown sugar
- 4–5 tablespoons boiling water for deglazing the pan

pineapple garnish

- butter for greasing the pan
- 8–10 canned pineapple slices, well drained
- 3–4 tablespoons dark brown sugar

salt
freshly ground pepper
Preheat oven to 350° F. For preparing pineapple slices set oven to broil position.

making the marinade

Place all the ingredients in a bowl, mix thoroughly, and set aside until ready to strain and use.

making the bouillon

Grease a roasting pan with oil and distribute the pats of butter. Put the bones in the pan along with the onion and herbs, place in the oven. Brown the bones for 10–15 minutes, turning them when necessary.

Remove the pan from the oven, transfer the bones, onion, and herbs to a heavy-bottomed enameled saucepan, and add the 2 cups of boiling water. Cook slowly until the liquid is reduced to about 1 cup. Strain into a small saucepan and set aside.

roasting the pork

Oil the roasting pan and distribute the butter pats. Stud the pork evenly with the cloves, slip a half clove of garlic under the skin at each end of the roast. Place the pan in the oven and brown the meat for about 20 minutes, turning it on all sides and seasoning with salt. As soon as the meat is browned, strain the marinade sauce and begin basting with it regularly—once every 10 minutes—until the end of cooking. Roast the meat for 1½–2 hours (after browning). About halfway through the cooking, sprinkle the meat with the brown sugar, which will cause it to look even more lacquered.

Transfer the roast to a board, set in a warm place, and let it rest for several minutes before slicing.

Deglaze* the roasting pan with the boiling water, scraping the bottom and stirring until all the caramel has been dissolved. Set the pan over medium heat, bring to a boil, and add to the reduced bouillon in the small saucepan. Cook slowly until slightly reduced. Taste and adjust seasoning. Set aside.

making the pineapple garnish

Butter a large oven pan generously and place the pineapple slices in it in one layer. Sprinkle with the brown sugar and broil (not too close to heat) for a few seconds until the slices begin to caramelize. Turn the slices, salt and pepper them lightly, and baste with the syrupy juice. Broil for another 2–3 seconds. Remove from the oven.

serving the meat

Carve the roast into thin slices and place them on a warmed oval platter. Arrange the pineapple slices around the edge of the platter.

Reheat the sauce and pour it into a warmed metal sauce bowl.

*The best accompaniment for lacquered roast pork is Creole Rice.**

Roast Loin of Pork with Vegetable Fritters
Carré de porc rôti aux fritots de légumes

Marinating the pork will enhance its flavor enormously, but it is not obligatory.

FOR 6–8 PEOPLE

marinade

    4–5 tablespoons peanut oil
    juice of 1/2–1 lemon
    2–3 sprigs of dried thyme
    1 bay leaf
    1 sprig of dried savory or 1 sage leaf
    a pinch of oregano or 1 small pinch of curry powder

pork

    margarine for greasing the roasting pan
    a 3–3 1/2 pound pork center loin, boned, rolled, and tied
    1/4 cup boiling water
    2 cloves garlic, unpeeled
    salt
    4 tablespoons boiling water for deglazing the pan juices
    1 pat butter or 1 teaspoon heavy cream
    Preheat oven to 350° F.

Mix the marinade ingredients together, place them in a shallow dish, and marinate the pork for 1 hour, turning it frequently.

roasting the pork

Grease the roasting pan, set in the roast, and place in the oven. Brown the meat for about 20 minutes, turning it on all sides.

Pour the 1/4 cup of boiling water around the edges of the pan and lay the garlic beside the meat. Season with salt, roast for about 1 1/2 hours (after browning), basting frequently. The meat is done when the point of a knife slips easily into the flesh.

Toward the end of roasting, cover the roast loosely with aluminum foil and reduce the oven temperature slightly. Transfer the cooked roast to a board and let it rest for 10 minutes before slicing.

making the sauce

Deglaze* the roasting pan with the 4 tablespoons of boiling water, scraping the bottom with a wooden spatula. Strain into a small saucepan and degrease.* Add the butter or cream, beat, adjust seasoning, and pour into a heated sauce bowl.

Carve the pork roast into even slices and arrange on a warmed metal platter.

Vegetable Fritters* are perfect with roast pork. An original idea is to garnish the platter with Grapefruit Fritters* or Corn Croquettes.*

Cold roast pork is delicious. Serve it with Cold Game Sauce* and a crisp salad.

HAM *Jambon*

Ham is the most practical meats, as well as one of the most delicious, for serving a large number of guests. A 10-pound ham will serve up to 18 people. Even if you are counting on fewer guests, it is a good idea to buy this much, for it will be very useful later. If you have 10 to 12 guests and a 10-pound ham, you will have enough left over to treat the innter circle to ham slices sautéed in butter with a pinch of minced shallot, accompanied by Cream of Mushroom Sauce* or Port Wine and Cream Sauce.* You may still have enough to serve cold on another occasion. Slice the remaining ham and ring the platter with ice-cold chopped Aspic* or garnish with Cherries in Vinegar.*

NOTE: *in the following two recipes use country-cured ham (Virginia, Smithfield, among others) whole and uncooked. All country-cured hams must be soaked to rid them of excess salt. The amount of soaking time depends on how salty the ham is; follow package instructions for desalting your ham.*

Ham Braised in Meursault *Jambon braisé au Meursault*

A recipe to glorify my favorite white wine, Meursault, either Meursault Perrières or Meursault Gouttes d'Or, both distinguished by the green-gold transparency and the incredible bouquet, not to mention the subtle hazelnut aftertaste. These are wines of great distinction not in the least impaired by cooking.

In this recipe the ham is first poached in an aromatic broth, then braised. You will need two large kettles and a large heavy braising pan (or large heavy-bottomed casserole) for making the dish.

FOR 16–18 PEOPLE

aromatic poaching broth

5½ quarts hot water
4 carrots, coarsely chopped
4 onions, 2 studded with a clove each and 2 cut in quarters
1 stalk of celery
a sprig of fresh or dried rosemary
a sprig of fresh or dried savory
3 fresh or dried sage leaves
1 *Bouquet garni classique**
12 coriander seeds, crushed
12 peppercorns, crushed
1 scant tablespoon curry powder

NOTE: *Do not add salt.*

---

ingredients for poaching the ham

a 10-pound uncooked country-cured ham, previously soaked (see the note at the beginning of the ham section)

2 bottles Meursault Perrières or Merusault Gouttes d'Or (½ bottle for poaching, the rest set aside)

2 veal knuckles, blanched for 5–7 minutes and refreshed in cold water

¼ pound fresh pork rind, blanched for 5 minutes, refreshed in cold water, and diced

5–6 cloves

braising ingredients

oil and butter for the braising pan and casserole

enough ham rind to line the braising pan

1 tablespoon butter

2 carrots and 2 onions, finely shredded

2 stalks celery, minced

4 tablespoons butter

4 tablespoons minced shallot

2–3 pinches of dark brown sugar

sauce caramel au Meursault (caramelized Meursault sauce)

3 tablespoons butter

1 onion and 1 carrot, chopped

the reserved fat from the ham

2 tablespoons brown sugar

the reserved half bottle of Meursault

1 teaspoon arrowroot dissolved in 2 teaspoons cold water (optional if thicker sauce is desired)

a few tablespoons Concentrated Essence of Mushrooms* (optional), or a few tablespoons sultana raisins macerated in hot tea until plump and soft, then strained (optional)

Preheat oven to 350° F.

preparing the aromatic poaching broth

Place the 5½ quarts of water in a large kettle, bring to a boil, add all the other ingredients, and cook at a slow boil for 20 minutes. Remove from heat and keep warm.

poaching the ham

Place the ham in another large kettle, cover with cold water, and bring to a boil. Boil for 2–3 minutes, then drain off the water. Pour the half bottle of Meursault over the ham and bring to a boil. Boil for 5 minutes, then put both the ham and wine in the poaching broth, adding water if necessary. The ham should be just barely covered with liquid. Add the veal knuckles and diced pork rind, cover the kettle, and poach the ham slowly for about 2 hours, adding more hot water if necessary. When the ham bone feels loose when touched

---

with the hand and the meat has slightly shrunk away from it, the poaching process is finished.

Transfer the ham to a board, cool slightly, then peel off the rind and remove some of the fat, leaving no more than ¼ inch on the ham. Set the rind and fat aside. Stud the ham with the cloves.

preparing the casserole and making the braising ingredients

Oil and butter the braising pan or casserole and line it with pieces of ham rind. Melt the 1 tablespoon butter in a small sauté pan, add the braising vegetables, and stir-cook for about 5 minutes. Spread over the ham rind and place the poached ham on top.

Melt the 4 tablespoons of butter in a small pan, add the 4 tablespoons shallot, and stir-cook for about 1 minute. Pour the second bottle of Meursault over the ham, sprinkle with the shallot, and heat on top of the stove. Then place the braising pan or casserole in the oven and cook for 1½ hours or a little longer, until the ham is golden brown and the bone completely loose. Baste now and then with pan juices. After about 1 hour of cooking, sprinkle the ham with 2–3 pinches of dark brown sugar to help the surface to brown.

When the ham is cooked, transfer it to a platter, cover with aluminum foil, and keep warm. Reserve the braising juices for the sauce.

preparing the caramelized sauce

Place the butter, onion, carrot, and ham fat in a small heavy-bottomed enameled saucepan over low heat. Sprinkle in the 2 tablespoons of brown sugar and heat the mixture, stirring, until it begins to caramelize. Pour in the wine. Raise heat and reduce the liquid slightly. Lower heat, cover, and simmer for 15 minutes, stirring now and then. Strain into a saucepan and set aside in a warm place.

Strain the braising juices into a saucepan through a sieve lined with dampened cheesecloth. Pick up the four corners of the cloth and twist so as to press out all the juice. Allow the fat to rise to the surface and degrease* carefully. Place the pan over medium heat, bring to a boil, skimming if necessary, until it is slightly reduced. Pour into the saucepan containing the wine mixture and simmer for 2–3 minutes, stirring.

To my mind, this sauce is perfect as it is, but if you wish to make it slightly thicker, dissolve 1 teaspoon arrowroot in 2 teaspoons cold water, add to the sauce, and simmer, stirring, for a minute or two.

Sometimes a tablespoon of heavy cream is stirred into the finished sauce. I prefer adding 2 pats of butter and letting it melt in the sauce after it has been poured into a heated sauce bowl.

carving the ham

Use a freshly sharpened knife with a long flexible blade. The slices should be thin and even.

Suggested accompaniments: Oval Tartlets* filled with spinach, Corn Croquettes,* large Stuffed Mushrooms,* or one or two purées. Your choice of purées will depend on the season: Chestnut Purée* or Celery Root Purée* in winter, or Green Bean Purée* or mousseline of green peas* in summer.

If you cannot find the Meursault indicated in the recipe, substitute dry red port wine or California champagne, the latter adding a delicious flavor that can be enhanced by a truffle poached in half cup of champagne then finely shredded.

Baked Ham with Port Wine Sauce   *Jambon rôti au Porto*

A poached ham, sliced and reconstructed, then baked and basted with red port wine. It is served with a port wine and cream sauce enlivened with pepper. Both ham and sauce can be prepared in advance. Allow about 30 minutes in a 300° oven for reheating the ham.

FOR 10–12 PEOPLE

poaching ingredients

    11 cups Beef Bouillon*
    4 carrots, coarsely chopped
    4 onions, 2 studded with a clove each and 2 cut in quarters
    1 stalk celery
    a sprig of dried or fresh rosemary
    a sprig of dried or fresh savory
    3 fresh or dried sage leaves
    1 *Bouquet garni classique**
    12 coriander seeds and 12 peppercorns, crushed
    1 scant tablespoon curry powder
    an 8-pound uncooked country-cured ham, previously soaked (see the note
        at the beginning of the ham section)
    boiling water if necessary

NOTE: *Do not add salt.*

ingredients for roasting the ham

    oil and butter for the roasting pan
    the poached-ham rind for lining the pan
    1 bottle red port wine (setting ½ cup aside for sauce)
    3 tablespoons dark brown sugar
    freshly grated nutmeg
    Preheat oven to 350° F.

Place the bouillon, vegetables, herbs, and condiments in a large kettle and bring to a boil. Put in the ham, turn down heat, and cook for about 2 hours, until the bone moves loosely when touched. Add boiling water to the poaching liquid if necessary.

Transfer the ham to a board and let it rest for 20 minutes.

Peel the rind off the ham and set aside. Remove and discard all but ¼ inch of fat. Cut the ham parallel to the bone in thin slices, turning them over as you proceed. Pile the slices on a sheet of aluminum foil in the same order as cut. Pressing down on the slices with one hand, turn the foil over so as to place the slices of ham back on the bone, remove the foil. Make any little adjustments necessary to align the slices.

Oil and butter a large roasting pan and line it with ham rind, fat side down. Carefully place the ham in the pan and bake for 25–30 minutes until the surface is golden brown.

Pour the wine over the ham and reduce oven heat to 300°. Sprinkle the top of the ham with a tablespoon of brown sugar along with some freshly grated nutmeg. Add the rest of the brown sugar at intervals during the baking. Bake the ham for about 1½ hours (this includes the preliminary half-hour browning), basting frequently.

About ½ hour before removing the ham from the oven, strain the poaching liquid, set over moderate heat, and reduce to 2–2½ cups to concentrate the flavors.

Remove the ham from the roasting pan and keep warm.

Port Wine and Cream Sauce   *Sauce au Porto et à la crème*

MAKES 2–3 CUPS (*depending on the amount of poaching liquid used*)

the reserved ½ cup red port wine
1–2 cups strained poaching liquid
¼ pound mushrooms, minced and prepared as in Bound Mushroom
    Duxelles*
3 tablespoons butter
2 cups heavy cream
freshly ground pepper (optional)

Deglaze* the roasting pan with wine, add the poaching liquid, bring to a boil, and strain into a heavy-bottomed enameled saucepan. Let the fat rise to the surface, then degrease* with care. Place over moderate heat and simmer for a few minutes, skimming if necessary. Remove from heat.

Place the mushroom duxelles in another heavy saucepan, set over low heat, and whisk in the butter and cream. Simmer for about 10 minutes, stirring constantly with a wooden spatula. Remove from heat and beat into the wine mixture. Place over low heat and simmer for a few minutes, stirring, until well blended.

Adjust the seasoning for the sauce: adding a little ground pepper will add to its piquancy. Do not add any salt. Pour into a warmed sauce bowl when ready to serve the ham.

Carefully transfer the ham to a heated large, metal platter. Surround with Oval Tartlets* of Chestnut Purée* or Oval Tartlets Filled with Cream-Puréed Spinach,* alternating with tartlets of Celery Root Purée.*

BEEF

Fillet Steaks, also known as Tournedos   *Tournedos*

These small round larded steaks cut from the tail end of the *filet* deserve special attention, for they are choice morsels. The weight of each tournedos should be about ¼ of a pound. They are usually about 2½ inches in diameter and 1 inch thick.

An attractive way to serve them is to set each one on a reheated round, golden-brown crouton, topping each fillet with a small amount of sauce.

The best way to prepare the steaks is to pan-broil them. They do not lend themselves very well to broiling, as their texture is too dry. Use a cast-iron skillet or sauté pan.

basic method for cooking tournedos

Lightly brush steaks and skillet with peanut oil. When the skillet is piping hot, put in the steaks. Do not crowd them. Press each one firmly against the bottom of the pan with a metal spatula, and cook for 3 minutes on one side and 2–2½ minutes on the other side if you want them rare. For medium-rare fillet steaks, add another minute of cooking time to each side. I do not advise cooking them any longer—they will be disappointingly tasteless. Salt and pepper each side after cooking, using freshly ground white pepper. Place each steak on a reheated crouton, top each with 1½ tablespoons of sauce. (See the following tournedos recipes for sauce suggestions.)

Tournedos with Valois Sauce   *Tournedos à la Valois*

FOR 3 PEOPLE (2 STEAKS PER PERSON)

1 recipe of Valois Sauce*
6 tournedos, each weighing about ¼ pound
6 Croutons,* made in advance and reheated at time of using
1 small bunch watercress for garnish

Prepare the sauce before cooking the steaks. Keep the pan of sauce warm by placing it over a saucepan of moderately hot water, off heat, stirring it from time to time. If the butter shows a tendency to rise to the surface, place the pan of sauce on a slab of marble or over a pan filled with ice-cold water and whisk until the sauce has returned to normal consistency.

Pan-broil the fillet steaks (using the basic method given above), place them on the reheated croutons, which have been arranged on a warmed platter. Spoon sauce over the top of each steak. Garnish one end of the platter with the watercress.

Accompany the steaks with Noisette Potatoes* or large Stuffed Mushrooms.*

Tournedos with Choron Sauce   *Tournedos, sauce Choron*

Follow the procedure in the recipe above, substituting Choron Sauce* for Valois Sauce.

Tournedos with Béarnaise Sauce   *Tournedos, sauce béarnaise*

This is one of my favorite tournedos sauces. Make the Béarnaise Sauce* before cooking the steaks. Keep the sauce warm, as described in Tournedos with Valois Sauce* above. Garnish the platter with a small bunch of watercress, and accompany the tournedos with Potatoes Dauphine.*

Sauce des trois gourmandes[1]

This very special "little" sauce can be served with any kind of pan- or oven-broiled steaks.

For 4–6 small steaks, each weighing about ⅓ pound, or 2 large steaks, each weighing about 1 pound.   MAKES ABOUT ½ CUP OF SAUCE

    4 tablespoons cognac
    2 pats of butter
    ½ cup dry white wine
    3 tablespoons finely minced shallot
    3 pinches of *Mignonnette** or 3 turns of the pepper mill
    1 tablespoon strong Dijon mustard
    2 teaspoons hot barbecue sauce
    ½ cup butter cut in small pieces

Place the cooked steaks on a heated platter and keep warm. Deglaze* the sauté pan or oven pan with the cognac and 2 pats of butter. Strain this juice into a bowl and set aside.

[1] Les Trois Gourmandes was the name of the cooking school that Mmes. Bertholle, Beck, and Child had in Paris.

Put the wine, shallot, and *mignonnette* or pepper in a small saucepan and reduce slowly to about 2 tablespoons. Mix in the mustard and barbecue sauce, add the deglazing liquid and heat through, stirring constantly. Off heat, beat in the pieces of butter. Taste and adjust seasoning. You may wish to add a little more pepper. Strain the sauce over the steaks and serve immediately.

Ground Round Steak *Steak haché*

Use a large cast-iron skillet or sauté pan for cooking the beef patties.

FOR 6 PEOPLE

about 1¾ pounds ground round steak, divided into 6 equal portions
1 tablespoon shallot or 1 tablespoon onion, squeezed through a garlic press (optional)
a little flour for dusting the patties
peanut oil for greasing the pan
salt
freshly ground pepper
6 tablespoons butter
1 tablespoon finely minced parsley

To the meat add a little shallot or onion before dividing it into portions. Form the meat into patties about ¾ inch thick. Dust each lightly with flour to keep the meat juices from seeping out. Set them on a rack for a few minutes to dry.

Brush the skillet lightly with peanut oil and heat until it is piping hot. Put in the patties, pressing down on each one with a metal spatula. Cook each side for about 3 minutes. If you want them less rare, cook each side for 4–5 minutes.

Transfer the patties to a heated metal serving platter and place over a pan of boiling water, heat off. Season them with salt and pepper.

Working rapidly, melt the butter in a saucepan, add a little more salt and pepper, and pour 1 tablespoon over each patty. Add a pinch of minced parsley on top of each and serve immediately.

Accompany with any of the following: French-fried potatoes, Sautéed Potatoes,* Buttered Green Beans* or Broiled Tomatoes* served on Rice Pilaf.*

Italian Sauce   *Sauce à l'italienne*

A French version of the Italian *bolognese* sauce that is delicious with pasta of all sorts, with Creole Rice* or as a garnish for zucchini or eggplant. Cooled and placed in a covered bowl or jar, it will keep for 2–3 days in the refrigerator.

FOR 6 PEOPLE

  6 tablespoons olive oil
  2 carrots, minced
  2 medium-size onions, minced
  3 slices packaged Canadian bacon, diced
  1 pound ground round steak[1]
  1 cup full-bodied red wine or 1 cup dry white Alsatian wine[2] (NOTE: if you use white wine, your sauce will have a nicer color)
  2 tablespoons tomato paste
  1 tablespoon sugar
  1 clove garlic, squeezed through a garlic press
  3¼ cups hot Beef Bouillon*
  1 *Bouquet garni classique**
  salt
  freshly ground pepper

Heat the oil in a heavy-bottomed enameled casserole and add the vegetables. Stir-cook them over moderate heat for 2–3 minutes. Mix in the diced bacon, cook for a minute or so, stirring, then add the ground meat. Stir-cook for 5 minutes, until the meat has browned. Remove the casserole from heat and pour in the wine, mixing well. Place the casserole over brisk heat and reduce the liquid almost completely, stirring with a wooden spatula and scraping the bottom of the casserole. Stir in the tomato paste, sugar, and garlic. Add the beef bouillon, bring to a boil, and add the *bouquet garni.* Season with salt and pepper. Lower heat, cover the casserole, and simmer, stirring from time to time, until the sauce is quite thick and reduced.

Before serving, discard the *bouquet garni,* partially degrease* the casserole with a spoon. Taste for seasoning.

For a richer sauce: sauté 2–3 chicken livers in 2 tablespoons of butter. Heat 1 tablespoon of cognac, pour into the sauté pan, and set aflame. When the flames have died down, crush the livers with a fork and add to the Italian sauce when it is finished.

You can also stir in a half recipe of Mushrooms Duxelles sautéed in butter, just before pouring the sauce into a serving dish.*

---

[1] You may substitute the same amount of raw veal or rabbit, finely ground in a meat grinder.

[2] If you prefer, substitute ½–¾ cup dry sherry or dry vermouth for the wine.

CASSEROLED BEEF

Beef Fillet Marinated in Game Sauce
Coeur de filet de boeuf venaison

The marinade enriches the meat and gives it a spicy, gamey taste. After being marinated, the meat is casseroled and served hot for a grand dinner party or cold for a buffet. This is a festive dish to present during the Christmas holidays.

It is important not to overcook the meat. When cut, the slices should be rosy pink.

FOR 6 PEOPLE

1 recipe of Master of the Hunt Sauce*
a 2½–3 pound beef fillet
1 recipe Cooked Marinade for Venison*
2 tablespoons peanut oil and 3 tablespoons butter for greasing the casserole
Preheat oven to 350° F.

Prepare the Master of the Hunt Sauce.

Wipe the fillet and place in the marinade for 24 hours (refrigerated), basting and turning the meat from time to time.

Remove the fillet from the marinade, pat dry, and place in an oiled and buttered casserole. Put the casserole in the oven and brown each side for about 10 minutes. Strain and heat the marinade and pour around the edge of the casserole. Baste the meat 3–4 times after browning. Cook for 15–18 minutes (not counting the browning time).

Reheat the sauce and pour it in a warmed sauce bowl.

Accompany the meat with Celery Root Purée and Chestnut Purée.**

Marinated Beef Fillet, Served Cold   *Filet de boeuf mariné, servi froid*

Marinate and cook the beef fillet as in the preceding recipe. Let it cool completely. Cut it into thin slices, place on an oval platter, and surround with a ring of ice-cold Chopped Aspic* made from 2 cups of Jellied Consommé* flavored with red port wine or cognac.

*Accompany the meat with Cold Game Sauce.**

BRAISED BEEF

Pot Roast *Boeuf mode*

A delicious as well as practical dish. It can be served hot for one meal and cold, molded in its own natural jelly, for another. The meat does not absolutely have to be larded, but larding makes it juicier.

Have the meat barded and tied, and ask your butcher to give you some sawed-up beef bones that have a little meat and fat clinging to them. The meat and bones are first browned in the oven, then transferred to a large braising pan or heavy-bottomed enameled casserole and simmered slowly for 3–3½ hours.

Marinating the meat is optional, but I, for one, am for it.

a 4-pound piece of rump chuck pot roast, or bottom round

marinade for the meat

1¾ cups dry white Burgundy wine
½ cup dry sherry or dry vermouth
1 onion and 1 carrot, sliced thin
a sprig of fresh or dried thyme
1 bay leaf

browning and braising ingredients

peanut oil and butter for oiling the oven pan used in browning
2–3 sawed-up beef bones
1 whole onion
1½ pounds whole carrots (set one aside, sliced, to add to the browning pan; the whole carrots may be used as garnish or for making Jellied Vegetable Loaf* to accompany the meat)
a sprig of dried or fresh thyme
1 bay leaf, broken in half
salt
butter for greasing the braising pan or casserole
½ pound pork rind, simmered for 10 minutes, refreshed in cold water, patted dry, and cut in 2-inch lengths
1 onion, quartered
1 calf's foot, split in half, blanched for 2–3 minutes, refreshed in cold water, and patted dry
the strained, heated marinade or 2 cups dry white Burgundy wine
about 7 cups hot Beef Bouillon,* degreased*
1 *Bouquet garni classique,** with a sprig each of tarragon and savory
1 clove garlic (optional)
a few coriander seeds (optional)
Preheat oven to 375° F. for browning the meat; reduce heat to 350° for braising.

marinating the meat

Marinate the meat for 8–12 hours, basting it twice and turning it once. Keep it refrigerated while it is marinating.

browning the meat

Oil and butter a large oven pan. Remove the meat from the marinade and pat dry. Place it in the pan and surround it with the beef bones, the whole onion, and the sliced carrot. Add the herbs. Place in the oven and brown the top side of the meat for 10 minutes, basting with the pan juices. Turn the meat and repeat the process. Baste and season with salt. When the meat and bones are good and brown and the pan juices have taken on a rich color, remove the pan from the oven, discard the herbs, and turn down oven heat.

braising the meat

Butter the braising pan or casserole. Place the strips of pork rind, fat side down, on the bottom and along the lower part of the sides. Put the meat in the middle of the pan and surround it with the browned bones and vegetables, whole carrots, and quartered onion. Place a half of calf's foot on each side of the pan, pour in the strained heated marinade and juices from the browning pan.

Heat the braising pan on top of the stove. When the liquid begins to boil, pour in the beef bouillon. Bring to a boil, add the *bouquet garni* and, if you like, the garlic and coriander seeds. Cover the pan and place in the oven for a slow braising of 3–3½ hours, checking from time to time to see that liquid is simmering gently. Lower oven heat if necessary.

When the meat is tender, transfer it, along with the carrots, to a heated dish, cover, and keep warm. Discard the bones. Strain the liquid into a saucepan through a sieve lined with dampened cheesecloth on which is placed an icecube to coagulate fat particles. Degrease.* Taste and adjust seasoning.

Reduce the cooking juices over low heat for a few minutes, skimming off all impurities that rise to the surface. Degrease* once more.

Slice the meat with a freshly sharpened knife. Arrange the slices on a heated metal platter and surround with the whole carrots. Cover the meat and vegetables with a few spoonfuls of reduced juices and serve the rest in a warmed sauce bowl.

The dish may also be accompanied with small Braised Lettuces or Stuffed Cabbage Leaves.**

Pot Roast Molded in Aspic   *Boeuf mode en gelée, moulé*

This dish is especially good for a buffet. The beef is prepared as in the preceding recipe, but with one more step: after straining and degreasing the braising liquid, clarify* it. Place the clarified liquid in a bowl and set it in the refrigerator until it has the consistency of thick syrup.

Allow the meat to cool completely and slice it. Then arrange the slices to look like the original piece of meat, pressing the slices one against the other firmly.

For molding the meat you will need a glass salad bowl with a wide top, large enough to hold the meat and its garnishes.

FOR 6-10 PEOPLE

the thickened jelly of the pot roast (2¾–3 cups)
the re-formed slices of pot roast

garnishes for the mold

6 cooked carrots (from the braising ingredients), sliced thin
5–6 fresh tarragon leaves, scalded, refreshed in cold water, and patted dry
1 canned pimento, drained, patted dry, and cut in narrow strips (optional)
a few lettuce leaves, washed and trimmed
2 tomatoes, peeled, seeded, and cut in quarters
10–12 small black olives

Assemble the pot roast jelly and the sliced meat.

garnishing the mold

Decorate the bottom of the bowl with the carrot slices, tarragon leaves, and, if you wish a note of color, the pimento. Spoon a layer of thickened jelly on top of the garnish and place in the refrigerator until set.

Holding the meat firmly and carefully, place it on top of the jellied decoration. Cover with the rest of the jelly. Return the bowl to the refrigerator until the jelly is completely set.

serving the beef in aspic

Place a few lettuce leaves in the middle of a round serving plate. Unmold the meat on these and garnish the dish with the quartered tomatoes and black olives.

for a more formal presentation

Prepare 1 recipe each of Glazed Carrots,* Small White Glazed Onions,* and Glazed Turnips.* Allow to cool.

Set the re-formed sliced meat in the middle of a long metal platter. Brush the meat with a layer of jelly and place in the refrigerator to set. Repeat this process three times until a shiny coating is obtained. Arrange the glazed vegetables around the meat in mounds, alternating the colors. Brush them lightly with a coating of jelly to make them glisten. Replace in the refrigerator until ready to serve.

In the springtime other cooked garnishes may be added: green asparagus tips, young leeks, Green Bean Salad, Family Style, glistening with a coating of the jelly. Still another idea is to place slices of Jellied Vegetable Loaf* around the edge of the round platter containing the meat.*

Casserole of Beef with Red Wine and Herbs   *Daube de boeuf*

Daube originated in the French Provençal region, and there are as many variations as there are fingers on your hands. But the principle remains the same: slow, long simmering of beef, left whole or cut in pieces (as in this recipe). The sauce is rich and fragrant and the meat fork-tender.

Use good wine in making *daube*. I recommend a Côtes-du-Rhône, which will keep its full-bodied flavor all through the cooking.

The word *daube* comes from the French word *daubière,* the name of the earthenware dish in which the meat was originally cooked. You may substitute a large, heavy-bottomed enameled (never metal) casserole with a cover.

FOR 6 PEOPLE

½ pound pork rind, simmered for 10 minutes, refreshed in cold water, and cut into narrow strips

½ pound barding fat, cut into ½-inch strips long enough to go around the middle of each piece of meat

2 tablespoons each finely minced parsley and garlic, mixed together and placed on a plate

3½ pounds lean chuck pot roast, bottom or top round, or other lean stewing beef, cut into 3-inch squares

3 tablespoons finely minced shallot

1 pound onions, sliced thin

½ pound packaged bacon, simmered for 10 minutes, refreshed in cold water, patted dry, and cut in 12 pieces

salt

freshly ground pepper

1 *Bouquet garni classique,** including a sprig of fresh or dried rosemary

2 tablespoons tomato paste

4½ cups Côtes-du-Rhône or other good, full-bodied red wine

4½ cups hot Beef Bouillon,* degreased*

*Beurre manié,** made from 1 tablespoon flour and 1 tablespoon butter

1 tablespoon minced parsley

Preheat oven to 350° F.

Lay half the strips of pork rind on the bottom of the casserole, fat side down. Roll the strips of barding fat in the parsley-garlic mixture until they are well coated. Then tie the strips around the pieces of beef. Arrange a layer of meat on top of the pork rind and sprinkle with half the minced shallot. On top of this place half the sliced onions. Repeat the process, starting with the pieces of beef. Slip the pieces of bacon in between the meat squares.

Place the casserole, uncovered, in the oven for 3–5 minutes to release the various flavors, then set on top of the stove over moderate heat. When the ingredients begin to steam, season with salt and pepper, add the *bouquet garni,* tomato paste, and wine. Bring to a boil and pour in the heated bouillon. Lay the rest of the pork rinds on top of the ingredients, cover the casserole, bring to a boil, and cook for about 5 minutes. Transfer the casserole to the oven and cook for 4–5 hours, checking every hour to see that the liquid is simmering gently and that the level of liquid is not too low. If necessary, lower oven heat slightly and add a little more bouillon and wine.

When the meat is tender, remove it from the oven, discard the barding strips, and place the meat in a heated metal serving dish with a cover.

Strain the cooking liquid into a saucepan and degrease* with care. Taste and adjust seasoning. Reduce the sauce very slightly over moderate heat. Remove from heat, whisk in the *beurre manié,* place over moderate heat for a minute or so, beating constantly. Spoon the sauce over the pieces of *daube.* Garnish with the pieces of bacon rescued from the strainer and the minced parsley.

Serve the daube *with Steamed Potatoes* or Creole Rice.* Whole Braised Chestnuts* or Stuffed Cabbage Leaves* make a delicious, if somewhat heavier, accompaniment.*

Beef Stew in Red Wine   *Boeuf bourguignon*

This universal favorite can be prepared entirely in advance, for it improves upon reheating.

Use two or three of the following cuts of meat in making the dish: bottom round, chuck pot roast, rump pot roast, or brisket. Have your butcher cut them in pieces.

FOR 6 PEOPLE

2 tablespoons butter and 1 tablespoon peanut oil (plus a tablespoon of each in reserve)
⅓ pound lean salt pork or bacon, simmered in boiling water for 10 minutes, refreshed in cold water, patted dry, and diced
2 onions, sliced
3 pounds stewing beef (see cuts above)
salt
freshly ground pepper
3 heaping tablespoons flour
3 cups red Burgundy wine
3 cups heated Beef Bouillon,* degreased*
1 carrot, sliced
1 tablespoon tomato paste
a good pinch of sugar
2 cloves garlic, crushed or squeezed through a garlic press
1 *Bouquet garni classique*
¼ cup warmed cognac, flamed in a ladle

garnishes for the bourguignon
These can be prepared while the meat is cooking.

16–18 Mushroom Caps Sautéed in Butter*
24 Small White Glazed Onions*
1 tablespoon finely minced parsley
12 triangular Croutons,* reheated before serving
Preheat oven to 350° F.

making the bourguignon

Heat the butter and oil in a large cast-iron or heavy-bottomed enameled casserole. Add the pieces of salt pork or bacon and the onions. Stir-cook these for a few minutes until they begin to color. Remove from the casserole with a slotted spoon and set aside.

Strain the fat from the casserole into a bowl. Wash and dry the casserole. Put the strained fat along with the reserved butter and oil into the casserole, heat, and add as much meat as the pan will hold comfortably. Brown the meat slowly, turning the pieces on all sides. Remove the meat to a platter as it is browned, add the rest of the meat, and brown in the same fashion and remove to the platter. If necessary, add more butter and oil. Salt and pepper the meat pieces as you arrange them on the platter.

Add the flour to the hot fat in the casserole, stirring slowly and patiently until the *roux* takes on the color of a hazelnut. Off heat, beat in the wine. Return to heat and boil for 1 minute. Reduce heat, pour in the warmed bouillon, bring to a boil, and put back the salt pork or bacon and the onion. Then add the carrot, tomato paste, sugar, garlic, *bouquet garni,* and the pieces of browned meat. Cover and place in the oven for about 2 hours, looking in every 20 minutes to see if more liquid is needed. If so, add more hot bouillon.

When the meat is tender, remove the casserole from the oven, discard the *bouquet garni,* and allow the fat to rise to the top. Skim off as much as you can with a spoon. Blot off the remaining fat with pieces of paper towel. Taste and adjust seasoning. Flame the cognac and stir into the casserole along with the sautéed mushrooms and glazed onions. Heat through on top of the stove.

serving the bourguignon

Transfer the pieces of meat to a heated large platter and spoon the sauce over them. Top with the mushrooms and onions. Sprinkle with parsley and place the reheated croutons between the pieces of meat.

This dish may be accompanied by Steamed Potatoes, Creole Rice,* or simply a dish of buttered noodles.*

LAMB

Noisettes of Lamb with Tarragon Sauce
Noisettes d'agneau à l'estragon

Noisettes are thick lamb chops cut from the loin of a boned saddle. Your butcher will prepare them for you. Each noisette should be hit with a cleaver to keep it flat while cooking.

In this recipe, the sauce is prepared first.

FOR 6 PEOPLE

sauce ingredients

ABOUT 1 CUP

> 2 cups strong Chicken Bouillon* or Chicken Consommé*
> 1 scant tablespoon tomato paste
> 1 teaspoon hot barbecue sauce
> 1 teaspoon ketchup
> a sprig of fresh or dried tarragon

other ingredients

> 6 noisettes of lamb
> peanut oil for the noisettes and sauté pan
> salt
> freshly ground white pepper
> 5 tablespoons butter
> 1 tablespoon finely minced shallot
> 2 tablespoons finely minced fresh tarragon
> 1 bunch of watercress

making the sauce

Mix all the ingredients together, place over medium heat, stirring, until reduced to about 1½ cups. Set aside.

preparing the noisettes

Brush each noisette with a little peanut oil. Lightly oil the sauté pan and place it over medium heat. When the pan is piping hot, put in the noisettes, pressing each against the bottom of the pan with a metal spatula. Cook them for 5–6 minutes on each side. Remove to a covered side dish, season with salt and pepper, and keep warm.

Deglaze* the sauté pan with 2 tablespoons of the butter. Stir in the minced shallot and 2–3 tablespoons of heated sauce, cook for 1 minute, stirring. Add another tablespoon or so of heated sauce and cook for 1–2 minutes. Strain into the pan of sauce and, constantly stirring, reduce to about 1 cup. Off heat, swirl in the remaining 3 tablespoons of butter. Taste and adjust seasoning. Stir in the tarragon.

Place the noisettes on a heated metal platter, top each with about 2 tablespoons of sauce, and garnish one end of the platter with the watercress.

Accompany with blanched Sautéed Potatoes* and Stuffed Mushrooms* or Green Bean Purée* or Potato Purée.*

Rack of Lamb with Mixed Vegetable Garnish
Carré d'agneau jardinière

A simple but elegant dish . . . the lamb is broiled, seasoned with salt and pepper, and served with a garnish of early-summer vegetables.

Have your butcher prepare the lamb so the chops are easily carved at serving time.

A large broiling pan equipped with a rack is needed for broiling the meat.

FOR 6–8 PEOPLE

ingredients for vegetable garnish, prepared ahead and kept warm

1 recipe of Green Peas, English Style*
1 recipe of Small White Glazed Onions*
1 recipe of Glazed Carrots*
6–8 large Stuffed Mushrooms*

meat ingredients

2 2–2½ pound racks of young lamb, each having 6 chops
peanut oil for the broiling pan
salt
freshly ground pepper
1 small bunch parsley for decorating the platter
Preheat the broiler.

Place the two roasts on the grill of the oiled roasting pan, fat sides up. Put the pan under the broiler, about 4 inches from heat. Brown for 10–12 minutes until the top is crisp and crackling. Season with salt and pepper. Turn the meat and repeat the process, seasoning with salt and pepper. Turn the meat a third time for a final browning of about 5 minutes.

Transfer the roasts to a board. Carve into chops and arrange them fanwise on a heated round platter with a bunch of parsley placed in the middle.

Serve the vegetables arranged with care on a heated metal serving dish.

Lamb en Brochette, Russian Style
Brochettes de mouton de pré-salé à la Russe

NOTE: *In France lambs or sheep that graze in the salty meadows of the coastal regions—Normandy and Brittany—are considered the choicest. They are known as* pré-salé *(salt-meadow) lamb or sheep, and do not have to be very highly seasoned with salt. Lambs or sheep that have not fed on these salty grasses should be seasoned, if possible, with coarse or fine sea salt.*

The Creole Rice* upon which the brochettes are unskewered can be made far in advance and reheated just before using.

The marinade for basting should be made first, since it needs to stand for at least one hour.

Have 6 skewers at hand.

FOR 6 PEOPLE

1 recipe of Creole Rice,* made ahead and reheated before using

marinade ingredients

1 cup aromatic Oil with Herbs from Provence*
a sprig of dried thyme
a sprig of dried savory
1 bay leaf
½ teaspoon crushed coriander seed or crushed black peppercorns
a few drops of lemon juice

other ingredients

6 slices packaged bacon, each slice cut into 6 pieces
2 pounds boned lamb meat (shoulder or leg) divided into 6 parts, each part weighing about ⅓ pound and cut into 6 pieces as regularly shaped as possible
1–2 bunches spring onions, washed, patted dry, root end cut off, and all but ½ inch of the green top discarded, then cut in 2-inch sections
salt
freshly ground pepper

garnishes

6–9 small Broiled Tomatoes*
6–9 raw spring onions, each with a ½-inch handle of green
1 lemon, cut in 6 sections, for squeezing over the lamb
Preheat the broiler.

making the marinade

Place the aromatic oil in a bowl and beat the herbs, condiments, and lemon juice into it. Allow to stand for at least 1 hour. Beat the marinade and strain it.

Skewer the ingredients in the following order: a piece of bacon, then of lamb, a piece of bacon and then of onion. Repeat this order to fill each brochette, ending with a piece of bacon. Arrange the skewers on a rack placed over the dripping pan of the oven and brush with half the strained marinade. Broil each side for 6–7 minutes, brushing the brochettes with the rest of the marinade after turning.

Remove the pan and rack from the oven and season the lamb and onions with salt and pepper.

Place the reheated Creole rice in a hot metal serving dish. Using a fork, unskewer the meat and onions onto the rice.

Place the broiled tomatoes, raw spring onions, and lemon sections around the edge of the dish.

Broiled Lamb Kidneys on a Nest of Greens
Rognons d'agneau grillés, en nid de verdure

An appetizing as well as attractive dish when prepared with care and seasoned with discretion.

Have your butcher remove the white membranes from the kidneys and cut them just a little more than halfway through. They should not be completely separated.

To make this recipe you will need two skewers and a heated metal platter large enough to hold the green garnish.

FOR 2 PEOPLE

4 fresh lamb kidneys

a small amount of peanut oil

salt

freshly ground pepper

1 pound Green Beans,* blanched, prepared ahead, and reheated in 2
    tablespoons of butter before serving

1 large bunch watercress

1 tablespoon finely minced parsley worked into 2 tablespoons butter,
    kept at kitchen temperature in a small saucepan

Preheat the broiler.

Skewer the kidneys through their middle sections so they lie flat, placing 2 kidneys on each skewer. Brush them lightly with oil and place them on the broiler grill. Broil for 4 minutes on one side and 3–4 minutes on the other. They should remain rosy and juicy inside.

Remove from oven and season with salt and pepper. Keep in a warm place.

Spread the reheated, buttered green beans over about two-thirds of the heated platter and place the watercress in the empty space. Heat the parsleyed butter in the saucepan. With the aid of a fork, unskewer the kidneys onto the green nest, pour the melted butter over them. Serve immediately.

LEG OF LAMB *Gigot d'agneau*

Many people have the idea that buying a leg of lamb is a wild extravagance, but actually, considering how many people you can serve with one, and how much of your valuable time you can save by preparing delicious but simple dishes with the leftovers, a leg of lamb is really not an extravagance at all!

Choosing a Leg of Lamb

Choose a leg that has a rounded shape rather than one that is long and flat. You can cut nicer-looking slices from a rounded leg.

Leg of lamb should be aged, for if it is too fresh the meat will be both dry and tough. If you know for a fact that a leg of lamb is very fresh, store it, lightly wrapped, in the refrigerator for three or four days before cooking it. Color is an indication of age: the best lamb has a pinkish-red color.

Roast Leg of Lamb, Basic Recipe

Have your butcher prepare the lamb for roasting. Ask him for all the bones (sawed up) and fat trimmings. These will be used in making the sauce. Before roasting the lamb, prepare the juice and set it aside.

FOR 8–10 PEOPLE
MAKES ABOUT I CUP

juice ingredients

the fat and sawed-up bones from the leg of lamb
3 tablespoons butter
2 tablespoons peanut oil
a sprig of fresh or dried thyme
a small piece of bay leaf
½ cup hot water
1 clove garlic
salt
freshly ground pepper

ingredients for roasting the lamb

a 6½–7 pound leg of lamb
1 clove garlic,[1] peeled and cut in 3 lengthwise
3 tablespoons softened margarine[2] for greasing the roasting pan and
  brushing on the meat
salt
freshly ground pepper
¼ cup hot water for deglazing the roasting pan
2 tablespoons butter
1 bunch watercress for garnish
Preheat oven to 350° F. for browning the bones, then raise oven temperature to
  365° for roasting the lamb.

making the juice

Put the lamb bones and fat along with 2 tablespoons of butter and 2 table-spoons of peanut oil into a heavy, preferably cast-iron, sauté pan. Add the herbs, place the pan in the oven, and brown the bones, turning frequently, for about 20 minutes. Remove the pan, discard the bones, and turn up oven heat.

Add the ½ cup of hot water and garlic to the pan, place over moderate heat, and reduce liquid by half. Off heat, stir in the remaining 1 tablespoon of butter. Add salt and pepper to taste. Strain the juice into a saucepan and degrease* carefully. Set aside.

roasting the lamb

Make 3 slits at the knuckle end of the leg and insert the garlic. Brush the roasting pan and leg of lamb with a generous coating of margarine.

Place the meat slightly below the middle of the oven, rounded side up. Brown for 15–20 minutes, turn the meat, season with salt and pepper, and baste with pan juices. Continue roasting, allowing 10–12 minutes a pound for rare meat, 12–14 minutes a pound for medium-rare meat, and 14–16 minutes a pound if you prefer your lamb well done (although I do not advise cooking lamb this much). Toward the middle of the cooking, lower oven heat slightly and cover the top of the meat with a piece of parchment paper if the lamb seems to be browning too much.

After cooking, leave the lamb in the oven, heat off, door open, for an 8-minute rest before slicing.

finishing the juice

Place the roasting pan over medium heat and deglaze* with the ¼ cup of hot water, stirring and scraping the bottom of the pan with the back of a fork.

---

[1] If you prefer, place 2 unpeeled garlic cloves, lightly crushed, alongside the lamb after it has been in the oven for 20 minutes.

[2] Butter should never be used in roasting lamb. It burns too easily and emits an acrid smell even if you use it along with peanut oil.

Lower heat and swirl in the 2 tablespoons of butter. Strain the liquid into the saucepan of reserved juice. Heat through, taste, and adjust seasoning, degrease if it seems necessary, and pour into a heated sauce bowl.

cutting the lamb

Have a heated metal platter at hand. Place the lamb on a board and cut slices of meat on the bias, that is, with the grain of the meat. Arrange the slices on the platter, alternating rare and better-done slices so as to be able to satisfy every taste.

The meat left next to the bone may be covered with aluminum foil and refrigerated for making leftover dishes.

Garnish one end of the platter with the bunch of watercress. Serve the meat as hot as possible, not forgetting to warm the dinner plates.

Suggested accompaniments: Sautéed (new) Potatoes,* Green Bean Purée,* Dried White Bean Purée,* and Onion Purée,* followed by a crisp salad.

TWO SAUCES FOR ROAST LEG OF LAMB

The best sauce for a leg of lamb is one made from its own juices (see the preceding recipe). But for those who like a change, here are two sauces admirably suited to roast leg of lamb. Both of these may be made ahead.

Garlic Sauce   *Sauce à l'ail*

MAKES ABOUT 1½ CUPS

¼ pound garlic cloves (or 2 bulbs of garlic)
1¼ cups cold water
1¼ cups cold Chicken Bouillon* (a little more if necessary)
salt
freshly ground pepper
a small amount freshly grated nutmeg
2 pats of butter
juice from a roast leg of lamb, degreased* (about 1 cup)

Peel the garlic cloves and put them to soak in the cold water for at least 3 hours to eliminate all trace of bitterness, changing the water 3 times. Drain and pat them dry.

Pour the bouillon into a small, heavy-bottomed enameled saucepan and add the garlic. Season lightly with salt, pepper, and nutmeg. Cover the saucepan and set over low heat. Simmer until the garlic has completely disintegrated and is easily crushed with a spatula. There should be about 2½ tablespoons of liquid left in the pan. If the liquid seems to be reducing too quickly, set the saucepan over an asbestos mat and add a little more bouillon.

Strain through a small sieve lined with dampened cheesecloth. Twist and squeeze the cheesecloth in order to press out all the flavor and juices.

Stir in the butter and whisk the mixture into the lamb juice. Heat through and serve in a heated sauce bowl.

Fresh Mint Sauce   *Sauce à la menthe fraîche*

MAKES ABOUT 1½ CUPS *(with lamb juice)*

1 cup finely minced fresh mint leaves, stems removed
1 tablespoon sugar
6 tablespoons cold water
1 cup wine vinegar
salt
freshly ground pepper
juice from a roast leg of lamb, degreased (about 1 cup)

Place the mint leaves, sugar, and 2 tablespoons of the water in a blender and process them.

Pour the vinegar into a small saucepan, set over medium heat, and reduce to 2 tablespoons. Add the remaining 4 tablespoons of water and the mint mixture. Season with salt and pepper and boil gently for 5 minutes. Strain through a small sieve lined with dampened cheesecloth. Twist and squeeze the cheesecloth to press out all the flavor and juices. Whisk into the lamb juice, heat through, and serve in a warmed sauce bowl.

Next-Day Leg of Lamb with Piquant Sauce
Lendemain de gigot, sauce piquante

The leftover lamb, cut in slices, is heated in a sauce heightened with vinegar and vinegar pickles.

enough lamb slices for 2–4 people

Piquant Sauce   MAKES ABOUT 2 CUPS OF SAUCE

¾ cup wine vinegar
2–3 shallots, finely minced
freshly ground pepper (2 turns of the mill)
2 tablespoons butter
2½ tablespoons flour
1 cup dry white wine
2¼ cups Chicken Bouillon* or chicken bouillon made from cubes
2–3 small vinegar pickles, finely minced

Put the vinegar, shallots, and pepper in a small enameled saucepan. Place over medium-low heat and simmer until reduced to 3 tablespoons. Set aside.

Using a heavy-bottomed enameled saucepan, prepare a blond *roux** with the butter and flour. Remove from heat and whisk in the wine and bouillon. Strain into the vinegar reduction and add the minced pickles. Place over low heat and simmer for 15–20 minutes, skimming if necessary, to obtain about 2 cups of sauce.

Place the lamb slices in a casserole, pour the sauce over them, and simmer very slowly for 8–10 minutes. Do not allow the sauce to boil, as this would toughen the meat. As a precaution, place an asbestos mat under the casserole. Remove from heat, taste, and adjust seasoning.

Transfer the meat slices to a shallow round dish and pour the sauce over them.

to make a milder sauce

Eliminate the vinegar reduction. Instead, stir-cook 2–3 shallots, finely minced, in 2 tablespoons of butter for 2 minutes and set aside. Follow the preceding recipe, and after stirring in the minced pickles, add 2–3 drops of wine vinegar. Heat the meat slices in the sauce and serve as above.

Suggested vegetable accompaniments: Potato Purée, Chestnut Purée,* or Potatoes Dauphine.**

Cold Leg of Lamb   *Gigot froid*

Cut all the remaining lamb off the bone in slices and neat pieces, arrange on a platter, and garnish with small vinegar pickles and a bunch of watercress. Accompany the meat with Mayonnaise* to which has been added a half clove of garlic, crushed.

Cold lamb may also be served with Green Mayonnaise* or French Dressing with Hard-Boiled Egg.*

Suggested salad accompaniments: Chicory with Garlic Crusts, Belgian Endive Salad,* or Dried White Bean Salad.**

Roast Leg of Spring Lamb Studded with Rosemary
Gigot d'agneau rosé, clouté de romarin

This is a recipe for people who shun garlic.[1]

FOR 6–8 PEOPLE

---

[1] For those who wish a taste of garlic to mingle with the fragrance of the rosemary, place 2 unpeeled garlic cloves on each side of the leg after about 20 minutes of roasting.

a 6½–7 pound leg of spring lamb
a good handful of dried rosemary leaves
salt
a small amount freshly ground pepper
Preheat oven to 365° F.

Using a fine larding needle, make small slits on the entire surface of the lamb. Stick a dried needle-shaped rosemary leaf into each slit. When you have finished, the lamb will resemble a hedgehog or a field of nicely spaced rosemary plants.

Prepare the meat as in Roast Leg of Lamb, Basic Recipe. Salt the leg halfway through the cooking. Use little (if any) pepper because rosemary and pepper do not go very well together.

Suggested accompaniments: Broiled Tomatoes,* Zucchini Fritters,* Sautéed Zucchini with Provençal Butter,* Green Bean Salad, Family Style.*

Roast Leg of Lamb with Provençal Herbs

Many people like to season a leg of lamb with herbs, such as dried thyme, to modify the naturally strong taste of an older lamb. If you must do this, go ahead, but let me give you a bit of advice. Do not add the herbs until after the meat has been thoroughly seared—about 30 minutes. If you put the herbs in the pan during the first part of the cooking, they will turn into little charred bits with a pronounced burned taste. When putting in the herb or herbs, add about ½ cup hot water to the lamb juices. Occasional basting will keep the herbs in good condition. Discard them after removing the lamb from the oven.

Roast Leg of Lamb with Green Peppercorns

Used with discretion, green peppercorns are particularly delicious with roast leg of lamb. When the roast is thoroughly seared—about 30 minutes—add 2 tablespoons of drained, slightly crushed green peppercorns to the roasting pan.

sauce made with green peppercorn pan juice   MAKES ABOUT 1½ CUPS
    2 tablespoons butter
    3 tablespoons heavy cream
    lamb juice (from Roast Leg of Lamb, Basic Recipe*)

Deglaze* the roasting pan with the butter and cream. Strain into a saucepan, add the lamb juice, and taste for seasoning. Heat through and pour into a warmed sauce bowl. This makes a sauce with a highly original taste.

A NOTE OF WARNING: *Do not use green peppercorns too frequently. Save it for special occasions so that the surprise and novelty will not wear off.*

Winter Lamb Stew with Turnips and Onions
Navarin d'hiver aux navets et aux oignons

Navarins are based on Simple Brown Roux Sauce.* They can be made with winter or summer vegetables, and both types are equally delicious and comforting.

Use two or three of the following cuts of lamb in making either recipe: shoulder, short ribs, neck, or breast. These cuts are much better than more expensive ones for stewing, as they do not dry out and become stringy.

FOR 6 PEOPLE

about 3½ pounds of a selection of lamb cuts listed above, boned, trimmed, and cut in pieces
salt
freshly ground pepper
a pinch of sugar
3 tablespoons lard, or 2 tablespoons butter and 2 tablespoons peanut oil
1 large onion, stuck with a clove
2 tablespoons flour
about 6½ cups lukewarm Beef Bouillon,* or bouillon made from bouillon cubes, or just plain water
1–2 tablespoons tomato paste
1–2 cloves garlic, crushed
1 *Bouquet garni classique**

ingredients for the garnish, cooked in advance

2 pounds Glazed Turnips,* cut in half, with ends rounded, set aside in their liquid
20 Small White Glazed Onions,* set aside in their liquid
1 tablespoon finely minced parsley for garnish
Preheat oven to 340° F.

cooking the meat

Lightly salt and pepper the meat pieces and sprinkle them with the sugar, which will help them to brown nicely.

In a large cast-iron or heavy-bottomed enameled casserole, heat the fat, add the onion, then the pieces of meat. Brown the meat evenly and slowly, turning it with a wooden spoon or spatula. Sprinkle it with flour and place in the oven for 5–6 minutes until the flour is golden brown. Remove the casserole from the oven, place over medium heat, and stir in the bouillon or water. The meat should be just barely covered. When the liquid comes to a boil, add the tomato paste, garlic, and *bouquet garni*. Cover and cook in the oven for about 1½ hours, testing for doneness after 1 hour.

Remove the casserole from the oven, discard the *bouquet garni,* and transfer the pieces of meat to a side dish. Let the fat rise to the surface of the sauce and degrease* with a spoon. Blot off any remaining fat with pieces of paper towel, passing them rapidly over the surface.

Wash and dry the casserole. Put in the meat pieces and strain the sauce over them. Add the glazed turnips and juice, bring to a simmer and cook, very slowly, for 10 minutes. Then add the onions and their juice and simmer for another 10 minutes.

Let the casserole stand, off heat, for a few minutes. Blot off any remaining fat with pieces of paper towel.

serving the navarin

Serve the meat, surrounded by the turnips and onions, in a warmed large platter. Cover with the piping hot sauce. Sprinkle the vegetable garnishes with minced parsley.

Leftover *navarin* is excellent warmed up. If you wish to add to the vegetable garnish, wash, peel, and trim to oval shapes 12 or so small potatoes. Place them in a saucepan of cold water, bring to a boil, add salt, and cook for 5–6 minutes. Finish the cooking in the *navarin* sauce.

If you are a little short on sauce, add 1 cup of bouillon when you put in the potatoes.

Lamb Stew with Spring Vegetables   *Navarin printanier*

It is hard to imagine a more attractive dish. Colorful and elegant in its simplicity, it will captivate the most difficult of your guests.

As in the preceding recipe, it is necessary to cook the vegetables separately, adding them to the *navarin* 15–20 minutes before serving the dish.

Fresh tarragon, fresh chervil, and fresh thyme will also add a springtime touch to the *bouquet garni.*

FOR 6 PEOPLE

See the ingredients and method in the preceding recipe. Only the garnishes change in this recipe. While the *navarin* is cooking, prepare the following vegetable garnishes:

about ½ pound fresh green peas
about ¼ pound fresh green beans
3 medium-size tomatoes or 4–5 small ones
about 1 pound small new potatoes

Put the shelled peas in a large amount of boiling water. Add a pinch of salt and a pinch of sugar. Blanch for 15–20 minutes or until tender. Drain and set aside.

Snip off the ends of the green beans and cut them into 1½–2-inch lengths; form these pieces into lozenge shapes, using scissors. Blanch the beans in boiling salted water for 10–12 minutes until they are tender but still crisp. Drain and set aside.

Scald each tomato for 30 seconds. Remove the cores. Peel, seed, and set aside.

Peel the new potatoes and trim them into small oval shapes with a vegetable peeler. Cover with cold water and set aside.

During the last 15–20 minutes of cooking, add the potatoes and tomatoes to the strained sauce and meat. When the potatoes are just tender, add the green beans and peas and cook for about 5 minutes. Remove the casserole from heat, tilt, and degrease* the sauce, using a spoon.

Place the meat on a heated deep platter, surround with the vegetables, making a colorful pattern, and pour the sauce over all. Sprinkle the vegetables with the fresh herbs if you possibly can.

Have the dinner plates piping hot for both these *navarins.*

Vegetables

Artichokes Cooked Whole, Basic Method
Artichauts cuits entiers

FOR 4 PEOPLE

4 artichokes
about 7 quarts water
2 tablespoons salt

Snap off the stem of each artichoke, thus detaching all the rough fibers of the heart. Snip off the points of the leaves with scissors and rinse the artichokes rapidly under the cold water tap.

Pour the water in a large kettle and bring to a boil. Add the salt and put in the artichokes, bottoms down. Cook for 30–45 minutes. The cooking time depends on the freshness and size of the artichokes. To test for doneness, strip a leaf from one of the artichokes and taste it. Do not overcook them, as overcooking makes them limp and tasteless. Drain them and set them on a rack, bottoms up.

Serve the artichokes hot or lukewarm on a platter covered with a napkin or a double thickness of paper towels.

If you serve the artichokes hot, accompany them with Béchamel Sauce,* Béchamel Sauce with Cream,* or with "Little Sauce" for Asparagus,* substituting the cooking water of the artichokes for the asparagus cooking water.

If you serve the artichokes lukewarm, accompany them with French Dressing* or French Dressing with Hard-Boiled Egg.*

NOTE: *Artichokes are not very good served cold. Cooling hardens them. If you make them in advance, reheat them in a large kettle of boiling water for 3–5 minutes. Drain as indicated above.*

Artichoke Hearts   *Fonds d'artichauts*

Whether they are topped with a sauce or garnished with, for example, sautéed mushrooms (see the end of the recipe), artichoke hearts are as delicious as they are attractive.

Unfortunately, few home cooks know the best way to prepare the hearts. They are usually cooked first, then stripped of their leaves until the heart and its choke are exposed. But in the process of stripping off the lower leaves, bits of the heart are torn off and the result is a rather mutilated spectacle.

A symmetrical, smooth, ready-to-cook artichoke heart is achieved only by beginning with a raw artichoke.

artichoke ingredients

    8–12 artichokes
    juice of ½ lemon

Blanc de légumes (bouillon)

    8–10 cups cold water (according to the amount of vegetables)
    2 tablespoons flour
    2 tablespoons cold water
    juice of 1 lemon
    2–2½ teaspoons salt
    1 Bouquet garni classique*

Snap off the stem of the raw artichoke as in the preceding recipe. With the thumb and forefinger grasp a leaf near the bottom and bend it back until it snaps off. Continue until all the leaves are removed and only the heart and choke remain.

Fill an enameled saucepan with cold water, squeeze in the juice of ½ lemon, and set aside.

Pare the bottom of the heart by turning it against the blade of a freshly sharpened knife, thus removing all bits of green and all stringy material. Turn the heart on its side and cut off the green stumps of the remaining leaves just above the choke. As each heart is prepared, drop it into the lemon-juiced water to keep it from darkening. Leave the hearts in the water for 3–4 minutes, then drain them and pat them dry.

cooking the artichoke hearts

First prepare the blanc de légumes. This is a kind of bouillon made with flour-thickened water, lemon juice, herbs, and salt. It is used in cooking delicate vegetables that would otherwise disintegrate when boiled.

Put the larger amount of water in an enameled or stainless steel (never aluminum) kettle. Mix the flour and the 2 tablespoons of cold water together in a bowl until smooth. Whisk the mixture into the kettle of water, add the lemon juice and salt, and heat slowly. When it comes to a boil, put in the bouquet garni. With a skimmer, lower the artichoke hearts into the boiling water and cook for 16–25 minutes. The amount of cooking time depends on the size and freshness of the hearts. Keep the water at a slow, steady boil throughout the cooking. The hearts should be tender-firm. In other words, do not allow them to become mushy.

Again using the skimmer, remove the hearts from the liquid and place them, bottoms down, on a board covered with 2–3 thicknesses of paper towels. Working delicately, remove the chokes with a spoon. Trim off any fibers or leaf ends with a sharp knife. The artichoke hearts may be served either hot or cold.

Mixed Vegetable Salad with Mayonnaise,* Celery Root with Mustard Sauce,* cold Ratatouille,* cold cooked shrimp bound with mayonnaise, leftover cold shredded fish in French Dressing with Hard-Boiled Egg.*

suggested garnishes for hot artichoke hearts

Fresh green peas; diced, blanched Sautéed Potatoes,* Mushroom Caps Sautéed in Butter,* green asparagus tips steamed in butter.

    Hot artichoke hearts may also be garnished with Artichoke Mousseline,* Celery Root Purée, or topped with Mornay Sauce* or Béchamel Sauce with Cream.*

Hot Poached Eggs on Artichoke Hearts with Hollandaise Sauce
Oeufs pochés chauds sur fonds d'artichauts, sauce hollandaise

FOR 6 PEOPLE

    3–4 tablespoons butter for reheating artichoke hearts
    6 cooked Artichoke Hearts,* made ahead and reheated
    1 shallot, finely minced (optional)
    6 Poached Eggs,* kept warm in a covered shallow dish over a pan of hot water, heat off
    1 recipe Hollandaise Sauce* kept hot (but not for too long) over a pan of hot water, heat off, and whisked from time to time

Heat the butter in a skillet, add the artichoke hearts and, if desired, the shallot. Heat the hearts through, allowing the bottoms of the hearts to remain in the butter and few seconds longer than the tops. Transfer them to a heated platter. Top each heart with a warm poached egg. Whisk the sauce one last time and spoon it over the eggs.

Cold Poached Eggs on Artichoke Hearts with Béatrice Sauce
Oeufs pochés froids sur fonds d'artichauts, sauce Béatrice

This recipe, including the sauce, can be made entirely in advance. Spoon the sauce over the egg-garnished hearts just before serving.

FOR 6 PEOPLE

    6 cooked Artichoke Hearts*
    lettuce leaves
    6 Poached Eggs,* well drained and cooled
    1 recipe Béatrice Sauce*

Arrange the artichoke hearts on a round platter spread with lettuce leaves. Garnish each heart with a poached egg. Keep cold until ready to serve, at which time top the eggs with spoonfuls of the sauce.

Artichoke Hearts Garnished with Artichoke Mousseline
Fonds d'artichauts à la mousseline d'artichauts

FOR 6 PEOPLE

6 cooked Artichoke Hearts*
1½ cups Artichoke Mousseline*
2 tablespoons heavy cream
freshly grated nutmeg
Preheat broiler

Garnish the artichoke hearts with the *mousseline*. Brush the tops with cream, grate a little nutmeg over each one, and set under the broiler for a second or two until lightly glazed.

These make a superb accompaniment for casseroled chicken, veal dishes, or as a garnish for sweetbreads.

ASPARAGUS   *Asperges*

TRANSLATOR'S NOTE: *In France the thick white Argenteuil asparagus is more common—though still a luxury—than the slim green variety commonly found in American markets. However, French white asparagus is not unknown in the United States. Both varieties are prepared and cooked the same way, with one small difference: white asparagus is cooked longer.*

Asparagus is one of the harbingers of spring; almost everyone looks forward to its arrival. This is rather strange, considering the peculiarities of the vegetable: it is expensive, and not only expensive but wasteful, since we peel away a good deal in preparing it and tend to leave less tender pieces uneaten on our plates; it is not easy to prepare or cook, and has a taste that can only be described as "bizarre"—yet it is one of the most sought after of all vegetables!

Asparagus, Basic Recipe

To get rid of the coarse, woody material that surrounds the stalks, asparagus must be peeled, and peeled deeply, rather than scraped. Either a sharp knife or a vegetable peeler can be used. Begin by cutting about two inches off the butt end of each stalk. Get rid of any small purple scales that may be attached to the stalks just below the tips. These contain sand that is next to impossible to rinse out. Hold the asparagus in your left hand with the tip facing you, then peel deeply from the tip down until the flesh is easily penetrated with one of your fingernails. Put each stalk into a large basin of cold water. Wash the asparagus as gently as possible so as not to bruise the delicate tips. Drain.

A platter of asparagus, with the tips broken off in cooking lying at one end, is a rather sad spectacle. Tips break off when the asparagus is laid flat in a kettle of boiling water, as the tender tips cook faster than the stalks and have a tendency to break off. To avoid this, the asparagus must be tied in bundles and placed upright in a deep, rather narrow kettle so that the stalks cook and the tips steam, and both are done at the same time.

Cut all the stalks the same length. Make bundles of 8–10 stalks. Tie them loosely about 2½ inches below the tips and about 2½ inches above the ends. Fill a deep kettle with water. Test the depth of the water with a bundle of asparagus—the water should be about 1½ inches away from the tips. Bring the water to a boil, add salt, and stand the bundles of asparagus in the water, leaning against one another. Put on the cover. If the tips peek out of the kettle, use an inverted saucepan as a cover. Cook the asparagus for 12–14 minutes from the time the water resumes boiling. If the stalks are very thick, add another 2–3 minutes to the cooking time.

As the season advances and asparagus becomes somewhat tougher, place a piece of dampened cheesecloth over them before setting the cover on. They can wait in the kettle, covered, heat off, for as long as 15 minutes.

Drain gently,[1] cut the strings, and place the asparagus in overlapping layers on a warmed platter covered with a napkin or a double thickness of paper towels. Serve the sauce in a separate bowl.

Asparagus Sauces

One of the nicest and quickest-to-make sauces consists of barely melted butter seasoned with salt, pepper, and a few drops of lemon juice. Two classical sauces for accompanying asparagus are Hollandaise Sauce* and Mousseline Sauce.*

Suggested cold sauces for warm asparagus: French Dressing,* French Dressing with Hard-Boiled Egg,* a Green Mayonnaise,* or Orange Mayonnaise with Cream.*

I strongly recommend the following "little sauce" for serving with asparagus. It is quickly made yet suggests one of the great classical sauces. And best of all, it will "wait," kept warm, for 10 minutes or so.

"Little Sauce" for Asparagus   *"Petite sauce" pour asperges*

MAKES 2 GOOD CUPS

> 2 tablespoons butter
> 2 tablespoons flour
> 1½ cups asparagus cooking water

[1] Save the asparagus water for using in soup or for making the next recipe.

---

2 egg yolks
4 tablespoons heavy cream
salt
freshly ground pepper
juice of ½ lemon
2 egg whites, stiffly beaten

Make a white *roux** with the butter and flour. Off heat, beat in the asparagus water. Place on heat and bring to a boil. Remove from heat.

Beat the egg yolks in a bowl, adding the cream gradually. Then whisk in the thickened asparagus water. Season with salt and pepper, stir in the lemon juice. Taste for seasoning.

Place the saucepan over low heat (using an asbestos mat is a good idea) and begin to whisk, adding large spoonfuls of the beaten egg whites. Let the sauce heat, beating constantly, and when it is smooth and thick, remove from heat, continuing to beat for a few more seconds. To reheat the sauce, beat it over very low heat for just a few seconds.

Asparagus with Two Sauces *Asperges aux deux sauces*

An elegant way to serve warm asparagus . . . two bowls of sauce, one hot or lukewarm, the other cold.

Select the two sauces from the following:

Hollandaise Sauce,* a Green Mayonnaise,* "Little Sauce" for Asparagus,* Orange Mayonnaise with Cream,* Hollandaise Sauce with Thickening,* Watercress Sauce,* Soft-Boiled Egg Sauce,* Lemon-Flavored Mayonnaise,* or Béatrice Sauce.*

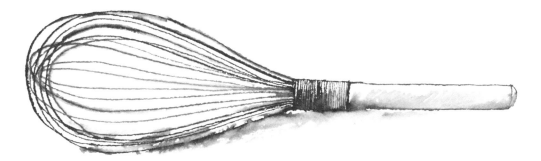

GREEN BEANS *Haricots verts*

Green beans, when prepared with care, are among the most delicious of vegetables. It goes without saying that they should be fresh and, if possible, stringless.

There is no point in making complicated dishes out of green beans. In the old days they were served with *béchamel* or other sauces or (as I found in one cookbook) "sautéed with onions for 20 minutes, until well-browned." Hard to believe!

Buttered Green Beans   *Haricots verts au beurre frais*

Use a large enameled or stainless steel kettle for making this recipe.

   2 pounds green beans, trimmed and washed
   6 quarts boiling water
   coarse salt
   4 tablespoons water
   4–5 pats of butter
   salt
   freshly ground pepper
   1 tablespoon mixed finely minced chervil, tarragon, and parsley for garnish
   2 pats of butter for garnish

preparing the beans for cooking

Snap off about ¼ inch from the ends of the beans. In case there are strings, lengthen the movement of snapping so that the snapped end glides down each side of the bean with the string trailing along. Put the beans in a large sieve and run cold tap water over them. Cook them as soon after this as possible. (It is a good idea to put the water on to boil while you are preparing the beans.)

cooking the beans

Plunge the beans by the handful into the boiling water. Stir gently with a long wooden spatula, cover, and let the water come to a boil again. Add coarse salt, stir, and cook the beans, uncovered, for 15–18 minutes. Taste a bean after 15 minutes. It should be slightly firm. Remember: the beans will cook a little more as they are buttered (or reheated). Beans become tasteless if overcooked.

Do not refresh the beans in cold water. Only refresh green beans that have somewhat overcooked. The cold water will make them firmer.

finishing the beans

Place the 4 tablespoons of water in a heavy-bottomed enameled saucepan. When it begins to steam, put in the beans, heat, and place the pats of butter on top. Cover the saucepan and heat for 2–3 minutes. Remove cover, stir the beans with a wooden spoon, add salt and pepper to taste, and transfer to a warmed vegetable dish. Use this same method for reheating beans if you have cooked them in advance, making sure that they are heated through. Sprinkle the top of the beans with the minced herbs. Place 2 pats of butter on top.

Green beans cooked in this manner can be used as an accompaniment for roasts of veal, pork, or lamb and are an essential ingredient in vegetable garnishes.

Green Bean Salad, Family Style
Salade de haricots verts, version familiale

Prepare and cook the same amount of green beans as in the preceding recipe, but do not warm them in butter. Let them cool to lukewarm, then season them with French Dressing* made with lemon or mustard. Double the recipe for the French dressing.

The salad can be garnished with a small piece of onion or garlic squeezed through a garlic press and mixed in with the dressing.

You can add a bright touch by decorating the salad with a peeled tomato cut in strips or diced.

Green Bean Salad, Dressed-Up Style
Salade de haricots verts, version habillée

> 2 pounds green beans, trimmed and washed
> 6 quarts boiling water
> coarse salt
> 1 double recipe of French Dressing*
> 2 canned pimentos, drained, patted dry, and cut into thin strips
> 2 spring onions, finely minced
> 1 tablespoons mixed finely minced chervil, tarragon, and parsley, or a few
>   leaves fresh basil, finely minced

Trim the beans, cutting them all the same length, and wash them. Divide them into bundles and tie each bundle loosely with string. Bring the water to a good boil, lower the bundles into it, and add some coarse salt. Cook until slightly firm. Do not butter as in the basic recipe.

Place the bundles on a round platter in the form of a pyramid, cutting away the strings as you pile the bundles of beans. Do not stir. Spoon the dressing over them. Decorate the top with the pimento strips, minced onion, and sprinkle with the mixed herbs or basil.

To make the salad larger, edge the platter with a ring of Potato Salad* or small peeled tomatoes cut in quarters and salted.

This is a lovely salad for a buffet. If necessary, double or triple the proportions.

Dried White Beans *Haricots secs*

The dried beans should be this year's crop. Stale beans will burst when cooked, and their flesh will be grainy.

> 1 pound dried Great Northern white beans
>
> enough lukewarm water to cover beans generously plus a kettle of almost boiling water for final cooking of the beans
>
> a sprig of fresh or dried savory
>
> salt
>
> freshly ground pepper
>
> 3–4 pats of butter
>
> 1 tablespoon finely minced parsley

Pick over and wash the beans. Soak them for 2 hours and drain. Place them in an enameled or stainless steel kettle, cover generously with lukewarm water, and slowly bring to a boil. Let them boil about 5 minutes. Drain them and put in the second enameled or stainless steel kettle of almost boiling water. Add the savory, bring the water to a boil, lower heat, and simmer, covered, until tender—about 2 hours. Strain the beans into a flameproof earthenware or porcelain casserole, season with salt and pepper, and stir in the butter. Heat through, stirring. Sprinkle with parsley and serve.

Dried White Beans, Breton Style *Haricots blancs à la bretonne*

Beans with tomatoes . . . especially good in the summer with garden-fresh tomatoes. This dish makes an excellent accompaniment for Leg of Lamb.* Serve them as they are or garnished with sautéed pork sausages.

> 1 pound dried Great Northern white beans
>
> enough lukewarm water to cover beans generously plus a kettle of almost boiling water for final cooking the beans
>
> a sprig of dried savory
>
> 2 medium-size onions, 1 stuck with a clove
>
> 1 leek white
>
> 1 clove garlic
>
> 1 *Bouquet garni classique**
>
> 1 tablespoon peanut oil
>
> 1 pound fresh tomatoes, peeled, seeded, and mashed
>
> a sprig of fresh or dried thyme
>
> ½ bay leaf
>
> salt
>
> freshly ground pepper
>
> 1 tablespoon finely minced parsley

Soak the beans for 2 hours and drain. Place them in a large enameled or stainless steel kettle, cover generously with lukewarm water, and slowly bring to a boil. Let them boil for about 5 minutes. Drain them and put them in the second enameled or stainless steel kettle of almost boiling water. Add the savory, onions, leek, garlic, and *bouquet garni.* Lower heat and cook, covered, until tender—about 2 hours.

Heat the oil in a small saucepan, add the tomatoes, thyme, and bay leaf. Season with salt and pepper and stir-cook for 5–6 minutes.

Drain the beans into a fireproof casserole, discard the *bouquet garni,* and stir in the tomato mixture. Simmer for about 15 minutes, stirring regularly. Place in a warmed serving dish and sprinkle with minced parsley.

Dried White Bean Salad *Salade de haricots blancs*

Cold leftover white beans cooked in the classical manner or Breton Style* make a delicious salad to be served along with other hors-d'oeuvre.

> 3 cups (or more) cooked dried white beans
> 1 teaspoon grated raw onion
> 4–6 tablespoons French Dressing with Mustard* (the amount of dressing depends on the quantity of beans)
> 1 tablespoon finely minced parsley

Put the beans, well drained, in a shallow salad bowl and add the grated onion. Mix in the dressing, sprinkle the salad with parsley, and serve.

Mixed Green and Baby Lima Beans *Haricots panachés*

In this original dish, green beans and baby limas are cooked separately, then mixed together and reheated.

FOR 6 PEOPLE

> 1 pound cooked Green Beans,* unbuttered
> 2 pounds baby lima beans, cooked in 2 cups of boiling salted water until tender (20–30 minutes)
> 3–4 tablespoons warm water
> 3–4 pats of butter
> 1 tablespoon finely minced parsley

Mix the two kinds of beans in a bowl, using the tips of the fingers.

Heat the water in a heavy-bottomed enameled saucepan add the mixed beans, and heat through slowly. When steam begins to rise, add the butter, stir carefully, and cover for another minute or so. When the beans are good and hot, transfer them to a warmed vegetable dish. Sprinkle with minced parsley and serve.

These are excellent served with all sorts of veal or Leg of Lamb.* *

BRUSSELS SPROUTS

Brussels sprouts are rather like miniature cabbages, though they have their own characteristic taste. Like cabbage, they must be blanched in a large enamel or stainless steel kettle of boiling salted water before final cooking.

NOTE: *In the United States, Brussels sprouts are usually washed and trimmed before being packed, so to prepare them for cooking, you need only cut off the stems. If you are lucky enough to have a garden or live near a place with fresh garden products, prepare the Brussels sprouts by trimming off exterior leaves and cutting off the stems. Wash abundantly in cold water.*

Brussels Sprouts Sautéed in Butter
Choux de Bruxelles sautés au beurre

FOR 4 PEOPLE

    2 pounds Brussels sprouts
    a kettle of boiling water
    salt
    6 tablespoons butter (cut half the butter into small pieces)

Prepare the sprouts as above. Drop them into an enameled or stainless steel kettle of vigorously boiling salted water and cook for 16–20 minutes or until almost tender. Taste a sprout after 16 minutes. Drain but do not refresh.

Heat 3 tablespoons of the butter in a large, heavy sauté pan. Put in the sprouts and sauté them, shaking the pan back and forth. Gradually add the cut-up pieces of butter. Cover the pan for a few minutes to allow the sprouts to steam in the butter. Test for doneness by inserting a fork in a sprout to see if it is tender all the way through. Taste for seasoning. Transfer to a heated metal serving dish.

Brussels sprouts cooked in this way can be used as a garnish for roasted or braised meats.

Braised Savoy Cabbage   *Chou vert braisé*

In this recipe the cabbage is blanched, then braised on a bed of vegetables, moistened with bouillon.

You will need a large enameled or stainless steel kettle and a round or oval braising pan or heavy-bottomed enameled casserole with a tight-fitting lid.

FOR 4–5 PEOPLE

a 2–2⅓ pound Savoy cabbage
boiling water for blanching cabbage
salt for the blanching water
oil and butter for the braising pan
2–3 carrots, sliced lengthwise
2 onions, sliced
¼ pound pork rind, simmered for 10 minutes, refreshed in cold water, and diced
1 *Bouquet garni classique**
5–6 juniper berries
4½ cups hot Beef Bouillon* (a little more if necessary)
2 tablespoons butter, cut in pieces
salt
freshly ground pepper
Preheat oven to 350° F.

Strip off the tough outer leaves from the cabbage, cut it in quarters, core, and wash thoroughly. Place it in a large uncovered kettle of boiling salted water and blanch for 15 minutes. In winter, when the cabbage is tough, set the cover on the kettle slightly askew.

Drain the cabbage and refresh it under the cold water tap. Place it on a board and chop it.

Oil and butter the braising pan, put in the carrots and onions, place over medium heat, and stir-cook for about 1 minute. Add half the diced pork rind.

Arrange the chopped cabbage on top, add the rest of the pork rind, the *bouquet garni,* and the juniper berries. Add enough hot bouillon just to cover the cabbage. Cover the braising pan with a piece of parchment paper, bring the liquid to a boil, cover, and place in the oven for about 2 hours, checking the amount of liquid every half hour and adding a little more if necessary. At the end of cooking, the bouillon should be entirely absorbed and the cabbage tender and succulent.

Stir in the pieces of butter and add salt and pepper to taste. Serve the cabbage in a heated vegetable dish garnished with broiled or sautéed sausages or crisply fried bacon.

Braised cabbage makes a good accompaniment for Roast Pork, Roast Pheasant,* or Roast Ham.**

Stuffed Cabbage Leaves   *Feuilles de chou farcies*

An original accompaniment for Roast Pork,* Roast Veal,* Roast Pheasant,* Casseroled Pheasant.*

Served cold with French Dressing* made with olive oil and lemon juice, then garnished with black olives and a sprinkling of chopped basil leaves, this dish makes a splendid entrée.

FOR 6 PEOPLE

12 large healthy cabbage leaves (use smooth green cabbage)
salt
about ½ pound leftover cooked meat (pot-au-feu, roast pork, roast chicken), finely chopped
1 onion, finely chopped and stir-cooked until slightly soft but not colored, in 2 tablespoons butter
2 tablespoons stale white bread pulp, moistened in a little bouillon, pressed out, and put through a food mill
1 egg
½ sprig of dried thyme, pulverized between the fingers
salt
freshly ground pepper
oil and butter for the braising pan or casserole
2–3 carrots, sliced lengthwise
2 onions, sliced in rounds
½ pound pork rind, simmered for 10 minutes, refreshed in cold water, and diced
1 *Bouquet garni classique**
12 coriander seeds
12 juniper berries
4½ cups hot Beef Bouillon* or Chicken Bouillon* (plus 1 cup in reserve)
Preheat oven to 340° F.

Put the cabbage leaves into an enameled or stainless steel kettle of boiling water. When the water begins to boil again, add salt. Blanch the leaves until they are supple—about 3–4 minutes. Refresh each leaf under the cold water tap and pat dry. Place them on a board and cut out and discard the base of the large vein from each leaf.

making the stuffing

Work the meat, onion, ground bread pulp, egg, thyme, salt, and pepper into a smooth mass, using a wooden spatula.

Place about 1 tablespoon of stuffing in the middle of each cabbage leaf. Close the leaf edges around it. Place a stuffed leaf in the corner of a clean kitchen towel. Pull the towel around it and twist gently to give the leaf a round shape. Repeat this operation for all the leaves.

cooking the cabbage

Generously oil and butter a braising pan or heavy-bottomed enameled casserole. Put in the sliced carrots and onions and stir-cook for 1 minute. Add half the diced pork rind.

Arrange the stuffed cabbage leaves on top, add the rest of the pork rind, the *bouquet garni,* coriander seeds, and juniper berries. Add enough hot bouillon just to cover the cabbage leaves. Cut a piece of parchment paper to fit the top of the braising pan and place it over the cabbage. Bring the liquid to a boil, set the lid on the pan, and place it in oven for about 1 hour 15 minutes, checking every 15 minutes to see if more bouillon is needed.

Serve in a heated vegetable dish or place the stuffed leaves around the edges of a platter of carved meat. Spoon a little bouillon over the leaves no matter how you choose to serve them.

Sauerkraut, Alsatian Style   *Choucroute garnie*

Sauerkraut is a delicious accompaniment for Roast Pork,* Roast Pheasant,* Casseroled Pheasant.* In France it is often eaten garnished, Alsatian style, as in the following recipe.

Before cooking, the sauerkraut must be thoroughly washed.

FOR 6-8 PEOPLE

3-3½ pounds fresh sauerkraut
¼ cup goose fat or lard
1 carrot, sliced
1 onion, stuck with a clove
1 tablespoon mixed coriander seed and juniper berries
2½ cups dry white Alsatian wine
2½ cups hot Beef Bouillon* or water
a 1-pound chunk bacon (rind removed), simmered for 20 minutes,
    refreshed in cold water, and drained
a 1-pound boneless shoulder butt
6-8 frankfurters
1 Polish Kielbasa sausage
Preheat oven to 350° F.

Put the sauerkraut in a colander and place under the cold water tap. Stir it around, separating the strands with the fingers, so the water reaches every part. When the water runs clear, let the sauerkraut drain for a minute or so. Then pick it up a handful at a time and press any remaining water out. Place on a board covered with paper towels for a few minutes to finish draining.

Put the sauerkraut in a heavy-bottomed enameled casserole over low heat. When it is warm, add half the fat, stirring it in with a wooden spatula until the sauerkraut is hot. Then add the carrot, onion, the rest of the fat, and the coriander seeds and juniper berries. Still stirring, heat for about 2 minutes, then add the wine. Cover the casserole, bring the liquid to a boil, and add the heated bouillon or water. Make places in the sauerkraut for all the meats, which should be covered with liquid. Cover the sauerkraut with a piece of parchment paper cut to fit, then put on the lid and place in oven for 2–2½ hours, removing the frankfurters and sausage as soon as they are cooked. Keep these warm. The rest of the meat can remain in the sauerkraut for the whole cooking time.

Stir the sauerkraut every half hour and lower oven heat when necessary to ensure a slow simmer. The liquid should be completely absorbed at the end of cooking.

serving the sauerkraut

Transfer it to a large heated platter and garnish with the shoulder butt and bacon cut in slices and the reheated frankfurters and sausage (the latter sliced). Decorate the top of the sauerkraut with the slices of carrot.

Serve beer or dry white wine with this dish.

CARROTS

Carrots are one of the healthiest of all vegetables, especially when they are cooked simply and not too long.

Carrots, Vichy Style   *Carottes à la Vichy*

Vichy is a world-renowned spa specializing in liver ailments. In all good hotels in Vichy, carrots are cooked in the mineral water that made the spa famous.

If you cannot get Vichy water, use ordinary tap water with a little baking soda added to it.

FOR 6 PEOPLE

> 2 pounds carrots
> warm water with 1 teaspoon baking soda to cover carrots
> salt
> a pinch of sugar (optional)
> 1 tablespoon butter, cut in pieces
> 1 tablespoon finely minced parsley

Peel or scrape the carrots thinly and cut them in fine slices. Place them in a wide saucepan and cover with the warm water and baking soda. Bring to a boil, lower heat, add salt and sugar. Cover the saucepan and cook the carrots for about 30 minutes, until they are tender and all the water has been absorbed. Add the pieces of butter, stir gently, and taste for seasoning. Replace the cover and let the carrots stand for 2–3 minutes. Transfer to a warmed vegetable dish and sprinkle with minced parsley.

Carrots with Béchamel Sauce with Cream and Egg
Carottes à la crème

FOR 6 PEOPLE

> 1½–2 pounds carrots
> about 4 cups warm water or light Chicken Bouillon*
> salt
> 2–3 sprigs of parsley
> a pinch of sugar

Peel or scrape carrots thinly and cut them in ½-inch slices. Place them in a saucepan of warm water or bouillon, add salt, parsley, and sugar. When the liquid begins to boil, lower heat, cover the saucepan, and cook the carrots until tender—about 35 minutes. Drain.

While the carrots are cooking, prepare the following sauce.

Béchamel Sauce with Cream and Egg
Sauce crème avec liaison à l'oeuf

MAKES ABOUT 1¾ CUPS

> 2 tablespoons butter
> 2 tablespoons flour
> 1 cup warmed milk
> ½ cup heavy cream beaten with 1 egg yolk
> salt
> freshly ground pepper
> freshly grated nutmeg

Make a Béchamel Sauce* with the butter, flour, and milk. Just before serving, beat in the cream and egg liaison. Season with salt, pepper, and a little grated nutmeg.

Transfer the drained carrots to a heavy-bottomed enameled saucepan, pour the sauce over them, and heat through without boiling. Serve in a warmed vegetable dish.

Glazed Carrots   *Carottes glacées*

A delicious and colorful garnish often served with Glazed Turnips* and Small White Glazed Onions.* The carrots are cooked in a small amount of liquid and butter, and when the liquid is almost completely reduced sugar is added, producing a glistening syrupy coating for the carrots.

FOR 4–6 PEOPLE

1¼ pounds carrots
2–3 tablespoons butter
1½ cups warm Consommé* or water
salt
freshly ground pepper
2 teaspoons sugar

Peel the carrots and rinse them. Cut each carrot into 2 or 3 pieces and with a sharp knife shape them into oblong pieces with angles rounded.

Melt the butter in a heavy-bottomed enameled saucepan just large enough to hold the carrots and liquid. Stir the carrots, shaking the pan from time to time, until they are all coated with butter. Pour in the consommé or water, cover, and cook for 10 minutes. Remove the cover and stir the carrots so that those on the bottom are on the top. Season lightly with salt and pepper, cover, and cook for 20–25 minutes or until carrots are tender.

When the liquid is almost completely reduced, add the sugar, cover the pan, and shake it back and forth for a minute or so. Uncover the pan and shake it once or twice. The carrots should be lightly browned and coated with a lustrous glaze.

Cauliflower au Gratin   *Chou-fleur au gratin*

FOR 5–6 PEOPLE

a 2-pound cauliflower
a few drops of vinegar (optional)
salt
butter for greasing the oven dish
1 recipe of Mornay Sauce* to which 3–4 tablespoons heavy cream has
    been added
3 tablespoons grated Swiss cheese and 1 tablespoon grated Parmesan
    cheese,[1] mixed together
a little freshly grated nutmeg
Preheat oven to 340° F. Then raise oven setting to broil.

Cut the stem of the cauliflower even with the base and strip off all outer leaves. Divide it into flowerets, trimming each stem to a length of about ½ inch. Place the flowerets in a basin of cold water to which may be added a drop or two of vinegar if there is any reason to fear slugs. These will then rise to the surface, where they can easily be disposed of. (This precaution is seldom necessary.) Drain the flowerets and cut a deep cross in the base of each stem to ensure quicker cooking.

[1] The addition of grated Parmesan cheese keeps the Swiss cheese from becoming sticky. It also brings out the flavor of the Swiss cheese.

Lower the flowerets into a large enameled or stainless steel kettle of boiling salted water. Cook quickly—15–20 minutes should suffice—for cauliflower develops a strong, unpleasant taste when cooked slowly. The flowerets should be tender-crisp, never mushy. Drain well.

Lightly butter a flameproof dish just large enough to hold the flowerets comfortably.

Make the Mornay sauce with its supplement of cream, spoon a thin layer of it on the bottom of the dish. Arrange the flowerets on top as closely together as possible. Using a spoon, coat each floweret with sauce.

Sprinkle the grated cheese on top, grate a little nutmeg over the cheese, and set the dish in the oven. After 8–10 minutes, heat the broiler and gratiné the cauliflower for 5–6 minutes, until the top is lightly browned.

Flowerets of Cauliflower Sautéed in Butter
Bouquets de chou-fleur sautés au beurre

FOR 5–6 PEOPLE

a 2-pound cauliflower, prepared for cooking as in preceding recipe
4 tablespoons butter
salt
freshly ground pepper
1 tablespoon finely minced parsley

Blanch the cauliflower as in the preceding recipe. Drain. Place the flowerets in a large skillet or sauté pan along with 2 tablespoons of the butter. Shake the pan back and forth so that the flowerets are all coated with butter. Add the remaining butter and cook, shaking the pan, until the flowerets have just begun to brown. Season with salt and pepper and transfer to a warmed vegetable dish. Sprinkle the top of the cauliflower with the minced parsley.

Sautéed cauliflower is excellent with veal or pork roasts, veal or pork chops.

See also Cauliflower Fritters* (Bouquets de chou-fleur frits.)

Raw Cauliflower Tidbits for the Cocktail Hour
Bouchées de chou-fleur cru pour l'apéritif

An American appetizer that is much appreciated by the French.

FOR 4–5 FLOWERETS PER PERSON

1 very firm small cauliflower
1 recipe of *Sauce Perrine** or *Sauce Françoise**

Cut the flowerets from the stalk of cauliflower, trimming each stem to a length of about ½ inch. Wash the flowerets in cold water and pat dry. Pierce each floweret with a toothpick. Place a bowl of sauce in the middle of a large round platter and arrange the flowerets around it in the form of a crown, the ends of the toothpicks facing outward.

CHESTNUTS *Marrons*

This delicious, mealy vegetable evokes Christmas goose or turkey for most of us. But chestnuts are also excellent, either braised or puréed, with all sorts of game. Many home cooks hesitate to make chestnuts because of the chore of peeling them. Here is a simple, quick way to perform this supposedly horrendous task.

Preheat oven to 400° F. Make 2 gashes on the flat side of each chestnut. Place chestnuts on a dripping pan and put in the oven for 4–5 minutes. NOTE: If the chestnuts are freshly gathered, leave them in the oven for only 3 minutes. Remove the chestnuts from the oven, shell, and peel.

Basic Method for Cooking Chestnuts

Chestnuts tend to fall apart when cooked in water or milk. If you wish to make whole chestnuts, follow this method: Cook them in chicken or veal stock (to cover) that has been bound by a small amount of flour or arrowroot diluted in water. This keeps the chestnuts from disintegrating.

Braised Chestnuts *Marrons braisés*

FOR 6 PEOPLE

butter for the oven dish
2¼ cups veal bouillon or Chicken Bouillon*
2 teaspoons arrowroot or flour dissolved in a little cold water
30 large raw chestnuts, peeled
3 tablespoons butter, cut in small pieces
1 *Bouquet garni classique** with a piece of fennel and a small celery leaf
a small amount salt
freshly ground pepper
Preheat oven to 350° F.

Butter a shallow oven dish large enough to hold all the chestnuts in one layer.

Heat the bouillon in a separate pan and stir in the dissolved arrowroot or flour.

Arrange the chestnuts in the oven dish, pour in the bouillon so that the chestnuts are just barely covered. Sprinkle on the pieces of butter, add the *bouquet garni,* and season with a little salt and pepper. Cover the dish with a piece of aluminum foil, place in the oven for about 45 minutes, basting once or twice, and checking the level of the bouillon, adding a little more if necessary. At the end of cooking, the chestnuts should be whole and tender.

Braised chestnuts are an excellent accompaniment for Roast Duck with Glazed Turnips and Glazed Onions,* Braised Duck,* Wild Rabbit,* or other furred game.

Corn Croquettes *Croquettes de maïs*

MAKES 20–24 CROQUETTES

2   16-ounce cans whole kernel corn
liquid from the cans of corn
2 tablespoons butter
3 heaping tablespoons flour
1 egg
salt
freshly ground pepper
3 egg whites, beaten to a light froth with a fork
3 handfuls white bread crumbs
3 cups peanut oil for deep-fat frying

Strain the liquid from the cans into a saucepan. Place over moderate heat, bring to a boil, and boil for 2 minutes.

In another saucepan make a white *roux** with the butter and flour. Off heat, stir in the corn liquid. Set over low heat and stir until the mixtures becomes very thick. Cool to lukewarm.

Pat the corn kernels dry with a kitchen towel.

Work the egg into the thick corn liquid, season with salt and pepper, and add the corn kernels. There should be just enough thickened liquid to bind the kernels. Let the mixture cool completely.

forming the croquettes

Take a tablespoon of the corn mixture out of the saucepan and roll it around in some flour on the board, until it is entirely coated with flour. Form into a small ball with your hands and set on a rack to dry. Repeat this operation until all the corn mixture has been used, renewing the flour on the board as needed. Next, roll each ball in the beaten egg whites,[1] then in the bread

---

[1] Corn croquettes rolled in beaten egg whites rather than whole eggs are easier to warm up because they stay firm. To warm up the croquettes: place them in a preheated 350° F. oven, door open, heat off, for about 10 minutes.

crumbs. Shape each ball into a cork-like form measuring about 1 by 1½ inches. They can be deep-fried immediately or allowed to stand for several hours.

cooking the croquettes

Heat the oil in a deep-fat fryer until the surface of the oil just begins to wrinkle. Cook the croquettes for 4–5 minutes, turning them once. They should be a light golden color. If they are allowed to become brown, they will be tough.

Remove the croquettes with a skimmer and place them on a heated metal platter covered with paper toweling. Salt lightly and serve.

These are a perfect accompaniment for fried or spit-roasted chicken, roast turkey or duck.

Salad of Corn Kernels *Salade de maïs*

FOR 5–6 PEOPLE

2 16-ounce cans whole kernel corn, well-drained
1 medium-size green pepper
1 pimento, drained, patted dry, and diced
2 medium-size tomatoes, peeled, seeded, juiced, and diced
2 small stalks celery, minced
7 tablespoons French Dressing* made with lemon juice, or 7 tablespoons Cream and Lemon Dressing*

decorations for the salad

3–4 thin onion rings
a handful of black olives
Preheat oven to 350° F.

Place the well-drained corn kernels in a salad bowl. Put the green pepper in the oven for 10 minutes to tenderize it. Allow to cool. Discard the core and seeds, then dice the pepper and add to the corn. Stir in the diced pimento, tomatoes, celery, and season with one of the dressings, mixing lightly but well. Taste and adjust seasoning. Decorate the salad with the onion rings and black olives.

Corn salad can be served along with other hors-d'oeuvre or as an accompaniment for cold chicken or cold roast pork.

BELGIAN ENDIVE *Endive*

NOTE: *Though this vegetable is known in the United States as "Belgian endive," it is also widely cultivated in France.*

Endive is a form of chicory that is as good cooked as it is raw in salads. The leaves have a mildly bitter taste that is not in the least disagreeable. But you must extract the core, which is an extension of the root end, because it is extremely bitter, and if not removed will ruin the taste of the endive. Cut around the core with the point of a knife and draw it out.

Wash each endive rapidly in cold water to rid it of sand. Dry thoroughly before blanching.

Do not attempt to cook endive before blanching. It will never become completely tender unless cooked so long that the outside leaves become discolored and the mild bitterness referred to above becomes overpowering.

basic method for blanching Belgian endive

Place the endives in an enameled or stainless steel kettle of boiling salted water, slightly acidulated with a squeeze or two of lemon juice. Cook the endives for 10–15 minutes (according to size). Drain them but do not refresh. Place each one between your hands and press out the water. Very thick endives may be cut in half lengthwise before proceeding with the recipe.

Blanched endive will keep for hours before being stewed or steamed.

Cooked endive makes an excellent garnish for veal or pork roasts or for roasted or braised poultry. And nothing is nicer than a crisp Belgian Endive Salad* after a hearty winter meal.

When I prepare cooked endive, I always make enough for two meals (counting two cooked endives per person). After blanching and pressing out the water, I wrap aluminum foil around them and place them in the refrigerator to be used two days later.

Belgian Endives Steamed in Butter   *Endives étuvées au beurre*

FOR 6 PEOPLE

2–2½ pounds Belgian endives
water for blanching the endives
salt for endive water
4 tablespoons butter plus 2 tablespoons in reserve
2 tablespoons peanut oil
salt
juice of ½ lemon

Peel the endives and blanch them in boiling salted water (see the Basic Method* preceding this recipe). Press out the water. In a large, heavy-bottomed enameled casserole melt 2 tablespoons of the butter and add the oil. Remove the casserole from heat and place the endives in it, alternating head and root ends. Place over low heat, add 2 more tablespoons of butter, and salt lightly. Place a piece of parchment paper over the endives, cover, and cook for 10–15 minutes, turning them once. When turning, add the reserved 2 tablespoons of butter and the lemon juice. The endives should be tender and lightly golden in color. Too much browning will bring out their bitter taste.

Serve the endives in a warmed vegetable dish or as a garnish for a platter of meat.

Oven-Braised Belgian Endives *Endives braisées au four*

FOR 6 PEOPLE

Preheat oven to 350° F.

Use the same amount of endives, butter, and oil as in the preceding recipe. Peel the endives, rinse and blanch them. Arrange them in a buttered, oiled casserole as in the above recipe. Steam on top of stove for 5–6 minutes. Cover with parchment paper, put the lid on the casserole, and place the endives in the oven for a braising of 20–25 minutes, turning them once and adding 2 tablespoon of butter cut in small pieces.

Belgian Endives with Bacon and Mornay Sauce au Gratin
Endives au bacon, sauce Mornay

FOR 4–6 PEOPLE

10–12 Belgian endives
10–12 slices packaged bacon, simmered for 10 minutes, refreshed, and patted dry
butter for the baking dish
1 recipe of Mornay Sauce*
2 tablespoons grated Swiss cheese or grated Parmesan cheese
Preheat oven to 350° F.; turn to broil position to gratiné the endives.

Peel, rinse, and blanch the endives (Basic Method*). Wrap each endive in a slice of bacon and arrange in a well-buttered baking dish. Place in the oven for 6–7 minutes or until the bacon is firm and lightly brown. Remove the dish from the oven, set to broil position.

Prepare the Mornay sauce, seasoning it well with the salt, pepper, and freshly grated nutmeg called for. Pour it over the bacon-wrapped endives. Sprinkle the top with grated cheese and place the dish under the broiler, not too close to heat, for 7–8 minutes, until the top is gratinéed.

Fennel Hearts Braised in Butter *Coeurs de fenouil étuvés au beurre*

Fennel is a delicate-tasting vegetable that imparts its anise taste to whatever fish or meat it accompanies.

FOR 6 PEOPLE

4–6 medium-size fennel bulbs
boiling water for blanching the fennel
coarse salt for the blanching water
6 tablespoons butter divided in 2 parts

---

salt

freshly ground pepper

Discard the coarse outer leaves of the fennel bulbs and snip off the feathery shoots. Keep the shoots, which are delicious diced finely and added raw to mixed vegetable salad or celery salad. They are particularly good when used as a garnish for steamed or sautéed potatoes.

Lower the fennel hearts into a kettle of boiling salted water and cook for about 20 minutes, uncovered. Test for tenderness with a fork. Drain the bulbs. Strip away all the outer leaves until the heart is exposed. Cut the hearts in half.

Melt half the butter in a large skillet, add the fennel hearts, and cook for about 5 minutes, partially covered. Turn the hearts, add the rest of the butter, and cook for another 5 minutes. Remove the fennel hearts when they begin to color and season with salt and pepper. Serve in a warm vegetable dish.

Fennel Hearts au Gratin   *Coeurs de fenouil gratinés*

FOR 6 PEOPLE

butter for greasing the oven dish

blanched fennel hearts (see the preceding recipe)

2 tablespoons grated Swiss cheese

½ teaspoon curry powder

Preheat oven to 350° F.

Butter an oven dish and arrange the halved fennel hearts in it. Sprinkle with grated cheese and curry powder, place in the oven until the top is golden brown.

This is a delicious accompaniment for fish of all kinds.

LENTILS   *Lentilles*

Lentils are both delicious and nourishing. Many people regard them as "uninteresting," cook them in a slapdash way, and never think of serving them to guests. But lentils, cooked properly, make an excellent accompaniment for all sorts of game and for dark-fleshed roasted poultry.

TRANSLATOR'S NOTE: *In the United States tan-colored lentils are the most commonly used. When green lentils are called for in the following recipes, you may substitute tan ones, for there is really not much difference in taste.*

Lentils, Basic Method for Cooking

a 1-pound package dried green lentils
lukewarm water for cooking them
1 onion stuck with a clove
1 medium-size carrot
1 *Bouquet garni classique**
*Beurre manié** (if necessary), made with 1 tablespoon butter and 1
    tablespoon flour
salt
freshly ground pepper

Soak the lentils for 1–2 hours, place them in an enameled (never metal) kettle, and cover them generously with lukewarm water. Bring to a boil and add the onion, carrot, and *bouquet garni.* Lower heat and simmer for about 1 hour 15 minutes, covered until the lentils are tender but still whole.

At the end the water should be entirely absorbed. As the level of water becomes lower, stir the lentils frequently so they do not stick to the bottom of the kettle. If a small amount of water remains in the kettle, bind it with *beurre manié.* Season the lentils with salt to taste and grind a little pepper over them. Place them in a warmed vegetable dish and serve.

Tomato-Flavored Lentils *Lentilles à la tomate*

1 recipe of Lentils, Basic Method for Cooking*
2 tablespoons tomato paste
3–4 tablespoons juice from whatever meat or game you are preparing

Cook the lentils for 50 minutes, strain the liquid into a saucepan, and return the lentils to the kettle, off heat.

Mix the tomato paste and meat juice into the lentil liquid, place over medium heat, and, stirring, bring to a boil. Pour the tomato mixture into the kettle of lentils, place over low heat, and cook for another 20 minutes, stirring frequently, until the lentils are tender. Serve in a warmed vegetable dish.

Braised Lettuce *Laitues braisées*

A delicious dish that I often have just as it is, without any meat accompaniment.

6 heads of lettuce, each weighing a little over ½ pound
1–2 drops of vinegar

boiling water for blanching the lettuce

salt for the blanching water

butter for the braising pan or casserole

¼ pound pork rind, simmered for 10 minutes, refreshed in cold water, and cut into 2-inch lengths

2–3 carrots, cut in small lengthwise pieces

2 onions, sliced thin

salt

freshly ground pepper

freshly grated nutmeg

1 *Bouquet garni classique**

2 cups Beef Bouillon,* not degreased

2 tablespoons butter, cut in pieces

Preheat oven to 330° F.

preparing the lettuce

Discard any wilted outside leaves. Trim the stems of each head to a point. Fill a bowl with cold water and add a drop or two of vinegar. Wash each head quickly, holding it by its stem and rotating it to remove all sand. Repeat the operation in cold water *without* vinegar. Drain the lettuce well.

blanching the lettuce

Heat water in a large enameled or stainless steel kettle until it boils. Lower the lettuce, tops up, into the water. Press lightly against the heads with a skimmer to force them deep into the water. Cover the kettle until the water boils again. Remove the cover, add salt, and cook, uncovered, for 5 minutes. Remove the heads of lettuce and refresh thoroughly under the cold water tap. Press the water out of each head by squeezing it gently between the hands. Cut each head in half, fold the top leaves inward so as to form small, rectangular "packages."

Generously butter a braising pan or heavy-bottomed enameled casserole. Put in the pork rind, fat side down, then add the carrots and onions. Place the lettuce packages on top, one against the other (slightly overlapping), in a single layer. Season with a little salt, pepper, and nutmeg. Push the *bouquet garni* into the center of the ingredients. The recipe can be made ahead to this point. Cover the pan if the dish is to wait.

braising the lettuce

Place the pan, uncovered, over medium heat and cook for about 5 minutes, until the juices begin to steam. Pour in the hot bouillon and bring to a boil. Place a piece of parchment paper over the lettuce, cover, and put the pan in the oven for a good hour of braising.

With a skimmer, transfer the lettuce to a heated metal dish, cover, and keep warm.

Strain the pan juices into a saucepan and degrease.* There should be about ⅓ cup of liquid that will be rich and syrupy due to the gelatinous elements in the pork rinds. Heat the juice through, then, off heat, add the pieces of butter, shaking the saucepan back and forth.

Braised lettuce make a delicious accompaniment for roast pork or roast veal. It is an excellent garnish for green beans to which Small White Glazed Onions* have been added.

CULTIVATED MUSHROOMS[1] *Champignons de couche*

Cultivated mushrooms should be fresh, firm, and creamy white with smooth, unblemished caps and stems. Small "button" mushrooms make elegant garnishes and are also the best size for mushrooms *a la grecque* (see Vegetables à la Grecques*). Medium-size mushrooms, cut in quarters or slices, are used in sauces and ragouts. Very large mushrooms may be stuffed.

A note on canned mushrooms: I do not advise using these for any recipe whatsoever. They sit in their cans of liquid, overcooked, tasteless, and rubbery, in contrast to their fragrant fresh brothers. Canned mushrooms may look like the real thing in a sauce, but they are utterly tasteless. It is far better to substitute a few drops of lemon juice or a sprig or two of fresh or dried herbs than to use mushrooms out of a can.

Mushroom Caps Sautéed in Butter
Capsules ou têtes de champignons, sautées au beurre

These may be used to garnish steaks and chops.

COUNT 4–6 PER SERVING

20–24 button mushrooms of roughly the same size
1 lemon, cut in halves
2–3 tablespoons butter plus 1–2 pats
salt
freshly ground pepper
a drop or two of lemon juice (optional)

Do not peel the mushrooms. Cut off the stems and wash the caps one by one under the cold water tap. Place them for a few minutes in a bowl of cold water into which you have squeezed the juice of one of the lemon halves. Rub each mushroom with the cut side of the unsqueezed lemon half, stir them around

---

[1] It is a great pity that we cannot include Mme. Bertholle's recipes for the famous wild mushrooms that are so prevalent in France: *cèpes, chanterelles, coulemelles, morilles,* and so forth. Some of these can be bought dried in the United States, and in this book we have included a recipe featuring dried morels (Chicken and Sweetbreads with Dried Morels and Cream.*)

in the water, drain them, and dry each one carefully with a clean kitchen towel. Fold them lightly in a dry towel while the butter heats.

Heat the 2–3 tablespoons of butter in a small sauté pan, put in the mushrooms, caps down, for 2–3 minutes, until they begin to color. Turn the caps over and cook for 3–4 minutes, adding 1–2 pats of butter. Transfer to a small heated dish, season with salt and pepper, and a drop or two of lemon juice.

Stewed Mushrooms   *Champignons cuits "à blanc"*

Prepare the same quantity of mushrooms as in the preceding recipe. Place the well-dried mushrooms in a small saucepan and add:

    2–3 pats of butter
    4 tablespoons cold water
    salt
    freshly ground pepper
    2–3 drops of lemon juice

Cook the mushrooms for 7–10 minutes. The amount of cooking depends on their size. Do not overcook: they should remain slightly firm.

Stewed mushrooms and their fragrant juice are added to sauces used in certain chicken recipes, Chicken Marengo,* for example, and to ragouts.

Concentrated Essence of Mushrooms   *Fumet de champignons*

    20–24 medium-size mushrooms
    3–5 tablespoons cold water
    1–2 tablespoons lemon juice
    4–5 pats of butter
    salt
    freshly ground pepper

After cutting off the stems, wash the mushrooms thoroughly, pat dry, and slice.

Place them in an enameled saucepan along with the water, lemon juice, and butter. Add a little salt and pepper and cook rapidly, uncovered, for 5–6 minutes or until the mushrooms have rendered their juices. Drain them into another, small saucepan. Reduce the cooking liquid until you have a highly concentrated essence. This makes a rich flavoring for sauces.

Stuffed Mushrooms *Champignons farcis*

Stuffed mushrooms are a classical garnish for vegetables, roast meats, poultry, or baked fish.

FOR 6 PEOPLE

12 large mushrooms, at least 2½ inches in diameter
a squeeze of lemon juice
the mushroom stems, finely minced
1 tablespoon peanut oil
1 slice boiled ham, finely minced
1 clove garlic, squeezed through a garlic press
2 slices stale white bread, crusts removed, moistened in water, pressed
    out, and put through a food mill
1 small shallot, finely minced
2 small pinches of dried thyme leaves, pulverized between the fingers
salt
freshly ground pepper
1 egg, lightly beaten
2–2½ tablespoons dried bread crumbs
2 tablespoons butter cut in small pieces
Preheat oven to 340° F.

Separate the stems of the mushrooms from the caps. Wash them all in cold water to which lemon juice has been added. Dry stems and caps with a clean kitchen towel. Set the caps aside, loosely covered with a dry towel.

Mince the stems finely, heat the oil in a small enameled saucepan, and stew them for 1–2 minutes, allowing them just barely to color. With a skimmer, transfer them to a mixing bowl. Add the ham, garlic, bread, shallot, thyme, salt, and pepper. Work these ingredients together with a fork. Bind them with the egg, mixing with a wooden spatula. Taste for seasoning.

Fill the mushroom caps, rounding the stuffing into dome shapes. Sprinkle the tops with bread crumbs and butter. Place the mushrooms one against the other in a flameproof oven dish just large enough to hold them. Bake for 18–20 minutes, until the top is lightly browned and the caps are tender-firm.

Mushrooms Duxelles *Duxelles de champignons*

Mushrooms *duxelles* are finely minced mushrooms cooked quickly in butter, seasoned with salt and pepper and sometimes a small amount of shallot or a few drops of lemon juice. They enrich and add fragrance to all sorts of sauces; they can be used as a garnish or filling for many vegetables, and they add a note of elegance to the simplest of dishes. Fish fillets baked *au naturel* become sumptuous dinner-party fare when laid on a bed of mushroom *duxelles* and covered with a rich sauce.

The process of making *duxelles* was "invented" by La Varenne, *officier de bouche*[1] of the Marquis d'Uxelles.

Classical Duxelles   *Duxelles classique*

The following recipe is for *duxelles* that can be used to enrich sauces, as a bed on which to serve fish fillets, as a garnish, or as a filling.

MAKES ABOUT 1 CUP

½ pound mushrooms
2 tablespoons butter plus 1 tablespoon held in reserve
2 small shallots, finely minced
salt
freshly ground pepper
a squeeze of lemon juice (optional)

Remove the mushroom stems and wash the caps. Drain and dry them thoroughly, slice them, then mince them as finely as possible, using a plain (not stainless) steel knife. Put the 2 tablespoons of butter, the shallots, and minced mushroom caps in a small sauté pan. Place over moderate heat and stir-cook for 3 minutes, adding the reserved butter and not allowing them to color. Do not overcook.

They are now ready to be used for whatever purpose your recipe calls for.

Do not let them stand in the sauté pan if it is metal. Remove them, along with their juice, to a glass bowl.

Dry Mushroom Duxelles   *Duxelles sèche*

The juices of the minced mushrooms are pressed out in this method of preparing *duxelles*. The natural juice of mushrooms runs brown when it is pressed out. This juice tends to be acrid, especially if the mushrooms are not perfectly fresh. Also, it might color sauces that are meant to be delicate and pale.

To press the minced mushrooms, put them in the corner of a clean kitchen towel. Twist and turn the towel to extract every bit of juice possible. The mushrooms will then be completely dry.

Cook them as in Classical Duxelles.*

[1] Table steward, especially for royalty.

Bound Mushroom Duxelles[1] *Duxelles liée*

Stir 2 tablespoons of heavy cream into the *duxelles* after cooking them.

For a firmer binding, use a large pinch of arrowroot dissolved in a teaspoon of water. Stir this into the *duxelles* after adding the cream.

These *duxelles* are especially good as a garnish for Artichoke Hearts.*

Small White Glazed Onions *Petits oignons glacés*

15–20 small white onions about 1 inch in diameter
2–3 tablespoons butter
1¼–2 cups Chicken Bouillon* or water
salt
freshly ground pepper
1 scant tablespoon sugar

Peel the thin outer skins from the onions, taking care not to cut into the flesh. With the end of a sharp knife cut a deep cross in the root end of each onion, so that the cooking liquid penetrates to the heart, thus ensuring even cooking.

Put the butter in a small, heavy-bottomed enameled saucepan and add the onions, which should be rather crowded together. Place the saucepan over medium heat and move it back and forth and shake it up and down until the onions are coated with butter. Continue cooking and shaking the pan until the onions are transparent and faintly yellow. Pour in enough bouillon or water to cover the onions barely. Season with salt and pepper. Cover the saucepan and simmer the onions over low heat for about 20 minutes, until the liquid is almost entirely reduced. Then add the sugar and shake the pan up and down a few times until the onions are covered with a lustrous glaze.

NOTE: *In winter when onions are stronger and tougher, it is a good idea to drop them into boiling water for about 5 minutes (after peeling) and then proceed with this recipe.*

Glazed onions are sometimes used in combination with Glazed Carrots and Glazed Turnips* for garnishing various dishes.*

FRESH GREEN PEAS *Petits pois*

Peas that are perfectly fresh have undamaged bright green, pods with no black spots. Avoid buying peas with dull, yellowish pods—they are sure to be tough and floury.

NOTE: *Medium-size to small fresh peas are the kind usually found in American markets, and the following recipes are based on these.*

---

[1] Bound mushroom *duxelles* may be made from classical *duxelles* or dry *duxelles*.

Green Peas, French Style *Petits pois à la française*

To my mind this is absolutely the best way to prepare fresh peas. The peas are steamed in very little water along with small heads of lettuce or lettuce leaves and a few small white onions. A generous amount of butter and a little sugar bring out the marvelous flavor of both peas and juice.

For cooking the peas you will need a good-size heavy-bottomed enameled saucepan. You will also need a shallow dish (a soup plate of the proper size will do) that will fit on top of the saucepan.

FOR 6 PEOPLE

2 small heads lettuce
boiling water for blanching the lettuce
6–10 small white onions
4 pounds unshelled green peas
a sprig of parsley with stem
a sprig of fresh or dried savory or thyme, or 1 fresh or dried sage leaf
6 tablespoons butter, cut in pieces, plus 2 tablespoons butter in reserve
1 lump sugar, broken into small bits
½ cup cold water
salt

Discard any wilted outer leaves of each head of lettuce and trim the stems even with the base. Wash the lettuce in a bowl of cold water. Drain, gently press out the water, and pat dry. Cut each head in half and fold the outer leaves over the cut sides. Tie each half lettuce around top and bottom with string to keep it from falling apart while cooking. Place the tied lettuce halves in a kettle of rapidly boiling water and blanch for 3 minutes once the water has resumed boiling. Drain.

Cut a cross in the root end of each onion to ensure even cooking. Place them in a small saucepan, cover with cold water, bring to a boil, and blanch for 5–6 minutes. Drain and set aside with the lettuce halves.

Shell the peas and put them in the heavy-bottomed saucepan along with the lettuce halves and onions. Push in the herbs, distribute the pieces of butter and bits of sugar, and add the ½ cup of water.

Cover the saucepan with a shallow dish filled with cold water. This maintains the humidity and concentrates the steam inside the saucepan. Renew the water in the dish when necessary.

The peas should be cooked over brisk heat rather than simmered. After they begin to boil—in about 8–10 minutes—add salt and cook for 20 minutes or until the peas are tender.

Remove from heat, discard the herbs, add the reserved butter, shaking the pan back and forth until the butter has melted.

Place the peas in a warmed vegetable dish. After snipping off the strings, arrange the lettuce halves on top and strew the onions around them.

Peas cooked in this manner form an essential ingredient of vegetable garnishes. They are a marvelous accompaniment for duck or roast or casseroled chicken.

Green Peas, English Style   *Petits pois à l'anglaise*

Both the English and the Americans like their peas to remain as green as they possibly can. They are cooked, uncovered, in a large quantity of boiling water. Salt is added after the peas are put in and the water has resumed boiling. This sets the color. An enameled kettle should always be used for boiling peas.

FOR 6 PEOPLE

4 pounds unshelled peas

9 cups boiling water

salt

6 tablespoons butter, cut in pieces

4–5 mint leaves, deveined and finely cut with scissors, or 3–4 leaves
    chervil, finely minced

Shell the peas. Cook them and add salt as indicated above. Medium-size peas take 25–30 minutes to cook, small peas take less time. Taste for tenderness.

Drain the peas and refresh them under the cold water tap. Let them drain a minute or so in a colander, then turn them out into a flat dish to remove all excess moisture. If the peas are wet when reheated and buttered, the butter will glide off them and form blobs of fat.

reheating the peas

Place one third of the butter in the bottom of a heavy-bottomed enameled saucepan, add the peas, the rest of the butter, and more salt. Cover, set the pan over low heat, and, holding the cover in place with one hand, move and shake the pan back and forth so as to coat the peas evenly with butter. Place the peas in a warmed metal vegetable dish and decorate with the mint leaves or chervil.

The peas can be served alone as a garnish, or accompanied with other vegetable garnishes (served in separate dishes) such as Noisette Potatoes,* diced cooked carrots, and cooked cauliflower.

POTATOES   *Pommes de terre*

Potatoes were introduced in France in the sixteenth century, but the French regarded them suspiciously, terming them "unsuitable for food" and "dangerous to eat because of their debilitating effects." Sometime later, the agronomist Antoine-Auguste Parmentier (1737–1817), who did not discover the potato but rather "promoted" it and subjected it to serious studies, succeeded in rehabilitating this frowned-upon tuber. His efforts were crowned with success, and for years potatoes have been considered a staple food in France.

Steamed Potatoes   *Pommes de terre vapeur*

It may seem odd to offer a recipe for steamed potatoes. But, like Soft-Boiled Eggs*
and other seemingly simple dishes, they are best when prepared correctly.

Steamed potatoes may be kept warm for 10–15 minutes standing covered, over
hot water (off heat), but they should never be reheated.

For this recipe you will need a double thickness of cheesecloth or a loose-
textured kitchen towel, and a strainer or colander with large holes.

FOR 6 PEOPLE

20 small, firm boiling potatoes of the same size
water for steaming the potatoes
coarse salt for the water

Peel the potatoes and wash them.

Fill a fairly large kettle about one third with cold water. Warm the water
and add salt. Line a strainer with a double thickness of cheesecloth, or a
kitchen towel, large enough to pull up and around the potatoes. Place the
potatoes on the cloth and fold them in. Set the strainer over the warm water,
not touching it. Bring the water to a boil, cover the kettle, and keep the water
boiling for 35–40 minutes, checking the water level from time to time. Test
the potatoes for doneness by sticking a larding needle or toothpick into them.
If it enters easily, the potatoes are done.

short-cut method of steaming potatoes

Put the potatoes in a kettle and cover with cold water. Add salt. Bring
the water to a boil and cook potatoes for 5 minutes. Put them immediately
into a cheesecloth-lined strainer (as in the preceding recipe) and set them
over a kettle of boiling water, one third full. Cover the potatoes with the cloth
and steam until tender. This method will save you 15 or more minutes.

SAUTÉED POTATOES   *Pommes de terre sautées*

Here are two methods for sautéing potatoes.

Sautéed Raw Potatoes   *Pommes de terre sautées à cru*

Use small boiling potatoes all the same size for this recipe. If only large potatoes are
available, peel them, then cut and shape them to resemble small potatoes, making
sure to round all the angles so they will roll easily in the butter.

FOR 6 PEOPLE

2 pounds firm boiling potatoes (for size see above)
2½ tablespoons peanut oil (keep a little in reserve)

---

6 tablespoons butter divided in half, plus 3 tablespoons butter to be added
    while the potatoes are sautéing

salt

3 pats of butter

1 tablespoon finely minced parsley, or 1 tablespoon chives, finely cut with
    scissors, for garnish

Peel the potatoes, rounding all the angles, wash them quickly, and dry them carefully with a clean kitchen towel.

Place the oil and 3 tablespoons of the butter in a large sauté pan and heat moderately. Put in the potatoes and allow them to warm for a minute or two. Grasp the handle of the pan firmly and shake the pan back and forth. Roll the potatoes toward the end of the pan (away from the handle) and shake the pan in such a way that the potatoes underneath will be on top. Cover the pan just long enough to form vapor that will help make the potatoes tender. Remove the cover and begin shaking the pan and rolling the potatoes again, adding the rest of the butter a tablespoon at a time. Pour a thin stream of the reserved oil around the edge of the pan. The potatoes will begin to brown after 15 minutes, and their entire cooking time will be 25–30 minutes, depending on their size. Test for doneness by pressing one of the potatoes with your finger to see if it is soft. Remove the potatoes with a skimmer and place in a warmed vegetable dish. Do not add the cooking fat. Salt the potatoes, distribute the pats of butter, and sprinkle with the parsley or chives.

Blanched and Sautéed Potatoes
Pommes de terre blanchies puis sautées

I have a preference for this method of sautéing potatoes because the natural juice of potatoes is acid and has a tendency to darken the butter and even to make it burn.

Use the same quantity of potatoes and fat as in the preceding recipe.

Peel the potatoes, rinse them, and place them in a large kettle. Cover with cold water, add salt, place over medium heat, and bring to a boil. Let the potatoes boil for 3 minutes, drain them, and dry them carefully with a clean kitchen towel or with paper towels.

Sauté the potatoes as in the preceding recipe. After preliminary sautéing, put the cover on the pan for 6–8 minutes, then remove the cover and continue to shake the pan back and forth. Roll the potatoes around in the fat until they are golden brown. The cooking time for blanched sautéed potatoes is 16–20 minutes. Test for doneness by pressing one with your finger to see if it is soft. Remove the potatoes with a skimmer to a warmed vegetable dish, add salt, butter pats, and garnish of minced parsley or chives.

Noisette Potatoes[1] *Pommes de terre noisette*

These small round potato balls are made with the same quantity of potatoes and fat as in the preceding recipes. They are sautéed raw (Sautéed Raw Potatoes*) and are used as a garnish for other vegetables.

Peel, wash, and dry the potatoes. Then, using a melonballer, form small balls from the potatoes. Heat the fat and sauté the potato balls, rolling them until they are golden brown and tender. The cooking time is shorter than in normal-size sautéed raw potatoes.

Potatoes Dauphine *Pommes de terre dauphine*

These are deliciously light potato croquettes made with potatoes cooked in very little water, put through a food mill, bound with Choux Pastry,* and deep-fried.

MAKES 20–24 CROQUETTES

choux pastry ingredients

½ cup water
4 tablespoons butter
½ cup all-purpose flour
2 eggs
a pinch of salt, taken with 3 fingers
1 egg white

other ingredients

2 pounds firm boiling potatoes
water for cooking the potatoes
salt for the potato water
6 tablespoons butter
4 egg yolks
salt
freshly ground pepper
freshly grated nutmeg
flour for coating the croquettes
3 cups peanut oil for deep-fat frying

Prepare the choux pastry (see its own recipe) and set it aside to rest.

Peel and wash the potatoes—if they are large, cut them into quarters. Place them in a pan, just barely cover with salted water, and cook until tender, drain well. Run them through a food mill, using the finest disk, and place them in a heavy-bottomed enameled casserole. Set them over low heat for a few seconds to dry them out, stirring vigorously with a wooden spatula.

[1] A *noisette* is a hazelnut.

Remove from heat. Add the butter tablespoon by tablespoon, working well with the spatula until it has been absorbed. Add the egg yolks one after the other, beating after each addition. Season with salt, pepper, and nutmeg.

Again working vigorously with the spatula, stir in the choux pastry by spoonfuls. Continue to work until the mixture is smooth and compact.

Spread a layer of flour on a board. Form the potato mixture into shapes resembling sausages and roll them in the flour. Cut the sausage-shaped pieces in half and form into small balls about the size of walnuts. Roll these in the flour, tapping off any excess of flour with your hands. Place the potato balls on a flat surface until time to deep-fry them.

deep-frying the potatoes

Pour the 3 cups of peanut oil into a deep-fat fryer and heat until the surface just barely begins to wrinkle. Fry the potato balls a few at a time, turning them, for about 3–5 minutes or until they are golden brown. Drain on paper towels and keep warm while you fry the rest.

reheating potatoes dauphine

Preheat oven to 300°F. Turn off the oven and place the potatoes inside, oven door open, until they are heated through.

Potatoes dauphine make delicious accompaniments for roast beef, Roast Leg of Lamb,*and Roast Chicken.* For a light meal, serve them with just a green salad.

Potato Nests   *Nids de pommes de terre*

These are charming garnishes for meals served during the Easter holidays. To make them, you need a special utensil consisting of two rather deep wire ladles (or scoops) hinged together. These can be found in shops specializing in Chinese kitchen equipment.

MAKES 3 NESTS

> 6 firm boiling potatoes
> 4½ cups peanut oil for deep-fat frying
> salt

Peel and wash the potatoes. Dry them thoroughly with a clean kitchen towel, then cut them in pieces the size of a matchstick. A *mandoline* cutter, if you have one, will make this work much easier. Lay the potato matchsticks on a piece of paper towel and pat them dry with a kitchen towel to get rid of every bit of dampness.

Start heating the oil in the deep-fat fryer. While it is heating, prepare the first nest: lay some of the matchsticks tightly together and horizontally in one of the hinged ladles (or scoops) as if you were building a nest. When the oil just faintly begins to wrinkle, bring the two ladles together and lower into the fat. After three minutes, remove the double ladle. The nest will be formed and almost firm. Remove the nest from the ladle, place it on a skimmer, and put it back in the fat for just a few seconds to make it firm and golden. Set the nest on a piece of paper towel to drain. Repeat this procedure until you have used up all the potatoes.

The nests can be reheated in an oven preheated to 300°F. with heat turn off and the oven door left open.

These lovely nests can be filled with Green Peas, English style* as a garnish for your Roast Leg of Lamb* for Easter. Serve another vegetable accompaniment separately.

Potatoes, Morvan Style   *Pommes de terre morvandelles*

This lovely dish consists of peeled large potatoes cut in the shape of kegs, hollowed out, and garnished with butter. At the end of cooking, cream replaces the absorbed butter and the potatoes are returned to the oven for a light glazing.

To bake the potatoes, use a dripping pan lined with a double thickness of aluminum foil.

FOR 6–8 PEOPLE

12 firm boiling potatoes, each weighing about ⅓ pound
⅓ cup butter, cut into 12 equal pieces
salt
freshly ground pepper
about ¾ cup heavy cream
freshly grated nutmeg
Preheat oven to 340° F. For glazing the potatoes raise oven heat to 350° F.

Peel the potatoes smoothly so there will be no sharp angles. With a sharp knife, narrow the two ends so the potatoes look like small kegs. Wash the potatoes and dry them thoroughly with a clean kitchen towel.

Using a sharp, pointed spoon or an apple corer, hollow out each potato, being careful not to penetrate the closed end. Fill each hollow with one of the pieces of butter and season with a little salt and pepper. Place the potatoes on the foil-lined dripping pan and put the pan in the middle part of the oven. Bake for about 40 minutes or until the potatoes are soft.

Remove the dripping pan from the oven and pour a good tablespoon of cream into each hollow. Add a little more salt and pepper and some grated nutmeg. Replace the pan in the oven (heat raised) until the cream is boiling and the top of each potato is lightly glazed.

Serve the potatoes with braised ham or braised beef or as one of the elements in a vegetable garnish. If you are using these potatoes with other vegetables, select small ones for baking, and adjust the butter and cream measurements.

René's Potato Cake   *Rösti de René*

An enchanting Swiss specialty, this is a handsome, golden-brown "cake" flavored with onion and cooked in lard in a heavy sauté pan on top of the stove. It is then unmolded on a round plate.

FOR 6 PEOPLE

18 firm medium-size boiling potatoes
2 onions, finely minced
½ pound lard in 2 pieces (1 piece slightly larger than the other)
salt
freshly ground pepper

Wash the potatoes and boil them in their skins, adding salt to the water, for 12 minutes only. Peel them, then grate them, using a grate with large holes. You should hear a slight rasping noise when you grate them. This is a sign that they have been correctly cooked. If overcooked, they will completely disintegrate while being grated, and your dish will be ruined.

Heat the larger part of the lard in the sauté pan. Then put in the potatoes and onions in any order. Cover the pan and cook over moderate heat for 10 minutes. During this period the potatoes should not color. Remove the cover, mix the potatoes once only with a wooden spatula. Add the second, smaller part of the lard, letting it glide along the sides of the potatoes near the edge of the pan. Cover and cook for another 10 minutes. Remove the cover. Season the potato cake with salt and pepper. You will notice the lard simmering and bubbling up along the edges of the pan. Raise heat and let the cake cook until the edges begin to brown and pull away from the sides of the pan.

To unmold: put a heated round plate over the top of the pan and turn the pan upside down. The *rösti* will be beautifully round and golden brown.

This dish is delicious served with Roast Leg of Lamb.* Since making it requires no oven, it can also be used in outdoor cooking and served along with various barbecued meats. For a simple light meal, serve the rösti *with a green salad.*

"Molded" Potatoes   *Manqué de pommes de terre*

These delicious potatoes look as if they had been baked in a pan like a cake. But looks can be deceiving . . . your family and guests will be amazed when you tell them how simple they are to make.

2 pounds large, firm boiling potatoes, unpeeled
½ cup butter, cut in pieces
salt
freshly ground pepper
freshly grated nutmeg
1 cup heavy cream
4 tablespoons grated Swiss cheese

Preheat oven to 340° for baking the potatoes; raise heat to 400° F. for browning the potatoes.

Wash the potatoes quickly under the cold water tap. Dry them thoroughly. Place them in a flameproof dish or on the oven dripping pan and let them cook gently in their skins for about 45 minutes or until soft.

Cut the potatoes in half lengthwise and extract all the flesh, placing it in a heated Pyrex bowl. Add the pieces of butter, salt, pepper, and a little nutmeg. Using a heavy fork, mash the potatoes and butter together without trying to get a perfectly smooth mixture. This is not a purée.

Put the mixture in the middle of a round flameproof platter, forming it into a round "cake," leveling the top, and making the sides the same height. Cover the cake with the cream, sprinkle with grated cheese and a little more grated nutmeg, and bake (oven heat raised) for about 10 minutes or until the cake is piping hot and golden brown.

POTATOES AU GRATIN *Gratins de pommes de terre*

Here are two highly original recipes I am sure you have never tried.

Gratin of Potatoes with Fennel Shoots
Gratins de pommes de terre aux pousses de fenouils

A flameproof earthenware dish, not too deep, will be needed for this recipe.

FOR 6 PEOPLE

2 pounds firm boiling potatoes, unpeeled
cold salted water for parboiling the potatoes
5–6 fennel bulbs with shoots
2 tablespoons butter for cooking the fennel
1 clove garlic, cut in half
peanut oil and 2 tablespoons creamed butter for greasing the oven dish
4 tablespoons butter, cut in pieces
salt
freshly ground pepper
1 bay leaf
a sprig of fresh or dried thyme
4 tablespoons grated Swiss cheese
Preheat oven to 350° F. for the baking dish, then preheat the broiler

Cover the washed but unpeeled potatoes with cold salted water. Cook them for 10–12 minutes only, just long enough to make them easy to peel. Peel the potatoes and cut them in thick slices. Set aside.

Strip away the coarse outside fennel leaves until you reach the small hearts. Mince these along with the slimmest of the fennel tops or shoots. Heat the 2 tablespoons of butter in a small saucepan and stir-cook the minced fennel for no more than 1–2 minutes. It should not be cooked, just softened.

Rub the inside of the oven dish with the cut sides of the garlic, then grease with a thin coating of peanut oil and the 2 tablespoons of creamed butter. Spread half the sliced potatoes in the dish and top with two thirds of the fennel and its juice. Distribute half the butter pieces on top. Add the rest of the potatoes in a tight layer. Top with the rest of the fennel. Season with salt and pepper. Put the bay leaf, thyme, and remaining butter pieces on top. Bake for 20–25 minutes. Baste the ingredients with the buttery juices after 15 minutes and once again just before removing the dish from the oven.

At the end of this time, remove the dish from the oven and preheat the broiler. Sprinkle the grated cheese over the ingredients and place under the broiler (not too close) for about 4 minutes, until the top is nicely browned.

This dish makes a splendid accompaniment for Roast Pork,* Roast Goose,* or a large baked fish.

Potato Gratin of the Cod Fisherman *Gratin des morutiers*

A hearty dish consisting of poached codfish, potatoes, onions, and the merest whiff of garlic. It makes a complete meal when accompanied by a green salad.

Use a flameproof earthenware dish, not too deep, for making this dish.

FOR 6 PEOPLE

1½ pounds firm boiling potatoes
cold salted water for cooking the potatoes
3 medium-size onions, sliced thin
2 tablespoons butter
2 tablespoons water
freshly ground pepper
¾ pound salt codfish poached in Court Bouillon* (leftover codfish would be fine)
1 clove garlic, cut in half
peanut oil and 2 tablespoons creamed butter for greasing the oven dish
1 recipe of Snail Butter,* made ahead
3 tablespoons grated Swiss cheese
Preheat oven to 350° F.

Cook the potatoes in the salted water, peel and slice them as in the preceding recipe, place them in a large bowl.

Cut the onion slices in half. Place them in a saucepan with the butter and stir-cook for a minute or so, just to soften them. Add the 2 tablespoons of water, cover the pan, and cook for 5 minutes, stirring frequently. Mix them and their cooking juice with the potatoes. Grind in a little pepper but do not salt.

Shred the poached codfish and add it to the potatoes and onions, mixing the ingredients together with 2 forks.

Have the snail butter at hand (at room temperature).

Prepare the oven dish by rubbing the inside with the cut sides of the garlic and greasing with a thin layer of oil and 2 tablespoons of creamed butter.

Place half the potato mixture in the dish and distribute half the snail butter on top. Repeat the process, ending with the rest of the snail butter. Sprinkle the ingredients with grated cheese, put the dish in the oven, and bake for 20–25 minutes until the potatoes are tender and a light golden crust has formed.

Ratatouille

A famous dish based on garden-fresh eggplant, zucchini, and tomatoes. It can be made entirely in advance and reheated or served cold.

You will need two large sauté pans with covers and a large, heavy-bottomed enameled casserole with a cover for making the dish.

FOR 6–8 PEOPLE

4–5 medium-size eggplants
4–5 medium-size zucchini
4 medium-size green peppers, cored, seeded, and diced
a large enameled kettle of boiling water
10 tablespoons olive oil
1½ pounds small white onions, peeled and sliced
2–3 tablespoons hot water
2 pounds ripe tomatoes, peeled, seeded, and cut in chunks
1 small red chili pepper, cored, seeded, and cut in half
1 *Bouquet garni classique,** including a sprig of rosemary and a small piece of fennel
a small piece of dried orange peel
a small pinch of curry powder
3–6 garlic cloves, peeled, finely diced, and pounded to a paste with 2 tablespoons olive oil
salt
freshly ground pepper

Partially peel the eggplants and zucchini by alternating peeled and unpeeled vertical strips. Cut in fairly large slices. Fill a large enameled kettle with water and bring to a boil. Add the slices of eggplant and boil for 1 minute, remove with a skimmer, and set to drain. Repeat this operation for the zucchini, then the green peppers. This step takes a little time, but it is worth it because it rids the vegetables of their acrid juices and keeps their colors fresh.

Heat 4 tablespoons of the olive oil in a sauté pan, add the slices of eggplant, and cook, turning, for a few minutes. Add 2 more tablespoons of oil, heat, and put in the slices of zucchini and mix with the eggplant. Cover the pan and cook for 8–10 minutes, stirring occasionally. Remove the pan from heat.

Heat the remaining 4 tablespoon of olive oil in the second sauté pan, put in the onions, and stir-cook for 3–4 minutes, adding the 2–3 tablespoons of hot water to keep the onions from coloring. Stir in the tomato and green pepper, cover the pan, and simmer, stirring occasionally, for about 10 minutes. Remove the pan from heat.

Place the contents of both sauté pans in the casserole and stir them together. Then add the chili pepper, *bouquet garni,* dried orange peel, and curry powder. Cover and cook over low heat for 1–1½ hours, stirring from time to time and seasoning with salt and pepper halfway through the cooking. Add the garlic paste about 15 minutes before the end of cooking. Taste and adjust seasoning.

Hot ratatouille is an admirable accompaniment for veal and pork roasts, and it goes wonderfully well with Pot-au-feu* made during the summer season.

Cold ratatouille, garnished with black olives and a little finely minced basil, makes a lovely hors-d'oeuvre. You can also use it to replace salad in a buffet featuring cold Chicken in Aspic* or Pot Roast Molded in Aspic.*

Leftover ratatouille can be reheated, spread on a round platter, and garnished with Fried Eggs, French Style.* If you have only a small amount of leftover ratatouille, use it to garnish an omelet or place it, reheated, in the middle of a dish of rice or spaghetti or inside a ring of molded rice.

RICE

Creole Rice Riz à la créole

This light, fluffy rice is a perfect accompaniment to dishes garnished with highly seasoned sauces such as Chicken Marengo.*

FOR 6 PEOPLE

½ pound converted long-grain rice
boiling salted water for cooking the rice
Preheat oven to 340° F.

Fill a large enameled or stainless steel kettle with water and bring to a boil. Add salt. Put the rice in the water, cover the kettle until the water resumes boiling. Remove the cover, stir the rice once and once only with a long wooden spatula, making sure that no grains are sticking to the bottom. Boil the rice for 13–16 minutes. Taste a grain before draining. The rice should be almost but not quite tender. Drain it and rinse it under the cold water tap to stop the cooking and set the starch. Do not touch the rice with your hands or any utensil. Bounce it up and down a little in the colander until all the grains are cool.

Put the rice in a shallow oven dish, place in the oven, and heat for 15 minutes or slightly more. Every 5 minutes, loosen the grains of rice on the bottom of the dish with a fork and bring them to the top. During this time, the rice will continue to swell and the grains will separate from each other.

The rice can wait for as long as 30 minutes in the turned-out oven if you place a piece of buttered parchment paper over the top of the dish and set on the cover. Leave the oven door open.

Indian Rice   *Riz à l'indienne*

This is best made with rice from the Bihar region of India. It may have to be washed (consult the package instructions).

FOR 6 PEOPLE

½ pound Indian rice
boiling salted water for cooking the rice
Preheat oven to 340° F.

Boil the rice as in the preceding recipe. After draining and cooling it, wrap it in a large clean napkin or kitchen towel and dry it out in the oven for 15 minutes.

Indian rice is a splendid accompaniment for all kinds of curries: chicken, meat, or fish.

Rice Pilaf   *Riz pilaf*

FOR 6 PEOPLE

2 tablespoons finely minced onion
½ pound converted long-grain rice
3 cups hot Chicken Bouillon* or 3 cups hot water
salt to taste
Preheat oven to 350° F.

Heat the oil slowly in a heavy-bottomed enameled casserole, add the onion, and stir-cook until the onion is lightly colored. Add the rice and cook, stirring constantly with a wooden spatula, until it has first a milky appearance and then becomes a light tan color. Pour in the hot bouillon or water and stir once. Cover the casserole and place in the oven for 17–18 minutes. At the end of this time the liquid will be completely absorbed and the rice grains beautifully distinct. In addition to tasting good, rice pilaf has a practical advantage: it can wait an hour or even a little longer in the casserole and then be reheated without losing its fine quality. It can be served as a simple meal in itself, followed by a green salad, or as an accompaniment to various sauced dishes. It makes an excellent garnish for mussels and shrimp, or for leftover chicken or roast ham cut in pieces.

Rice with Saffron and Curry   *Riz au safran et au curry*

FOR 6 PEOPLE

1 recipe of Rice Pilaf* (given above)
a pinch of saffron, taken with 3 fingers
2 pinches of curry powder, taken with 3 fingers
Preheat oven to 350° F.

As soon as you have added the bouillon or water in the recipe for rice pilaf, stir in the saffron. Place in oven as in the preceding recipe. When the bouillon or water has been completely absorbed, remove the rice from the oven. Add the curry powder, mixing gently so as not to crush the rice grains. Taste for seasoning.

This is a delicious accompaniment to fish and shellfish.

Suggestion for a buffet: Make the recipe above and garnish it with 1 quart of shelled *Mussels Marinière, Paris Style,* or with 1 cup of cooked, shelled shrimp, or with a small can (about ½ cup) of flaked crab meat. Top with thinly sliced onions that have been sautéed in a little oil, drained on paper towels, and sprinkled with salt and a pinch of curry powder.*

Rice, Vietnam Style   *Riz à la vietnamienne*

A rice recipe that can be cooked entirely on top of the stove. To make it, you will need a heavy-bottomed enamaled casserole with a tight-fitting cover.

FOR 6 PEOPLE

4½ cups water
1 teaspoon salt
½ pound converted long-grain rice
3–4 tablespoons butter

Pour the water into the casserole, bring to a boil, add salt, and pour in the rice as slowly as possible so as not to interrupt the boiling. Stir once. Cook for 8 minutes. Drain the rice and cool it under the cold water tap until it becomes transparent.

Place 2½ tablespoons of butter in the casserole. Add the rice, spreading it evenly in the pan with the fingers. Cover and place over very low heat for 10–12 minutes. The rice will finish cooking in its steam. Lift the cover twice and add the rest of the butter along the sides of the casserole (not on top of the rice).

Rice, Canton Style   *Riz à la cantonnaise*

A colorful, beautifully seasoned dish . . . perfect for a buffet. If you are having a large buffet party, double the quantities.

FOR 6–8 PEOPLE

marinade ingredients

- 4 tablespoons soy sauce
- 2 tablespoons honey
- 2 tablespoons mango chutney
- 1 tablespoon ketchup
- 3 slices canned pineapple, finely diced
- 4 tablespoons pineapple juice

other ingredients

- ½–¾ pound lean cooked pork, finely diced
- 1 2-egg Omelet,* cooked in oil and left flat (unfolded)
- 2 tablespoons peanut oil
- 1 recipe of Creole Rice,* using ⅔–1 pound rice
- 4 small cooked pork sausages, cut in half after cooking
- ⅓ cup sliced mushrooms, sautéed in 1 tablespoon oil, salted, peppered, and anointed with a squeeze of lemon juice
- 1 small leek white, cut in thin strips and cooked in 1 tablespoon peanut oil until tender but not colored
- 12 small canned shrimp, lightly sautéed in 1 tablespoon peanut oil (optional)

Preheat oven to 350° F.

Mix the marinade ingredients together and marinate the diced pork for 15–20 minutes. Remove it from the marinade and set aside. Strain the marinade and set aside.

Place the omelet in the oven for a minute or so to dry the surface. Remove it from the omelet pan, cut in fine strips, and set aside.

Heat the oil in a small sauté pan and stir-cook the diced pork until the pieces are slightly caramelized. Set these aside.

assembling the dish

Place the cooked Creole rice in a flameproof dish, garnish with the diced pork, sausages, mushrooms, leek, and shrimp. Heat the strained marinade, then pour it into the rice mixture, stirring it in gently. Finally, add the omelet strips, working lightly with two forks.

Fit a piece of parchment paper over the dish, cover, and place in the oven for 10–15 minutes until heated through.

SORREL *Oseille*

This delicious, slightly but pleasantly sour-tasting vegetable must be picked in "all the green freshness of its youth." Allowing it to mature ruins not only its bright beauty but its taste. The fresh savor of sorrel lasts from May to the end of June. After that, it becomes more acid and even acrid.

Fresh sorrel does not have to be blanched. All you need to do is pick out the stems, remove any large ribs, wash it abundantly, and drain it well.

Stewed Sorrel   BASIC METHOD   *Fondue d'oseille*

FOR 2 PEOPLE

2 pounds sorrel, picked over, washed, and drained
3–4 tablespoons butter
2 tablespoons heavy cream
salt
freshly ground pepper
freshly grated nutmeg

Place the sorrel in a heavy-bottomed enameled casserole along with the butter, stir-cook for a few minutes until it has released its juices and become limp. Stir in the cream, then whisk the sorrel vigorously until all the cream has been absorbed. Season with salt, pepper, and nutmeg to taste. Place in a warmed vegetable dish.

Older sorrel must be blanched before preparing in this way. Simply plunge it into a large kettle of boiling water and drain immediately, as soon as the sorrel wilts. Press out the water by squeezing out handfuls, place on a board, and chop finely with a stainless steel knife. Then prepare as in the basic method, above.

Sorrel is a superb accompaniment to veal and fish, especially poached fish. For still another method of cooking sorrel, see Poached Salmon Trout with Sorrel Butter.*

See also Sorrel Purée.*

Sorrel Ribbons   *Chiffonade d'oseille*

An excellent and original way to enliven leftover soup. After picking over, washing, and draining about 1 pound of sorrel, roll the leaves into the shape of cigars and cut them in slices. Unrolled, they will look like green ribbons. Heat the soup through—almost but not quite to the boiling point—drop in the sorrel, add 2–3 pats of butter, and place in a hot soup tureen.

Chopped Spinach Stewed with Butter   *Épinards à l'étuvée*

Always use a stainless steel or enameled kettle for cooking spinach. Aluminum will darken it and give it a metallic taste.

FOR 6 PEOPLE

3–4 pounds fresh spinach
1 tablespoon salt
4 tablespoons butter
salt for later seasoning
freshly ground pepper
freshly grated nutmeg
2 tablespoons heavy cream (optional)

Sort over the spinach, remove any wilted or damaged leaves, trim off the root ends and large stems. Wash in several waters to eliminate any traces of sand. Drain well.

Fill a large kettle with water and bring to a boil. Put the spinach in by handfuls so the water keeps boiling. Push the spinach into the water with a skimmer, and when the water is boiling at a gallop, add the 1 tablespoon of salt to set the color. Boil the spinach for 5 minutes, pour into a colander, and refresh under the cold water tap until the spinach is completely cool. Pick up the spinach by handfuls and press out the remaining water. Once this process is completed, the spinach will keep for as much as 24 hours, refrigerated.

finishing the spinach

Put the spinach on a board and chop it with a stainless steel knife. In a heavy-bottomed enameled casserole, melt half the butter, add the spinach, mix it with a wooden spatula. Add the rest of the butter gradually, continuing to stir the spinach. Season with salt, very little pepper, and a small amount of nutmeg. Add the cream at this time, spoonful by spoonful, continuing to stir. Adjust for seasoning. Serve immediately in a warmed vegetable dish.

NOTE: Winter spinach sometimes has a rather acrid taste. To alleviate this, add a pinch of sugar taken with 3 fingers while you are mixing the spinach and butter. The cream will also soften the taste.

Leftover spinach can be used as a garnish, as in Crêpes with Spinach.* These can be served as a first course, as an accompaniment to veal or ham, or, as a dinner for two, use in Fish Fillets, Florentine Style.*

Croutons Garnished with Spinach   *Petites croûtes aux épinards*

An elegant yet easy way of embellishing a platter of sliced roast pork or veal. The meat is arranged in the middle of the platter and surrounded by the spinach-garnished croutons.

FOR 4–6 PEOPLE

8–12 rectangular Croutons,* made ahead and reheated before using
16–18 tablespoons Chopped Spinach Stewed with Butter*

Arrange the reheated croutons around the platter and top each with chopped spinach.

Ham and Spinach au Gratin   *Jambon aux épinards*

Here is an excellent entree using chopped spinach.

FOR 4–6 PEOPLE

8–12 rectangular croutons, made ahead and reheated before using
enough slices of boiled ham to cover the croutons
16–18 tablespoons Chopped Spinach Stewed with Butter*
1 recipe of Mornay Sauce,* kept warm over hot water, heat off
2 tablespoons grated Swiss cheese
Preheat oven to 400° F.

Arrange the croutons in an oven dish. Place a slice of ham on each, cover with a tablespoon or so of spinach, top with a tablespoon of Mornay sauce (whisked before using), and sprinkle with grated cheese. Place in the oven until the croutons are hot and the top golden.

Tomato Coulis   *Coulis de tomates*

The tomatoes are cooked with various condiments and herbs. A note of warning: the taste of fresh tomato should predominate, so please do not overdo the herbs. A small *bouquet garni* with a sprig of tarragon, a little dried basil, or a small amount of oregano is all you need.

FOR 6 PEOPLE

2 tablespoons olive oil or peanut oil
1 small shallot or 1 small onion, finely minced
2½ pounds ripe tomatoes, peeled, seeded, juiced, and diced
1 lump sugar
1 *Bouquet garni** (see above)
salt
1 clove garlic, minced and pounded with a few drops of olive oil (optional)
freshly ground pepper
2 pats of butter

Heat the oil slightly in a heavy-bottomed enameled casserole, add the shallot or onion, and stir-cook for 2 minutes. There should be no coloration whatsoever. Stir in the tomatoes, add the sugar, and *bouquet garni,* and salt. Stir in the garlic. Cover the casserole, bring the tomatoes to a boil, lower heat, and cook for about 20 minutes. At the end of this time, whisk the *coulis* for a minute or so, add the pepper and the pats of butter. Taste for seasoning.

This delicious sauce can be mixed into rice, noodles, or spaghetti, and it is excellent with Poached Eggs,* but first bind the sauce with Beurre manié* made with 1 tablespoon of flour and 1 tablespoon of butter.

And for a delicious light meal make Veiled Eggs* with tomato sauce. First heat the oven to 350° F. Spread the sauce on the bottom of a lightly buttered round flameproof dish. Make hollows in the coulis *with the back of a tablespoon. Carefully crack an egg into each hollow. Place on top of the stove for a minute or two, drizzle a little melted butter over the eggs, and place the pan in the oven until the eggs are lightly "veiled." Remove the dish, salt and pepper the eggs, and serve immediately.*

Another quickly made elegant meal: sauté a cut-up chicken in a mixture of oil and butter until the pieces are almost tender and just beginning to color. Pour the tomato sauce into a heavy-bottomed enameled casserole, add the chicken pieces, cover the casserole, and cook until the chicken is tender and the sauce reduced. Degrease* the sauce if necessary.

Tomato Fondue   *Fondue de tomates*

Cooled, placed in a jar, and hermetically sealed, this sauce will keep for 10 days in the refrigerator.

Use the same ingredients as in the preceding recipe, but cook for 20 more minutes. At the end of this time you will have a rich, reduced sauce (or purée), marvelous for garnishing Poached Eggs* that have been placed either on reheated Croutons* or in reheated round tartlets made of Simple Puff Pastry.* This amount of sauce (about 2 cups) is enough for garnishing 6 poached eggs.

Tomato Sauce   *Sauce tomate*

The best tomato sauce is based on Tomato Fondue* (the preceding recipe), which may have a delicate liaison of *Beurre manié.** It should never be thickened with flour paste (*roux**).

MAKES ABOUT 2 CUPS

 2 cups Tomato Fondue*
 Beurre manié,* made with 2 teaspoons butter and 2 teaspoons flour
 1 tablespoon finely minced fresh tarragon or basil

Put the tomato *fondue* through a food mill, using the finest disk. Place in an enameled saucepan and set over low heat. Gradually whisk in the *beurre manié.* When the sauce is slightly thickened, add the tarragon or basil, and pour into a warmed sauce bowl.

Tomato Sauce Made from Unpeeled Tomatoes
Sauce tomate avec tomates non pelées

A delicious, quickly prepared tomato sauce.

MAKES ABOUT 2 CUPS

    2 tablespoons olive oil
    2 pounds unpeeled ripe tomatoes, cut in half, juiced, seeded, and diced
    1 small green onion, finely minced
    1 clove garlic, squeezed through a garlic press
    a sprig of fresh or dried thyme
    ½ bay leaf
    a sprig of fresh or dried tarragon (optional)
    a pinch of sugar (optional)
    salt
    freshly ground pepper
    *Beurre manié,** made as in the preceding recipe (optional)

Heat the oil in a heavy-bottomed enameled saucepan, add the tomatoes, onion, garlic, herbs, and sugar, stir together. Season with salt and pepper. Cover and simmer for 15–20 minutes, stirring occasionally. Remove from heat, discard the herbs, and put the sauce through a food mill, using the finest disk. Return the sauce to saucepan and reduce over low heat until it has a smooth consistency. (If you wish to bind the sauce a little more, whisk in the *beurre manié.*) Adjust for seasoning and pour into a warmed sauce bowl.

Broiled Tomatoes   *Tomates grillées*

A colorful garnish consisting of small garden-fresh tomatoes baked a few minutes in a well-oiled oven dish, then broiled. Colorful placed around a platter of sliced meat.

FOR 6 PEOPLE

    9 small tomatoes, all the same size
    2 tablespoons peanut oil or olive oil
    salt
    freshly ground pepper
    9 small pieces butter (about ½ pat to a piece)
    1–2 tablespoons finely minced parsley
    Preheat oven to 350° F. for preliminary baking, then preheat the broiler

Cut the stem caps off the tomatoes, turn them over, and lightly press out the seeds and juice. Let them drain upside-down for a few minutes. Set them in a well-oiled oven dish, place in the middle of the oven, and bake for about 15 minutes until the tomatoes are heated through. Remove from the oven, baste them with the oil in the dish, season them with salt and pepper, and place a piece of butter on top of each one. Set the dish under the broiler, not too close to heat. Broil until the top edges of the tomatoes begin to brown. Remove from the oven and sprinkle with parsley.

Tomatoes Stuffed with Vegetables *Tomates farcies de légumes*

Mushroom *duxelles* give these stuffed tomatoes their inimitable flavor.

FOR 6 PEOPLE

10–12 small round tomatoes
a little salt

stuffing ingredients

1 recipe Dry Mushroom Duxelles,* cooked with 1 tablespoon mixed minced onion and shallot
1–2 slices white bread, crust removed, soaked for a moment in milk, pressed out, then put through a food mill (you should have 2 tablespoons)
salt
freshly ground pepper
freshly grated nutmeg
2 tablespoons mixed finely minced chervil, tarragon, and parsley
1 small egg or ½ large egg, lightly beaten with a fork

other ingredients

butter for the baking dish
1–2 tablespoons white bread crumbs
10–12 small pieces butter (about ½ pat each)
Preheat oven to 350° F.

Cut the stem caps off the tomatoes. Scoop out the pulp and seeds with a small spoon and discard. Press out the juice. Let the tomatoes drain upside-down for a few minutes, then wipe out the insides with a paper towel and season lightly with salt.

making the stuffing

Prepare the dry mushroom duxelles and place in a bowl. Work in all the other stuffing ingredients, using a wooden spatula. Taste for seasoning.

filling and baking the tomatoes

Butter an oven dish just large enough to hold the tomatoes. Fill the tomatoes with the stuffing, making dome shapes. Top each with a sprinkling of bread crumbs and a piece of butter. Bake for about 35 minutes, checking toward the end to see if the tomatoes are not browning too much. If necessary lower heat and place a piece of parchment paper over the dish.

The tomatoes may be made ahead and reheated in the oven before serving.

These make excellent garnishes for roasts of all sorts, especially Roast Leg of Lamb.*

For an especially sumptuous garnish alternate the stuffed tomatoes with artichoke hearts garnished with fresh green peas.

Stuffed Tomatoes, Provençal Style   *Tomates farcies provençales*

One of the most delicious of all summer garnishes . . . firm, ripe tomatoes cut in half and stuffed with a garlicky bread crumb mixture. In Provence and the southeast of France the tomatoes are sometimes topped with minced capers, or two or three anchovies, diced and pounded with olive oil (depending on what they are to accompany).

FOR 6 PEOPLE

9 firm, fresh, ripe tomatoes
salt

ingredients for stuffing

2 cloves garlic, squeezed through a garlic press, then pounded with 1 tablespoon olive oil
2 tablespoons finely minced parsley
½ cup dry white bread crumbs
½ cup olive oil (keep the bottle of oil at hand)

other ingredients

olive oil for greasing the oven dish
a sprig of dried or fresh thyme (optional), or a sprig of dried or fresh savory (optional), or a dried or fresh sage leaf (optional)
Preheat oven to 330° F.

Cut the tomatoes in half after slicing off the stem caps. Gently press out the seeds and juice. Sprinkle each half with salt.

Delicately knead the stuffing ingredients together either with the tips of your fingers or a fork. Fill the tomato halves.

Using olive oil, lightly grease an oven dish large enough to hold the tomato halves in one layer. Arrange the tomatoes in it and place the dish in the oven. Bake for 15 minutes, then place one of the herbs in the dish. Bake for about 1 hour, basting two or three times with the pan juices and a little extra olive oil. At the end of this time the tomatoes should be fragrant with olive oil and lightly browned.

These make a delicious accompaniment for Roast Leg of Lamb.* Carve the lamb and ring the platter with the tomato halves, or place the tomatoes on top of Dried White Beans Purée.* They can also be used as a garnish for roast chicken or roast veal.

Another idea is to serve them with a bowl of noodles or spaghetti, accompanied by a mixture of grated Swiss cheese and grated Parmesan cheese.

They can also be used as a base for Scrambled Eggs,* Poached Eggs,* or Fried Eggs, French Style*—the tomato halves taking the place of croutons.

Tomatoes Stuffed with Meat   *Tomates farcies de viande*

Leftover *Pot-au-feu** meat, veal, and chicken, finely ground, may be used for these delicious stuffed tomatoes.

FOR 6 PEOPLE

> 8–10 medium-sized tomatoes
> a little salt

stuffing ingredients

> ½ pound finely ground leftover meat (see above)
> 2 tablespoons finely minced onion, stir-cooked for a minute or so in 2
> tablespoons peanut oil
> a small piece of garlic, squeezed through a garlic press and mixed with the
> stir-cooked onion
> the flesh of 1 tomato, diced
> 1 tablespoon finely minced parsley
> 1 egg, lightly beaten with a fork
> salt
> freshly ground pepper
> freshly grated nutmeg

other ingredients

> oil for the baking dish
> 1–2 tablespoons white bread crumbs
> 8–10 small pieces of butter (about ½ pat each)
> *Preheat oven to 350° F.*

Cut the stem caps from the tomatoes, scoop out the pulp and seeds, and discard (reserve the pulp of one tomato, diced, for the stuffing). Press out the juice. Let the tomatoes drain upside-down for a few minutes. Wipe out the insides with a paper towel and season lightly with salt.

making the stuffing and baking the tomatoes

Work all the ingredients together, using a wooden spatula, until they are well blended and smooth. Fill the tomatoes.

Oil a baking dish and set the tomatoes in it. Top each with a sprinkling of bread crumbs and a piece of butter. Bake for 45 minutes or a little more, basting from time to time with the pan juices.

Serve the tomatoes, lightly browned, in the baking dish.

Small Tomatoes Stuffed with Fish Mousseline
Petites tomates farcies de mousseline de poisson

Ring a platter of braised, baked, or grilled fish with this elegant garnish.

FOR 6 PEOPLE

  10 small, firm ripe tomatoes
  salt

mousseline ingredients

  2 flounder fillets (or other fine white fish), each fillet weighing about ¼
      pound
  1 egg plus ½ egg white
  ½ cup heavy cream
  salt
  freshly ground pepper
  1 tablespoon dry sherry or dry Madeira
  oil for the flameproof dish
  1 tablespoon finely minced parsley or tarragon, or parsley for garnish
  Preheat oven to 340° F.

Cut the tomatoes in half after slicing off the stem caps. Gently press out the juice and seeds, leaving the flesh intact. Turn them upside-down on a board to drain, then wipe them out with a paper towel and sprinkle lightly with salt.

making the mousseline

Cut the fish fillets in small pieces and put them through a food mill or blend them in a blender. Place the resulting purée in a bowl and, using a small wooden spatula, work in the whole egg, then little by little the cream until completely absorbed. Still using the spatula, work in the egg white until it is thoroughly blended into the mixture. Season with salt and pepper. Stir in the sherry or Madeira. Blend well and place the mixture in a pastry bag.

Lightly oil a flameproof dish large enough to hold all the tomatoes in one layer. Arrange the tomato halves in the dish and squeeze a small portion of the mousseline mixture on each tomato half. Place the dish over moderate heat until it begins to sizzle (1–2 minutes), put the dish in the oven, and cook for about 10 minutes. The mousseline filling should be firm but must not be allowed to brown.

Garnish the platter of fish with the tomato halves, sprinkling the tops with one of the minced herbs.

An idea for a more elaborate garnish is to alternate tomato halves with "packages" of Braised Lettuce* or with Fennel Hearts Braised in Butter.*

Glazed Turnips   *Navets glacés*

These are prepared in the same way as Glazed Carrots.* The amount of turnips and other ingredients remains unchanged. One small difference: turnips take less time to cook than carrots, so begin testing for doneness after 15 minutes.

Glazed turnips are often used in combination with Glazed Onions* and Glazed Carrots* as a colorful and tasty garnish. They go wonderfully well with Roast Duck.*

All glazed vegetables may be made in advance.

Sautéed Zucchini with Provençal Butter
Courgettes sautées au beurre provençal

Zucchini sautéed in oil then garnished with Provençal butter are much lighter and aromatic than zucchini sautéed in the usual Provençal manner. In this method the butter is added after the zucchini are cooked. This makes them much tastier, and you have no burned herbs to contend with.

FOR 6 PEOPLE

3 pounds medium-size zucchini (all the same size)
boiling salted water for blanching them
5 tablespoons peanut oil (keep the oil bottle at hand)
1 recipe of Provençal Butter*
salt
freshly ground pepper

Do not peel the zucchini. Cut off the ends, wash, and cut each into 3 or 4 pieces. Round the ends of the pieces so they will roll in the pan easily when they are sautéed.

Bring the water to a boil in a good-size enameled kettle and add salt. Lower the zucchini pieces into the water, cook for 2–3 minutes after the water resumes boiling. This is just enough cooking to get rid of the vegetable juices, which have a tendency to burn when the zucchini pieces are sautéed. Drain the zucchini and pat dry.

Heat the oil in a large sauté pan, add the zucchini, and begin sautéing, moving the pan back and forth so the pieces roll around and become coated with oil. After 3–4 minutes, reduce heat, cover the pan, and continue cooking, moving the pan back and forth and occasionally shaking it up and down (holding onto the cover). Continue sautéing for 15 minutes. Remove from heat.

Drain all the cooking oil from the sauté pan. Spread the zucchini pieces with the Provençal butter. Over low heat begin rolling the zucchini around as in the sautéing. Cover the pan and allow the zucchini to heat through completely. Place them in a warmed metal serving dish, season lightly with salt and pepper, and serve.

This dish goes beautifully with casseroled chicken and almost all roast meats.

Jellied Vegetable Loaf   *Cake de légumes en gelée*

A perfect accompaniment for cold Pot Roast* or almost any cold roasted meat.

Use a heavy rectangular cake pan with a 10 by 4-inch top and a 9 by 3-inch bottom.

FOR 6 PEOPLE

3 cups Jellied Consommé,* placed in the refrigerator until almost firm
2–3 canned pimentos, patted dry and cut in fine strips
a few chervil leaves, scalded, then patted dry
a good handful of canned peas
a good handful of cooked Green Beans*
7–8 cooked carrots, cut in thin lengthwise slices (the carrots can be left
      over from some other dish, such as Pot Roast*)

It is important that all these ingredients are perfectly dry. If any moisture remains on them, the load will not gell. Rinse the canned vegetables under the hot water tap before patting them dry.

decorating the mold

Set the cake-pan mold in a large pan containing ice cubes. Spoon a layer of the almost-set jelly on the bottom. Arrange half the strips of pimento on top of the jelly along with half the chervil leaves and a few green peas. Distribute some of the string beans vertically along the edges of the mold. Spoon a layer of jelly over these. Arrange the slices of carrot in the middle of the mold surrounded on both sides by the rest of the green beans and peas. Cover with a layer of jelly, add the rest of the pimento strips and chervil leaves. Cover with jelly. The mold should be about three quarters full, place in the refrigerator until the jelly is firmly set (at least one hour).

unmolding the loaf

Loosen the loaf by passing a sharp stainless steel knife around the inside edges of the mold, making sure to reach all the way to the bottom. Turn the mold upside down over a platter, rap the mold sharply, and lift it from the loaf.

Slice the loaf with a freshly sharpened stainless steel knife, dipped quickly into hot water and dried.

Arrangement of slices for a round platter: Cut fairly thin slices of the loaf and arrange them on a slant, overlapping and leaning against the sliced meat.

Arrangement of slices for a long platter: Cut only two thirds of the meat and vegetable loaf and arrange them in two lines down the platter. Place the uncut meat and uncut vegetable loaf at each end of the platter. This is the more picturesque arrangement.

DEEP-FAT FRYING *Friture*

People who are horrified at the idea of deep-fat frying are usually those who do not take the necessary steps to eliminate odors.

It is essential to have a well-functioning ventilator in your kitchen. This should be turned on before you begin to heat the oil. If this is done, you will have no smoky odors whatsoever.

The savory, succulent vegetable fritters included in this section make delightful garnishes for all kinds of roasts.

An excellent idea is to ring a platter of sliced roasted meat with a variety of these light, easy-to-digest fritters.

Fritter Batter *Pâte à frire*

A light, supple batter that is neither too thick nor too thin.

    1 cup all-purpose flour
    a small pinch of salt
    1 egg yolk
    2–3 tablespoons cold water
    2 tablespoons peanut oil
    ½ cup light beer
    1 egg white plus a pinch of salt, stiffly beaten

Sift the flour into a bowl. Make a well in the center and put in the salt, egg yolk, water and oil. Using a wooden spatula, fold the flour over the ingredients in the well and work the ingredients into a paste. Whisk vigorously or beat with an electric beater for a minute or so. Then stir in the beer.

Set the batter aside to rest for about 1 hour. Just before using, fold in the stiffly beaten egg white with a pinch of salt.

VEGETABLE FRITTERS

Zucchini Fritters   *Beignets de courgettes*

ENOUGH FOR 4–6 PEOPLE

3 medium-size zucchini
flour for dusting the zucchini slices
1 recipe of Fritter Batter*
about 3 cups peanut oil for frying the fritters
salt

Wash and dry the zucchini. Do not peel them. Cut them into ½-inch slices, pat dry, and wrap them in a dry kitchen towel for about 15 minutes. Dust them with flour, shaking or tapping off any excess.

Start heating the oil. When the surface just barely begins to wrinkle or reaches 375° F., dip the slices of zucchini in the batter and fry them a few at a time. Turn them once. Remove the fritters and place on paper towels to drain. Sprinkle with salt, continue frying the rest of the fritters. Between cooking batches, remove and discard any pieces of batter that may be floating in the oil.

Ring a platter of sliced roast meat with these delicacies. For a novelty, use three kinds of fritters.

NOTE: *on keeping fritters warm: after draining them on paper towels, place them on a heated plate set over a pan of boiling water, then turn off heat. Use this method for all fritters in this section.*

Cauliflower Fritters   *Bouquets de chou-fleur frits*

MAKES ENOUGH FOR 6 PEOPLE

1 small, firm cauliflower
boiling salted water for blanching the cauliflower
1 recipe Fritter Batter*
3 cups peanut oil for frying the fritters
salt

Strip off the green leaves, cut off the heavy stem at the base, and wash the cauliflower thoroughly in cold water. Plunge it into an enameled kettle of boiling salted water, blanch for 12 minutes, and drain. Divide the cauliflower into flowerets, leaving each with about ½ inch of stem. Dry the flowerets carefully and allow them to cool completely. Holding the flowerets by the stems, plunge them one by one into the batter. Place them in the heated oil (about 375° F.) a few at a time until they become golden brown. Between cooking batches, remove and discard any pieces of batter that may be floating in the oil. Drain the fritters on paper towels, sprinkle with salt, and keep warm while you are making the rest.

Brussels Sprouts Fritters *Beignets de choux de Bruxelles*

I highly recommend these delicious little golden balls. Count six Brussels sprouts per person.

Follow the procedure described in the preceding recipe. Spear the blanched Brussels sprouts with a fork when you dip them in the batter.

Grapefruit Fritters *Beignets de pamplemousse*

These can be served as a "vegetable" garnish. Of all fritters these are the most intriguing. One small problem: how to keep the grapefruit juice from oozing out into the batter and ruining your fritters. The answer is simple: you need a different kind of batter—one that coats the grapefruit wedges more heavily and makes them "leakproof."

ingredients for grapefruit fritter batter
  1½ cups all-purpose flour
  1 whole egg plus 1 egg yolk
  a pinch of salt
  ¾–1 cup water

other ingredients
  3 large seedless grapefruit
  flour for dusting grapefruit wedges
  3 cups peanut oil for frying fritters
  salt

Mix the batter as in regular Fritter Batter* and set aside to rest for an hour.
  With a freshly sharpened knife remove the peel from the grapefruit. Cut deeply so as to rid the fruit of all the bitter white pith. Proceeding from the edge to the center, cut the grapefruit into wedges, each having the thickness of about 1½ sections of grapefruit. Place these wedges on a large sheet of paper towels and cover with another sheet. Let them stand for 1 hour. At the end of this time, dry each wedge with a clean kitchen towel. Dust the wedges lightly with flour and let them dry for a few minutes.

Heat the oil in the fryer to 375° F. Dip the grapefruit wedges in the batter, holding them with a fork. Place 6 in the oil and cook until golden brown, turning once. Remove the fritters to paper towels to drain, sprinkle lightly with salt, and continue cooking the rest. Between batches remove and discard any pieces of batter that may be floating in the oil.

PURÉES OF VEGETABLES

Binding purées made of floury or mealy vegetables presents no problem because of their starch content.

Binding purées made from artichokes, celery root, mushrooms, turnips, and onions is another story. These vegetables give off much liquid after having been blended or puréed, and they must be somehow dried out. To accomplish this, place the purée in a heavy-bottomed enameled saucepan, set over low heat, and stir constantly with a wooden spatula until all the liquid has evaporated.

Spinach, sorrel, and green beans also contain a great deal of liquid and are a little more difficult to deal with than the vegetables mentioned above. Each of these vegetables requires its own special liaison, which you will find in the recipes. A word of warning: do not bind watery vegetables by putting them through a food mill or blender along with cooked rice or cooked potatoes. This method deprives the green vegetable of its savor and makes it "heavy."

Three vegetable purées, served in separate dishes, are an original accompaniment for poultry, game, roasts, and other festive fare. But they should be chosen to harmonize with each other and with the dish they are to accompany. I have indicated various combinations in the recipes that follow.

Purées can be made in advance and kept hot over a pan of hot water. Beat them before placing them in a heated vegetable dish.

Apple and Potato Purée   *Purée aux deux pommes*

A purée of unsweetened apples is given body by a small amount of leftover Potato Purée.*

FOR 4–6 PEOPLE

3 pounds tart cooking apples
½ lemon
a small piece of lemon peel
¼ cup water
¾ cup leftover Potato Purée, placed over a pan of hot water
salt
freshly ground pepper
freshly grated nutmeg or a small pinch of cinnamon
2 pats of butter

Peel, core, and quarter the apples. Rub the cut side of the lemon over each apple quarter. Cut the quarters into slices and place in a heavy-bottomed enameled saucepan, along with the lemon peel and the ¼ cup of water. Cover and cook until tender, stirring frequently. The cooking time depends on the kind of apples you use.

Place the apples in the blender and process them, adding the puréed potatoes (which have been standing over hot water). Place the purée in a saucepan, heat through, and stir in the seasonings. Then beat in the butter. Serve immediately in a warmed vegetable dish.

This is a delicious accompaniment for Braised Ham,* Roast Duck,* or Goose.*

Spiced Apple Purée, Used as a Vegetable Garnish
Purée de pommes fruits épicée

An unsweetened apple purée seasoned with salt, pepper, and mango chutney. It makes a delicious garnish for goose, Roast Duck,* Roast Saddle of Venison,* as well as hot or cold Braised Ham.*

FOR 6–8 PEOPLE

2 pounds tart cooking apples
½ lemon
a small piece of lemon peel
½ cup water
3 pinches of salt, each taken with 3 fingers
freshly ground pepper
1–2 tablespoons mango chutney, depending on your taste

Peel, core, and quarter the apples. Rub the cut side of the lemon over each apple quarter. Slice the quarters and place in a heavy-bottomed, enameled saucepan, along with the piece of lemon peel and the ½ cup of water. Cook the apples until they are tender and have disintegrated, stirring frequently. Season with salt and pepper.

Discard the lemon peel and put the apples through a food mill, using the finest disk. Stir in the chutney and taste for seasoning. Serve lukewarm or cold.

Artichoke Mousseline   *Mousseline d'artichauts*

Use large artichokes for making this delicious purée.

FOR 5–6 PEOPLE

10–12 Artichokes Cooked Whole*
1 egg
3 tablespoons heavy cream
salt
freshly ground pepper
freshly grated nutmeg
a few drops of lemon juice
3–4 pats of butter

Break the leaves off the cooked artichokes and, using a sharp-edged spoon, scrape the flesh from each leaf into a bowl. Discard the chokes, trim the hearts, dice, and put in the same bowl. Run through a food mill while still warm. With a wooden spatula work in the egg, then 1 tablespoon of cream. Beat the mixture with an electric beater, adding the rest of the cream 1 tablespoon at a time.

Place the mixture in a heavy-bottomed enameled saucepan and set over moderate heat. Beat in the salt, pepper, nutmeg, lemon juice, and the pats of butter until the mixture is light and fluffy. Serve immediately in a warmed vegetable dish.

This goes wonderfully with veal.

Canned White Bean Purée   *Purée de haricots en boîte*

FOR 6 PEOPLE

3 large cans vegetarian-style white beans (without tomato sauce)
1 cup warmed milk or 1 cup warmed cream
a sprig of dried or fresh savory, or a sprig of fresh or dried thyme
1 tablespoon raw onion squeezed through a garlic press
salt
freshly ground pepper
1 pat of butter
1 tablespoon mixed finely minced chervil, tarragon, and parsley, or 1
    tablespoon finely minced parsley

Put the beans in a colander and rinse them thoroughly under the hot water tap. Place them in a heavy-bottomed enameled casserole and add the warmed milk or cream, one of the herbs, onion, salt, and pepper. Heat, stirring constantly, to prevent the milk or cream from boiling over. Remove from heat and allow to stand for 15–20 minutes.

Discard the herbs and put the beans through a food mill, using the finest disk. Add the butter, adjust seasoning, and heat through. Place in a warmed vegetable dish, sprinkle with the minced herbs, and serve.

Dried White Bean Purée   *Purée de haricots secs*

This purée will please everyone, especially those who have trouble digesting the skins of cooked white beans.

FOR 6–8 PEOPLE

1½–2 pounds dried Great Northern white beans
enough lukewarm water to cover the beans generously, plus a kettle of almost-boiling water for the final cooking of the beans
a sprig of fresh savory
½ tablespoon raw onion squeezed through garlic press
2 tablespoons butter, cut in pieces
2 tablespoons heavy cream
salt
freshly ground pepper

Pick over and wash the beans. Soak them for 2 hours and drain. Place them in an enameled or stainless steel kettle, cover with lukewarm water, and bring to a boil. Let them boil for about 5 minutes. Drain the beans and put them in a second kettle of almost-boiling water. Add the savory, bring the water to a boil, lower heat, and simmer the beans until tender—about 2 hours. Discard the savory, put the beans through a food mill twice, using the finest disk, or use a blender. Stir in the onion, butter, and cream, season with salt and pepper, heat through, and serve in a heated vegetable dish.

This purée *is delicious with roast pork, leg of lamb, or shoulder of lamb.*

Green Bean Purée   *Purée de haricots verts*

This is one of the most delicious of vegetable purées, if the beans are garden-fresh or almost garden-fresh. Because they contain a great deal of liquid, it is necessary to bind the purée, and this presents a problem because a liaison of cream and butter is not enough. The purée will continue to give off moisture, even when you try to dry it out by placing it over low heat, and it will not only be unattractive, but it will have a rather flat taste.

After much experimenting, I finally discovered a method of making a purée of green beans that is not drowned in liquid and that preserves the full flavor of fresh beans. Cream and butter are used as binding, but the secret ingredient is . . . see the recipe following.

3 pounds green beans, washed and trimmed

about 7 quarts of boiling salted water

1 cup canned *flageolets*[1]

4 tablespoons milk

2–3 fresh or dried basil leaves or 1 sprig fresh or dried savory

2–3 tablespoons heavy cream

salt

freshly ground pepper

3–4 pats of butter

Prepare the green beans, rinse them under the cold water tap, and blanch them in boiling salted water until tender-firm. Do not refresh them. Put them through a food mill while still hot, using the finest disk, into a heavy-bottomed enameled casserole.

Rinse the canned *flageolets* (or canned white beans) under the cold water tap. Place them in an enameled saucepan along with the milk and basil or savory. Heat, stirring, for a minute or two. Discard the herbs, put the *flageolet* mixture through a food mill (using the finest disk), whisk into the green bean purée a tablespoon at a time. Set the casserole over low heat and whisk in the cream. Add salt and pepper to taste. Beat in the butter and transfer the purée to a warmed vegetable dish.

This purée goes beautifully with Roast Leg of Lamb* and Sautéed Veal Chops with Mushrooms.* For a grand dinner party, when you are serving three separate purées, serve with Dried White Bean Purée* and Onion Purée.*

Celery Root Pureé   *Purée de céleri-rave*

A delicious and nourishing winter purée that goes with roast pork, various kinds of veal, ham, game, especially venison and wild rabbit.

This tasty purée is bound with eggs, lightened with cream, and enriched with butter.

FOR 5–6 PEOPLE

a 3–3½ pound celery root

water for cooking it

coarse salt

2 eggs

¾ cup heavy cream

salt

freshly ground pepper

1–2 tablespoons butter, cut in pieces

---

[1] Canned *flageolets* can be found in some specialty shops, but if you cannot find them, substitute ½ cup of canned white beans.

Cut off the root end of the celery root, scrub in cool water, and peel deeply. Cut into chunks and place in an enameled saucepan. Cover with cold water, add coarse salt, bring to a boil, and cook for 25–30 minutes or until tender. Drain and put through a food mill, using the finest disk. Then process in a blender for 1 minute along with the eggs. Remove to a saucepan, beat in the cream a tablespoon at a time, and place over moderate heat until piping hot. Add salt and pepper, beat in the pieces of butter. Then put the purée in a warmed vegetable dish and serve.

Serve this in combination with other purées, such as Chestnut,* Spiced Apple,* or Mushroom,* for gala occasions.

Chestnut Purée   *Purée de marrons*

FOR 6 PEOPLE

4¼ pounds chestnuts, peeled
6¾ cups water
1 stalk celery, coarsely cut
1 *Bouquet garni classique**
salt
freshly ground pepper
3–4 tablespoons butter, cut in small pieces

Place the chestnuts in a large enameled saucepan and cover them with water. Bring to a boil, add the celery and *bouquet garni*. Reduce heat and cook the chestnuts until tender, about 45 minutes.

Drain the chestnuts and put them through a food mill, using the finest disk. Transfer to a metal or Pyrex dish, season with salt and pepper, and set over a pan of boiling water. Stir in the pieces of butter and beat the purée with a whisk. Serve it piping hot in a warmed vegetable dish.

Purée of chestnut is a delicious accompaniment for turkey and all kinds of furred game.

Lentil Purée   *Purée de lentilles*

A delicious dish to serve with roast goose, roast or braised duck, or roast partridge.

FOR 6 PEOPLE

1 pound lentils, prepared as in Basic Method for Cooking*
the neck (cut in 3 pieces) of whatever poultry you are using, plus all the
   bone trimmings

Place the neck and bone trimmings in with the lentils at the beginning of cooking. Add the rest of the ingredients in the lentil recipe, cook until they are tender. Strain them, then put them through a food mill, using the finest disk, or process them in a blender for 1 minute.

NOTE: *If you are using a food mill put the lentils through twice to achieve a lighter mixture.*

*See also Lentil Salad.**

Mushroom Purée   *Purée de champignons*

An elegant, rich purée to serve as a single garnish or in combination with other purées.

FOR 4–6 PEOPLE

2¼ pounds firm, fresh mushrooms
½ lemon
4 tablespoons butter
1 tablespoon minced shallot
*Beurre manié,** made with 2 tablespoons butter and 2 tablespoons flour
2–3 tablespoons heavy cream
salt
freshly ground pepper
a squeeze of lemon juice (optional)

Cut off the sandy root end of the mushrooms. Wash them in a basin of cold water in which you have squeezed the juice of the half lemon (leaving the squeezed skin in the water). Drain the mushrooms and dry them one by one with a clean kitchen towel. Chop the caps and stems, then mince them finely. Put them, yes raw, through a food mill, using the coarsest disk, or grind them in an electric grinder.

Put the ground mushrooms and half the butter in a sauté pan and stir-cook for about 2½ minutes. Add the rest of the butter and the shallot and stir-cook for another 2 minutes. Drain the mushroom juice into a bowl and set aside.

If you want a smoother purée, place the cooked mushrooms in a blender and process for 1 minute, or put them through the food mill once again.

Place the purée in a heavy-bottomed enameled saucepan. Reduce (if necessary) the mushroom juice to 3–4 tablespoons.

Pour the reduced mushroom juice into the saucepan of purée and mix well. Pick up bits of the *beurre manié* with the end of a whisk and mix into the purée. Then, using a spatula, work in the cream little by little. Season with salt and pepper, tasting. Heat through, allowing the purée to bubble up once or twice. A few drops of lemon juice may be added at this time, especially if the purée is to accompany Fish Fillets.*

Serve in a warmed vegetable dish.

Purée of mushrooms makes an excellent accompaniment for roast veal, roast chicken, veal chops or veal scallops, saddle of hare, young partridges, or pheasants.

Suggestion for serving with fish fillets: Place a layer of mushroom purée on a heated oval platter and lay the fish fillets on top. Top the fillets with whatever sauce you have chosen.

Onion Purée   *Purée d'oignons*

There are various ways of preparing onion purée. In one classical recipe, rice and onions are cooked slowly together, then put through a food mill, the rice serving as a liaison. In another, the puréed onions are bound with a Béchamel Sauce.* I find that in both these methods the onions lose their essential taste and strength. Years ago, a talented chef gave me the following recipe for onion purée and I have used it ever since.

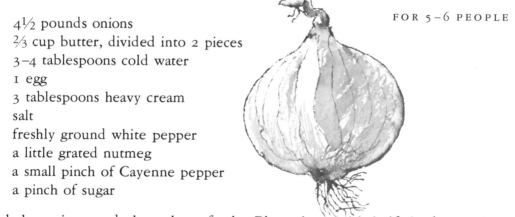

FOR 5–6 PEOPLE

4½ pounds onions
⅔ cup butter, divided into 2 pieces
3–4 tablespoons cold water
1 egg
3 tablespoons heavy cream
salt
freshly ground white pepper
a little grated nutmeg
a small pinch of Cayenne pepper
a pinch of sugar

Peel the onions and chop them finely. Place them with half the butter in a large, heavy sauté pan or heavy-bottomed enameled casserole. Set the pan over low heat and stir-cook the onions for a few minutes, until they are coated with butter. Reduce heat, pour in the 3–4 tablespoons of water, and cook for 20–25 minutes, stirring frequently, adding the rest of the butter a little at a time. At the end of the cooking time the onions should be tender to the point of melting and faintly yellow.

Put them through a food mill twice, using the finest disk, or blend them for 1 minute in a blender.

Spoon off any excess of butter. Place the purée in a heavy-bottomed enameled saucepan and add the egg. Set over low heat, gradually work in the cream. Season with salt, white pepper, nutmeg, Cayenne pepper, and sugar. Taste and adjust seasoning if necessary. Heat the purée until it reaches the boiling point. Serve in a warmed vegetable dish.

Here is a little trick for giving the purée the taste of fresh onion: Grate a small piece of raw onion over it after it has been placed in the serving dish.

Onion purée makes an admirable accompaniment for pork roast, lamb chops, roast leg of lamb, and for some game meats such as venison.

Fresh Green Pea Purée   *Purée de pois frais*

FOR 6 PEOPLE

2 pounds shelled peas (about 6 pounds unshelled peas)
boiling water for cooking them
6–7 fresh green lettuce leaves, rolled and sliced[1]
1 green onion, cut in half
1 *Bouquet garni classique** or 1 sprig of fresh or dried thyme
⅔ cup heavy cream
a pinch of sugar
salt
1–2 pats of butter

Put the peas in a large saucepan of boiling water and add the lettuce slices, onion, and *bouquet garni* or thyme. Cook for about 20 minutes until the peas are tender—taste one to make sure. Discard the *bouquet garni* or thyme and put the peas and lettuce through a food mill, using the finest disk.

Place the purée in a heavy-bottomed enameled saucepan, set over low heat, and bit by bit work in the cream with a wooden spatula. Add sugar and salt and taste for seasoning. Whisk the purée vigorously, adding the pats of butter. Serve the purée in a warmed vegetable dish.

This is excellent with spring lamb and braised meat of all kinds. It is delicious with broiled pork sausages.

Split Pea Purée   *Purée de pois cassés*

FOR 6 PEOPLE

1½ pounds split peas, soaked in cold water for 2 hours and stirred twice during this time
1 small carrot, peeled
1 medium-size onion, cut in half
1 *Bouquet garni classique**
salt
a small saucepan of boiling water to be used if necessary
3 tablespoons butter, cut in small pieces
freshly ground pepper
a small pinch of oregano
2 tablespoons heavy cream (optional)

Drain the soaked peas and place them in a large, heavy-bottomed enameled casserole. Cover generously with cold water, bring to a boil, skim, and add the

[1] The lettuce brightens up the green color of the peas, which tend to fade slightly when cooked.

carrot, onion, and *bouquet garni*. Salt lightly—the main salting comes after the peas are puréed. Cover the casserole and cook over low heat for 1½–2 hours, stirring with a wooden spatula from time to time to prevent the peas from sticking to the bottom. During the first hour of cooking you may add a little boiling water from the saucepan if the liquid seems too thick.

Remove the casserole from heat, discard the carrot, onion, and *bouquet garni,* and purée the peas either by putting them through a food mill twice, using the finest disk, or by blending them in a blender.

Place the purée in a saucepan, set over low heat, and stir in the butter a piece at a time. Remove from heat, add the salt, pepper, and oregano to taste.

If you would like a creamier purée, stir in the cream.

Purée of split peas makes an excellent accompaniment for veal (chops or scallops), pork sausages, braised ham.

Potato Purée   *Purée de pommes de terre*

Purée of potatoes can be a sad affair—weak and watery, with a peculiar, almost sandy texture.

A perfect potato purée should be smooth with just the barest suggestion of graininess. Instead of being as white as the driven snow, it should have a faint ivory tint. The following recipe produces the most delicious potato purée I know of.

FOR 6 PEOPLE

2 pounds of firm boiling potatoes (to yield about 1½ pounds after peeling)
coarse salt
⅓ cup butter, cut in pieces
¾ cup boiling hot milk
salt
freshly ground pepper
freshly grated nutmeg

Peel, wash, and drain the potatoes. Cut them in quarters, put them in an enameled or stainless steel kettle, cover with cold water, add salt, and boil, uncovered, for 16–20 minutes. Do not overcook them, for they will absorb too much water and will not have the proper consistency when puréed. Pick out a potato and press it lightly between thumb and forefinger. If it yields to the pressure, it is done enough.

Drain the potatoes and put them through a food mill, using the finest disk, into a saucepan set over a pan of hot water. Stir them with a wooden spatula, then work in the pieces of butter. Alternate the addition of butter with tablespoons of boiling hot milk until all the butter and milk have been incorporated. Then whisk the purée briskly until it is nice and light.

The labor can be shortened if you purée the potatoes a minute or so in a blender, adding butter and milk as above. Season with salt, pepper, and a little nutmeg. Taste and adjust seasoning if necessary. Heat the purée thoroughly and place in a warmed vegetable dish in the shape of a dome. Starting at the bottom, stripe the sides of the purée upward with the tines of a fork so the stripes meet at the top of the dome.

Purée of potatoes can be served with just about everything. It dresses up the simplest of dishes and sets off the complicated ones.

Cake of Potato Purée   *Gâteau de pommes de terre*

What should one do with leftover purée of potatoes? Since they are not very well adapted to simple reheating, the best thing is to make an entirely new dish—a "cake" of leftover potato purée. The dish requires few ingredients and very little labor. And best of all, it is delicious.

To make the dish you will need a not-too-high soufflé mold, well buttered and sprinkled with a little grated Swiss cheese.

FOR 4–5 PEOPLE[1]

2 cups leftover Potatoe Purée*
4 tablespoons boiling hot milk
3 egg yolks
salt
freshly ground pepper
freshly grated nutmeg
3 egg whites, beaten stiffly with a pinch of salt
6 tablespoons grated Swiss cheese
Preheat oven to 350° F.

Put the purée of potatoes in a heavy-bottomed enameled saucepan, place over low heat, and stir in the hot milk, first working with a wooden spatula, then beating with a whisk.

Work in the egg yolks one after the other, beating after each addition. Taste and add salt if needed. Stir in a little pepper and nutmeg. Fold in the stiffly beaten egg whites alternately with half the grated cheese.

Place the mixture in the prepared soufflé mold (see the introduction to this recipe). Sprinkle with a little more grated cheese and some grated nutmeg.

Place the mold in the oven, bake for 7–8 minutes, reduce oven heat to 340°, and bake for another 8–10 minutes until the cake is well risen and golden. Serve the dish in the mold.

---

[1] 1 cup of leftover potato purée will serve 2–3 people. Use 2 egg yolks and 2 beaten whites instead of 3.

Sorrel Purée *Purée d'oseille*

2 pounds sorrel
3 tablespoons heavy cream
1–2 tablespoons thick Béchamel Sauce* (if necessary)
salt
freshly ground pepper
freshly grated nutmeg
3–4 drops lemon juice (if necessary)

Pick over and wash the sorrel. Place in an enameled kettle of boiling water and blanch for 3–5 minutes until it is limp and soft. Drain. Take handfuls of sorrel and gently press out the water. Purée the sorrel either in a blender or by putting it through a food mill twice, using the finest disk. Put the sorrel in a heavy-bottomed enameled saucepan, set over low heat, and stir in the cream. If the sorrel seems too liquid, bind it with the *béchamel* sauce. Season with salt, pepper, and nutmeg. Taste and adjust seasoning. If the sorrel has a slightly acrid taste, stir in a few drops of lemon juice.

Sorrel purée makes an excellent garnish for halved Hard-Boiled Eggs,* 5- or 6-Minute Boiled Eggs,* or Poached Eggs* served on hot Croutons.*

Cream-Puréed Spinach *Epinards à la crème*

3 pounds fresh spinach
2 tablespoons butter, cut in pieces
4 tablespoons heavy cream
salt
a pinch of sugar
freshly ground pepper
freshly grated nutmeg
9 triangular Croutons,* made ahead and reheated before using
2 pats of butter

Sort over, wash, blanch, and chop the spinach as in Chopped Spinach Stewed with Butter.* If you like, place the blanched spinach in a blender and process for 1 minute.

In a heavy-bottomed enameled casserole, slowly heat half the butter. Add the spinach, turning and stirring constantly with a wooden spatula. Add the other half of the butter, continuing to stir and turn the spinach. Work in the cream, add the seasonings, and taste. Beat the spinach vigorously and pile it, dome-shaped, in a warmed serving dish. Stripe the surface with the tines of a fork, put the reheated croutons around the sides of the dish, put the pats of butter on top, and serve.

For a light meal: make round croutons, spread them with the spinach, and top with a warm Poached Egg.*

Oval Tartlets Filled with Cream-Puréed Spinach
Barquettes aux épinards

An elegant garnish for braised ham, veal roast, or fish fillets served with Mornay Sauce.*

Make Oval Tartlets* using Short Crust Pastry Dough.* Allowing 2 per person, fill with domes with Cream-Puréed Spinach.* Surround the platter of meat or fish with these marvels.

Turnip Purée   Purée de navets

Why do we associate turnips with poverty, cheap boardinghouses, or soup kitchens? It is a perfectly delicious vegetable, especially the tender, early-crop turnips with their sweet juices. It is these spring turnips that make the most delicious purée.

FOR 4–6 PEOPLE

3–4 pounds spring turnips
salt
freshly ground pepper
a pinch of sugar
2 tablespoons butter, cut in pieces
3 tablespoons heavy cream

Peel the turnips, cut them in quarters, and wash them. Place them in a heavy-bottomed enameled casserole and just barely cover them with cold water. Add salt, pepper, sugar, and half the pieces of butter. Cover the pan and cook over medium-low heat, shaking the pan up and down now and then, for 25–30 minutes until the turnips have absorbed all the water and are shiny and meltingly tender.

Drain the turnips, place them on a board, and chop them coarsely. Put them in a blender and process for a minute or so, adding the rest of the butter and the cream. (This operation can also be done with a food mill.) Taste and adjust seasoning. Place the purée in a saucepan, set it over low heat, and whisk until heated through. Serve in a warmed vegetable dish.

Purée of turnips is a marvelous accompaniment for Roast Duck. It is a good idea to serve turnip purée as one of the purées in a group of three. Suggestions for the two other purées: Mushroom,* Fresh Green Pea,* or Green Beans.*

Watercress Purée   *Purée de cresson*

This delicious purée takes a good deal of patience and courage to make. But when you have tasted the finished product, you will not regret the time you have spent preparing the watercress.

FOR 4 PEOPLE

    8 bunches watercress
    a scant ½ cup heavy cream
    1 tablespoon butter
    salt
    freshly ground pepper
    ½ teaspoon strong Dijon mustard

Wash the watercress meticulously in several waters, drain well. Cut away all the thick stems. Make little bouquets of the watercress, each with 4 or 5 leaves. Plunge them into a kettle of rapidly boiling water and pour them through a colander before the water has begun boiling again. For this operation, you will have to pay close attention.

Refresh the watercress under the cold water tap, using your fingers to stir the leaves around so they all become cool. Take bundles of cress in your hands, press out the water, place in a bowl, and then put it through a food mill twice, using the finest disk. Place the purée in an enameled saucepan and set it over low heat to dry out, stirring constantly. This operation takes only a few seconds. Then slowly stir in the cream. Do not use any more cream than indicated. Too much cream will cause the cress to lose its bright green color. Stir in the butter, salt, pepper, and mustard. Taste and adjust seasoning.

Watercress purée is wonderful served with steaks of all kinds, with veal kidneys, and broiled lamb kidneys.

MIXED VEGETABLE GARNISHES OR "GARDENS"

Here are two mixed vegetable garnishes I serve on special occasions, according to the season.

The first one (see below) is as colorful and beautiful as it is delicious. It belongs to the spring and, in a way, to me . . . for when I served it for the first time, a friend cried out, "Why, it's Louisette's garden!" And it has been called that ever since.

All the vegetables in this "garden" must be cooked separately and kept hot.

Use a large oval flameproof (preferably metal) platter for arranging the vegetables.

Louisette's Garden   *Le Jardin de Louisette*

FOR 6 PEOPLE

    1 pound Noisette Potatoes*
    1 pound Glazed Carrots*

---

24 Small White Glazed Onions*

1 pound fresh green beans cooked tied together (Green Bean Salad*)

6 small Broiled Tomatoes*

6 large Stuffed Mushrooms*

a little finely minced parsley

Prepare the vegetables and keep them hot in flameproof dishes set on an electric hot tray. Heat the metal serving platter before arranging the vegetables on it.

arranging the vegetables on the platter

Place the hot vegetables in small piles on the platter, snipping the strings from the green beans after they are placed on the platter. Contrast the color in the following manner: green (beans), white (potatoes, onions), red (tomatoes, carrots), then white, green, red, and so on. Try to keep the arrangement as regular as possible. Dot the piles of glazed onion and noisette potatoes with the tiniest bit of parsley. Surround the platter with the stuffed mushrooms.

If the dish must wait for a few minutes, cover the platter with a piece of parchment paper and place it in an oven preheated to 350° F. and turned out just before you set the platter inside. Do not let the dish wait more than 10–15 minutes.

This colorful vegetable garnish can be used to dress up all sorts of roast or casseroled beef dishes; it is excellent served with casseroled veal and will make any dinner party a "thing of beauty and a joy for ever."

Winter Vegetable Garnish *Jardin d'hiver*

This garden is somewhat less colorful than the preceding one, but it is almost as sumptuous and will set off a roast turkey, a braised duck, a roast of pork, or roast of veal with striking success.

FOR 6 PEOPLE

30 Braised Chestnuts* or 6 Oval Tartlets* made with Short Crust Pastry Dough* and filled with well-buttered Chestnut Purée,* or 1 pound Brussels Sprouts Sautéed in Butter,* or 12 Flowerets of Cauliflower Sautéed in Butter,* or 12 Brussels Sprouts Fritters*

for a very grand dinner

6–8 round Tartlets* made with Short Crust Pastry Dough* filled with Cream-Puréed Spinach* and 6 Fennel Hearts Braised in Butter* then gratinéed.

Arrange the vegetables nicely on a heated metal platter.

Desserts

Today desserts are not as much in demand as they used to be. We are no longer used to eating huge meals, and the dessert course is frequently omitted. Most people are now satisfied to end their meal with the cheese course.

Nevertheless, certain meals, moods, and occasions still call for desserts.

With desserts, as with most things, it is wise to avoid complications. Simple homemade desserts are the most popular. They are especially successful when they are prepared from the freshest ingredients and attention is paid to the finishing touches.

Floating island and baked *pots de crème* can be enjoyed at all times. Rich chocolate desserts are welcome in the winter. Ice creams and sherbets are fashionable at the moment. Light, flaky-crust tarts, served fresh from the oven, have a faithful following. Italian cookery has renewed interest in fruit compotes by making them more exciting.

In recent years cake has made a comeback. I have noticed that men, when they have time, like to stay on at the dinner table and dawdle over a piece of cake and a glass of wine. Dessert wines, which go so well with cake, should be brought back: Frontignan, from southern France; Jurançon, from the Pau region; the amber-colored Vin de Paille from Arbois, as well as the Sauternes. These wines should be served in glasses that have been chilled in the refrigerator for 15–20 minutes; the wine itself should be cold but not ice cold.

Sugar Syrup *Sirop de sucre*

Sugar syrup is used to sweeten fruit compotes, fruit salads, and certain iced drinks.

Concentrated Sugar Syrup

    4 cups granulated sugar
    2 cups water

Bring the sugar and water to a boil and remove from heat immediately.

Mild Sugar Syrup

    4 cups granulated sugar
    4 cups water

Follow the procedure above.

Syrup of the Islands *Sirop des îles*

I first tasted this exotic sugar syrup in the punches served on a famous transatlantic steamship line I used to travel with. I asked the barman about it, and he amiably told me what the "secret" ingredients were.

> 4 cups concentrated Sugar Syrup*
> 2 vanilla beans
> 2 nutmegs
> 2–3 coriander seeds
> 2–3 white peppercorns
> 1 strip orange peel 2–3 inches long
> 1 strip lemon peel 2–3 inches long

Pour the sugar syrup into a large, wide-necked glass bottle. Make 2 incisions in each of the vanilla beans to release the flavor, and add them to the syrup along with the other ingredients.

Make a temporary cork out of cotton or a piece of paper towel to allow the air to circulate freely during fermentation.

Put the bottle in the cellar or other cool place. After a week or ten days, exchange the temporary cork for a real one.

This syrup will keep for a year.

Candy Syrup *Sucre filé*

> 2 cups mild Sugar Syrup*

Place the syrup in a copper or stainless steel saucepan. Bring the syrup to a boil.

The different stages of sugar syrup used in making various confections are as follows:

thread stage

This stage can be tested by first dipping your thumb and forefinger in cold water, then placing a drop of syrup between them. Let the syrup cool and separate your fingers: if the syrup has reached the thread stage, you will see thin threads forming between thumb and finger.

Cooking temperature: 223° F.

ball stage

Cook the syrup beyond the thread stage. Dip your thumb and forefinger into cold water and repeat the operation above. The syrup should now form a semi-solid ball when you separate thumb and finger.

Cooking temperature: 244° F.

DESSERTS   398

hard-crack stage

Prolong the cooking beyond the ball stage and test as above. A thin, brittle layer of sugar should detach itself from your thumb and forefinger when you separate them. It will be hard and crunchy when you bite into it.

Cooking temperature: 257° F.

Here is one way to use the hard-crack stage of sugar syrup.

Glazed Fruit Sections *Tranches de fruits glacées*

2 cups Sugar Syrup,* cooked to Hard-Crack Stage*
24 tangerine sections, or 18 orange sections, or 12 grapefruit sections

Remove all the pith and filaments from the fruit sections.

Bring the sugar syrup to the hard-crack stage, remove from heat, and let it stand until it has cooled somewhat. Using a fork, dip each fruit section in the hot syrup. Remove quickly, drain for a second, and place on a marble slab. Continue until all fruit sections have been coated with a thin, crunchy layer of syrup.

When the sections are completely cool, transfer them to a serving plate with a metal spatula.

Glazed fruit sections can be served instead of petits fours *at the end of a meal. They are also used to decorate fruit sherbets (see Tangerine Sherbet*).*

CAKE ICINGS

Icings give cakes a refined as well as professional touch, and almost all of them are simple to make. One of the most delicious icings is made with white fondant.

White Fondant, Basic Recipe *Fondant blanc*

4 cups granulated sugar
2 cups water
2 tablespoons kirsch, raspberry or plum liqueur
(For less icing cut the recipe in half.)

Boil the sugar and water together until it reaches the Thread Stage.* Remove from heat and pour onto a clean grease-free marble slab or plastic work surface.

With a small wooden spatula work the warm syrup round and round and back and forth until the mass thickens and becomes opaque and creamy.

If you are using the fondant immediately, transfer it to a small saucepan; otherwise store it in a covered jar or bowl.

Gently heat the fondant. Add one of the liqueurs, stirring constantly. Do not allow the fondant to become more than barely warm. If it overheats it will revert to its former syrupy state and all your work will have been for nothing! If it shows any sign of losing its creamy whiteness, remove it from heat immediately, place it over a pan of cold water, and beat vigorously with a wooden spatula until the whiteness is restored.

Quick Icings Made From Confectioner's Sugar

Quick White Icing   *Glaçage blanc minute*

This is one of my favorite quick icings.

MAKES ENOUGH FOR 1 LAYER

¼–½ pound confectioner's sugar (according to how much icing you wish
    to make)
2, 3, or 4 tablespoons kirsch or other clear fruit brandy

Sift the sugar into a bowl. Add the brandy and work vigorously with a wooden spatula until the sugar and brandy are blended and creamy (about 6–8 minutes) and the mixture oozes off the spatula in a broad ribbon.

Quick Chocolate Icing   *Glaçage minute au chocolat*

A soft, creamy icing that spreads easily. The butter gives it a lustrous sheen.

MAKES ABOUT 1 CUP

3–4 ounces semi-sweet chocolate
2–3 tablespoons strong brewed coffee
4–5 tablespoons cold unsalted butter, cut in small pieces

Over low heat melt the chocolate with the coffee. When a thick, creamy mixture has been obtained, remove from heat and allow to become lukewarm. Work in the butter piece by piece until it is thoroughly blended.

Allow the icing to cool before frosting the cake.

frosting the cake

Place the cake on a rack set over a shallow dish. Heat a metal spatula in hot water and dry it well. Carefully pour the icing on top of the cake and spread it with the spatula, working from the center to the edge of the cake. Cover the sides thoroughly. Scoop up and use any icing that may have dripped off the cake into the dish.

Royal Icing *Glaçage royal*

This firm, snow-white icing should be included in your repertory.

MAKES ABOUT 1 CUP

1 egg white
¾ cup (packed) sifted confectioner's sugar
3 drops acetic acid (use 5–6 drops of lemon juice if you cannot get acetic acid)
1 tablespoon all-purpose flour (optional)

Put the egg white in a bowl and work in the sugar little by little with a wooden spatula. Add the acetic acid or lemon juice and beat vigorously until the icing stands in a peak when dribbled off the spatula.

If you wish to glaze a cake or cookies in the oven, beat the flour (sifted) into the mixture.

Traditional Chocolate Icing *Glaçage classique au chocolat*

MAKES 1 LARGE CUP

2 ounces semi-sweet chocolate
2–3 tablespoons strong brewed coffee
¾ cup and 1 tablespoon sifted confectioner's sugar
2 tablespoons warm water plus 1–2 drops lukewarm water

Melt the chocolate with the coffee in the top of a double boiler. Do not cook the mixture. Just allow it to become creamy.

Using a wooden spatula, work the confectioner's sugar together with the water until a whitish paste has formed.

Blend the two mixtures, working until the icing runs off the spatula in a broad ribbon.

Place the mixture over hot water until it is lukewarm, adding a drop or two of lukewarm water to give it the proper consistency for spreading.

---

hints for making icings shiny

One way to make your icings glimmer and gleam is to add a small piece (about ½ pat) or two of cold butter when the mixture has been removed from the heat.

Another trick is to . . . But let me start the story at the beginning. An outstanding *cordon bleu* friend passed away, taking all her secrets with her. But thanks to a curious accident, I had learned one of these well-guarded "secrets." I was in the kitchen one day while she was baking and she asked me to go and get a bottle of glycerin. "For my ears," she said. Since it was obvious that she had no earache, I guessed, that the glycerin was to be used as an ingredient in her cake icing. And I was right. If you try this trick, use one drop and one drop only.

CREAM FILLINGS AND CUSTARDS

Butter Cream Filling   *Crème au beurre*

Very few of us can resist a rich, well-flavored butter cream filling. These fillings can be made with a base of sugar syrup or a base of custard. There is also a quick butter cream filling that needs no cooking.

Butter Cream Filling with Sugar Syrup   *Crème au beurre au sirop*

MAKES ABOUT 2 CUPS *(enough for filling a 2-layer cake)*

⅔ cup granulated sugar
⅓ cup water
4 egg yolks
⅔ cup unsalted butter
4 tablespoons Grand Marnier or Cointreau, or 3½ ounces semi-sweet chocolate melted with 1 tablespoon instant coffee powder, or 3 tablespoons instant coffee powder

Make the Sugar Syrup* with the sugar and water, boiling it just slightly beyond the Thread Stage* to the Ball Stage.*

In a metal bowl beat the egg yolks while adding the syrup in a slow, gradual stream. Continue beating until the mixture is cool and frothy.

Cream the butter and work it into the egg-syrup mixture. Whisk it until you have a perfect blend. Stir in whatever flavoring you have decided on.

Let the butter cream stiffen somewhat before filling the cake.

Butter Cream Custard Filling, English Style
Crème au beurre à l'anglaise

A butter cream filling based on Vanilla Custard Sauce.*

MAKES ABOUT 2 CUPS *(enough to fill a 2-layer cake)*

½ cup granulated sugar
4 egg yolks
¾ cup boiling hot milk
1 cup unsalted butter, creamed
flavoring (see the preceding recipe for choices)

Make the vanilla custard sauce by beating the sugar and egg yolks together in a heavy-bottomed enameled saucepan over very low heat, until the mixture has lightened in color and runs off the spatula in a broad ribbon.

Remove from heat and slowly beat in the hot milk. Return to heat and cook, stirring constantly, until the mixture coats the spoon. (This is done over very low heat.) Let the mixture stand until it is barely lukewarm. Add whatever flavoring you have decided on and gradually beat in the creamed butter.

Let the filling cool completely before using it.

Quick Butter Cream Filling   *Crème au beurre minute*

A butter cream filling that requires no cooking and is especially adaptable for Genoese Cake* and rolled cakes.

MAKES ABOUT 4 CUPS *(enough to fill a 2-layer cake)*

3 eggs
½ cup granulated sugar
1–1¼ cups unsalted butter, creamed
flavoring: see choices in Butter Cream Filling with Sugar Syrup,* or use 2
    tablespoons finely minced candied orange peel, or 2 tablespoons
    orange marmalade

Beat the eggs and sugar in a double boiler over hot water, off heat, until the mixture swells and thickens. Remove from the hot water and continue to beat until the preparation becomes light and frothy.

Whisk in the creamed butter gradually. Stir in the desired flavoring. Let the butter cream filling become firm before using it.

Custard Cream Pastry Filling   *Crème pâtissière*

This cream filling is basically a vanilla custard slightly thickened by a small amount of flour.

Being less "runny" than Vanilla Custard Sauce,* it is ideal as a topping for various fruits. An excellent dessert consists of canned, halved pears, well drained and covered with custard cream filling, then decorated with slivered toasted almonds.

Custard cream filling can also be used as a filling for Dessert Crêpes,* which are then glazed in the oven or flamed.

It has no equal as a filling for cream puffs or Profiteroles with Chocolate Sauce.* It is often used as a filling for Genoese Cake* when you do not want a richer butter cream.

For a lighter filling, use only 3 egg yolks and no whole eggs.

MAKES ABOUT 2–2¼ CUPS

2 cups milk

1 teaspoon vanilla extract

2 whole eggs

3 egg yolks

½ cup granulated sugar

3–4 tablespoons sifted all-purpose flour

1 tablespoon unsalted butter

Heat the milk and the vanilla extract together. Put the eggs, egg yolks, and sugar in a heavy-bottomed enameled saucepan and place over low heat. Work these together with a wooden spatula, then add the flour all at once, whisk until smooth.

Off heat, beat in the hot milk and vanilla. Put the saucepan back on heat and bring the contents to a rolling boil, stirring constantly with the whisk.

Remove the saucepan from heat and beat the mixture vigorously. Strain through a sieve to give it extra gloss, blend in the butter. This prevents the formation of a surface film. Beat the custard cream to help it cool.

Custard cream pastry filling will not separate when boiled or heated to a high temperature in the oven.

Custard Cream Saint-Honoré   *Crème Saint-Honoré*

This is Custard Cream Pastry Filling* lightened with stiffly beaten egg whites and flavored with kirsch, Cointreau, or rum.

MAKES ABOUT 2 CUPS

½ cup granulated sugar plus 1 tablespoon

4 egg yolks

2–3 tablespoons all-purpose flour

1 cup very hot milk

1 tablespoon unsalted butter

2–3 tablespoons kirsch, Cointreau, or dark rum

4 egg whites, stiffly beaten with a pinch of salt

The basic procedure for this recipe is the same as in custard cream pastry filling.

Put the sugar and egg yolks in a heavy-bottomed enameled saucepan, place over low heat, and work together until the mixture becomes pale and runs off the spatula in a broad ribbon. Add the flour all at once and whisk until smooth.

Off heat, whisk in the hot milk gradually. Place back on heat, bring to a rolling boil, continuing to whisk.

Remove from heat and stir in the butter and one of the flavorings. Add a pinch of salt to the egg whites, beat until stiff, and add a tablespoon or two to the custard cream to lighten it. Then beat the hot custard into the remaining beaten egg whites, and continue beating until the custard is light and frothy.

Use a metal spatula dipped in hot water and well dried for spreading the custard cream.

In the "old days" custard cream made in this way was used as a garnish for a crown of choux puffs (*Saint-Honoré à la crème*); it formed the traditional ending for First Communion luncheons.

If you want to make a splendid dessert that does not take quite so much time, buy a ready-made *Savarin* (a large crown of baba puffs baked in a ring mold). Pour a little of the flavoring you have used in the custard cream over it, then fill the center of the crown with the custard cream. Decorate the outer edges of the crown with candied cherry halves alternating with candied angelica leaves.

Pithiviers or Frangipane Custard Cream
Crème Pithiviers ou crème frangipane

A rich custard cream flavored with powdered almonds, orange-flower water, and dark rum.

MAKES ABOUT 2 CUPS

1 egg
3 egg yolks
½ cup granulated sugar plus 1 tablespoon
1 tablespoon sifted all-purpose flour
1–1½ cups milk (depending on how thick you want the cream)
⅔ cup powdered almonds (make sure they are not rancid)
1 tablespoon unsalted butter in small pieces
1–2 tablespoons orange-flower water
1–2 tablespoons dark rum

Beat the egg, egg yolks, sugar, and flour together until they are smooth. Bring the milk to a boil and add the powdered almonds. Remove from heat and allow the almonds to steep for about 10 minutes. Strain the powdered almonds from the milk and stir them into the egg-sugar mixture. Gradually whisk in the hot milk (using only 1 cup if you want a thick cream).

Place the cream over very low heat and beat vigorously until it has thickened. Do not allow the mixture to boil. Remove from heat and allow to cool before working in the butter and adding the flavoring.

This delicious custard cream can be used to fill an Epiphany Galette* *or a large* tourte *(double crust tart) or several small ones. Place the custard cream in the middle of the* galette *or* tourte, *as it will spread out while baking.*

Vanilla Custard Sauce   *Crème à la vanille ou crème anglaise*

This is a light, semi-liquid custard sauce that contains no starch and is never allowed to boil.

MAKES ABOUT 4 CUPS

a scant 1½ cups granulated sugar
10–12 egg yolks (depending on the size of the eggs)
4 cups milk
2 vanilla beans, slit (or ½ tablespoon vanilla extract)

In a heavy-bottomed enameled saucepan gradually whisk the sugar into the egg yolks. Continue whisking until the mixture is thick and pale yellow and runs off the whisk in a broad ribbon.

Pour the milk into another heavy-bottomed enameled saucepan. Add the vanilla beans or vanilla extract. Bring the milk just to the boiling point, then gradually pour it into the egg yolk mixture, whisking all the time. Place the saucepan over low heat, and with a wide, circular motion stir the custard until it approaches a boil, that is, when the foam on the top has disappeared. At this point, the custard will coat the spoon and should be removed from heat. Strain the custard into a serving dish and beat gently until it is cool.

Vanilla custard sauce has many uses: it forms the base for Vanilla Ice Cream* and can be served as an accompaniment for numerous cakes and other desserts. It is one of the basic components of Floating Island.*

Coffee Custard Sauce   *Crème anglaise au café*

1 recipe of Vanilla Custard Sauce*
⅓ cup water
3 tablespoons freshly ground coffee beans

Make the vanilla custard sauce. Boil the ⅓ cup of water, add the coffee, and let it steep until it is very strong. When the coffee is cool, strain out the grounds and stir it into the cooled custard.

Chocolate Custard Sauce   *Crème au chocolat*

A smooth, light custard made according to the procedure for Vanilla Custard Sauce.*

FOR 6–8 PEOPLE   MAKES ABOUT 4 LARGE CUPS

8–9 egg yolks (depending on the size of the eggs)
¾–1 cup granulated sugar (depending on how sweet you like it)
½ pound semi-sweet chocolate, cut in small pieces
2–3 tablespoons water
4 cups milk (with 2–3 tablespoons removed for adding to chocolate)
1 slit vanilla bean (optional)

Beat the egg yolks and sugar in a large, heavy-bottomed enameled saucepan until the mixture is thick and light yellow and runs off the whisk in a broad ribbon.

Melt the chocolate along with the 2–3 tablespoons each of the water and milk in a small, heavy-bottomed enameled saucepan, stirring constantly with a wooden spatula. Remove from heat just before the mixture boils.

Heat the rest of the milk in a saucepan, adding the slit vanilla bean, bring to a boil, then let it stand off heat for a few minutes while the vanilla bean steeps. Discard the vanilla bean.

Beat a little of the hot milk into the melted chocolate, then pour the chocolate mixture into the saucepan of milk, scraping all the chocolate out with a rubber spatula. Heat the milk and chocolate mixture until it reaches the boiling point, then whisk it into the beaten eggs and sugar.

Place over low heat and stir with a wide circular motion until the mixture begins to thicken. Withdraw the saucepan from the heat when the boiling point is near, that is, when the foam on the custard disappears. Beat the custard vigorously and strain it into a serving dish. Continue beating until almost cool to prevent the eggs from curdling.

Place the custard in the refrigerator, stirring it once or twice while it is chilling to prevent the formation of a surface film.

The custard may be used as an accompaniment for Epiphany Galette or served with Meringue Shells.**

Zabaglione with Port Wine   *Sabayon au Porto*

A light foamy dessert with a base of egg yolks and sugar. It is flavored in this case with red port wine, but if you prefer, use Madeira, Maraschino, Marsala, Frontignan, or one of the sweet Sauternes.

FOR 6 PEOPLE

6 large egg yolks
¾–1 cup granulated sugar
1¼ cups red port wine
a squeeze of lemon juice
a dash of nutmeg
½ teaspoon arrowroot plus 1 tablespoon red port wine (optional)

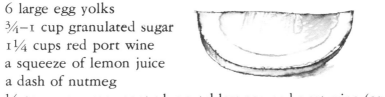

Place the egg yolks and sugar in a heavy-bottomed enameled saucepan and whisk them together until they become thick and light yellow and run off the whisk in a broad ribbon. Stir in the wine.

Place the saucepan on an asbestos mat over low heat. Beat gently and continuously until the custard is light and frothy. Stir in the lemon juice and nutmeg. Serve immediately in individual cups. If it is not served immediately after being made, the custard will separate; consequently, you must prepare this dessert at the last minute—when everyone is ready to eat it.

If you cannot serve the *zabaglione* immediately, mix the arrowroot with a tablespoon of red port wine and beat it into the egg-sugar mixture just before adding the full quantity of wine.

Accompany the zabaglione *with small cookies, Meringue Shells* or fresh macaroons.*

An idea for a quick dessert: pears or peaches coated with zabaglione: *use canned pears or peaches. Drain them thoroughly and set them on paper towels to absorb all the moisture. Place two pear or peach halves in each cup and coat each one with* zabaglione. *Decorate with a handful of currants or sultanas which have been soaked in a little cognac until plump and juicy.*

Praline Nut Brittle *Pralin*

This confection is sometimes used to fill cakes and charlottes. It makes a delicious addition to custard creams and ice creams. Praline is made from a mixture of dried nuts: almonds, walnuts, and hazelnuts, which are heated, coated with caramel, then crushed.

MAKES ABOUT ½ POUND PRALINE NUT BRITTLE

¼ cup unblanched whole almonds
¼ cup unblanched whole hazelnuts
½ cup unblanched whole walnuts
¼ pound lump sugar
about 2 tablespoons water for moistening the sugar lumps
Preheat oven to 325° F.

Spread the nuts in one layer on a baking sheet and heat them in the oven without actually toasting them. Turn them occasionally.

While the nuts are heating, make the caramel syrup: Put the sugar in a copper or copper-bottomed or stainless steel saucepan with just enough water to moisten it. Heat until the sugar turns amber color and caramelizes.

Add the heated nuts to the caramel and stir them around for a few seconds before turning them out onto a greased marble slab.

Allow the caramelized mass to harden, then break it into pieces. Crush the praline with a rolling pin or by grinding it in a coffee mill or putting it through a blender for a second or two. Do not completely pulverize the praline. It should remain rather coarse. Praline nut brittle will keep a day or two if placed in a tightly covered jar and stored in a cool, dry place.

Chocolate Praline Filling   *Crème au praliné chocolatée*

MAKES ENOUGH TO FILL A LARGE THREE-LAYER GENOESE CAKE

8 ounces semi-sweet chocolate
3–4 tablespoons strong brewed coffee
1 cup Custard Cream Pastry Filling*
1 cup unsalted butter, cut in small pieces
1 recipe of Praline Nut Brittle*
1 Genoese Cake* cut into 3 layers

Melt the chocolate in a double boiler with the coffee. Stir this mixture into the custard cream pastry filling, beat in the pieces of butter gradually. Add the praline nut brittle. Let the filling become completely cool before filling the cake.

After filling it, frost it with one of the icings in the icing section.

Floating Island with Pink Pralines   *Île flottante aux pralines roses*

A lovely, quickly-made dessert consisting of beaten egg whites and crushed pink pralines surrounded by vanilla custard sauce. If you have trouble finding pink pralines, use Praline Nut Brittle* or freshly ground toasted almonds.

For this recipe you will need an 8-cup metal charlotte mold.

FOR 6 PEOPLE

4 egg whites
a pinch of salt
1/3 cup granulated sugar
1/4 teaspoon vanilla extract
3–4 ounces pink pralines, or 3 ounces Praline Nut Brittle,* crushed, or 3 ounces freshly ground toasted almonds
10–12 sugar lumps
about 2 tablespoons water for moistening the sugar lumps

vanilla custard sauce ingredients

    6 egg yolks

    ⅓ cup granulated sugar

    2 cups milk

    ¼ teaspoon vanilla extract

    Preheat oven to 325° F.

Beat the egg whites with the pinch of salt until stiff peaks have formed. Fold in the sugar, vanilla, and the pralines or one of the substitutes.

Caramelize the charlotte mold by putting the sugar lumps in it and adding enough water just to moisten them. Place the mold over low heat, moving it back and forth, until the sugar has melted and a rich golden syrup has formed. Remove the mold from heat and, wearing padded mitts, turn and tilt the mold until every side is coated with the syrup. Set it aside to allow the caramel to cool and harden.

Fill the caramelized mold with the egg white mixture and place it over a pan of hot water. Heat the water on top of the stove until just before it begins to boil, then place the pan of water and the mold in the oven for 25–30 minutes.

While this is baking, prepare the Vanilla Custard Sauce* (see that recipe), using the egg yolks, sugar, milk, and vanilla given here. Beat the cream two or three times while it is cooling.

Remove the charlotte mold from the oven and allow to cool before unmolding into a deep serving dish. Coat the "floating island" with a few spoonfuls of vanilla custard sauce, then pour the rest around it so that the island seems to be floating.

Snowy Peaks with Caramel Marbling
Oeufs à la neige marbrés au caramel

To produce the finest texture and firmest shape, cook the beaten egg whites in well-sweetened water flavored with vanilla. The caramel marbling gives this dessert an unusually attractive and original appearance.

FOR 6 PEOPLE

    4 egg whites

    a pinch of salt

    ⅓ cup granulated sugar

    ½ teaspoon vanilla extract

    water for poaching the beaten egg whites

    2 tablespoons granulated sugar and 1 teaspoon vanilla extract for adding to the poaching water

    1 recipe of Vanilla Custard Cream,* strained and cooled

    10–12 sugar lumps

about 2 tablespoons water for moistening the sugar lumps

a few drops of lemon juice if necessary

Beat the egg whites with the pinch of salt until they stand in stiff peaks, add the sugar a tablespoon at a time, and stir in the vanilla.

cooking the egg whites

Boil enough water for poaching the egg whites in a wide saucepan and add the mixed sugar and vanilla. Lower heat until the water is just barely simmering. Using a tablespoon, scoop out ovals of the beaten egg white and slip them into the water. When they have cooked for 1 minute, turn them with a fork. After another minute remove the egg white ovals and set them on paper towels to drain.

assembling the dish

Place the cooled, strained vanilla custard sauce in a serving dish and arrange the egg whites on top.

making the caramel

In a copper or copper-bottomed saucepan (stainless steel will do in a pinch) heat the sugar lumps with just enough water to moisten them. When a syrupy golden caramel forms, remove the saucepan from heat and spread the caramel over the egg whites and custard sauce in a marble pattern. Keep in the refrigerator until you are ready to serve it.

NOTE: *If the caramel shows signs of hardening too fast to spread, squeeze in a few drops of lemon juice while the syrup is still bubbling.*

Molded Caramel Lemon Custard   *Crème caramel renversée au citron*

Haven't you often noticed that when caramel custards are served there is usually never enough caramel sauce to coat the custards?

A simple solution is to make extra caramel sauce, and that is what we have done in this recipe.

By adding a garnish of orange, tangerine, or pineapple pieces cut in small triangles and glazed in caramel syrup, you will create a classic dessert, refined yet simple.

You will need a 7- or 8-cup metal charlotte mold for baking the custard.

FOR 6 PEOPLE

10–12 sugar lumps

about 2 tablespoons water for moistening the sugar lumps

ingredients for the lemon custard

> 2 cups milk
> 1 teaspoon vanilla extract
> 3 egg yolks
> ½ cup granulated sugar
> 3 whole eggs
> grated rind of 1 or 2 lemons (according to taste)

caramel sauce ingredients

> ½ pound granulated sugar
> ½ cup cold water
> ½ cup hot water for diluting the caramel
> *Preheat oven to 325° F.*

Place the lumps of sugar in the charlotte mold and add just enough water to moisten them. Heat the mold, moving it back and forth across the heat, until a golden-brown caramel syrup forms. Remove the mold from heat and, wearing padded mitts, turn and tilt the mold so that the syrup coats the sides evenly. Set it aside.

making the custard

In a heavy-bottomed enameled saucepan, bring the milk to a boil, add the vanilla, and remove the pan from heat.

In another saucepan work the egg yolks and sugar together with a wooden spatula until they are thick and pale yellow and flow off the whisk in a broad ribbon. Add the whole eggs one by one, whisking vigorously after each addition.

Beat the hot milk slowly into the egg and sugar mixture. Stir in the lemon rind. Allow the mixture to rest for a minute before pouring it into the caramelized mold. Once it is in the mold, stir it gently for a second or so.

Set the mold in a pan of hot water and place in the oven for 35–40 minutes. The secret of a good custard is to keep the oven at a steady, fairly low temperature throughout the baking. If the oven temperature is raised, the eggs will curdle and the custard will become watery. Test the custard for doneness by inserting a larding needle or toothpick into the center. If it comes out clean, the custard is done. The top should be golden and the edges a little darker and slightly pulled away from the edges of the mold.

Remove the mold from the oven. Set it aside to cool completely at room temperature. Then chill in the refrigerator.

While the custard is cooling, prepare the caramel sauce.

preparing the caramel sauce

Heat the sugar and cold water in a copper or copper-bottomed or stainless steel saucepan until a thick amber syrup forms.

Remove the saucepan from heat and, holding it at arm's length, very slowly and carefully add the hot water, gently rotating the saucepan. Place over low heat and bring to a simmer, stirring and scraping the bottom of the pan.

Using a wooden spatula, transfer the caramel sauce to a sauce bowl and let it cool at room temperature.

serving the custard

Unmold the custard into a deep serving dish. Let the caramel sauce flow out of the mold over the custard and add 2–3 tablespoons of the extra caramel sauce as well. Accompany the custard with the bowl of caramel sauce.

Special garnishes for this dessert: In winter, decorate the custard with prunes that have been poached in Sugar Syrup* flavored with a little lemon rind, or garnish with orange sections or pineapple slices cut into triangles. Another idea is to use glazed fruit sections as a garnish. In summer, use fresh quartered peaches as a garnish. Another good idea is to garnish the custard with strawberries poached in sugar syrup, or with raspberry compote.

Small Pots de Crème in Three Flavors
Petits pots de crème aux trois parfums

Pots de crème are delicious and have a charming simplicity; they are popular with everyone whether they are for a farmily meal or for a buffet. The best containers for cooking and serving them are small flameproof porcelain pots equipped with lids. These specially designed little pots are just the right depth to prevent the *crèmes* (or custard, if you like) from drying out while baking. The lids are set on after baking. If you do not own any of these pots, use small flameproof ramekins or, in a pinch, small Pyrex dishes.

FOR 6 PEOPLE

12 *pots de crème* in one of the three flavors (recipes are given below)

FOR A BUFFET

8–12 chocolate *pots de crème** (given below)
8–12 vanilla *pots de crème** (given below)
8–12 coffee *pots de crème** (given below)

Chocolate Pots de Crème *Petits pots de crème.au chocolat*

FOR 6 POTS *(for 12 pots double the recipe)*

> 2 cups milk (each pot will have about 5 tablespoons of milk in it and should be about ¾ full)
>
> ½ teaspoon vanilla extract
>
> 4 egg yolks or 3 egg yolks and 1 whole egg
>
> 3 tablespoons granulated sugar
>
> 6 ounces semi-sweet chocolate
>
> 4 tablespoons water or 1 teaspoon instant coffee powder dissolved in 4 tablespoons boiling hot water
>
> butter for pots
>
> *Preheat oven to 325° F.*

Bring the milk to a boil and stir in the vanilla. Remove from heat.

Beat the egg yolks, or the egg yolks and whole egg, with the sugar until thick and light yellow.

Melt the chocolate with the water or instant coffee and water. Dilute the chocolate with the hot milk by pouring the milk in gradually and whisking until thoroughly blended. Strain the mixture to remove any lumps and to give it a smooth gloss. Blend into egg-sugar mixture and strain once more to ensure perfect smoothness.

Butter the pots and fill them about three quarters full, as the custard swells somewhat while baking.

baking the custard

Put some hot water from the tap into a shallow oven dish and place the pots of custard in it. The water should reach about halfway up the cups. Heat the dish on top of the stove until the water begins to simmer, then place in oven for 15–18 minutes, at which time the top of the custards should be lightly puffed. To test for doneness: press your forefinger against the top of a custard. If the custard gives a little, it is done. Custard tends to separate if it is cooked too long.

Remove the pots from the oven, place them on a rack to cool completely before putting them in the refrigerator.

Vanilla Pots de Crème *Petits pots de crème à la vanille*

These are prepared according to the basic instructions for chocolate *pots de crème* (the preceding recipe) with slight variations. It is a good idea to use vanilla extract and a vanilla bean.

FOR 6 POTS

5 tablespoons milk per pot
1 vanilla bean slit plus 1 teaspoon vanilla extract
1 heaping tablespoon granulated sugar for boiling in the milk
1 egg yolk per pot plus 1 whole egg for the entire mixture
1 heaping teaspoon granulated sugar per pot
a little butter for greasing the pots
Preheat oven to 325° F.

Put the milk, vanilla bean, and vanilla extract in a saucepan and stir in the sugar. Bring to a boil. Remove from heat and allow to steep for about 15 minutes.

Whisk the egg yolks and whole egg with the heaping teaspoons of sugar until the mixture becomes thick and pale yellow and flows off the whisk in a broad ribbon. Slowly pour the hot milk mixture into the egg and sugar mixture, whisking vigorously as you pour. Continue whisking for a minute or two, strain the custard into pots, and bake as in chocolate *pots de crème.* Test for doneness after 15 minutes.

Coffee Pots de Crème *Petits pots de crème au café*

These are made the same way as the preceding recipe—without vanilla, of course.

coffee flavoring
3 heaping tablespoons instant coffee powder
1/3–1/2 cup boiling water
1 tablespoon granulated sugar

Dilute the instant coffee in the boiling water, stir in the sugar and add it to the boiling milk of the preceding recipe. Allow to steep for about 5 minutes. Continue with the recipe.

WHIPPED CREAM

TRANSLATOR'S NOTE: *On Crème Fraîche: Anyone who has lived in France knows the characteristic flavor of* crème fraîche, *especially noticeable when it is served with strawberries or other fresh fruit or is used as a topping for desserts. The taste is hard to describe. It is not exactly sour, but on the other hand it is not really sweet (though cream that tastes just like American heavy cream can be found in Brittany, Normandy, and other dairy-farming regions). Crème fraîche* is *cream that has been allowed to mature. In maturing, the natural ferments produce the distinctive flavor of the cream. It has nothing in common with American sour cream.*

In some parts of the United States it is now possible to buy genuine crème fraîche
*(though be warned: it is very expensive). If you prefer, and if you can buy it, we suggest that
you try* crème fraîche *in this dessert section. If you cannot find any, your desserts (or any
other dishes, for that matter) will not suffer in the least if you use American heavy cream,
though avoid the "ultra-pasteurized" products. We have not specified* crème fraîche *in any
of the recipes.*

What is better than heavy cream that is whipped until it forms soft peaks and then
sweetened? For the best results whip the cream over a basin containing ice cubes and
water. Once beaten, the cream will have doubled in volume.

Recipe I

1¼ cups cold heavy cream
½ of an ice cube, finely crushed
⅓ cup granulated sugar
¼ teaspoon vanilla extract
(a half-dozen or so ice cubes and 2–3 cups of water for placing in the basin
      over which cream is whipped)

Put the cream with the crushed ice cube in a large metal bowl and place it
over a basin containing the ice cubes and water. Beat the cream steadily and
continuously with an egg beater or whisk until it becomes foamy and firm: the
beater or whisk should leave tracks in the cream when you run it through. Do
not overbeat the cream, as butter curds will form and ruin the preparation.
Blend the sugar and vanilla into the cream with a wooden spatula. Place the
cream in the refrigerator to chill.

Recipe II

This second recipe will ensure the freshness and firmness of whipped cream if you
must make it ahead of serving time. Glucose and beaten egg whites are often used in
restaurants and pastry shops to provide a constant supply of firm whipped cream.

½ cup water
⅓ cup granulated sugar
2 tablespoons glucose
vanilla extract to taste (about ¼ teaspoon)
3 egg whites
a pinch of salt
1¼ cups heavy cream

Cook the water, sugar, glucose, and vanilla until the mixture reaches the Ball
Stage* (see Candy Syrup*).

Beat the egg whites with the pinch of salt until they form stiff peaks. Pour the boiling hot sugar syrup into the egg whites and beat vigorously. Allow to cool completely.

Whip the cream and incorporate the syrup and egg white mixture into it.

ICE CREAMS

Vanilla Ice Cream   *Glace à la vanille*

REMEMBER: In all ice creams the cream must be kept in the refrigerator until it is ready to be used. The metal mixing bowl must also be thoroughly chilled.

MAKES ABOUT 1½ QUARTS (*enough for 8 people*)

4 cups milk
2 vanilla beans, slit, or ½ tablespoon vanilla extract
10–12 egg yolks (depending on the size of the eggs)
1–1⅓ cups granulated sugar
2 cups cold heavy cream

Make the Vanilla Custard Sauce* with the milk, vanilla beans or extract, egg yolks, and sugar. When it has cooled completely, strain it into the chilled metal bowl. Beat in 1 cup of cold heavy cream. Place the bowl in the freezer for 1 hour. Remove, set the bowl over ice, work in the rest of the cream, and beat thoroughly for at least 5 minutes, using an electric beater if possible. Place the bowl in the freezer for 1–2 hours, remove, place over a bowl of ice, and beat for another 5–6 minutes, using an electric beater. Place the bowl in the freezer until you are ready to serve.

Vanilla ice cream is delicious garnished with strawberries or raspberries. It can also be served with Raspberry Sauce* or Chocolate Sauce.*

Vanilla ice cream is the basic component of the recipe that follows—Peach Melba.

Peach Melba   *Pêche Melba*

An especially luscious dessert consisting of vanilla ice cream crowned with lightly poached fresh peaches covered with fresh raspberry sauce garnished with slivered almonds. Canned peach halves and frozen raspberries may be used, but the dessert will not be nearly as fine.

Peach Melba is usually served in ice-cold champagne glasses or cups. Chill them in the refrigerator until you are ready to use them.

FOR 6 PEOPLE

---

1 recipe Vanilla Ice Cream* (recipe preceding)
6 ripe, unblemished peaches (choose big ones, all the same size)
½ lemon
1 cup granulated sugar
1¼ cups water
½ teaspoon vanilla extract
additional granulated sugar
a few drops lemon juice
slivered almonds, for garnishing
1 recipe of Raspberry Sauce* (recipe follows)
a few fresh raspberries for garnish (optional)

Make the vanilla ice cream in advance and keep it in the freezer.

Peel the peaches and rub them with the cut side of the lemon.

Prepare a sugar syrup by mixing the sugar, water, and vanilla together and bringing to a boil. Lower heat, put the peaches in the syrup, and poach them gently for 5–6 minutes, just long enough to make them tender. Remove them with a skimmer and set them on a rack for at least one hour to drain and become firm. Then pit the peaches and shake a little sugar over each one.

assembling the peach Melba

Place 2 rounded tablespoons of vanilla ice cream in each chilled champagne glass. Put a peach on top, cover with raspberry sauce and top with a few slivered almonds. If you wish, garnish with fresh raspberries.

Serve with rolled wafers or other simple, vanilla-flavored cookies.

Raspberry Sauce   *Sauce aux framboises*

FOR 6 PEOPLE

1 pound fresh raspberries (the same amount of frozen raspberries may be substituted)
3 tablespoons granulated sugar
a few drops of lemon juice
1 jigger warmed framboise (raspberry brandy), for flaming (optional)

Press the fresh or thawed raspberries through a sieve into a heavy-bottomed enameled saucepan. If you prefer a thicker sauce or wish to flame it, leave the raspberries whole.

Boil the berries and sugar together, stirring, for 5–6 minutes, then add a few drops of lemon juice. Taste for sweetness.

If you wish, flame the sauce with the warmed framboise.

Raspberry sauce can also be used as a garnish for vanilla ice cream or as an accompaniment for Galette des rois* *or* Galette Naomi.*

Another idea for a simple but lovely dessert: Flame the raspberry sauce with framboise and pour it over poached fresh peaches or drained canned peach halves.

Pears with Vanilla Ice Cream and Chocolate Sauce   *Poire Hélène*

Peach Melba inspired this original dessert, which uses lightly poached fresh pears, vanilla ice cream, and a luscious chocolate sauce.

FOR 6 PEOPLE

1 recipe of Vanilla Ice Cream,* made ahead and stored in the freezer
6 ripe pears, peeled, halved, cored, and poached in Sugar Syrup* (see
      Peach Melba* above)
½ lemon for rubbing on the raw pear halves
1 recipe of Chocolate Sauce* (given below)
a handful of toasted, slivered almonds for decorating

See Peach Melba* for preparation and assembling. Remember to chill your champagne glasses before using.

Chocolate Sauce   *Sauce au chocolat*

This rich, smooth, semi-liquid sauce is usually served hot, and it can be used as an accompaniment for many other desserts including Vanilla Ice Cream,* Coffee Ice Cream,* Profiteroles with Chocolate Sauce,* and cakes made with Chestnuts.*

MAKES ABOUT 2 CUPS

8 ounces semi-sweet chocolate
1 tablespoon instant coffee powder
2 cups boiling water
½ teaspoon vanilla extract
4–5 tablespoons unsalted butter

Melt the chocolate in a double boiler along with the coffee dissolved in 2 tablespoons of the boiling water. Stir until the chocolate is perfectly smooth and fluid.

Add the remaining water and the vanilla. Bring to a boil and continue boiling gently for a minute or so, stirring constantly. Remove from heat and whisk in the butter little by little.

The resulting sauce will have a high luster and will be just the right thickness for pouring over a dessert. It can also be served cold. If you make the sauce in advance and want to reheat it, use a double boiler, stirring the whole time it is heating.

Profiteroles with Chocolate Sauce   *Profiteroles au chocolat*

Profiteroles are cream puffs made of sweetened choux pastry, filled with Vanilla Ice Cream* or with chilled Custard Cream Pastry Filling,* then piled up to form an elegant pyramid and served with hot Chocolate Sauce* (the preceding recipe).

This is a truly festive dessert that may tactfully be served to replace the traditional birthday cake for a senior "birthday child" who isn't up to blowing out all those candles! I was recently treated to a *profiterole* pyramid on my birthday and enjoyed it immensely.

Profiteroles filled with vanilla ice cream are delicious but must be served at once and cannot be glazed with candy syrup, as this would melt the ice cream.

Sweetened Choux Pastry   *Pâte à choux sucrée*

MAKES 45–50 SMALL PUFFS OR ABOUT 24 LARGE ONES

1 cup water
½ cup butter
a pinch of salt
1 tablespoon granulated sugar
1 cup all-purpose flour
4 whole eggs plus ½ unbeaten egg white

Refer to Choux Pastry* for preparing and baking the puffs.

Profiteroles can be filled with custard cream pastry filling. To fill, make a small incision in the bottom of each puff. After filling, glaze with Candy Syrup* cooked to the Hard-Crack Stage.* Dip the top of each *profiterole* in the syrup for a second. Set the puffs upright on a rack to allow the glaze to dry.

serving the profiteroles

Pile the *profiteroles* in the shape of a pyramid on a large round serving platter. Accompany the dish with a bowl of hot chocolate sauce. The recipe (2 cups) will be just right for 6–8 people.

If the *profiteroles* are filled with ice cream, do not glaze them. Build them into a pyramid, sprinkle them with confectioner's sugar and a few crushed pink pralines or ground pistachios.

Coffee Ice Cream   *Glace au café*

This delicious ice cream is based on Coffee Custard Sauce* to which cream has been added.

FOR 6–8 PEOPLE

---

12 egg yolks

1½ cups granulated sugar

4 cups hot milk

3 tablespoons instant coffee powder dissolved in ⅓ cup boiling water

3 cups heavy cream, kept in the refrigerator until time to use

4 ounces candied coffee beans (optional)

Prepare the sauce with the egg yolks and sugar, adding the hot milk and cooking the mixture over low heat without letting it boil. Strain the custard into a metal bowl and cool, stirring occasionally.

Make the instant coffee and let it cool. Stir it into the cooled custard and fold in one-third of the cream.

Place the bowl in the freezer for 1 hour. Whip the rest of the cream until it forms soft peaks. Remove the bowl from freezer and fold in the whipped cream. Beat the mixture over ice for a good 5 minutes. Return to the freezer for 1–2 hours. Remove and beat vigorously over a bowl of ice for at least 5 minutes. Return to the freezer and repeat the beating process after 1 hour. Keep the ice cream in the freezer until ready to serve.

Serve a large scoop of ice cream in individual dishes, or mound it in a crystal bowl. If you like, garnish the top with a few candied coffee beans.

Coffee Parfait *Parfait au café*

This recipe makes absolutely marvelous parfait. It is richly flavored with coffee and has just the right amount of creaminess. Use freshly ground coffee, if possible, for best results.

FOR 6 PEOPLE

3 heaping tablespoons freshly ground coffee

¾ cup boiling water

1–2 drops coffee extract (optional)

1 cup heavy cream

2 ice cubes

1 scant cup granulated sugar

5 large egg yolks

3 ounces candied coffee beans or 18–20 candied violets for decoration (optional)

Steep the ground coffee in the boiling water until it is very strong. Taste it. If it does not taste strong enough add a drop or two of coffee extract. What I am trying to get at is that the coffee should taste TOO strong at this moment.

Start whipping the cream in a metal bowl containing the 2 ice cubes. Remove the cubes before they melt. Continue whipping, and when the cream forms soft peaks, stir in 2 tablespoons of the sugar, allow the mixture to become firm in the refrigerator.

Whisk the egg yolks and the rest of the sugar in a heavy-bottomed enameled saucepan until they turn pale yellow and flow off the whisk in a broad ribbon.

After straining out the coffee grounds, add the hot coffee to the sugar and egg mixture and place over low heat until the custard thickens. Stir continuously during this operation.

Remove the saucepan of custard from heat, place it over a basin of cold water, and continue stirring until the custard is completely cool.

Beat the custard into the chilled whipped cream and return to the refrigerator until it is good and firm. Then beat it vigorously with a whisk and return to the refrigerator. Repeat this procedure three times, beating at least 5 minutes each time.

serving the parfait

Place two scoops of parfait into chilled champagne glasses or form it into a mound in a crystal serving dish. Garnish with candied coffee beans or candied violets if you wish.

Praline Ice Cream   *Glace pralinée*

A light ice cream with a nutty chocolate flavor. In this recipe you must whip the ice cream in a chilled metal bowl over a dish of ice cubes.

FOR 8 PEOPLE

1 recipe of Chocolate Praline Filling* with butter left out, made ahead
2 cups heavy cream
1 ice cube
1¼ cups granulated sugar

Prepare the chocolate praline filling.

Start whipping the cream in a metal bowl containing the ice cube. Remove the ice cube before it melts. Adding the sugar gradually, beat the cream until it forms soft peaks.

Stir 1–2 tablespoons of whipped cream into the chocolate praline filling to make it more malleable, then blend the filling into the bowl of whipped cream.

Put the concoction into freezer trays and allow to chill for a good 2 hours. Remove the trays, place the ice cream in a chilled metal bowl set over a dish of ice cubes, and beat it thoroughly for 5–6 minutes. Replace in the trays for another hour (more if necessary).

Serve the ice cream in individual dishes or mounded in a crystal bowl.

Meringues

If the following three rules are adhered to, meringues have every reason to come out successfully:
1. The standard proportion is always ¼ cup granulated sugar to each egg white
2. A metal bowl, preferably copper, should be used for beating the egg whites
3. Meringues should be baked in a very slow oven. They should, in effect, dry (without browning) rather than cook

Meringue Shells *Coques de meringues*

MAKES 12 LARGE SHELLS OR 24 MEDIUM-SIZE SHELLS

4 fresh egg whites
a pinch of salt
1 cup granulated sugar
butter for greasing and flour for dusting the baking sheet
a little confectioner's sugar for sprinkling on the meringues
Preheat oven to 240° F.

Beat the egg whites with the salt in a metal bowl until they are firm and form stiff peaks. Beat a heaping tablespoon of sugar into the whites to help maintain their firmness.

Place the bowl in a shallow pan of hot water (off heat) and beat the egg whites steadily, using a balloon whip or strong whisk while you sprinkle in the rest of the sugar. The consistency of the egg whites will change with the addition of the sugar. When they run off the whip or whisk in a broad ribbon, remove the bowl from hot water and continue to whip or whisk until the meringue paste has cooled.

forming the meringue paste

Butter a baking sheet and lightly dust it with flour.

Fill a pastry bag fitted with a plain tip about three quarters full with meringue paste—this is rather a chore unless you have someone to help you hold the bag open. Shape the meringues into oblongs on the baking sheet, then lift the tip of the bag abruptly to stop the flow of paste and to form a peak on each meringue. When the meringues are formed, sprinkle them with a little confectioner's sugar and allow them to stand for about 10 minutes.

cooking the meringues

Place them in the oven for 1 hour or a little more. When done they should be an off-white color and have little irregular beads of sugar scattered on their surface. Remove them from the baking sheet with a metal spatula.

If you are planning to fill the meringues, now is the time to make a small cavity by pressing your thumb into the bottom of the shell.

Place the meringues on a rack until they are cool. They can be stored in a tightly covered tin or jar in the refrigerator for 1–2 days, but they will never be as tender as when freshly baked.

Meringue shells can be served on top of Chocolate Custard Sauce,* Vanilla Custard Sauce,* or Coffee Custard Sauce* to replace oeufs à la neige. *Marble the meringues with Caramel Sauce* (see under Molded Caramel Lemon Custard*).*

Meringues with Whipped Cream *Meringues à la crème Chantilly*

FOR 6 PEOPLE

12 Meringue Shells*
2 cups Whipped Cream* (Recipe I)

Make a cavity in each meringue while it is still warm. Fill each cavity with whipped cream and lightly fit two meringue shells together. Fill the space between them with a fluting of whipped cream, using a pastry bag with a star-shaped tip. Repeat the procedure for all the other meringues.

Meringues with Ice Cream *Meringues glacée*

FOR 6 PEOPLE

12 Meringue Shells*
12 scoops Vanilla Ice Cream* or Coffee Ice Cream*
½ recipe of Whipped Cream (Recipe I)

Make a cavity in each meringue while it is still warm. Fill each cavity with a scoop of ice cream and lightly fit two meringue shells together. Fill the space between them with a fluting of whipped cream, using a pastry bag with a star-shaped tip. Repeat the procedure for all the other meringues.

Meringues with Strawberry Ice Cream *meringues glacées aux fraises*

The fresh strawberry ice cream in this recipe is extremely good and makes a lovely springtime treat for your family or guests.

FOR 6 PEOPLE

---

12 Meringue Shells*

5 pounds fresh strawberries (rinse and set aside 12 of the handsomest with their stems)

1 ¼ cups granulated sugar

1 tablespoon lemon juice

2 cups heavy cream

1 unbeaten egg white

½ recipe of White Fondant*

a little confectioner's sugar

Prepare the meringues ahead of time, making a cavity in each one while it is still warm. Set aside on a rack.

making the ice cream

Hull the strawberries (except for the 12 you have set aside. Rinse them quickly, drain thoroughly, and put through a food mill (using the finest disk) into a metal bowl. You should have about 1 quart of strawberry purée. Stir in the sugar and lemon juice.

With a strong whisk beat the cream into the purée a small amount at a time. When all the cream has been added, keep beating steadily until the mixture is light and fluffy. Add the unbeaten egg white and whisk vigorously for at least 5 minutes. The addition of the egg white will prevent ice crystals from forming in the ice cream. This trick of using an unbeaten egg white is used in all fruit ice creams and sherbets.

Put the bowl of purée into the freezer and chill for 1 hour. Remove and beat vigorously over ice for at least 5 minutes. Repeat this process two more times, allowing an interval of 1 hour of freezing between beatings. Keep the ice cream in the freezer until ready to use.

making the strawberry garnish

Prepare the white fondant. While it is still warm,[1] dip the strawberries in it one at a time, holding each by its stem. Allow them to dry on a marble slab that has been lightly dusted with confectioner's sugar.

serving the dessert

Fill each meringue with a large scoop of ice cream, and press two meringues together. Line a round serving dish with a paper doily and build the meringues on it, working quickly in the form of a pyramid (as in Profiteroles with Chocolate Sauce*).

Decorate the pyramid with the fondant-iced strawberries by placing them in the spaces between the meringues.

---

[1] If you have made your fondant in advance, warm it in a double boiler until it is of the proper consistency.

Frozen Chocolate Mousse and Meringue Dessert
Mousse au chocolat meringuée glacée

A delicious, fabulously light frozen dessert that contains no eggs. It can be prepared ahead of time and kept in the refrigerator until you are ready to unmold it. It is served with vanilla custard sauce or coffee custard sauce.

To make this dish, you will need an 8-cup metal charlotte mold.

FOR 6 PEOPLE (*large portions*)   FOR 8 PEOPLE (*smaller portions*)

8 ounces semi-sweet chocolate
I cup very strong coffee
½ cup granulated sugar
3 cups heavy cream
⅓ cup Cointreau or Grand Marnier
6 Meringue Shells* or 4 large macaroons broken in two
3 ounces candied coffee beans (optional)
I recipe of chilled Vanilla Custard Sauce* or chilled Coffee Custard Sauce*

Slowly melt the chocolate with the coffee in a double boiler (or in a saucepan placed on an asbestos mat). Do not allow the chocolate to boil.

Remove from heat and beat in the sugar. Beat the chocolate as it cools and do not stop beating until it is cool.

Whip the cream until it forms soft peaks, reserving 3 tablespoons for final decoration. Fold the cream into the cooled chocolate, add the Cointreau or Grand Marnier, and work the mixture together thoroughly for at least 6 minutes.

Moisten the inside of the charlotte mold, shaking out any drops of water. Place a piece of parchment paper cut to fit on the bottom of the mold.

Fill the mold with alternate layers of chocolate mousse and meringues or macaroons, sprinkling each layer with a few candied coffee beans, if you wish.

End the layering with the meringues or macaroons to give the mousse a firm base after it is unmolded.

Put the mold in the freezer for a minimum of 2 hours.

In the meantime, prepare the vanilla or coffee custard sauce. Beat it gently until it is cool and store in the refrigerator until ready to serve.

unmolding the frozen mousse

Wrap a towel that has been dipped in lukewarm water and wrung out around the base of the mold and gently ease the chilled mousse into a serving dish. Using a pastry bag, decorate it with roses formed from the reserved whipped cream.

Accompany the dessert with the cold custard.

CHESTNUT DESSERTS

Chestnut desserts are traditionally served in France for Christmas or New Year's dinners.

Preparing fresh chestnuts is a demanding task, especially when a large number of guests is expected. That is why I recommend canned chestnut purée, which saves time and spares the cook's temper. There are two kinds of canned chestnut purées: one is sweet and is made of puréed glazed (or candied) chestnuts (*crème de marrons glacés*) and the other is made of unsweetened chestnuts. In the first of the following desserts only *crème de marrons glacés* is used, and in the second both unsweetened and sweetened purées are used.

NOTE: *Both unsweetened chestnut purée and* crème de marrons glacés *can be found in specialty shops. You will also find broken or whole glazed (or candied) chestnuts* (marrons glacés), *which are sold in bulk or handsomely boxed and in France are regarded as one of the most perfect Christmas gifts.*

Chestnut Parfait *Parfait aux marrons*

For making this recipe, you will need an 8-cup metal charlotte mold.

FOR 6–8 PEOPLE

- 2 pounds canned sweet chestnut purée (*crème de marrons glacés*)
- 1 jigger Maraschino liqueur or dark rum
- 2½ cups heavy cream
- ⅔ cup granulated sugar
- ½ teaspoon vanilla extract
- 4–5 ounces crumbled glazed chestnuts (*marrons glacés*)
- peanut oil for greasing the charlotte mold
- 5–7 chestnuts preserved in Maraschino, or 5–7 whole glazed chestnuts (*marrons glacés*), or a few candied violets, or a few candied cherries as a last resort

Put the cans of chestnut purée in a bowl and blend in the Maraschino or rum. Make Whipped Cream* (Recipe I), using the sugar and vanilla. Refrigerate ⅓–½ of the whipped cream, which will be used in decorating the parfait. (If you are making the parfait the day before, whip only the cream to be used in making the parfait. Store the rest of the cream in the refrigerator for last-minute whipping.)

Fold ½–⅔ of the whipped cream into the purée and refrigerate until it becomes fairly firm. Remove the bowl and carefully stir in the crumbled glazed chestnuts.

Lightly oil the charlotte mold, fill with the chestnut and cream mixture, and place in the refrigerator for several hours until it is firm enough to unmold easily.

Unmold the parfait on a round serving plate that has been covered with a paper doily. Put the reserved whipped cream in a pastry tube fitted with a star tip and make fluted designs around the edges of the parfait. Top the parfait with a whipped-cream swirl, and around this arrange the whole glazed chestnuts or whatever decoration you have chosen.

Chestnut Surprise   *Surprise aux marrons*

Another lovely chestnut dessert made with unsweetened chestnut purée and puréed glazed (or candied) chestnuts (*crème de marrons glacés*). It is flavored with kirsch and topped with chocolate icing.

For making this recipe you will need an 8-cup metal charlotte mold.

FOR 6–8 PEOPLE

2 pounds canned unsweetened chestnut purée

3 teaspoons hot milk

¾ cup unsalted butter

½–⅔ cups granulated sugar (depending on how sweet you like it)

1 jigger kirsch

1 half-pound can glazed (or candied) chestnut puree (*crème de marrons glacés*)

peanut oil for greasing mold

1 recipe of Chocolate Icing* (choosen from the icing section)

7–9 cherries preserved in kirsch (or other liqueur) and coated with chocolate

Put the unsweetened chestnut purée through a food mill, using the finest disk, into an enameled saucepan. Stir in the 3 teaspoons of hot milk, place the saucepan over hot water, and stir until the purée is smooth and almost fluid.

Cream the butter and work in the sugar. Then work this mixture into the warm chestnut purée until thoroughly blended. Put through a food mill, using the finest disk.

Stir in the kirsch. Add the chestnut purée a tablespoon at a time, working thoroughly with a wooden spatula after each addition.

When the mixture is perfectly smooth, pour it into the lightly oiled charlotte mold and refrigerate for several hours until firm enough to unmold.

serving the chestnut surprise

Unmold as in the preceding recipe. Frost the dessert with chocolate icing and decorate with the preserved cherries.

If you wish, serve the dessert with Vanilla Custard Sauce,* substituting kirsch for the vanilla.

DESSERTS   428

SHERBETS

Tangerine Sherbet   *Sorbet à la mandarine*

This is a wonderfully fine, light, and refreshing dessert. It is worth the trouble to prepare glazed tangerine sections (see Glazed Fruit Sections*). These will embellish and add character to the delicate sherbet. If you possibly can, use cane sugar when you make the glazed fruit sections.

Set 8 champagne glasses in the refrigerator to chill before starting the dessert. The metal bowl should also be chilled.

FOR 8 PEOPLE

> 4–5 pounds tangerines
> 1½ cups granulated sugar (a little more if you like the sherbet on the sweet side)
> juice of 1–1½ lemons
> 1 egg white, unbeaten
> 1 recipe of Glazed Fruit Sections,* using tangerines

Juice the tangerines to obtain about 1 quart (or a little more) of juice, strain through a fine sieve, place in the chilled metal bowl, and add the sugar and lemon juice gradually, tasting for sweetness. Work in the egg white. Then whisk the ingredients for 3–4 minutes until frothy.

Place the bowl in the freezer. After an hour, when the sherbet begins to set, remove the bowl and whisk it again for 3–4 minutes. Freeze for another hour, remove the bowl, and beat, this time with an electric beater, for 2–3 minutes. Return the bowl to the freezer until ready to serve. The sherbet should freeze for a total of 3 to 4 hours.

Serve it in the chilled champagne glasses or mounded in a crystal serving dish. Decorate with the glazed tangerine sections.

Pear and Glazed Chestnut Sherbet
Sorbet aux poires et aux marrons glacés

A fabulous dessert for a festive meal. Use unblemished, just-ripe pears. If the pears are somewhat coarse-grained or bitter, poach them for 2 minutes (as Pears with Vanilla Ice Cream and Chocolate Sauce*) before puréeing.

Set 8–10 champagne cups in refrigerator to chill, before you start making the dessert. Chill the metal bowl as well.

FOR 8–10 PEOPLE

8–10 just-ripe pears
½ lemon
1 egg white, unbeaten
1 jigger pear liqueur
½ pound broken pieces of glazed chestnuts (*marrons glacés*)
½ cup Whipped Cream* for decorating the sherbet
8–10 candied violets for decoration

Peel, core, and quarter the pears. As soon as you finish quartering each one, rub them with the cut side of the lemon to prevent them from turning brown. (See the note in the introduction to this recipe about poaching the pears.) Cut the quarters into small pieces and put them through a food mill, using the finest disk, into the chilled metal bowl. Work in the unbeaten egg white. Whisk the mixture vigorously for 4–5 minutes. Place the bowl of puréed pears in the freezer for 35–40 minutes. Remove, add the pear liqueur,[1] beat vigorously, and return to freezer for 1 hour. Remove the bowl and stir in the pieces of *marrons glacés*. Return to the freezer until ready to use.

serving the sherbet

Place 1 or 2 scoops of sherbet in each chilled champagne glass. Decorate with a swirl of whipped cream squeezed from a pastry bag, top each scoop with a candied violet. Serve the sherbet with "Cigarette" Cookies.*

COOKIES

The following recipes are among the best for cookies that accompany ice creams, sherbets, and custards.

Almond Tiles   *Tuiles aux amandes*

The tiles are thin and somewhat transparent. They are baked for only two or three minutes.

MAKES ABOUT 24 TILES

2 egg whites
a pinch of salt
½ cup granulated sugar
½ teaspoon vanilla extract
½ cup sifted all-purpose flour

---

[1] It is important to add the pear liqueur at this time. If you add it after stirring in the glazed chestnuts, your sherbet will not set properly.

¼ cup unsalted butter, melted
¼ cup ground almonds
butter for greasing the baking sheet
Preheat oven to 375° F.

Using a fork, beat the egg whites with the salt until they are light and frothy. Add the sugar, vanilla, flour, and melted butter, blend thoroughly.

Lightly butter a baking sheet, drop the mixture on it a tablespoonful at a time, allowing plenty of room between to be able to spread them. Using the back of a small spoon, spread each tablespoon of mixture thinly enough to see the baking sheet underneath. Sprinkle the tops of the dough with ground almonds.

Place the sheet in the oven and bake the cookies for 2–3 minutes. They are done when the edges are lightly golden. Use a metal spatula to lift them off the baking sheet, place them, top side down, in the bottom of a ring mold to give each tile a gentle curve. When the tiles have cooled enough to hold their shape, remove them to a rack until completely cool.

"Cigarette" Cookies *Cigarettes*

MAKES ABOUT 48 "CIGARETTES"

4 egg whites
a pinch of salt
⅔ cup granulated sugar
¾ cup all-purpose flour
2–3 tablespoons powdered almonds
½ teaspoon vanilla extract
grated rind of 1 lemon
2 tablespoons unsalted butter, melted
butter for the baking sheet
Preheat oven to 375° F.

Beat the egg whites with the salt until they are light and frothy. Sift the sugar and flour and blend into the egg whites along with the almonds. Add the vanilla, stir in the lemon rind and butter.

Put as much of the mixture as you can in a pastry bag with a simple round top and force small blobs of the dough onto a buttered baking sheet. Set the blobs well apart. Place them in oven for just a few minutes. These cookies bake rapidly and must be watched with care.

Remove them from the oven when the edges are golden, and immediately wrap the cookies around the round handle of a wooden spoon. Press the flap edge against the table top to seal the "cigarette" so it will not unroll. Place the baked cigarettes on a rack to cool, and continue baking until all the cookies are done.

Sand Cookies, Alsatian Style   *Petits sablés alsaciens*

> 2 cups all-purpose flour
> ¾ cup granulated sugar
> a pinch of salt
> ½ cup plus 2 tablespoons unsalted butter
> ½ teaspoon vanilla extract
> 2–3 tablespoons dry white Alsatian wine
> butter for greasing the baking sheet
> *Preheat oven to 370° F.*

Sift the dry ingredients into a bowl. Add the butter, vanilla, and wine, gently work the ingredients together with the tips of your fingers. Turn the dough out onto a lightly floured board and roll to a thickness of ⅛ inch.

Using a fluted-edge cookie cutter 1½ inches in diameter, cut out the cookies and lay them on a lightly buttered baking sheet. Bake for about 8 minutes until the cookies are slightly colored. Remove from the oven and place them on a rack to cool.

hints on keeping cookies

Cookies will stay fresh and firm for 3 or 4 days if stored in a tightly covered tin or jar and kept in the refrigerator. When you serve stored cookies, it is a good idea to preheat the oven to 350°, turn heat off, and place the cookies inside until they are just warm. Let them cool completely before serving them; they will have a "freshly baked" taste. Most cookies will keep for at least 2 weeks in a tightly closed plastic container.

CHOCOLATE CAKES

Good chocolate cakes are always very popular. Here is a selection of recipes for you to choose from. The first is the traditional French chocolate cake; the second is the traditional chocolate cake turned into a birthday cake; the third, *kalouga,* is halfway between a cake and a molded "pudding"; the last one, with the royal name, is sweetened with honey and originated in Provence.

Traditional French Chocolate Cake   *Le classique au chocolat*

A delicious cake with a creamy, moist interior. It must be tested carefully while being baked. Too much baking will dry its velvety center.

Use a round cake pan 1¾–2 inches deep with a 9-inch bottom diameter.

a little butter for greasing the cake pan
a small amount flour for dusting the cake pan
4 egg yolks
1 cup granulated sugar
7 ounces semi-sweet chocolate
3 tablespoon water or 3 tablespoons strong brewed coffee
¾ cup unsalted butter at room temperature
2 tablespoons all-purpose flour
4 egg whites
a pinch of salt
1 recipe of Chocolate Icing* (choosen from the icing section)
Preheat oven to 350° F.

Lightly butter the cake pan and dust it with flour. Turn it upside down and tap out any excess flour.

Whisk the egg yolks and sugar together until the mixture is light-colored and creamy and runs off the whisk in a broad ribbon.

Slowly melt the chocolate with the water or coffee in a heavy-bottomed enameled saucepan, stirring constantly. Do not allow to boil. Stir the chocolate into the egg-sugar mixture, then carefully blend in the slightly softened butter. Blend in the flour, work the mixture with a wooden spatula for 2–3 minutes.

Beat the egg whites with the salt until they form stiff peaks. Add 2 tablespoons of the beaten whites to the chocolate mixture to thin it, then gently fold the rest of the whites into the chocolate mixture.

Pour the batter into the cake pan, bake for 18–23 minutes (a little longer if necessary.) Begin testing for doneness after 16 minutes by sticking a larding needle or thin knitting needle into the middle of the cake. The needle should come out lightly coated with chocolate; if the chocolate drips from the needle, the cake needs a few more minutes of baking. Test again in 2 minutes. Keep in mind that the needle must have chocolate on it. If it comes out moist but devoid of chocolate, your cake, alas, is overdone. It won't be completely ruined, but it won't have that superb velvety center spoken of in the introduction to the recipe.

Remove the cake from the oven and allow it to cool on a rack. When it is completely cool, unmold it onto a cake plate that has been covered with a paper doily. Frost the cake with the chocolate icing.

If you do not have time to make icing, dust the cake lightly with confectioner's sugar, removing any spilled sugar from the edge of the plate.

Chocolate Birthday Cake   *Gâteau d'anniversaire*

A delicious two-layer birthday cake that follows the Traditional French Chocolate Cake* recipe (given above) but uses two cake pans, one larger than the other.

Make the larger cake using the same ingredients and cake-pan size as in the preceding recipe. Unmold the cake onto a cake plate covered with a paper doily.

For the small cake, use a pan 2 inches deep with a 6½-inch bottom diameter. Here are the proportions for the smaller cake:

3 egg yolks

½ cup plus 1 tablespoon granulated sugar

4–5 ounces semi-sweet chocolate

2 tablespoon water or 2 tablespoon strong brewed coffee

½ cup unsweetened butter at room temperature

1½ tablespoons all-purpose flour

3 egg whites

a pinch of salt

a few pink Jordan almonds (*dragées*) or pink pralines for decorating the cake

1 double recipe of Chocolate Icing* chosen from the icing section

Preheat oven to 350° F.

After the larger cake has been made, mix and bake the small cake according to the method in the preceding recipe, not forgetting to butter and dust the cake pan with flour. Allow the cake to cool on a rack, unmold it onto a plate, then carefully place it on top of the larger cake.

Make the chocolate icing and frost the outside of both cakes. When the icing is just dry, decorate the top of the double cake with Jordan almonds or pink pralines. For the birthday touch, put pink birthday candles around the edge of the larger cake and, if you wish, around the edge of the top cake.

Kalouga

Kalouga is a rich chocolate dessert. It is easy to make and can be baked in a 9-inch square cake pan or in an 8-cup charlotte mold and covered with chocolate icing. If you make it in the mold, it is delicious accompanied with vanilla custard sauce or coffee custard sauce. If it is made in a cake pan, it may be cut into squares and served in fluted paper cups as *petits fours*. Whether you use a cake pan or mold, the dessert is always baked over hot water.

FOR 6–8 PEOPLE

9 ounces semi-sweet chocolate, grated

1¼ cups granulated sugar

1½ tablespoons water or brewed coffee

a pinch of allspice

1 cup unsalted butter, cut in pieces

4 egg yolks

1 tablespoon sifted all-purpose flour

4 egg whites

a pinch of salt

butter and flour for the cake pan or charlotte mold

1 recipe of Chocolate Icing* (chosen from the icing section)

1 recipe of Vanilla Custard Cream* or Coffee Custard Cream* (if you are baking the dessert in a charlotte mold)

a sprinkling of confectioner's sugar (in case you do not use the chocolate icing)

Preheat oven to 350° F.

Melt the chocolate, sugar, and the water or coffee in a double boiler over low heat. Stir in the pinch of allspice. Remove from heat, allow to cool somewhat, then blend in the butter piece by piece until all has been absorbed. Scrape the mixture into a bowl.

Beat the egg yolks with the flour in a bowl. When thoroughly blended, beat into the chocolate mixture.

Using a fork, beat the egg whites with the pinch of salt until they are light and frothy. Mix them into the batter.

Lightly butter the cake pan or charlotte mold and dust with flour. Turn the pan upside down and tap out any excess flour. Fill with batter and set in a pan of hot water. Put on top of the stove over medium heat until the water begins to simmer, then place in the oven and bake for about an hour, until a larding needle or thin knitting needle comes out lightly coated with chocolate. Begin testing for doneness after 45 minutes. Check from time to time to see that there is enough water in the pan. If necessary, add boiling water.

Remove from the oven and set on a rack to cool. Unmold on a cake plate covered with a paper doily. Frost with your favorite chocolate icing.

If you have no time to make icing, let the cake cool, then place it in refrigerator for about 2 hours, remove, and dust generously with confectioner's sugar.

If the dessert has been made in a charlotte mold, serve it with vanilla custard sauce or coffee custard sauce.

Queen Bee Chocolate Cake   *Reine des abeilles*

A rich, dark chocolate cake known in some regions as Queen of Sheba or Queen of Ethiopia. This Provençal version is sweetened with honey—hence its apiarian name.

You will need a 10-inch round cake pan for this recipe.

FOR 8–10 PEOPLE

9 ounces semi-sweet chocolate

1 cup thick, light-colored honey

1 cup unsalted butter, creamed

5 egg yolks

¾ cup flour

2 teaspoons baking powder

½ cup chopped, toasted hazelnuts,or 2 tablespoons candied orange peel,
    finely chopped, or 3 tablespoons seedless raisins soaked in a jigger or
    so of dark rum until plump then patted dry, or ½ cup Praline Nut
    Brittle*

butter and flour for dusting the cake pan

Preheat oven to 350° F.

Melt the chocolate in the top of a double boiler. Using a wooden spatula, stir it until it is completely smooth.

Heat the honey in a saucepan—it should be just lukewarm. Pour into a bowl and stir in the melted chocolate. Then blend the butter into the honey-chocolate mixture, working with a spatula. Add the egg yolks one by one, again using a wooden spatula to work them in.

Sift the flour with the baking powder and blend it gradually into the mixture. Then add the hazelnuts or candied orange peel or raisins or nut brittle.

Butter the cake pan. Dust with flour, tapping out any excess. Fill the cake pan with the batter, place in the oven, and bake for 45–50 minutes. Test for doneness after 35 minutes by sticking a larding needle (or other needle) into the middle of the cake. If it comes out moist but clean, the cake is done.

Remove the cake from the oven and let it cool for about 10 minutes on a rack. Unmold on a cake plate covered with a paper doily.

If you wish to make the cake two or three days in advance, store it in a tightly covered tin or well-sealed plastic container and keep in the refrigerator.

SEVERAL CLASSIC CAKES

Genoese Cake *Génoise*

This famous cake may be served just as it is with simply a dusting of confectioner's sugar, or sliced into two or three layers (depending on your skill) and filled with jam or butter cream filling, then frosted with an icing of your choice.

Use a round 9 by 2-inch cake pan.

FOR 8 PEOPLE

4 eggs

⅔ cup granulated sugar

1¼ cup all-purpose flour

5 tablespoons unsalted butter, clarified*

grated rind of 3 oranges, or grated rind of 2 lemons

butter and flour for the cake pan

garnish suggestions

confectioner's sugar

apricot jam, orange marmalade, strawberry or raspberry jam

a little Cointreau or Grand Marnier

1 recipe of chocolate Butter Cream Filling (contains chocolate) with Sugar Syrup*

1 recipe of cake icing (chosen from the icing section)

Preheat oven to 350° F.

Break the eggs into the top of a double boiler and add the sugar. Place over low heat and whisk until the mixture has expanded and become creamy.

Remove from heat and continue to beat for 8–10 minutes until the mixture has doubled in volume. (NOTE: if your double boiler is not large enough for this operation, use a fairly large enameled saucepan placed over a pan of hot water.) This whisking process is of utmost importance and you must not skimp on the time. Set your timer for 10 minutes and sing a song or two while you whisk.

Blending in the flour is a delicate operation and requires care. Sift the flour onto a piece of paper, then dip the whisk into the egg-sugar mixture, then into the flour and sprinkle this flour over the egg mixture. Repeat this operation two or three times at least to ensure that the flour is introduced gradually. Then, using a slotted spoon, fold in the rest of the flour. After all of it has been added, gently stir in the clarified butter and the grated orange or lemon rind.

Butter the cake pan. Dust with flour, tapping out any excess. Pour in the batter. Bake for about 35 minutes. The cake will be done when the top is spongy to the touch and the edges have shrunk away a little from the pan.

Remove the cake from the oven and set on a rack. Unmold when it is lukewarm.

When the cake has completely cooled, cut it into two or (if possible) three layers.

If you use apricot jam or orange marmalade for filling the cake, put them through a food mill, using the finest disk. Strawberry or raspberry jam can be used as is.

Dribble a little Cointreau or Grand Marnier over each layer before filling with a generous amount of jam. Brush the top and sides of the cake with a little jam to help make the icing adhere.

If you prefer, use chocolate butter cream filling instead of jam.

Frost the cake with one of your favorite icings. I myself prefer chocolate.

NOTE: *Chocolate icing can also be used as a filling for the cake. If you decide on this, dribble a generous amount of Cointreau or Grand Marnier on each layer before covering with icing.*

Quick Genoese Cake   *Génoise minute*

If you want a nice dessert and are pressed for time, buy a ready-baked, good-quality Genoese cake and transform it with a quickly made filling and icing.

Cut the cake into two or three layers. Fill the layers with raspberry jam or orange marmalade (the latter having been put through a food mill). Brush the sides and top with a thin coating of the jam to help the icing adhere. Frost the cake with Quick White Icing.*

Another idea: cut the cake in two or three layers and fill with Custard Cream Pastry Filling flavored with kirsch or rum or orange marmalade. Frost with Quick Chocolate Icing.**

Almond Cake   *Pain de Gênes*

A rich, moist cake flavored with powdered almonds and kirsch.

Use a 9 by 2-inch round cake pan.

FOR 6–8 PEOPLE

½ cup powdered almonds (taste to see that they are not rancid)

¾ cup granulated sugar divided into 2 equal parts

⅔ cup unsalted butter

3 large eggs

⅓ cup flour

a pinch of salt

2 tablespoons kirsch

butter and parchment paper for the cake pan

Preheat oven to 350° F.

Using a wooden spatula, mix the powdered almonds with half the sugar. Cream the butter with the remaining sugar and combine with the almond-sugar mixture. Whisk in the eggs one by one, pausing momentarily after each addition. Do not worry if at this point the batter does not appear to be well blended. Continuing to whisk, beat in the flour, salt, and kirsch until the batter is smooth and creamy.

Butter the cake pan and fit a round piece of buttered parchment paper on the bottom. Pour the batter into the pan and bake for 35–40 minutes. If the cake seems to be browning too quickly, lower oven heat to 325°.

Test for doneness by sticking a larding needle or fine knitting needle into the center of the cake. The needle should come out moist but free of batter when the cake is done.

Serve with vanilla, Chocolate Custard Sauce* or Coffee Custard Sauce.* The cake is delicious with red port wine or dry sherry.

Basque Cake   *Gâteau basque*

For making this cake you will need a deep 9 by 3-inch round cake pan.

FOR 6–8 PEOPLE

1 recipe of Custard Cream Pastry Filling* flavored with 2–3 pinches of grated lemon rind and 2 tablespoons dark rum
4½ cups all-purpose flour
a pinch of salt
2½ teaspoons baking powder
grated rind of 1 lemon
1¼ cups unsalted butter, creamed
1¼ cups granulated sugar
3 egg yolks
1 whole egg
½ cup dark rum
butter and flour for the cake pan
1 egg yolk diluted with 3 drops of water for glazing the top
Preheat oven to 350° F.

Make the custard cream pastry filling and set it aside to cool.

Sift the flour, salt, and baking powder into a bowl, stir in the lemon rind. Make a well in the center, add the creamed butter, the egg yolks and the whole egg, which have been beaten together, and the sugar. Work these ingredients into the flour with a spatula or fork. Then knead with the fingertips of one hand while adding the rum. Do not attempt to get a smooth mixture at this time. Form a ball with the dough and let it rest at room temperature for 20–30 minutes. Butter the cake pan. Dust it with flour, tapping out any excess.

Divide the ball of dough into two equal parts. Dust a board with flour and lightly roll out one part to fit the bottom and sides of the cake pan.

Beat the custard cream filling, heap it in the middle of the dough, do not spread it out to the edge of the pan.

Roll out the second part of the dough and fit it on top of the pan. Press the edges of the dough together to seal in the filling. Brush the top of the dough with the diluted egg yolk lightly beaten with a fork. Make a latticework design on the top with the point of a knife. Put in the oven and bake for 45–50 minutes, checking after 30 minutes to see that the top is not browning too quickly; if it is, lower oven heat to 325°.

Remove from the oven and set on a rack. When cool, unmold on a plate covered with a paper doily.

A glass of Sauterne or Jurançon wine goes extremely well with this cake.

Walnut Bread *Pain aux noix*

This recipe, which comes from the Limousin region, is not exactly a cake, but it is close enough to be included in this section. Cut in slices and buttered, it makes a lovely accompaniment to afternoon tea. See the end of this recipe for other serving suggestions.

For making the bread you will need a loaf pan 10 inches long, 4½ inches wide, and 3½ inches deep.

SERVES 6 OR 7 TEA GUESTS

1 egg
½ cup granulated sugar
3 pinches of salt, each taken with 3 fingers
2 cups flour
2 teaspoons baking powder
1 cup finely chopped walnuts
1 cup cold milk
a little butter for greasing the loaf pan
Preheat oven to 350° F.

In a large bowl, work the egg, sugar, and salt together, using a wooden spatula. Add the flour, sifted with the baking powder, and blend. Stir in the chopped nuts and gradually work in the milk. Stir until the ingredients are well blended.

Butter the loaf pan and pour in the mixture, cover with a towel, and set in a warm place to swell for 35–40 minutes.

Bake the walnut bread for 1–1¼ hours. It is done when the top is golden and the sides have slightly shrunk away from the pan. Unmold it immediately and set it to cool on a rack.

More servings suggestions: cut slices of walnut bread in half and spread them with Roquefort cheese paste, or spread whole slices of the bread with raspberry jam or red currant jelly and decorate each slice with a walnut.

DESSERTS

Epiphany Galette *Galette des rois*

Galettes are traditionally served on January 6, the twelfth day of Christmas. They are made of puff pastry—in this case simple 4-turn puff pastry—and baked with a small porcelain "favor" that comes to light when the *galette* is cut and served. Whoever has the good luck to find the favor in his or her piece of *galette* becomes "king" and is presented with a golden crown made out of lacy stiff paper. Sometimes two golden crowns are presented to the "king," who confers the title of "queen" on someone of his or her choice.

There is always a breathless hush when the *galette* is cut and distributed. For becoming "king" is a momentous affair—especially if you are a child. But you do not have to be a child to appreciate the lightness and tastiness of this delicious holiday cake.

FOR 6–8 PEOPLE

1 recipe of Simple Puff Pastry,* made ahead and refrigerated

1 small Epiphany "favor"—there are many kinds to choose from: an effigy of one of the Three Kings, the Christ Child, the Virgin Mary, a crown, a star, a bean, and others.

1 egg yolk, lightly beaten with 2–3 drops of water

Preheat oven to 400° F.

Remove the puff pastry from the refrigerator. When it has reached room temperature, form it into a ball so it can be rolled in a circle about 8 inches in diameter and ¾ inch thick.

Do not try to make a perfect circle, as part of the charm of this *galette* is the slightly uneven "homemade" look. Cut shallow, regular slits around the sides of the *galette* and pinch the dough between them to create a fluted edge.

Wipe a baking sheet with a damp cloth or sponge and place the *galette* on it, top side down. Lift part of it off the baking sheet, making a small horizontal incision, and slip the favor into the dough, taking care to seal it in so it doesn't stick out and ruin the surprise!

Paint the surface of the *galette* with the diluted egg yolk. This will produce a nice glaze when it has finished baking. Bake for 20–25 minutes, checking occasionally to see that it is not browning too much. Lower oven heat if necessary.

Serve the *galette* slightly warm. It can be reheated by heating the oven to 350°, turning it off, and placing the *galette* inside for about 10 minutes. A *galette* served cold is a trifly heavy and not quite as tasty.

The galette may be accompanied by heavy cream, Whipped Cream (Recipe I), or a pot of slightly warmed raspberry and red currant jelly. It can also be served with cold Chocolate Custard Sauce.**

Galette Naomi   *Galette de Naomi*

Through the good offices of an American friend, I was finally able to get hold of the recipe for this famous *galette,* which originated in the oldest inn in France.

In the old days the *galette* was baked in a stone bread oven that was heated with branches of acacia and broom. These imparted their aromatic fragrance to the cake.

ENOUGH FOR 6–8 PEOPLE

1 cake yeast
½ cup lukewarm water
¼ cup sugar
grated rind of 1 lemon
4 cups all-purpose flour
a pinch of salt, taken with 3 fingers
1 large egg
½ cup unsalted butter divided into 2 parts
extra sugar for sprinkling on the *galette*
Preheat oven to 440° F.

In a slightly warmed bowl dissolve the yeast and sugar in the lukewarm water, working with 3 fingers. Stir in the lemon rind.

Sift the flour with the salt, place half of it in a large bowl. Make a well in the center, drop in the egg and half the butter. Gradually work the flour in from the sides until the mixture is blended. Work in the yeast mixture little by little.

Mix in the remaining flour with the tips of your fingers or a fork, working lightly and quickly. When the dough no longer sticks to your fingers, cover the bowl with a towel and set it in a warm place to rise for 1½ hours.

When the dough has risen, roll it into a circle about 8 inches in diameter and ⅛ inch thick. Lightly dampen the baking sheet with a cloth or sponge and set the rolled-out dough on it. Dot the dough with the remaining butter cut in small pieces, and a sprinkling of granulated sugar.

Bake the *galette* for 5–8 minutes. It is usually done in about 6 minutes, so be on your guard! It is done when it is golden and shiny.

DESSERT CRÊPES

You can make sweet dessert crêpes by following the recipe for savory Crêpes* and adding 1 teaspoon—no more—of granulated sugar. Too much sugar will cause the batter to stick to the pan.

The following recipe makes delicious sweet crêpes. Because of the added egg yolks they are lighter than savory crêpes but just a bit harder to handle until you have the knack.

Sweet Crêpe Batter, Basic Method   *Pâte à crêpes sucrées*

1½ cups all-purpose flour
a pinch of salt
1 teaspoon granulated sugar
1 whole egg
2 egg yolks
5 tablespoons milk
10–12 tablespoons cold water
5 tablespoons melted butter
2 tablespoon dark rum

Beat the ingredients together and cook as in savory crêpes.

Sweep crêpes must always be served piping hot on warmed plates.

A simple way of serving them is to dust them with a little granulated sugar and fold them into rectangular "packages."

They are delicious with a thin trickle of dark rum, kirsch, Cointreau, or Grand Marnier poured over them. They may also be spread with raspberry jam, red currant jelly, or orange marmalade. My favorite garnish for crêpes is blackberry jam accompanied by a bowl of heavy cream.

FLAMED CRÊPES

Flamed crêpes are a very popular dessert, not only because they taste good, but because of their dramatic effect.

Here are two of the most typical recipes in the large family of flamed crêpes: those filled with custard cream filling and crêpes Suzette.

Flamed Custard Crêpes   *Crêpes à la crème patissière flambées*

This is a practical as well as delicious dessert, for the crêpes can be made well ahead of time, then reheated and flamed at the last minute.

MAKES 12 CRÊPES

1 recipe of Sweet Crêpe Batter* that has rested for 1 hour
1 recipe of Custard Cream Pastry Filling*
grated rind of 1 orange
grated rind of 1 lemon
2–3 tablespoons curaçao or Grand Marnier or Cointreau
2 tablespoons butter for the crêpe dish
½ cup dark rum or armagnac or cognac, heated

After making the crêpe batter, prepare the custard filling and let it cool, beating it occasionally. Stir the grated orange and lemon rinds into the custard and whichever of the orange liqueurs you have chosen.

Cook the 12 crêpes and fill each with the custard cream filling. Fold them into well-sealed rectangular "packages" (Crêpes with Crème de Fromage*). Place them in a buttered flameproof dish.[1] Up to this point they can be made ahead.

When you are ready to serve them, reheat, then douse them with the warmed rum or armagnac or cognac. Set them aflame and bring the dish to the table in all its flaming glory.

NOTE: *In case you do not wish to flame the crêpes, pour a little melted butter over each after filling, sprinkle with granulated sugar, and place under the broiler for a minute or so to glaze.*

Flamed Crêpes Suzette   *Crêpes Suzette flambées*

This is a famous French dessert, but it is not always as good as it should be, even when accompanied by the most theatrical gesturing and pouring. Many cooks use too much orange juice in making crêpes Suzette, and the result is usually rather soggy crêpes.

In the following recipe, the crêpes are spread with Suzette butter, which I find absolutely indispensable, and I am sure that once you have tried it you will agree.

Let me give you a few hints and words of advice about making successful crêpes Suzette:

The crêpes will be firmer and easier to handle if they are cooked the night before and stored in the refrigerator. The Suzette butter may also be made the night before and kept covered in the refrigerator.

The chafing dish should be buttered and sugared before the crêpes are heated in it. When the butter and sugar are heated, a light caramel will form which will ensure the flaming.

The crêpes must be thoroughly heated before they are flamed. Did you know that the butter and sugar combination actually helps in flaming crêpes, while an excess of orange juice is a hindrance?

One final thing: the brandy (armagnac or cognac) is not added until you are ready to flame the crêpes.

12 crêpes made from Sweet Crêpe Batter,* made the day before and
stored in the refrigerator until about 1 hour before using

ingredients for the Suzette butter made the day before and stored in the refrigerator

2 oranges

6–8 sugar lumps

⅓ cup unsalted butter, creamed

3 tablespoons curaçao or Grand Marnier or Cointreau

[1] You can do the reheating and flaming of the crêpes at the table by using a chafing dish. See the following recipe, Flamed Crêpes Suzette,* for explicit directions.

chafing dish
2 tablespoons butter for the chafing dish
2 tablespoons granulated sugar for the chafing dish
juice of ½ lemon or 4 tablespoons orange juice
a little granulated sugar for final dusting of the crêpes
glass containing 2 jiggers warmed armagnac or cognac
a fork and a spoon
the bottle of orange liqueur with which you have flavored the Suzette
    butter

making the Suzette butter

Wash and dry the oranges. Rub the sugar lumps over the oranges so they pick up the maximum amount of rind and taste of orange.

Pound the orange-impregnated sugar in a heavy bowl. Gradually add the creamed butter and the orange liqueur you have chosen. Work the mixture until smooth. (Remove from refrigerator about ½ hour before using.)

preparing the crêpes for flaming

Spread each unfolded crêpe with Suzette butter and fold them into triangles. Arrange the crêpes at one end of a serving platter so they overlap a little.

flaming the crêpes

Light the lamp under the chafing dish. Put the butter in the dish and sprinkle the sugar on top. Allow to brown slightly. Tilt the dish in all directions so it is evenly coated with the lightly caramelized mixture. Add the lemon or orange juice.

Heat the crêpes three at a time, turning them once, and storing them at the far end of the dish when they are hot. Dust each crêpe with a little sugar before storing it. When all the crêpes have been heated in this manner, douse them with armagnac or cognac and set them aflame. Using a spoon and fork, turn the crêpes in the hot liquid. When the flames have died down, spoon the sauce over the crêpes and arrange them on the serving platter.

One final, glorious touch: Holding the bottle high, pour a little orange liqueur over the crêpes. If the bottle is not equipped with a pouring spout, hold your thumb over three quarters of the top while pouring. This procedure takes a bit of practice, but once you have mastered the technique, the effect will be memorable!

TARTS

Apple tarts are the most traditional of all French tarts; they are splendid when the crust is light and flaky and the apples are not cooked into applesauce.

There are many recipes for apple tarts, including numerous, often disappointing versions of the famous *tarte Tatin* (Upside-Down Apple Tart*). I can imagine the originator of this recipe, Stephanie Tatin, turning in her grave at the cemetery of La Motte-Beuvron in Sologne if she knew some of the things that were done to her famous recipe!

Here are two recipes: traditional apple tart and the original *tarte Tatin*.

Apple Tart, Village Style *Tarte aux pommes à la villageoise*

This is the one that is made and sold on Sunday mornings in the bakeries of villages all over France. The apples are baked in Sugar Crust Pastry Dough.* Choose apples that do not cook to pieces when they are baked. Golden apples are a good choice.

To make the tart you will need an 8- or 9-inch tart pan.

FOR 6–8 PEOPLE

1 recipe of Sugar Crust Pastry Dough,* made ahead (even the day before)
2–2¼ pounds golden apples or other apples that keep their shape when baked
1 lemon, cut in half
4 tablespoons granulated sugar
a dash of cinnamon or a little grated lemon rind
4–5 tablespoons apricot jam, slightly warmed then strained
2 tablespoons unsalted butter, cut in pieces
½ cup apple, quince, or lemon jelly (optional)
Preheat oven to 350° F.

Roll the dough in a circular shape a little larger than the tart pan and about ⅛ inch thick. Line the tart pan with it and set in the lower part of the refrigerator until you are ready to use it.

Peel the apples and rub the cut side of the lemon halves over them to keep them from turning brown. Cut them in quarters and remove the cores. Cut the quarters into thin even slices, place in a bowl, and mix with 2 tablespoons of sugar and the cinnamon or lemon rind. Cover the bowl.

Remove the tart pan from refrigerator and spread the cooled, strained apricot jam over the bottom.

Starting at the center, fill the lined tart pan with concentric circles of apple slices, alternating the direction of the slices every other row. Sprinkle with the remaining 2 tablespoons of sugar and dot with butter.

Bake for 40–45 minutes, reducing oven heat to 325° for the last half of the baking. For a sophisticated tart, glaze with one of the jellies in a very hot oven for a minute or so.

Upside-Down Apple Tart
La tarte des demoiselles Tatin (ou tarte à l'envers)

I have eaten all sorts of *tarte Tatin* in Sologne, as well as variations—some better than others—in Parisian restaurants. Now a little bit of history about the original *tarte Tatin*.

It was first made in the Sologne district at the end of the nineteenth century, when Sologne, with its great forests and lakes, was still a hunter's paradise. The demoiselles were the two Tatin sisters (maiden ladies) who operated the family hotel in the village of La Motte-Beuvron. Let me add that this hotel, located opposite the railroad station, is still in operation, but it has lost its character.

Caroline, the elder sister, spent little time in the kitchen and was more interested in real estate, giving precious advice to the wealthy Parisians who were then buying up large tracts of forest land and establishing estates. She appears to have been a very great lady and was often referred to by her clients as "the empress of Sologne."

Of the two demoiselles it was Stephanie, known as "Fanny," who achieved immortality in her own quiet way by "inventing" the apple tart that became so famous that it was given the family name. It was originally made by Fanny in a country oven with "beds of coal above and below." This, of course, is no longer possible. Though close to the original, the present recipe has been somewhat adapted to modern cooking methods. Originally the tart was made in a special copper baking dish, but you will get just as good a result if you use an aluminum, flameproof earthenware, or Pyrex baking dish 9–10 inches in diameter and 2½–3 inches high.

FOR 6–8 PEOPLE

apple filling

a little over 4 pounds golden apples or other apples that keep their shape when cooked

⅓ cup granulated sugar

a little cinnamon

⅔ cup melted unsalted butter (this includes butter for greasing the dripping pan

2 tablespoons granulated sugar (optional)

sugar crust pastry dough
(see the Index for its preparation)

1⅓ cup all-purpose flour

a pinch of salt

1 tablespoon granulated sugar

⅓ cup unsalted butter

1 egg

about 2 tablespoons cold water

(*see preparation in Molded Caramel Lemon Custard**)

> 12–14 sugar lumps
> 2 tablespoons water
> *Preheat oven to 350° F.*

Peel, core, and quarter the apples. Cut the quarters in fairly thin, even slices and place them in a bowl. Mix in the sugar and a sprinkle or two of cinnamon. Let the apples stand for 15–20 minutes, then place them in the well-buttered dripping pan and bake for 30–45 minutes, basting frequently with the rest of the melted butter. If you wish, dust the apples with the granulated sugar to facilitate their browning. After cooking, transfer the apple slices to a large, flat dish.

Make the sugar crust pastry dough and place in the refrigerator for at least one hour.

Caramelize the baking dish with the sugar lumps and water.

assembling and baking the tart

Roll out the dough in a circular shape a little larger than the baking dish; it should be about ⅛ inch thick.

Lay the apples in the caramelized baking dish, browned sides down. Place the pastry dough on top of the apples, tucking the dough *under* all around the edges of the dish. Prick the middle of the crust to allow steam to escape. Bake for 25–30 minutes or until crust is lightly golden and pulls away from the dish. If it seems to be browning too quickly, lower oven temperature a little and cover the dish with a piece of aluminum foil.

Remove from the oven and set on a rack to cool. Then unmold the tart onto a round flameproof serving dish.

If the apples are not sufficiently caramelized, sprinkle a little granulated sugar on them and place under the broiler for a few seconds.

Lemon Tart from Peyrudette *Tarte au citron de Peyrudette*

I discovered this tart in the small town of Peyrudette. It was served to me along with a glass of chilled Sauterne . . . a delectable experience!

The tart shell is partially baked before it is filled with the lemon custard. This short (15-minute) preliminary baking "sets" the dough and prevents the crust from becoming limp and soggy when you bake it again with the filling inside.

Follow the steps for making the honey-clear custard carefully: it must never, never boil!

For making the tart you will need a 8–9-inch tart pan.

FOR 6–8 PEOPLE

1 recipe of Sugar Crust Pastry Dough,* made ahead and kept in the refrigerator; remove from the refrigerator about ½ hour before rolling

lemon custard filling

4 eggs
1¼ cups granulated sugar
grated rind and juice of 2 lemons
Preheat oven to 350° F.

Roll out dough as in the preceding recipes (about ⅛ inch thick) and line the tart pan. Cut out a round piece of parchment paper or aluminum foil and place on the dough. Strew a few pebbles or dried white beans on top of the paper or foil. This will keep the pastry flat while it is baking. Place the pan in the oven and partially bake the dough (about 15 minutes). It should not be allowed to brown. Remove from the oven, set aside to cool.

making the lemon custard

Place all the ingredients in a heavy-bottomed enameled saucepan and set over low heat. Stir gently and patiently with a wooden spatula until the mixture begins to thicken. Be sure not to let the custard boil. If necessary, place an asbestos mat under the saucepan. Remove the slightly thickened custard from the heat and continue stirring until it is cool. As it cools, it will thicken more. When it is entirely cool, whisk it for a minute or so.

Pour the custard into the partially baked pastry shell and bake until the top begins to glaze and turn lightly golden in color.

NOTE: *The partially baked shell and the lemon custard may be kept separately in the refrigerator for as long as 24 hours. About 45 minutes before filling the tart, heat the oven to 400°, turn off heat, and set the shell inside for a few minutes. Allow to cool before adding the custard and glazing.*

Orange Tart *Tarte à l'orange*

This tart is filled with orange-flavored Custard Cream Pastry Filling.* If you wish, you may add a little Cointreau or Grand Marnier to heighten the orange flavor.

An 8–9-inch tart pan will be necessary.

FOR 6–8 PEOPLE

1 recipe of Sugar Crust Pastry Dough,* partially baked as in the preceding recipe
1 recipe of thick Custard Cream Pastry Filling*
6 tablespoons orange juice
a few drops of lemon juice
2 pinches of grated lemon rind
3 tablespoons Cointreau or Grand Marnier (optional)

garnishing ingredients

> 2 washed and dried oranges, sliced and fluted (Fluted Lemon Slices*), each slice cut in half
>
> granulated sugar for dusting the orange slices
>
> 18 glazed orange sections (see Glazed Fruit Sections*)
>
> ½ cup orange marmalade, strained and diluted with 1–2 tablespoons warm water for glazing the tart
>
> *Preheat oven to 350° F.*

Make the custard cream filling and stir in all the other ingredients. Taste for flavoring. Set aside to cool, stirring occasionally.

Dust the fluted orange slices with sugar and set aside to dry. Prepare the glazed orange sections.

Fill the partially baked pastry shell with the orange-flavored custard. Arrange the orange slices around the edges of the tart so they overlap and form a kind of crown. Coat the surface of the tart with the lightly diluted strained marmalade.

Set in the oven just long enough—about 3–4 minutes—to obtain a nice glaze. Place the tart on a rack to cool. Garnish the center with the glazed orange sections arranged in pinwheel fashion.

SPRING AND SUMMER FRUIT TARTS

Strawberry and raspberry fruit tarts are made of sugar crust or simple puff pastry dough. Just before serving, the tart is garnished with jelly and the uncooked ripe fruit.

Use an 8–9-inch tart pan for all these tarts.

Strawberry Tart *Tarte aux fraises*

FOR 6–8 PEOPLE

> 1 recipe of Sugar Crust Pastry Dough* or Simple Puff Pastry*
>
> 1½ pounds firm, ripe strawberries, hulled
>
> a scant ½ cup red currant and raspberry jelly
>
> 1 tablespoon water for diluting the jelly
>
> 2 tablespoons granulated sugar
>
> *Preheat oven to 350° F.*

Roll out the dough to about ⅛-inch thickness and line the tart pan. Cut a round of parchment paper or aluminum foil and place on the dough. Strew a few pebbles (or dried white beans) on top of the paper or foil. This will keep the pastry flat while it is baking. Place in the oven and bake for 17–18 minutes (a longer baking than the semi-cooked shells, because this tart does not go back in the oven). Remove from the oven and set on a rack to cool.

Place the strawberries in a colander and rinse them quickly under the cold water tap. Gently fold them in a triple thickness of paper towels so that all the moisture drains off. This is a vital operation. If the strawberries are wet, not only will the pie shell become soggy, but the jelly coating will not adhere to the fruit.

Melt the jelly with the tablespoon of water over low heat. Allow it to become lukewarm. Spread the jelly over the bottom of the tart shell in a thin layer. Put one large strawberry in the center of the jelly and arrange the rest of the strawberries around it, hulled ends down, in concentric circles, so there are no unfilled spaces. Sprinkle the strawberries with the sugar, then coat the top with a layer of lukewarm jelly. Serve immediately.

Raspberry Tart   *Tarte aux framboises*

FOR 6–8 PEOPLE

1⅔–2 pounds ripe raspberries, hulled and washed quickly under the cold water tap and folded into a triple thickness of paper towels until all moisture has drained out

For the procedure follow the recipe above, using the same kind of jelly.
Serve immediately, as with strawberry tart.

Cherry Tart   *Tarte aux cerises*

Making a successful tart with fresh cherries is a rather delicate affair. The cherries must be pitted with care so as not to ruin their shape, and the tart must be baked as soon as it is filled, before the cherry juice seeps into the tart dough, making it soggy. Fresh cherries, when used for a tart, should be poached first; that is, set in a wide saucepan over low heat until their juices are released. They should then be drained (in a single layer) on a triple thickness of paper towels for ½–1 hour.

In the recipe below, canned pitted Bing cherries are used. No poaching is necessary, and the tart shell is baked before the cherries are added. The tart is then lightly glazed in the oven.

An 8–9-inch tart pan is necessary.

FOR 6–8 PEOPLE

1 recipe of Sugar Crust Pastry Dough,* baked as in Strawberry Tart*

2 16-ounce cans pitted Bing cherries (you will probably use less)

½ cup red currant jelly, diluted with 1 tablespoon water, heated, then cooled to lukewarm

¼ cup granulated sugar

Preheat oven to 350–400° F.

After making the crust, strain the cherries and set them on a triple thickness of paper towels to drain for at least ½ hour. Spread a layer of the lukewarm red currant jelly on the bottom of the cooked tart shell. Arrange the cherries on top, openings facing the crust, dust them with sugar, and coat the top with the rest of the jelly. Place the tart in the oven for 3–4 minutes until it is nicely glazed.

Serve immediately.

Blackberry Tart *Tartes aux mûres*

The best blackberries are those picked along country byways at the end of the month of August. If you are denied the pleasure of blackberrying, choose the biggest ones you can find in your market, for these are the juiciest.

For this recipe, as for all the other tarts mentioned in this section, use an 8–9-inch tart pan.

FOR 6–8 PEOPLE

1 recipe of Sugar Crust Pastry Dough*
2–3 pounds fresh blackberries
2 tablespoons granulated sugar plus as many tablespoons of sugar as tablespoons of blackberry juice
3 tablespoons red currant jelly
confectioner's sugar for dusting the top of the tart
Preheat oven to 350° F.

Roll out the dough to about ⅛ inch thick and line the tart pan. Cover the bottom with a round of parchment paper or aluminum foil. Strew a few pebbles or dried white beans on top to keep the pastry flat while it is baking. Bake the pastry for 5–6 minutes. Remove the tart shell from the oven and set on a rack to cool.

preparing the blackberries

Working delicately, pick over and rinse the blackberries under the cold water tap. Place them in a heavy-bottomed enameled saucepan, sprinkle with the 2 tablespoons of sugar, and set over low heat. Cook, without stirring, for 6–8 minutes or until all the juice has been released.

Strain the blackberries and place them on a triple thickness of paper towels to drain. Put the juice with an equal amount of sugar into another saucepan and cook for 6–8 minutes or until the blackberry syrup falls in drops when poured from a spoon.

Remove the syrup from heat and stir in the red currant jelly. Allow to cool and thicken. Paint the bottom of the tart shell with some of the syrup.

Arrange the cooled, well-drained blackberries on the shell as in Strawberry Tart.* Cover the blackberries with 2–3 tablespoons of the syrup, put the tart in the oven, and bake for 10 minutes. Cool to lukewarm before serving.

Just before serving, spoon the rest of the syrup over the top of the tart and sprinkle with a little confectioner's sugar.

If you wish, accompany the tart with a bowl of Whipped Cream* (Recipe I).

Greengage Plum Tart   *Tarte aux reines-Claudes*

Juicy, sun-ripened greengage plums make delicious tarts. For this tart, the crust is cooked along with the fruit.

As usual, use an 8–9-inch tart pan.

FOR 6–8 PEOPLE

1 recipe of Sugar Crust Pastry Dough*
2¼–2½ pounds ripe greengage plums
2 tablespoons water
3–4 tablespoons granulated sugar
¾ cup apricot jam
Preheat oven to 350° F.

Roll out the dough to ⅛ inch thickness and line the tart pan.

Wash and pit the plums. Place them in a heavy-bottomed enameled saucepan along with the water and sugar. Cook over low heat for about 10 minutes. Strain the plums and mix the plum juice with the apricot jam. Place over medium heat for a few minutes to thicken and reduce. Strain and allow to cool.

Brush the bottom of the uncooked pastry shell with the syrup. Arrange the well-drained plums on top and pour on the rest of the syrup. Bake for 35–40 minutes.

Serve the tart lukewarm.

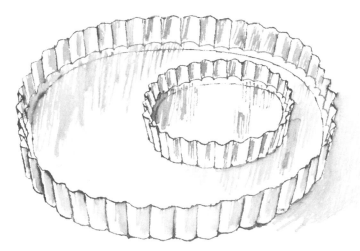

FRUIT COMPOTES

Fruit compotes make a refreshing dessert after a heavy meal. A particularly nice way to sweeten them is with spiced sugar syrup.

Always make a large quantity of compote, as it keeps for several days in the refrigerator.

Spiced Peach Compote   *Pêches au poivre*

3–4 pounds ripe peaches
2 cups cold water
½ cup Syrup of the Islands* or ½ cup cane sugar or granulated sugar
2 cloves
1 teaspoon coriander seeds
1 teaspoon black peppercorns
2 strips orange rind, each about 2 inches long
1 strip lemon rind about 2 inches long

Wash the peaches and pat dry. Put the cold water in a heavy-bottomed enameled saucepan, add the syrup or sugar, and place over low heat. Stir in the spices and fruit rinds, increase heat, and bring the liquid to a boil, reducing it somewhat. Remove from heat, cover, and allow to steep for about 10 minutes.

Put the peaches in the warm syrup and add water if necessary, so the peaches are three quarters covered. Place the cover on the saucepan and bring the liquid slowly to a boil. Cook for about 10–15 minutes or until the peaches are tender. Remove them from the liquid with a slotted spoon and skin them. Transfer the peaches and syrup to a large bowl and allow to cool before refrigerating.

Prunes Stewed in Tea   *Pruneaux au thé*

4 cups hot brewed Chinese "smoky" tea
2 cloves
2 thin strips (1 inch long) of lemon rind
2 pounds "tenderized" California prunes
3–5 tablespoons granulated sugar

Pour the hot tea into a large bowl, add the cloves, lemon rind, and prunes, and let them steep in the liquid. When the prunes are plump, transfer them and their liquid to an enameled saucepan, add the sugar, and cook for 10 minutes. Place the prunes in a bowl, using a slotted spoon. If you like, reduce the spiced tea liquid and pour it over the prunes. Cool before placing in the refrigerator.

Stewed Pears with Orange Sections   *Poires à l'orange*

    2 16-ounce cans pear halves in syrup
    2 large oranges
    a little kirsch or dark rum (optional)

Drain the pear syrup into an enameled saucepan and set the pears aside.

Using a vegetable peeler, remove the orange rind. Cut the rind into shreds, cover with cold water, bring to a boil, and cook for about 3 minutes. Drain the rind, rinse under the cold water tap, and pat dry.

Put the rind in the pear syrup and boil for 10–15 minutes until the rinds are somewhat glazed. Remove the rind shreds with a slotted spoon and place them on a work surface to become firm.

Divide the oranges into sections, removing all pith and filaments.

Place the pear halves in a glass dish, pour the hot syrup over them, and decorate with the shredded orange rind and orange sections. Cool and refrigerate.

If you like, pour a little kirsch or dark rum into the syrup before you add the pear halves and orange garnishes.

Index

Aiguillettes, 217–20
Aioli, for Provençal fish
    stew, 131–32
Aioli sauce (garlic mayon-
    naise), poached salt
    cod with, 167–68
Alcohol vinegar, 22
Allspice, 8
Almond
  cake, 438–39
  tiles (cookies), 430–31
Anchovies (anchovy)
  butter, 29
    red mullet broiled
      with, 176
    cucumber stuffed with
      tuna and, 79
    eggs stuffed with, 139
    mayonnaise, 34
    sauce Bellini, 90
Apple(s)
  cooked, Normandy style,
    casseroled pheasant
    with, 251–52
  goose with, 230–31
  and potato purée,
    382–83
  purée, spiced, as a vege-
    table garnish, 383
  tarts, 445–48
    upside-down, 447–48
    village style, 446–47
Aromatic bouillon (aroma-
    tic broth)
    small lobsters in,
      200–1
    vegetables à la grecque in,
      81
Aromatic oils, 20–21
  garlic oil, 20–21

    with herbs from Prov-
      ence, 21
  limes preserved in olive
    oil, 21
  with savory, 21
Aromatic pepper, 8
Aromatic vinegar(s), 23–24
  cherries in, 24
  cider, 22
  elderberry flower, 24
  malt, 22
  mint, 24
  shallot, for winter, 23
  tarragon, 23
  wine, 22–23
Arrangements and decora-
    tions, table, 57–62
  baking dish cover made
    of pastry, 61–62
  canapés, 59
  croutons, 58–59
  finishing touches and dec-
    orations, 58
  lemon and herbs used for,
    58
  pastry scallop shells, 62
  puff pastry crescents, 60
  serving dishes, choice of,
    57
  tartlets
    oval, 61
    savory, 60
Artichokes (artichoke
    hearts), 322–25
  cold poached eggs with
    Béatrice sauce on,
    324–25
  cooked whole, basic
    cooking method,
    322

    garnished with artichoke
      mousselline, 325
  hot poached eggs with
    hollandaise sauce on,
    324
  mousseline (purée), 325,
    383–84
  sweetbreads Colbert with
    béarnaise sauce on,
    284–85
Asparagus, 325–27
  basic recipe, 325–26
  "little sauce" for, 326
  sauces, 326–27
  soup, velouté of, 114–15
  tips, scrambled eggs on
    canapés with, 151
  with two sauces, 327
Aspic
  chicken in, 220–23
  chicken livers in, 223
  chopped, for garnish, 110
  fish in, 172–73
  hare in, Alsatian style,
    262–64
  patchwork chicken in,
    221–22
  poached eggs in, 144–
    45
  pot roast molded in,
    304–5
  tarragon chicken in,
    220–21
Au gratin, 7
  Belgian endives with
    Mornay sauce, 344
  cauliflower, 338–39
  fennel hearts, 345
  gratiné method, 7
  ham and spinach, 370

potatoes, 361–63
with cod, 362–63
with fennel shoots,
361–62
See also Gratin (*gratiné*)
Aurora sauce, 43–44

Bacon
Belgian endives with
Mornay sauce and,
au gratin, 344
dandelion salad with, 103
garbure with, 119–20
Île de France meat and
vegetable soup with,
124–25
Bagna cauda (sauce Bellini),
90
Baked fish. *See under* Fish,
specific kinds, rec-
ipes
Baked ham with port wine
sauce, 296–97
Baked sea bass stuffed with
salmon *mousseline,*
177–79
Baked stuffed carp, Oriental
style, 181–83
braising ingredients, 182
stuffing ingredients, 182
Baked tuna with *ratatouille,*
180
Baked whiting, 181
Baking dish cover made of
pastry, 61–62
Barding meats before roasting, 4, 5
Basil, 8
salade Niçoise with, 88–89
vegetable soup with gar-
lic, and (*pistou*),
120–21
Basque cake, 439–40
Basque fish soup, 128–29
Bastard saffron. *See* Safflower
Batter
crêpe, 153–54, 443
sweet, 443
unsweetened, 153–54
fritter, 379

Bay leaf, 8
Beans. *See* Dried white
beans; Green beans;
Lima beans; White
beans; specific re-
cipes
Béarnaise sauce, 48–49
sweetbreads Colbert on
artichoke hearts
with, 284–85
tournedos with, 299
Béatrice sauce, 35–36
cold poached eggs on ar-
tichoke hearts with,
324–25
Béchamel sauce, 40
with cream, 41
egg, 337
and egg and carrots,
337
with curry, 41
ham *mousseline* with, 163
Mornay, 40
See also Mornay sauce
roux, 40
thickening, 40
Beef, 298–308
bouillon, 106
bourguignon (stew in red
wine), 307
braised, 303–8
pot roast, 303–4
pot roast molded in as-
pic, 304–5
stew in red wine,
307–8
with red wine and
herbs, 306–7
casserole(d), 302
with red wine and
herbs, 306–7
consommé, 106
degreasing, 5–6
garnishes, 109
cooking techniques and
terms, 3–7
degreasing bouillons,
juices, and sauces,
5–6
fillet marinated in game
sauce, 302

served cold, 302
ground round steak,
300–1
Italian sauce, 301
patties, 300–1
marrow, canapés with,
123–24
oven cooking, 4–5
pot roast, 303–4
molded in aspic, 304–5
roast, preparing, 4–5
salad, Paris style, 92
tournedos (fillet steaks),
298–300
basic cooking method,
298
with *béarnaise* sauce,
299
with Choron sauce,
299
marinated in game
sauce, 302
with *sauce des trois
gourmandes,* 299–300
with Valois sauce,
298–99
See also Meat; specific
cooking methods,
ingredients, kinds,
recipes
Beets, borsch with, 126–27
Belgian endives, 342–44
with bacon and Mornay
sauce au gratin, 344
basic cooking method,
343
oven-braised, 344
salad, 101
steamed in butter, 343
Bellini sauce (*bagna cauda*),
90
Beverages, 63–70
cup au champagne, 69
cup au vin blanc, 69
punch au thé, 70
sangría, 68–69
wine, 63–69
See also Wine
Birds, game. *See* Game birds
Birthday cake, chocolate,
434

chicken, 6–7, 209–12
  in wine, 210–12
pheasant, 251–52
  with cooked apples,
    251–52
-roasted duck, 233–34
-roasted guinea hen with
    fruit sauce, 226–28
-roasted loin of veal,
    286–87
saddle of rabbit, 255–56
See also specific ingre-
    dients, recipes
Cauliflower, 338–40
  au gratin, 338–39
  flowerets sautéed in but-
    ter, 339
  fritters, 380–81
  raw tidbits for the
    cocktail hour,
    339–40
Caviar
  -flavored consommé,
    iced, 110
  red, crêpes with, 157
Cayenne pepper, 9
Celery, 75–76
  root, in julienne strips
    with mustard sauce,
    75–76
  root mixed salad, 76
  root purée, 386–87
  stuffed with Roquefort
    cheese paste, 74–75
Champagne, 64
  cup au, 69
  fillets of flounder with,
    186
  serving, 64
  vinegar, 23
Champagne region wines,
    63
Charcuteries (pork prod-
    ucts), wines to serve
    with, 67
See also Ham; Pork
Chaud-froid sauce, chicken
    strips on canapés
    with, 217–18
Cheese
  cream, tomatoes with

chives and, 86
crème de fromage, crêpes
    with, 154–55
croûtes, 123
crown of *choux* with, 56
hors d'oeuvre, 74–75
  celery stuffed with
    Roquefort paste,
    74–75
  dressing, Roquefort,
    97
  omelet, 148–49
  puffs, 55–56
  salad dressing,
    Roquefort, 97
  wines to serve with, 67
  See also Au gratin; Gratin;
    specific ingredients,
    kinds, recipes
Cherries (cherry)
  tart, 451–52
  in vinegar, 24
Chervil, 10
Chestnut(s), 340–41
  basic cooking method,
    340
  braised, 340–41
  desserts, 427–28
    parfait, 427–28
    pear and glazed
      chestnut sherbet,
      429–30
    surprise, 428
  purée, 387
Chicken, 204–25
  in aspic, 220–23
  bouillon, 107
    degreasing, 6
    making, 224–25
  breaded deep-fried strips,
    220
  broiled, 204–6
    squabs with *sauce diab-
      lesse,* 204–6
  casseroled, 209–12
    in wine, 210–12
  consommé, 107–10
    clarifying, 107
    jellied, 109–10
    suprême, 109
    velouté, 108–9

Île de France meat and
    vegetable soup,
    124–25
leftover, seashell maca-
    roni with Madeira
    for, 223–24
livers. *See* Chicken liver(s)
Marengo, 207–9
minute, with tarragon,
    206–7
patchwork, 221–22
Périgord, with stuffed
    cabbage "sausage,"
    215–17
poached, 215–17
poêler (to casserole), 6–7
roast, with *sauce finan-
    cière,* 214–15
sauced, 212–15
sautéed, 206–9
seashell macaroni with
    Madeira with,
    223–24
split-roasting in the oven,
    5
stock, 225
strips *à la meunière,* 219
strips on canapés, 217–19
suprêmes (boned breasts),
    217–20
  breaded deep-fried
    strips, 220
  chaud-froid sauce,
    217–18
  sabayon sauce, cold,
    218–19
  strips *à la meunière,*
    219
  strips on canapés,
    217–19
and sweetbreads with
    dried morels and
    cream, 212–14
in tarragon aspic, 220–21
valouté, 108–9
in wine, casseroled,
    210–12
wines to serve with, 66
Chicken liver(s)
  in aspic, 223
  butter, 30

See also Wild rabbit

Haunch of venison with master of the hunt sauce, 266

Hearts of lettuce and romaine salad, 98

Hen, guinea. See Guinea hen

Hen, pheasant. See Pheasant

Herb(s), 8–18

bouquet garnis, 9

butter, 26

and butter enrichment for soups, 306–7

casserole of beef with red wine and, 306–7

eggs stuffed with, 137

marinade for broiled sea bass, 176–77

mixed, 12

Provençal, roast leg of lamb with, 318

and seasonings and spices, listed and described, 8–18

soup garnish, 105

See also specific kinds, recipes

Herbe à tortue (mixed herbs), 12

Herring

fresh, grilled or broiled, with mustard sauce, 174–75

smoked, 91, 93–94

fillets marinated in oil, 93–94

and potato salad, 91

Hollandaise sauce, 47

hot poached eggs on artichoke hearts with, 324

mousseline, 48

with thickening, 48

Hors d'oeuvre, 73–94

canapés for. See Canapés

cantaloupe sherbet, 74

celery root with mustard sauce, 75–76

celery stuffed with Roquefort cheese

paste, 74–75

chicken liver mousse with port wine, 90–91

cold stuffed eggs, 139

See also Stuffed eggs

cucumbers

with cream and lemon dressing, 78–79

filled with crab meat, 80

with mint, 78

stuffed boats, 79

stuffed with tuna and anchovies, 79

egg salad, hard-boiled, 78

lentil salad, 86–87

mackerel with white wine, 94

mixed celery root salad, 76

mixed vegetable salad with mayonnaise, 77

mushrooms

à la grecque, 82

with cream, 80

with mayonnaise, 81

onions, small white

à la grecque with tomato sauce, 82

with seedless raisins, 83

potato salad

beef salad and, 92

with Périgord sauce, 88

and smoked herring salad, 91

raw vegetables, Mediteranean style, 89, 90

salade niçoise with basil, 88

smoked herring, 91, 93

fillets marinated in oil, 93

and potato salad, 91

tomato(es)

with cream cheese and chives, 86

salad, 84

sherbet, 73–74

stuffed with pimentos, 85

with tapénade, 85–86

vegetables à la grecque, 81, 82

See also specific ingredients, recipes

Horseradish sauce, 34–35

Hot poached eggs on artichoke hearts with hollandaise sauce, 324

Hot stuffed eggs. See Stuffed eggs, hot and cold

Hot tray, electric, use of, 57

Ice cream, 417–22

coffee, 420–21

cookies to accompany, 430–32

meringues with, 424–25

meringues with strawberry, 424–25

peach Melba, 417–18

pears with vanilla ice cream and chocolate sauce, 419

praline, 422

profiteroles with vanilla ice cream and chocolate sauce, 420

raspberry sauce, 418–19

vanilla, 417

Iced caviar-flavored consommé, 110

Icings, cake, 399–402

hints for making them shiny, 402

quick, made from confectioner's sugar, 400–2

quick chocolate, 400–1

quick white, 400

royal, 401

traditional chocolate, 401–2

white fondant, basic recipe, 399–400

Île de France meat and vegetable soup, 124–25

Indian rice, 365

Italian sauce, 301

veal roast with, 224
Mace, 13
Mackerel
    fillets, Normandy style,
        189–90
    with white wine, 94
Madeira wine, seashell
        macaroni with,
        223–24
Malt vinegar, 22
Marengo chicken, 207–9
    sauce, 208–9
Margarine, 3–4
    cooking in, 3–4
    short crust pastry dough
        with, 52
    See also Butter
Marinades
    game meat, 272–74
        cooked, for venison,
            274
        dry, 274
        furred game, 273
        wild rabbit, special
            light, 273
    lacquered roast pork, 290
    See also specific ingre-
        dients, recipes
Marinated beef fillet in
        game sauce, 302
    served cold, 302
Marinated fillets of smoked
        herring, in oil, 93–94
Marjoram, 13
Master of the hunt sauce,
        266
    haunch of venison with,
        266
Matelote, 193–94
Mayonnaise, 31–34
    anchovy, 34
    egg salad, hard-boiled, 78
    garlic (aioli sauce), 33,
        167–68
        poached salt cod with,
            167–68
    green, 39
    keeping a day or two, 32
    making, 31–32
    mixed vegetable salad
        with, 77

orange, with cream, 37
pimento, 33–34
pink sauces, 37–38
raw mushrooms with, 81
serving on a warm day, 32
watercress sauce, 39
without eggs, 32–33
Meat, 277–321
    beef, 298–308
    See also Beef; specific
        recipes
    cooking techniques and
        terms, 3–7
    degreasing bouillons,
        juices, and sauces,
        5–6
    ham, 293–98
    See also Ham
    lamb, 309–21
    See also Lamb
    oven cooking (roasting),
        4–5
    pork, 290–93
    See also Pork
    serving, 57
    stock (demi-glace), 46
    tomatoes stuffed with,
        375
    veal, 277–89
    See also Veal
    and vegetable soups,
        121–25
        Île de France, 124–25
        pot-au-feu, 121–25
    wines to serve with,
        66–67
    See also Beef; Furred
        game; Game birds;
        Ham; Lamb; Pork;
        Poultry; Veal;
        specific cooking
        methods, ingre-
        dients, recipes
Mediterranean style raw
        vegetables, 89–90
    dressings for, 90
Meringues and meringue
        desserts, 423–26
    frozen chocolate mousse
        and, 426
    with ice cream, 424

shells, 423–24
    with strawberry ice
        cream, 424–25
    with whipped cream, 242
Metal serving dishes, use of,
        57
Meursault wine
    caramelized sauce, 294,
        295
    handbraised in, 293–98
Mignonnette, 13
Mild sugar syrup, 397
Milk thickening for soup,
        104
Mint, 13
    cucumbers with, 78
    sauce, fresh, for roast leg
        of lamb, 316
    vinegar, 24
Minute chicken with tarra-
        gon, 206–7
Mirepoix, brown sauce with,
        45
Mixed celery root salad, 76
Mixed green beans and
        baby lima beans,
        331–32
Mixed grill of veal scallops,
        277–78
Mixed herbs. See Herbe à tortue
Mixed vegetable garnishes
        ("gardens"), 395–96
    Louisette's garden,
        395–96
    rack of lamb with, 310
Mixed vegetable salad with
        mayonnaise, 77
Molded caramel lemon cus-
        tard, 411–13
Molded mousselines and
        mousses. See
        Mousseline(s) and
        mousse(s)
"Molded" potatoes, 360–61
Molded rice pilaf with
        scrambled eggs and
        tomato sauce, 152
Morels. See Dried morels,
        chicken and sweet-
        breads with cream
        and

Mornay sauce, 40
   Belgian endives with
      bacon and, au gratin,
      344
Mousse (dessert), frozen
      chocolate, meringue
      dessert and, 426
Mousseline(s) and mousse(s),
      as entrees, 159–63
   artichoke, 325
      artichoke hearts gar-
      nished with, 325
      purée, 383–84
   chicken liver
      loaf, Bresse style, 162
      with port wine, 90–91
   cold salmon, 161–62
      baked sea bass stuffed
      with, 177–79
   fish
      baked sea bass stuffed
      with cold salmon,
      177–79
      cold salmon, 161–62
      baked sea bass stuf-
      fed with, 177–79
      in a ring mold, 159–61
      shrimp bisque, 160–61
      small tomatoes stuffed
      with, 376
   ham, 163
   sauce, 48
   shrimp bisque, 160–61
   tuna, 92
   See also Soufflé(s)
Mullet. *See* Red mullet
Mushroom(s), cultivated,
      348–52
   caps sautéed in butter,
      348
   concentrated essence of,
      349
   duxelles, 350–51
      bound, 352
      classical, 351
      dry, 351
      tomatoes stuffed with,
      373
   eggs stuffed with, 138–39
   lié, for fish fillets *gratiné,*
      188–89

   purée, 388–89
   raw
      with mayonnaise, 81
      salad with cream, 80
   sauce, cream of, 51
   sautéed veal chops with,
      279–81
   stewed, 349
   stuffed, 350
   velouté of, 116–17
Mussel(s)
   marinière, Paris style,
      197–98
   pilaf, with saffron and
      curry, 198–99
   salad, 199–200
   with snail butter, 198
Mustard
   butter, 29
   French dressing with, 100
   sauce, 75–76, 175
      celery root with, 75–
      76
      fresh herring grilled or
      broiled with, 174–75
Mutton. *See* Lamb

Next-day leg of lamb with
      piquant sauce,
      316–17
Noisette(s)
   of hare on canapés,
      261–62
   of lamb with tarragon
      sauce, 309–10
   potatoes, 357
Normandy sauce, rolled
      flounder fillets with
      shrimp butter and,
      192–93
November goose with fall
      apples, 230–31
Nut brittle
   chocolate praline filling,
      409
   floating island with pink
      pralines, 409–10
   praline, 408–9
   praline ice cream, 422
Nutmeg, 13

Oil(s), 19–21
   aromatic, 20–21
   fillets of smoked herring
      marinated in, 93–94
   garlic, 20–21
   with herbs from Pro-
      vence, 21
   for making mayonnaise,
      31
   olive, 19–20
      limes preserved in, 21
      See also Olive oil
   peanut, 19
   with savory, 21
   walnut, 20
      chicory salad with, 101
   See also Fat(s); specific in-
      gredients, kinds, rec-
      ipes, uses
Olive oil, 19–20
   aromatic oils, 20
   limes preserved in, 21
   ordinary, 20
   refined, 20
   three categories of,
      19–20
   virgin, 19
Olives, duck with, 237–38
Omelet(s), 146–50
   cheese, 148–49
   with croutons, 148
   gratin of fresh tomato,
      149
   pan for, 147
   plain, basic recipe,
      147–48
   potato, 148
   recommendations, 147
   sorrel with ham, 149–50
Onion(s)
   described, 14
   green peas with, French
      style, 353
   lamb stew with turnips
      and, 320–21
   purée, 389
   soup, Paris style, 111
   varieties and uses of, 14
   white, small
      à la grecque with to-
      mato sauce, 82

stewed in tea, 454–55
Puff pastry, 53–56
　baking dish cover made
　　of, 61–62
　cheese puffs, 55–56
　choux, 54–55
　　See also *Choux* pastry
　crescents, 60
　decorations, 60–62
　galettes, 441–42
　oval tartlets, 61
　savory tartlets, 60
　scallop shells, 62
　simple (half-pastry,
　　rough-puff pastry),
　　53–54
　tartlets, 60, 61
　　oval, 61
　　savory, 60
Punch au thé, 70
Purées, fruit. *See under*
　　Fruit; specific kinds,
　　recipes
Purées of vegetables, 382–95
　apple and potato, 382–83
　artichoke *mousseline,*
　　383–84
　celery root, 386–87
　chestnut, 387
　　dessert, 427–28
　green bean, 385–86
　green pea, fresh, 390
　lentil, 387–88
　mushroom, 388–89
　onion, 389
　potato, 391–92
　　and apple, 382–83
　　cake of, 392
　　serving, 57
　sorrel, 393
　spiced apple, 383
　spinach, cream-puréed,
　　393–94
　　oval tarlets filled with,
　　394
　split pea, 390–91
　turnip, 395
　watercress, 395
　white bean, 384–85
　　canned, 384–85
　　dried, 385

Quail. *See* Partridge
Quatre épices. See Four spices
Queen Bee chocolate cake,
　　435–36
Quick butter cream filling,
　　403
Quick cake icing, 400–2
　chocolate, 400–1
　royal, 401
　white, 400
Quick Genoese cake, 438

Rabbit, wild. *See* Wild rabbit
Rack of lamb with mixed
　　vegetable garnish,
　　310
Ragouts
　cooking techniques and
　　terms, 3, 5–6
　degreasing, 5–6
　See also Stew(s)
Raisins, seedless, small
　　white onions with,
　　83
Ramekins, eggs with cream
　　in, 141–42
　with tarragon cream, 142
Raspberry
　sauce, 418–19
　tart, 451
Ratatouille, 363–64
　baked tuna with, 180
Raw cauliflower tidbits for
　　the cocktail hour,
　　339–40
Raw mushroom(s)
　with mayonnaise, 81
　salad with cream, 80
　See also Mushroom(s), cul-
　　tivated
Raw sautéed potatoes,
　　355–56
Red caviar, crêpes with, 157
Red meats, oven cooking
　　(roasting), 4–5
　See also Beef; Roasting;
　　specific kinds, re-
　　cipes
Red mullet, broiled with
　　anchovy butter, 176

Red pepper (cayenne pep-
　　per), 9
Red peppers (pimentos). *See*
　　Pimento(s)
Reducing water or a liquid,
　　3
Red wine, 63, 64
　beef stew in, 307–8
　butter flavored with shal-
　　lot, 28
　casserole of beef with
　　herbs and, 306–7
　port
　　baked ham with cream
　　　sauce and, 296–98
　　chicken liver mousse
　　　with, 90–91
　sangría, 68–69
　　fantasie, 68–69
　serving, 63, 64, 66, 67
　sherry, veal kidneys
　　sautéed with,
　　285–86
　vinegar, 22–23
　See also Wine; Wine vin-
　　egar; specific kinds,
　　recipes
Refreshing blanched vege-
　　tables, 7
Regional soups (*potées*). *See*
　　under Vegetable
　　soups); specific
　　kinds
René's potato cake, 360
Rib roast
　spit-roasting in the oven,
　　5
　See also Roast beef; Roast-
　　ing
Rice, 364–67
　Canton style, 367
　Creole, 364–65
　Indian, 365
　pilaf, 365–66
　　molded, scrambled
　　　eggs with tomato
　　　sauce and, 152
　　mussel, with saffron
　　　and curry, 198–99
　with saffron and curry,
　　366

of corn kernels, 342
crudités, 89–90
dandelion greens, 102–3
  with bacon, 103
  with shallots and
    croutons, 102–3
dressings, 95
  See also Dressing(s),
    salad; specific kinds,
    recipes
dried white bean, 331
egg, hard-boiled, 78
field, 102
general information, 95
green beans, 329
  dressed-up style, 329
  family style, 329
lentil, 86–87
lettuce, 98, 99
  hearts of romaine and,
    98
  with orange, 98
  ribbons with fruit, 99
mixed vegetables with
  mayonnaise, 77
mushrooms, raw, 80, 81
  with cream, 80
  with mayonnaise, 81
mussel, 199–200
niçoise with basil, 88–89
potato, 87–88
  beef salad and, 92
  with Périgord sauce, 88
  with smoked herring, 91
preparation of, 95
raw vegetables, Mediter-
  ranean style, 89–90
sardine paté, 93
smoked herring and
  potato, 91
spring and summer, ten-
  der leafed, 98–99
tomato, 84
watercress, 99
winter, 100–3
Salmis, 243–44
  of duck, 243–44
  sauce, 243–44
Salmon
  mousse (*mousseline*), cold,
    161–62

baked sea bass stuffed
  with, 177–79
smoked, butter, 29
trout, poached with sorrel
  butter, 169–71
Salt (sodium chloride,
  NaCl), 16
Salt cod, 167–69
  croquettes, 169
  poached with garlic and
    cream, 168–69
  poached with garlic
    mayonnaise, 167–68
Sand cookies, Alsatian
  style, 432
Sangría, 68–69
  fantaisie, 68–69
Sardine(s)
  fresh, grilled or broiled,
    174
  pâté, canned, 93
Sauce(s), 35–51
  aioli, 167–68
  for asparagus, 326–27
  Aurora, 43–44
  béarnaise, 48–49
    making, 48–49
    sweetbreads Colbert
      on artichoke hearts
      with, 284–85
    tournedos with, 299
  Béatrice, 35–36
    cold poached eggs on
      artichoke hearts
      with, 324
  béchamel (white), 40 *See
    also Béchamel* sauce
  Bellini (*bagna cauda*), 90
  blanquette, 282–83
  blond, 41–44
  brown, 44–46
  Burgundy, 146
    with poached eggs,
      145–46
  butters for binding, 25–26
  caramelized Meursault,
    293–96
    ham braised in, 293–96
  chaud-froid, 217–18
  chicken strips on canapés
    with, 217–18

Choron, 49
  poached eggs on *crous-
    tades* with, 145
  tournedos with, 299
civet, 46, 260–61
  jugged hare with,
    260–61
cold, 31ff., 276
  See also specific kinds,
    recipes
Colliosure, 90
concentrated essence of
  mushrooms as flavor-
  ing for, 349
covlis, 126, 127
  making, 370–71
crab, *à l'américaine,*
  195–96
cream of mushroom, 51
with curry powder, 35
  See also Curry powder
degreasing, 5, 6
demi-glace, 46
des trois gourmandes,
  299–300
  tournedos with, 299–
    300
diablesse, 205–6
  squab chickens with,
    204–6
financière, 42–43
  roast chicken with,
    214–15
for fish fillets, 184–85,
  187, 188, 192
Françoise, 37
fruit, casserole-roasted
  guinea hen with,
    226–28
game, 46, 275–76
  beef fillet marinated in,
    302
  cold, 276
garlic, 315–16
  for roast leg of lamb,
    315
green, 38–39
  mayonnaise, 39
  tartar, 38
  watercress, 39
hollandaise, 47

baked, stuffed with salmon *mousseline,*
177–79
broiled with fennel,
176–77
Sea salt, 16
Seashell macaroni with
Madeira, 223–24
leftover chicken with,
223–24
veal roast with, 224
Seasonings, herbs, and
spices, 8–18
See also specific kinds,
recipes, uses
Serving dishes, choice of,
57
Shallot(s), 17
butter, 27
dandelion salad with
croutons and, 102–3
vinegar for winter, 23
Shellfish, 197–203
crab in the shell, au gratin, 201–2
See also Crab (crab
meat)
fish *mousseline* in a ring
mold, 159–61
lobsters, small, in aromatic bouillon, 200–1
mussel(s)
marinière, Paris style,
197
pilaf, with saffron and
curry, 198–99
salad, 199–200
with snail butter, 198
scallops and shrimp
cocktail, 203
shrimp. *See* Shrimp
wines to serve with, 66
See also Fish; specific
kinds, recipes
Shells, meringue, 423–24
See also Meringues and
meringue desserts
Sherbet(s), 429–30
cantaloupe, 74
cookies to accompany,
430–32

pear and glazed chestnut,
429–30
tangerine, 429
tomato, 73–74
Sherry
veal kidneys sautéed
with, 285–86
vinegar, 23
Shirred eggs, 140
with pork sausages, 141
Provençal style, 141
veiled, 140
with visible yolk, 140
Short crust pastry dough, 52
with butter, 52
with margarine, 52
Shrimp
bisque, 160–61
butter, 29
rolled flounder fillets
with Normandy
sauce and, 192–93
fish *mousseline* in a ring
mold, 159–61
and scallops cocktail, 203
Simmer (to cook slowly in a
liquid), 3
Simple French dressing, 96
Skimming (to skim), 7
Small lobsters in aromatic
bouillon, 200–1
Small *pots de crème* in three
flavors, 413
Small tomatoes
with cream cheese and
chives, 86
stuffed with fish *mousseline,* 376
with *tapénade,* 85–86
See also Tomato(es)
Small white onions, 352
à la grecque with tomato
sauce, 82
glazed, 352
eel stew with, 193–94
roast duck with glazed
turnips and, 232–
233
with green peas, French
style, 353
with seedless raisins, 83

See also Onion(s)
Smoked herring
fillets marinated in oil,
93–94
and potato salad, 91
Smoked salmon butter, 29
Snail butter, 28
mussels with, 198
Snowy peas with caramel
marbling, 410–11
Soft-boiled eggs, 134–35
5- or 6-minute, 135
sauce, 36
3-minute, 134
Sorrel, 368
butter, 170–71
salmon trout with,
169–71
flounder of halibut fillets
with, 185–86
omelet with ham, 149–50
purée, 393
fricandeau of veal with,
278–79
ribbons, 368
stewed, 368
Soufflé(s), 164–66
basic recipe, 164
copper bowl and balloon
whip for, 164
crab, unmolded, 165–66
onion soup with, 111–12
serving, 166
See also Mousseline(s) and
mousse(s)
Soup(s), 104–33
asparagus, *velouté* of 14–15
Basque fish, 128–29
beef
bouillon, 106
consommé, 5–6, 106,
109
borsch, 126–27
chervil, cream of, 114
chicken
bouillon, 105
consommé, 107–10
velouté, 108
clarifying, 107–8
croutons to accompany,
105, 129

Stuffed tomatoes, 373–76
  with fish *mousseline,* 376
  with meat, 375
  Provençal style, 374–75
  with vegetables, 373–74
Stuffing(s)
  for baked stuffed carp,
    Oriental style, 182
  simple, for baked fish,
    179
  See also specific ingre-
    dients, kinds, recipes
Sugar crust pastry dough,
  53
  See also specific recipes,
    uses
Sugar syrup(s), 397–99
  butter cream filling with,
    402
  candy, 398–99
  concentrated, 397
  of the Islands, 398
  mild, 397
Summer savory, 16
Suprême (egg and cream
    soup thickening),
    104, 108, 109
  chicken *velouté,* 108
  consommé, 109
  liaison suprême, 108
Suprêmes of chicken,
    217–20
  breaded deep-fried strips,
    220
  chaud-froid sauce, 217–18
  sabayon sauce, cold,
    218–19
  strips *à la meunière,* 219
  strips on canapés, 217–19
Suzette butter, for crêpes
  Suzette, 444–45
Sweating (to sweat) food, 4
Sweetbreads
  and chicken with dried
    morels and cream,
    212–14
  Colbert on artichoke
    hearts with *béarnaise*
    sauce, 284–85
Sweet crêpe batter, basic
  method, 443

Sweetened *choux* pastry,
  420
Syrup(s), sugar, 397–99
  butter cream filling with,
    402
  candy, 398–99
  concentrated, 397
  of the Islands, 398
  mild, 397

Table arrangements and
  decorations. *See* Ar-
  rangements and dec-
  orations, table
Tangerine
  sections, glazed, 399
  sherbet, 429
Tapénade, small tomatoes
  with, 85–86
Tarragon, 17–18
  aspic, chicken in, 220–
    21
  butter, 26–27
    green, 27
  cream, eggs in ramekins
    with, 206–7
  minute chicken with,
    206–7
  sauce, noisettes of lamb
    with, 309–10
  vinegar, 23
Tartar sauce, 38
Tarte Tatin, 447–48
Tartlets
  oval, 61
    filled with cream-
      puréed spinach, 394
  savory, 60
  See also Tarts
Tarts (fruit tarts), 445–53
  apple, village style, 446
  blackberry, 452–53
  cherry, 451–52
  fruit, spring and summer,
    450–53
  greengage plum, 453
  lemon, from Peyrudette,
    448–49
  orange, 449–50
  raspberry, 451

upside-down apple,
  447–48
  See also Tartlets
Tea
  prunes stewed in, 454–55
  punch, 70
Temperature for serving
  wines, 64, 65, 397
Tender-leafed spring and
  summer salads,
  98–99
Terrine of hare, aspic for,
  269–70
Thyme, 18
Tiles, almond (cookies),
  430–31
Tomato(es)
  balls, jellied consommé
    with, 110
  broiled, 372–73
  cold stuffed small, 85–86
  coulis, 126, 127, 370–71
    making, 370–71
  dressing and garnish, 84,
    105
  with dried white beans,
    Breton style,
    330–31
  -flavored lentils, 346
  fondue, 371
  omelet, gratin of, 149
  peeling and cutting, 84
  ratatouille, 363–64
  salad, 84
  sauce. *See* Tomato sauce
  sherbet, 73–74
  soup, fresh, 117–18
  stuffed, 85–86, 373–76
    with cream cheese and
      chives, 86
    with fish *mousseline,* 376
    with meat, 375
    with pimentos, 85
    Provençal style,
      374–75
    with *tapénade,* 85–86
    with vegetables,
      373–74
Tomato sauce, 371–72
  coulis, 126–27, 370–71
    making, 370–71

fondant, basic recipe, 399–400
 quick, 400
 royal, 401
White fondant, (cake icing), basic recipe, 399–400
 See also White cake icings
White meats, oven cooking (roasting), 5
 See also specific kinds, recipes
White onions, small. *See* Small white onions; specific recipes
White sauces, 39–41
 béchamel, 40
  with cream, 41
  with curry, 41
  See also Béchamel sauce
 butter, 50
 liquid used in, 40
 Mornay, 40
  Belgian endives with bacon and, au gratin, 344
White wine, 63, 64, 66
 braised veal with curry powder and, 288–89
 cup au champagne, 69
 cup au vin blanc, 69
 for game meat marinades, 272, 273, 274
 ham braised in Meursault, 293–96

mackerel with, 94
sautéed wild rabbit *chasseur,* 253–54
trois gourmandes sauce, 299–300
See also Wine; specific kinds, recipes, uses
Whiting
 baked, 181, 191
 cold rolled fillets of, 191
Wild boar, roast loin of young, 266–67
 sauce for, 267, 275
Wild fowl liver butter, 272
Wild rabbit, 253–57
 marinade, 273
 poacher's *pot-au-feu,* 256–57
 rillettes of, 270–71
 saddle of, Vouzeron style, 255–56
 sautéed *chasseur,* 253–54
 stew, 255
 See also Hare
Wild thyme, 18
Wine, 63–69
 basket, use of, 65
 braised veal with curry powder and, 288–89
 cellars, 65
 champagne, 64
  See also Champagne
 chicken in, 210–12
 choice of, 63
 cup au vin blanc, 69

decanting, 65
dessert, 67, 397
glasses for, 65
marinades for furred game, 272, 273, 274
serving, 63
temperature for, 64, 65, 397
uncorking, 64–65
vinegar. *See* Wine vinegar
what to serve with what foods, 66–67
See also Red wine; White wine; specific kinds, recipes, uses
Wine vinegar, 22–23
 saddle of rabbit, Vouzeron style, 255–56
Winter lamb stew with turnips and onions, 319–20
Winter salads, 100–3
Winter savory, 16
Winter vegetable garnish, 396

Zabaglione with port wine, 407–8
Zucchini
 fritters, 380
 ratatouille, 363–64
 sautéed with Provençal butter, 377–78

Index of French Recipe Titles